NEW WORKS
IN ACCOUNTING
HISTORY

Richard P. Brief, *Series Editor*

*Leonard N. Stern School of Business
New York University*

A Garland Series

CARL THOMAS DEVINE

Essays In Accounting Theory
A Capstone

edited with a preface and notes by
HARVEY S. HENDRICKSON

GARLAND PUBLISHING, Inc.
A MEMBER OF THE TAYLOR & FRANCIS GROUP
NEW YORK & LONDON / 1999

Published in 1999 by
Garland Publishing Inc.
A Member of the Taylor & Francis Group
19 Union Square West
New York, NY 10003

10 9 8 7 6 5 4 3 2 1

Library of Congress-in-Publication Data is available from the Library of Congress.

Carl Devine, essays in accounting theory: a capstone / edited by Harvey Hendrickson.

ISBN 0–8153–3263–7

Contents

v

Carl Thomas Devine
1911–1998

Editor's Preface

This collection of thirteen essays (actually fifteen since two have two parts) provides a capstone to the previous five volumes that were published by the American Accounting Association in 1985 as Studies in Accounting Research No. 22. The essays included here were distributed by the author as Volume VI, and his foreword to them shows the continuing evolution of his personal philosophy, research, thinking, and writing during his six decades of "laboring in the vineyard"—studying, reflecting, writing, and/or discussing in offices, seminar- and class-rooms, and libraries at universities in the U.S., Canada, and Indonesia.

Carl wrote the essays over a period of many years. They are a manifestation of the practice he began as a graduate student of writing brief comments that he filed, later retrieved and revised several times until they were substantive thought pieces; these then were published as articles, presented at symposia, or compiled into a privately printed volume. These essays are classics that present glimpses from a lifetime of study by a person who ranks at or near the top of a short list of the most literate, most insightful, and most ethical accounting professors and scholars.

A major purpose of his study and thinking appears not only to have been a love of ideas and learning, but a lifelong search for concepts and ideas that relate and/or could apply to enrich the study of accounting—which long has been recognized as interdisciplinary. Carl seems to have been searching for relevance in hitherto unrecognized areas. In these essays, he relates the findings of his extensive research to accounting. In so doing, the reader gains insight into new areas and a broader understanding of accounting. Thus, the reader broadens and deepens her/his knowledge of accounting and many other areas.

Merely by scanning any essay, one quickly discovers the richness and integration of his breadth and depth of knowledge. He covers a wide range of disciplines, subjects, concepts, topics, and personalities associated with them. Typically he begins with an exploration of one or more subject areas and then applies relevant concepts to accounting and/or auditing. Thus, these essays, like those in the earlier volumes, provide the basis for a broad science, literature, and arts education that also enhances one's understanding and appreciation of accounting and auditing.

This volume plus the earlier five should viewed as a set since many of the ideas presented here enlarge upon earlier discussions, often with references to the earlier essays. The entire set should be considered required reading for doctoral studies in accounting and auditing. Many of the earlier volumes were printed privately by professors and distributed to their students at universities in Florida, Colorado, North Carolina, and Texas as required and/or supplementary readings in doctoral and other courses.

The coverage in this volume includes the absurd, art, economics, ethics, mathematics, metaphysics, physics, psychology, psychometrics, sociology, statistics, many areas of philosophy (e.g., belief, climate of opinion, coherence theories, correspondence theories, deconstruction, conceptualism, dogmatism, empiricism, exegesis, existentialism, gestaltism, hermeneutics, homiletics, fuzzy logic, logic, logical positivism, positivism, modernism, postmodernism, pragmatism, scientism, situationalism, solipsism, structuralism, subjectivism, symbolic interaction, symbolic logic, symbolism, epistemology, morphology, ontology, phenomenology, teleology, topology, typology, rhetorics, and semantics) as well as behavioral and financial accounting, auditing, and auditing independence. He also refers to many persons whose ideas he explores, among them are Albert Camus, Rudolf Carnap, Stuart Chase, Auguste Comte, John Dewey, Noam Chomsky, Irving Fisher, S. I. Hayakawa, Martin Heidegger, Edmund Husserl, Alfred Korzybski, Karl Marx, Karl Pearson, Bertrand Russell, Jean-Paul Sarte, B. F. Skinner, Robert Penn Warren, and Alfred North Whitehead. Many of these areas and persons are introduced in his stimulating, probing first essay: "Accounting Theory: A Personal Journey."

This volume includes many areas and ideas that were not explored in the first five volumes and adds to many that were. An index is included in this volume to facilitate cross-referencing among the essays; this in turn can be used to continue research in all of the essays of the earlier volumes for which comprehensive indexes are provided at the end of Volume V.

An intensive attempt has been made to proof all quotations, to verify all citations and references, to provide citations where none were provided, and to verify the spelling of names and terms; only a very few quotations (fewer than five) could not be traced to a primary or secondary source for verification. Attempts also have been made to correct typographical errors, and to lightly edit the syntax, grammar, readability, and accuracy of the text and footnotes without altering Carl's style or intended meaning. A number of editorial notes have been inserted to clarify meaning and document sources, but many insertions and corrections have not been documented out of deep respect for the author. Carl obviously put extreme effort and care into interpreting and presenting many diverse subjects and sources; his interpretations and insights seem to be impeccable. In the editing process I probably also may have made or added errors, so any that remain must be attributed me.

I have had the privilege of knowing Carl for some 30 years, and attempted to touch base with him on a fairly regular basis, usually by telephone. I continue to be amazed by his thirst for—and breadth of—knowledge, and his enthusiasm for exploring ideas, concepts, interfaces, and insights. It was a rare call that lasted less than 30 minutes because he would get on a train of thought that had many branches—often it was an essay that he had been working on, other times it would be on reminisces of published articles, presentations, discussions, ideas, and/or colleagues. To Carl, nuances of thought were essential aspects of life, and he approached each with an enthusiasm that was not unlike that of a precocious child with a new toy. He kept writing until the final months of his life when his cancer entered the terminal phase. His papers include drafts of numerous essays, eight of which he marked for a volume seven. His powerful intellect and great sense of humor continued to the last days of his life.

Many thanks are due to my Research Assistant, Milagros Garcia, whose persistence and ingenuity in searching data bases and pursuing sources has been invaluable. Thanks also are due to Douglas Hasty and his interlibrary loan staff at the Florida International University Library for their untiring assistance in locating upwards of one-hundred books, monographs, articles, and pieces that were essential to completing the editorial task. Special thanks also are due to the publisher for permitting the inclusion of revisions that Carl made in several of the essays during the last months of his life but that were not found until the page proofs had been revised.

The following is based on the Memorial that Professor Edward McIntyre of Florida State University prepared for the Early Fall issue of the American Accounting Association's *Accounting Education News:*

Carl Thomas Devine was born in West Virginia, and received the first six years of his education in a one-room schoolhouse. During the depression years, he attended Davis and Elkins College where he taught commercial subjects while majoring in mathematics and physical sciences, graduating as valedictorian. In 1936 he began studies at the Graduate School of Business of the University of Michigan. In 1938 he received the M.B.A. and in 1940 he received the Ph.D., the seventh awarded in business administration by the University of Michigan.

He was a professor of accounting at Florida State University from 1965 to 1976. Prior to this appointment, he was a faculty member at the University of Florida, the University of Southern California, the University of Pennsylvania, and Johns Hopkins University. He also held appointments as Visiting Professor at the University of California (Berkeley), the University of British Columbia, the University of Chicago, the Massachusetts Institute of Technology, and the Universitas Indonesia.

Professor Devine was a leading accounting scholar of the Twentieth century. In breadth and depth of knowledge, he had few peers. Over his career he published numerous scholarly articles, essays, reviews, chapters, books and monographs, a number of which are now referred to as classics. He is credited with stimulating interest in the field of behavioral research in accounting with his observation that "accountants seem to have waded through their relationships to the intricate psychological network of human activity with a heavy-handed crudity that is beyond belief." In 1983 Professor Devine received the American Accounting Association's Outstanding Accounting Educator Award.

Professor Devine had the uncommon ability to link the study and practice of accounting to a variety of fields, especially philosophy. In his later years he produced five volumes of essays that covered a wide range of topics and demonstrated the breadth of his scholarship. The subjects of these essays varied from the practical (Auditing—An Appraisal and Some Recommendations) to the more philosophical (Description, Phenomenology, and Value-Free Science). These essays were first printed privately by the Florida State University Department of Accounting, and later published by the American Accounting Association as Studies in Accounting Research No. 22. On the basis of these essays, Professor Devine received the American Accounting Association's 1986 Notable Contributions to Accounting Literature Award. In his last years he continued to write essays, completing volume six in 1993.

Carl Devine was a genuine scholar who believed that being a bookworm was an honorable pursuit. His dedication to scholarship, and the integrity that he displayed in all aspects of his life, served as a model for other faculty and produced a lasting influence on many former students and colleagues. He was 87 when he died at his Tallahassee home on September 12, 1998. Professor Devine is survived by his wife Drue, his son Steven, and his daughter Beth.

Author's Foreword

A note on the genesis of these essays may be of interest. The first two volumes were mimeographed in 1962. Volume III dates from 1971, Volume IV from 1977, and Volume V from 1985.

The idea for these essays dates back to graduate-school days (thirties) when I adopted the practice of writing brief comments and tossing them into an informal file—"Topics in Accounting Theory." Upon retrieval many notes that once excited insomnia turned out to be trivial. Some items were leftovers from my dissertation. Others were used in a futile attempt to change the traditional course of cost accounting. My efforts on depreciation and amortization were plundered for a handbook contribution. The original opening essay for Volume I became, with some modification, a 1958 presentation to the AAA Ivory-Tower Committee and a 1960 article in the *Review*. Materials on measurement theory were ransacked in 1966 for a contribution to an AAA symposium on measurement.

In the original plan Volume I was to contain broad interdisciplinary relationships and Volume II was to be devoted to more practical accounting matters. Historically the second volume with the exception of the notes on scientific methods and scattered emendations came first and dates from the forties. This latest volume is composed of scraps and leftovers reshuffled to emphasize my own accounting-world view and sets forth some recent more personal conceptions.

This current volume belongs to my post-scientific thinking. Over the years I have been enthusiastic about combining hypothetico-deductive processes with the flexibility of empirical methods and have argued that this combination should be applied to the field of accounting. There are obvious advantages to grouping individuals and concepts, responding to them in terms of their commonalities instead of their uniqueness, and placing discourse in an antecedent-consequent relationship. Clearly I have not abandoned scientific methods and their dependence on shared experiences for their grounding.

In spite of meticulous care in giving detailed attributions some of the ideas are now so interwoven and overlapping that it is no longer possible to dissociate them or even speculate about their origins. For example the exciting work of Murray Hilibrand (an unpublished doctoral dissertation) on the importance of "source credibility" was later found to be an extension of ideas set forth more than a decade earlier by Carl Hovland and his associates. It is humiliating to reflect on countless other deserving innovators who may have been victims of similar neglect.

Certainly there is more to accounting than mathematical manipulation, computer literacy, statistical transformations on the one hand and agonizing soul searching to uncover the mysteries of existence on the other. Blatant scientism is simply inadequate. Yet the obvious merits of deconstruction, discourse, symbolic interaction and hermeneutic interpretation cannot lead to universal explanation. My sympathies for the latter groups are expressed clearly in this volume, but they too must "ground" their arguments and "privilege" their positions. Argumentation in the hands of experts can trivialize discourse and both scientists and their opponents sooner or later must fall back on sheer faith to support their beliefs and make their explanations convincing.

At an earlier time I was enthusiastic about the merits of symbolic logic, mathematics and precisely constructed languages. I am now more sympathetic to polysematic interpretations and the use of common languages with their quick acknowledgement of ambiguities and uncertainties. Emphasis on logic, in my current opinion, encourages extremists of the go-no-go variety and naive believers in absolute truth and other non-negotiable positions. Scientists have softened their positions by supporting *tentative* conclusions but have maintained some of their dogmatic standards for acceptance and refutation. Ironically advocates of discourse and deconstruction agree with scientists on the tentative nature of belief, and hermeneutic interpretations allow ample room for ordinary ambiguities and uncertainties. Certainly I have no compulsion to stand firmly with either of these attractive groups at the exclusion of the other. A free spirit must often stand alone and alienated from deeply respected colleagues and friends.

Some critics have remarked about my changing accounting views, but at least I have remained a consistent and unreconstructed subjectivist. To me the distinction between *self* and the environment (me and thou, subject and object) is definitional, and I simply prefer a unifying merger rather than the traditional two-dimensional separation. In the tradition of Marcus Aurelius "I am a part of all I've met" and following Ortega "the past is I." The philosophical result is a strange mixture that more or less rejects both dualism and monism in favor of a William-James-like, many faceted concept of reality—a constructed reality.

On the level of particulars I have always been a moderate humanist and an unreserved advocate of intellectual freedom. From this perspective the current trend toward political correctness is an abomination. Yet clearly rational discourse has no place for shouting and jeering by intimidating and threatening mobs. Making life disagreeable for all who disagree is a sorry basis for interpersonal relations.

I view the current stress on ethnicity with severe reservations. In the present world unrestrained tribalism (and its big brother nationalism) simply will not do. This age-old problem of conflicting group identifications requires a balance that permits satisfying identification with ethnic traditions and folkways with enough broader community spirit to avoid the rise of ungovernable mobs. A sense of communal responsibility for *all* of mankind must not give way to unbridled what's-in-it-for-me or what's-in-it-for-my-little subgroup even if the subgroup is a flourishing national state.

Put simply, I consider the balance of our responsibility to humanity with the desires of individuals and their responsibilities to smaller identity groups—ethnic or otherwise — to be the major problem of the day. Recently in America this general dilemma has been centered on the more manageable interpretation of the First Amendment and the so-called right to privacy. With the help of psychiatrists and related therapists, who concentrate on the individual and consider social constraints to be machinations of the enemy, the scales have been tilting in favor of the individual. It is clear that I have much more respect for community responsibilities than some of my new-left friends. I remain convinced that a considerable level of social responsibility is necessary for even an anarchistic state to operate and to survive.

In view of my disenchantment with universities that forget their intellectual mission and administrators who are too often anti-intellectual, a word of praise for some universities may be in order. Rarely did university administrators (some with scanty resources) fail to give encouragement and support my efforts. Some gatekeepers (department heads and deans) did not understand the relevance of my work to either scholarship or accounting. Others were simply not interested in either accounting or accountants unless the profession is involved directly in the latest computer technologies or the arithmetic of decision making. Fortunately for me a surprising number were willing to support my rambling efforts even though by their standard accounting is a poor vehicle and my chosen paradigm (based on discourse) a capricious choice.

The uneven quality of university libraries should be noted. Most librarians were supportive and were pleased to help with my endless offbeat inquiries. A very few employees (usually lower-level assistants) were surly in responding to detailed and persistent demands, but fortunately library professionals showed respect for their materials and for the tedious requirements of intense inquiry. Special thanks are due the librarians of Penn's Lippincott library and the libraries at Johns Hopkins and Chicago. Many others were efficient but detached, while one (Stetson), with severely limited resources, made strangers feel welcome and at home.

Thanks are due to a host of student associates and to the universities that made them available. My practice has been to acquire my own copies of important volumes, mark passages for possible quotation and depend on student typists to copy these passages, and order them for quick accessibility. This procedure is highly recommended. These files can be the equivalent of well constructed outlines and can convey a firsthand feeling for each author's beliefs and methods.

Thanks are due to Joseph Icerman and Jane Reimers for generous clerical assistance from limited departmental resources and to Elise Hiatt, whose patient decoding of atrocious copy has been a monumental exercise in effective cryptology. Finally (again) special thanks to Edward McIntyre for the usual steadying hand and quiet encouragement.

Sincere and loving appreciation goes to Drue, Steve, Beth and numerous household animals who wandered freely about the house without interfering greatly with the tedious and sometimes lonesome work. Finally appreciation is due the Thomases for honest genes and the Devines for providing an intellectual oasis in the middle of early twentieth-century rural Appalachia. In many ways I did not fully utilize these advantages, but these rambling essays, for all their limitations, are about the best I can do.

Tallahassee
Carl Thomas Devine, 1993

CARL THOMAS DEVINE

ESSAYS IN ACCOUNTING THEORY

A Capstone

ESSAY 1

Accounting Theory: A Personal Journey

It is a commonplace that the orientation of a theorist to his particular field is likely to be an extension of his general world view. In my own case it is impossible to separate arguments about accounting theory from more inclusive philosophical and sociological views.

The organization of this essay is simple. First, attention is given to my extremely subjective view of the world and the influence of this view on such accounting concepts as depreciation, goodwill, inventories, loss recognition, objectivity, neutrality, professional functions and ethics generally. Second, the influence of some training in mathematics and interest in the semantic aspects of language (communication) is traced and assessed. Third, my interest in pragmatism is discussed in terms of concern for interpersonal (social) relations and its early transfer to what is now known as "behavioral" accounting. Finally, my lifelong interest in ethics and the frailty of the human condition is discussed in terms of the necessary value structures that lie behind human actions and especially the values that lie behind simple market supply-demand surrogates. The impossibility of ever escaping value judgments and the futility of expecting the profession to be neutral, fair and provide justice for all should then be clear.

While my highly subjective orientation has been fairly consistent, it has never been so extreme as to deny the possibility of an outside world and the need to correlate our responses with experiences over which we seem to have little conscious control. To carry on a successful life it is necessary to accept the presence of other entities whose interactions and responses are only partially correlated with ours. In any case it is neces-

1

sary for accountants to assume the presence of events (or related entities) that need to be interpreted and translated into accounting language, and it is essential that auditors assume the presence of others who make these interpretations and translations. Moreover accountants cannot avoid some degree of dualism for they require the assumption of external events that have influences that need to be recorded.[1] In my own case I have incorporated enough dualistic (n-tuplistic?) concepts to escape the "egocentric predicament," and have accepted the existence of events to be symbolized, and the presence of others to interpret them.

In one important area my respect for the rigorous arguments of Carnap (*The Logical Syntax of Language,* 1959) may have done more harm than good. Carnap insisted on the separation of semantics (symbols to things) from pragmatics (symbols to human reactions), and, in spite of my uneasiness with dualistic philosophy, I tended to emphasize the semantic aspect of language instead of the pragmatic aspect that is more consistent with my long commitment to a subjective framework. The general semantics of Korzybski combines semantics and pragmatics and is certainly more congenial for one who thinks of *things* in terms of stable experiences. My version may have been influenced by the feeling that Korzybski, in spite of his brilliance, was an intellectual blowhard and by Chase and Hayakawa who emphasized "finding referents." After a decade or two my natural pragmatism reasserted itself and returned to communication as human intercourse rather than a relationship between symbols and things.

While there has been a consistently subjectivistic thread in my thinking, there have been times when the assumption of a more or less objective world has been relatively more important. During the early forties my thinking was dominated by language and referents that are grounded in experience. The second period of emphasis was in the late fifties, when mathematicians were seeking interpretations for their variables, logicians were seeking rules of correspondence for their symbols and model-makers were concerned with models that were isomorphic to external data.

This strong subjective approach to philosophy had some interesting and important practical consequences. One important consequence is that I seldom took an unequivocal stand for any accounting alternative as being superior in all situations. Accountants who believed in objectivity, neutrality and the like, were in a better position to take rigid stands on such matters as historical versus current exit costs. Once appropriate objective factors had been specified Littleton could support historical costs,

Paton could defend current costs, Chambers could thunder for exit values, Carl Nelson and a host of others could be confident that Fisher and Canning had discovered the stone tablets that spoke for discounted expectations.

A subjective orientation develops an uneasiness over objective criteria and an appreciation for differences and unlike situations. Clearly there are limits to the subjective approach or thinking degenerates into solipsism and an egocentric labyrinth. At some point even the most subjective philosopher must place individual experiences into classes and respond to them in terms of their commonalities rather than their differences. The important point here is for the investigator to recognize when he is making such aggregations and not trying to defend them by vague references to objectivity or by constructing physical analogies to support his beliefs. Unfortunately those with subjective inclinations are at a disadvantage in arguing with dogmatic people. Extremists have a body of staunch friends and supporters along with the advantage of a consistent position. A situationalist is much more vulnerable and must become accustomed to charges of vacillation and indecision.

My revolt against models and the science of *things* came early in my accounting study and later led to what amounted to a behavioral basis for accounting theory with emphasis on language, interpretation and the need for endless value judgments. My dissertation (1940) was devoted largely to expectations and their relationship to accounting gains and losses. The intuition that the movement of physical goods has no relation whatever to values was then generalized to cost or market and to the view that losses (except for evidentiary matters) are usually related to breaching original revenue-getting *expectations*.[2] Optimistic increases in expectations after purchase but before disposal are (within the traditional structure) not sufficient to support recognizable gains, while reductions of original expectations on the downside traditionally are a sufficient condition for showing accounting losses. Whether this decrease is brought about by physical damage, obsolescence or by more general reductions in sales potential (perhaps, from lower replacement costs) *is important only* as *evidence* for the lowered expectations. This subjective view was then expanded moderately to include speculation about the behavioral effects of taking inventory gains slowly as the goods are sold and taking losses more rapidly through the cost or market formula. Certainly there are important influences on entrepreneurial expectations, private investment decisions and the business cycle generally.

The subjective orientation leads to certain practical positions. Inventory valuation, for example, can be completely separated from the movement of physical goods. The specific invoice calculation recommended by many accountants as the standard to judge the various inventory formulas becomes irrelevant. In my early years I preferred the average inventory formula. It seemed obvious that with stable economic conditions selling one of ten gallons of identical alcohol results in giving up one-tenth of the income potential (value) regardless of any cost figures marked on a particular bottle. It was just as obvious that with rising prices one-tenth of the pooled cost was a poor measure of sacrifice for a continuing concern, and my preference shifted to LIFO (really current costs) with supplementary balance-sheet disclosure of current values.

In a similar fashion the subjective orientation carried over into problems of depreciation and depletion. It was obvious that tons of unmined coal might be equivalent along some measurement scales that might be worthless as measures of value. Some tons may be easy to extract and others difficult with exorbitant costs of removal. In a similar manner physical conditions and capacities of fixed assets are appropriate only to the extent that they are surrogates for service potentials. For example it was argued that a tobacco barn with a physical life of twenty years need not be depreciated over each of the twenty years if it was constructed only to hold bumper crops from a few productive years. In short it seemed that costs should be matched with revenues when the expected revenues (or other benefits) were received rather than on some physical or other "objective" basis. In general physical inventories became sales expectations, physical buildings became anticipated shelter plus future tax deductions, insurance contracts became assurances of less risk, (so that different rates of return may be appropriate), oil wells became revenue generators, dollars of sales became measures (often poor ones) of accomplishment, and so on.

My early writings reveal unusual attention to replacement methods of depreciation. This method allocates capital consumption to periods by using periodic expenditures (after initial acquisition). Traditional depreciation methods divorce expenses and expenditures and "smooth" the periodic expense by what are essentially statistical procedures for handling lags and leads. This attitude then was expanded to the problem of finding an acceptable depreciating unit. The selection of a building for the depreciation unit, for example, smoothes the original cost of painting, roofing, heating, etc., over the expected life of the entire building. The accountant then expects the costs of all replacements to average-out sufficiently to make the additional work of selecting smaller depreciating units unnecessary. This preliminary discussion also was used to introduce distribution reserves and composite depreciation.

At one time the cost of purchased goodwill was permitted to remain unchanged on the books over the life of the firm. Here too future costs to buttress the firm's intangible position were presumed to be uniform enough to make the separation of expense and expenditure unnecessary. Incidentally the current 40-year provision consciously smoothes only 2½ percent of the original cost and still depends on the spacing of expenditures to provide a sensible overall measure of capital consumption.

This subjective attitude has continued throughout my accounting career, although there has been some change in interpretations. In an economic sense it has resulted in my favoring value-in-use over the more objective value-in-exchange. Thus I have never been a rabid (or consistent) supporter or critic of either historical or current market costs. In the early years I was satisfied with the historical cost process that feeds shrewd acquisitions, obsolescence and inflation factors into income as the assets are used and revenues recorded.

My early criticism of market prices was that they do not represent actual subjective values of either the buyer or the seller unless both are at the margin. Certainly market prices do not express the subjective values of any of those who failed to participate in exchanges. It is true that current market values may represent possible alternatives that may be open to the entity. However these alternatives are never exercised by a firm that is *not* in the market and may be irrelevant for a going concern committed to continued operations. Fortunately I remain genuinely concerned about periodic income numbers that include changes in market values that do not enter into interfirm transactions and are therefore possible alternatives that are never taken.

The belief that accountants account only for events that actually transpire is an attractive one for those who feel comfortable with the concept of objectivity. It is my belief that this attitude has done far more harm than good to those who are expected to profit from accounting information. In this area economists have been well ahead of accountants by making subjective sacrifice the defining cornerstone for cost. To be operational, economists too must employ simplifications. Their practical measure of sacrifice is the best alternative known to have been foregone and is an extremely difficult rule to implement.

The importance of language in stabilizing beliefs and even in determining reality itself is illustrated here, and in this instance limiting the world covered by accounts to transactions and disbursements does not come off well. Far too many businessmen (and no doubt others) have been influenced to make foolish decisions. Examples are too numerous for comment, but the most common and pernicious is the widespread feeling that there is no interest cost when major acquisitions are made for cash. Larger down payments do not automatically lower the acknowledged cost of such purchases!

More importance was attached to current market values when the price-level began rising during World War II, although I have never taken a doctrinaire stand for any particular income definition or measurement. It is clear that proper economic proportioning of the factors of production requires current costs and that changes in ways of doing business, e.g., leases give them wider relevance for a continuing concern. LIFO replaced averages as my preferred inventory procedure, not because it attempts to keep *physical* capital intact, but because it is a surrogate for current sacrifice.

While I never took a strong position on general-price-level adjustments as a routine part of the reporting system, it seemed to me that one of management's *functions* is to keep monetary assets and equities reasonably balanced and therefore specific monitoring of this function should be a part of the accounting service. Oscar Nelson convinced me (1942) that market prices for specific assets include an estimate of obsolescence, and I later concluded that the chief difference between general and specific levels was (for the longrun) due in part to specific obsolescence. In any case it seemed that balance-sheet adjustments for specific asset changes (through reserves and appraisals) along with a reasonable balancing of dollar denominated assets and liabilities could often serve as a substitute for more complete general price-level adjustments.

My interest in Irving Fisher's approach to income was naturally favorable and has remained so. Clearly he was the most subjective of business economists, and I was captivated by a definition of income entirely in terms of expectations. His later recommendation for equating consumption expenditures to income is hardly consistent with his earlier views even though it does include important incentives for investment expenditures and avoids some well known difficulties in traditional income measurement.

It is clear that Fisher's income, defined entirely in terms of discounted expectations, offers numerous opportunities for managerial manipulation and non-auditable fraud. Its advantages too seem obvious, e.g., new information is incorporated quickly. The scope of this new information is broadened to include expectations about general business conditions, new product acceptance, etc. Finally the Fisher measure is particular to the firm in that the expectation estimates are made for each individual firm rather than by the market process of forming general estimates from a broad spectrum of firms.

LANGUAGE

The interest in the relationship of accounting to language came shortly after my first serious study of accounting. Stuart Chase, a CPA, brought out *The Tyranny of Words* in 1938, the year I encountered *The Meaning of Meaning* (Ogden and Richards, 1923). Chase became intrigued with populist social movements and demonstrated less interest in accounting as a communication device. Many accountants did mention accounting as the language of business, but none developed the theme or expanded to the wider concept of communication. In those years I was something of a frustrated English scholar and had retained some interest in this discipline. On one of numerous *ad hoc* discussions that ranged from old Icelandic to endless interpretations of Ulysses, some imaginative student (Susan Lee Heines?) suggested that accounting might be viewed as a system of metaphors designed to evoke predictable responses from a specialized reading audience. This paradigm fitted well with my interest in pragmatism and led to my view that accounting is a set of constructions that need interpretation and finally to a behavioral view of accounting. In some ways the term "behavioral" is a misnomer and dredges up memories of Watsonian physical responses to outside stimuli. My own usage was intended to emphasize *user* interpretations in terms of individual ends in view.

It is clear that accountants employ elementary mathematics as a specialized form of expression. It is also obvious that applied mathematics itself is a language (perhaps not a very rich one) and finally that both accounting and mathematics are related to poetry and other literary forms. Poets select their audiences, choose from a wide variety of impressions they wish to create and employ a wide variety of linguistic devices. Mathematics has a narrower field of application with less emphasis on emotive reactions, but mathematicians too try to express their output to further understanding and help readers intuit new relationships. Accountants adopt a still narrower view and restrict their efforts mainly to wealth (its changes and potentials) and direct their efforts to a limited audience interested in such considerations.

My deep-seated uneasiness with the new criticism in literature and with "transformational" (generative) grammar extends to its converse as set forth by Merleau-Ponty.[3] It seems that Chomsky and Ransom are brothers under the skin and it seems further that both are close to the position of the young Russell and other early boosters of symbolic logic. The metaphysical reality attributed to symbolic logic and grammar is precisely opposite to the direction I wish to go. Yet I cannot imagine "meaning" without a grammar covering operating rules—even if the language is simply pointing. Nor can I imagine a pointing grammar without specified relationships for the required gestures. Certainly human beings need to structure their sensations and the need for structuring rules (whether called grammar or logic) is simply not arguable.

Symbolic logicians who attempt to separate the structure (grammar) from meanings (semantical interpretation) are in trouble immediately for they must employ undefined terms and various interpretations and semi-interpretations that permit them to recognize the structural concepts and understand how they are related and manipulated. On the practical level formal classes can be established by stipulation but before they can be used they must be related to the world of experience by overlooking all sorts of ambiguities and outrageous analogies. It is my contention that the grays of ambiguity must be an important part of any language and that a language defined without considering them is a form of extreme idealism. (Consider the belated popularity of "fuzzy" logic.)

I have never been a structuralist in the traditional sense except in so far as its advocates must at some point adopt pragmatic criteria. Vague references to "inner logics" and to "internal dynamics" never seem to be fruitful. This suspicion has been with me a long time (perhaps from 1940) and I simply cannot understand (much less support) the internal literary criticism of Robert Penn Warren, John Crowe Ransom and their followers. It seems to me that poetic criticism without outside (pragmatic) considerations does not make sense except possibly in the way that symbolic logic makes sense. The same feeling applies to some aspects of Noam Chomsky's attempts to define language in terms of grammar alone. Yet it is difficult to argue against Chomsky or the interpretative sociologists and deny the usefulness of treating language as problematic in all research endeavors.

The record on my association with hermeneutics and deconstruction is not entirely clear. To some extent I have always grounded my beliefs in a modified coherence theory of truth in that by some definition of "coherence" the statements of a system must hang together and cohere. This basis for grounding is based in large part on language and a unified understanding of the symbols that others are expressing (objectivizing?). Interest in language and persuasion as determinants of beliefs and opinions goes back many decades.

As a Dewey disciple I have been a practicing situationalist, but there has always remained the realization that intellectual effort *must* group clearly disparate experiences and respond to them as well as manipulate them in terms of group commonalities. Even ostensive pointing to express "here-now" requires responses in terms of space groupings and time intervals for cognition. The newer critics are on target in complaining about scientists and others who "privilege" certain bases for belief and "ground" their arguments in a presumed dualistic world. Yet my support has been restrained because hermeneuts themselves must ground their arguments and privilege certain forms of evidence.

My long career as a traditional subjectivist means that my sympathies are with the new critics, but I have always been aware of the need to accept *some* basis for grounding and privileging. The benefits of discourse and consensual understanding cannot be denied, but again I have always shied away from dependence on invisible (or visible) hands that guide the course of dialectics. The older privileging of physical manifestations and substantive evidence has always been troubling, but I have hesitated to depend entirely on soul stirrings and the powers of rhetoric for a complete "understanding." All inquirers privilege something and ground their arguments somewhere. One important aspect is that accountants understand the necessity for foundations to support foundations, and so on and on. Specific groundings in specific situations may be far less important than recognizing this necessity.

While it is essential that all believers and persuaders privilege something, I have never been convinced by references to vague "inner logics" or inner dynamics or mysteriously constructed structures. It is always possible to *define* or *stipulate* the desired qualities of, say, a musical composition and then evaluate the quality of any particular composition by applying these defining guidelines. In this sense it is possible to omit pragmatic considerations (effects on listeners) from the defining process and be an expert music critic (judge the merits of an individual composition) without leaving the prescribed stipulations. Such criticism uses only the properties expressed in the definition. All evaluations no doubt proceed in this general manner, but ultimately someone must devise the standards. In my own case it is difficult to evaluate propositions or actions without recourse to pragmatic consideration. In an important sense the most abstract mathematics and logic survive because they are relevant to the human condition. Yet to hold that the richness of human existence should be governed importantly by a narrowly-defined, go-no-go system for exposing certain kinds of contradictions is no longer appealing. My antagonism toward phenomenologists and those who wish to employ only morphology for their structures started early and has continued. Attempts by morphologists to form typologies with complete disregard to function may provide interesting intellectual exercises and qualify for exciting entertainment, but such aimless system building can scarcely support an entire philosophical structure. Even the formalization of mathematics and logic has well established objectives and the *surviving* rules of transformation must serve some social purpose.

Phenomenologists wish to reduce particulars to "basic essences" and group (bracket) them on this basis. Presumably they can perform this task without any explicit basis for classification other then some innate ability to recognize fundamental essences. In this respect they remind me of the AICPA's search for *fundamental* postulates without guidelines to identify observations that are fundamental, and of those who wish to identify *critical* events among the myriad of happenings that are not critical. Nor have I been able to identify with those who select *fundamental flows* to support transactions or those who divide the world into inputs and outputs that affect accounting and those that do not.

Uneasiness with the true-false distinction and with the concept of absolute truth also go well back in my thinking. Early pragmatic worry over the warrantedness of assertions was soon accompanied by positivist worry over verification, confirmation, and possible ways of distinguishing between truth and falsity. Thus while I have always had great admiration for the precision of formal logic and great respect for those who practice its forms, I have never been an all-or-none investigator, and as a result my writing has seemed to be more difficult because of the numerous shades of gray that demand attention. I still maintain that the logical postulates "if *p*, then *p*" and "if *p* or *q*, then *p*"—the laws of identify—are impossible to implement except by stipulation. In practice the investigator must work with various degrees of similarity, imperfect rules of interpretation, and the use of near and not-so-near analogies.

In the early *Essays* I was intellectually seduced by Carnap and Ayer into believing that there is some *important* difference between analytic and synthetic explications. Thus I argued that there was some important structural difference between such expressions as "the sky is blue" and "Beth is beautiful." The second statement was thought to be about a *belief* while the first in some mysterious way was true or false by criteria other than belief. The ridiculous nature of this distinction is obvious when it is realized that observational methods are necessary to determine whether the analytic rules are properly applied. Others have argued that the second statement is different because it is a "preference" statement (or an expression without a predicate), but it should be clear that both are *belief* statements even though the methods of arriving at belief may not be similar. Such statements assert that some particular is a member of some class, but the interesting discussion is about ways of getting support for this belief.

SCIENCE: A STRONG EMBRACE—A MILD REVOLT

It seems to be a giant step from my subjective background to an embrace of scientific methods and the elements of semantics that relate language symbols to some conception of an external world. This transition was easy enough, because by that time I had been introduced to Whitehead and Russell and their conceptions of reality. The elementary *things* of physics became bundles of direct or indirect experiences with certain accepted stability patterns and they differed only in details from revenues, income and similar accounting constructions. In other words by 1940 my concept of science was reasonably modern and was not encumbered by the burden of the older physicists and philosophers speculating about the "true nature" of a world composed of things. Science became a way of organizing and talking about common and uncommon experiences.

Science as a model for accounting was for those times a relatively sophisticated paradigm, but the first quotation in Essay One, Volume I[4] and numerous subsequent statements indicate caution and extreme skepticism over the dualistic philosophy upon which traditional science is based.

Essay One contains quite a few warnings about naive scientists. The emphasis on Bridgman[5] indicates a more traditional view of science, but there also is mention of his own emphasis on the *personal* nature of science and the necessity for *mental* operations (Essay One, p. 6). Even today I insist that *comparing, evaluating* and *ordering* are operational, and that, if we can recognize differences and evaluate them, we should in principle be able to correlate experiences with certain number systems and thus measure them. Thus I have had few problems with presenting summaries of accounting measures (surrogates) for well-offness, value added, strength of belief and expectations so long as they share a common dimension. This dimension is an expectation of well-offness (wealth). While accountants may not be able to add apples and oranges they can and *must* be able to add *something* about disparate items, e.g., number of calories, number of hemispherical items, number of food objects, market value.

My background in elementary science and quantitative methods meant that Russell became a favorite and I remained a loose disciple until his mystical associations between logic and reality reduced my commitment. My introduction to positivism came not from Comte but from Karl Pearson (*circa* 1938), whose no-nonsense view of science has remained an influence to this day. The positivism of Pearson led naturally to an interest in earlier writers from the new field of semantics, which at that time seemed to combine the best of subjective association with symbols that relate to an external, *mutually acknowledged* world. Nevertheless I have never been a card-carrying dualist, and accordingly became intrigued with the interpretations that often surround symbols. Moreover I was influenced by William James' (*Pragmatism*) argument that dualism is a simplification of an n-dimensional framework based on particular situations in which each individual is an active participant. This background is consistent with my long interest in solipsism—a toe-in-the-water haven for those to whom dualism becomes unbearable. It was about this time that (despite my respect for Skinner) gestaltism began to replace my more simple behavioralist S→R structure, but it took some time for conceptualism to replace the older operationalism that had shaped my early thinking.[6]

My interest in models and systems was a natural outgrowth of the earlier interest in semantics and languages. Semantic problems revolve about the well-known triad of symbol-concept-event and require associations in the form of individual interpretations and organized rules of correspondence for correlating members of the triad. A deep respect for applied mathematics and its requirement to translate the conditions of a situation into symbolic relationships seemed appropriate for the field of accounting. Classroom accounting requires a translation of the language of an exercise into events in the business universe and the retranslation of *certain aspects of these events* into the language of accounting. Wealth claims, transfers and potentials are manipulated and summarized according to rigid (semi-mathematical) rules. Thus I found little conceptual difference between the preparation of a balance sheet for bankers and, for example, an analysis of a bridge with its stresses, strains, moments and the like.

In any case my already declining faith in causation was largely destroyed, and I turned to a poorly structured concept of associative correlation as an acceptable substitute. This statistical concept is in accord with Pearson and Russell's idea that one never knows *why* anything ever happens and must be content to predict *how* it happens. Moreover this concept was more in keeping with intermediate mathematics where functional relations in both implicit and explicit forms made the concept of causation unnecessary. (Observe however that mathematicians must still isolate relevant variates and either neglect or randomize the remainder of the environment.) I remain uneasy when anyone introduces the concept of causation even though the concept is clearly useful in the social sciences, where goals are often fed back in to arguments as causes for actions. To accommodate this need I turned to the Dewey framework, which requires decisions about variables that are critical and manipulatable. These variables are defined as causes.

Those with minimum philosophical training recognize the shakiness of scientific foundations and the simplistic philosophy (ontology and epistemology) behind the concepts. Most scientists are dualists who make a sharp distinction between the "I" and the external world that is assumed to be independent of the investigator, even though Russell pointed out two-thirds of a century ago that the scientist can only observe what is going on in his own mind, i.e., science must contain an element of psychology. Most scientists assume regularities in subjective experiences that can be loosely correlated to events in a presumed external world. This correlation is supported by the belief that the subjective experiences can be shared with others and that agreement among *qualified* investigators leads to scientific truth. Thus confidence is increased when experiences are stable through time or over repeated testings and can be shared with others. Accordingly in a roundabout way traditional scientists may (if they wish) substitute belief in the shared reactions of other scientists for belief in the external existence of things.

For scientists shareable experiences are privileged and provide firmer grounding than day dreams, hallucinations and personal feelings. The psyche along with emotional stirrings are as far as possible removed from the human scientific condition. In any case repeated (stable) experiences are used to support the concept of *things*. Shared experiences become a modified concept of objectivity and lead to the belief that the external part of dualistic philosophy does exist.[7] My own scientific training was not so dogmatic, and early on (*circa* 1940) I began to question the concepts of neutrality and objectivity. Unfortunately my uneasiness with the two concepts did not (at that time) extend to independence. This recognition came a decade or so later when I became acquainted with the extension of the Marxian concept of ideology to the more general concept of the sociology of all knowledge. A nagging question then became unbearable: How can auditors be independent when they are creatures of their society, and are taught to observe, infer, reason, interpret, remember, and report in similar ways?

It was not for another decade or more that I began to generalize and to think of research in non-scientific terms and to think of science as a belief system that—like religions—at some point must rest on sheer faith. Sooner or later the most sophisticated scientist is forced to confess that his proofs lead to an endless regress and at some point he must *accept* the assumptions and, like the prophets themselves, rely on simple faith. At some stage the support for observations, objectivity, existence, being and the like no longer qualifies for the standards set by science itself. In these cases he must give up asking for *whys* and retreat, like Karl Pearson, to the position that scientists only describe relationships and must have faith that they will continue.

It should be obvious to the most unsophisticated reader that scientific methods cannot capture all important aspects of the human condition. Clearly science does a poor job of explaining religious fervor and emotive experiences. Logical positivists had trouble explaining Hitler's non-rational outcries or the successes of such leaders as Oral Roberts and fellow fundamentalists. Some casual attempts to explain a science of values have been made, but clearly science neglects major parts of the human experience by simply ignoring them. A gnawing and continuing question: How then are such experiences to be studied? By *expanded* scientific methods? Expanded in what ways? Along what dimensions? The road is now open for deconstruction and hermeneutics.

What science does, it does very well indeed, and I have never been serious about rejecting the scientific outlook. However, science is virtually useless for the delicate, sensitive task of intuiting useful hypotheses. Moreover, the rigorous physical anchoring has proved to be far too rigid to certify many hypotheses that make up my current ethical and esthetical beliefs.

BEHAVIORAL ACCOUNTING

My interest in the behavioral aspects of accounting date from the dissertation days (1938–40) and acquaintance with Fritz Schmidt's *Rechenfehler,* in which he argued that inconsistent accounting rules for recognition of gains and losses are a substantial cause of business cycles. The Schmidt effort reinforced my existing interest in language interpretation and traditional pragmatism.

In retrospect my efforts in cost accounting (1940-7) were woefully inadequate in emphasizing the behavioral aspects of the profession. At that time I stubbornly argued that it was not the duty of the accountant to enforce standards, and accordingly concentrated on techniques of variance reporting and analysis. Even the attention devoted to profit planning had an industrial engineering flavor with mathematics of finance over-emphasized for handing decisions variables. Even before the text was completed, I became concerned with the lack of behavioral content and, without making major changes, added a discussion of ethics and tried to restructure profit planning to include additional behavioral overtones. Neither operation turned out well.

The immediate influence for the interest in behavioral studies (my chief concern of the fifties) was the realization of the appalling ignorance of reader interpretations and responses to accounting reports. It was clear that accountants made wide use of behavioral assumptions with only limited knowledge of psychology, sociology or the embryonic decision sciences. Moreover accountants were practically ignorant of traditional scientific methods and the hypothetico-deductive method for structuring arguments. It was also obvious that while Paton and some other leaders were extremely skilled in argument and persuasion, they used behavioral hypotheses that often were little more than unsupported conjectures. Often these hypotheses were presented as bare-bone assertions and as naturalistic self-evident truths.

In the early years interest in behavioral work grew out of my respect for pragmatism and the teleological underpinning of all service professions. It was clear that practicing accountants knew almost nothing about the important revolution in psychological theories and that most of their statements about reader reactions and the superiority of specific accounting rules were the result of observation by amateurs.[8] In some cases the behavioral consequences were simply ignored or supported by the most simplistic assumptions. My own dissertation, for example, contained a study of the influences of inventory costing methods on periodic profits with little consideration for the effects that differences in reported profits might themselves have on purchasing and inventory policies. A former colleague also presented a dissertation that assessed the effects of alternative accounting rules on business cycles without empirical data, substantial knowledge of user behavior or, for that matter, the relevant German literature.

In retrospect it is clear that my avid *first* embrace of the behavioral sciences also grew out of early interest in applying scientific methods to accounting. As my own interest in psychology and sociology increased, my emphasis on strict empiricism was strangely reduced. Obviously there was a great need for statistical (empirical) evidence to support professional beliefs and to permit useful generalizations. Yet later researchers almost without fail emphasized the technical (statistical) features of their behavioral work in accounting. This technical approach did solidify some previous speculations about human behavior in an accounting context and confirmed a few established conclusions. Meanwhile my own interests returned to a highly subjective view of accounting interpretation that left me stranded on a lonely road while my intellectual companions frantically were paving new roads with their newly discovered statistical weapons. It is still my stubborn belief that much of accounting cannot yet be supported by the endless statistical tables and Greek-letter operations favored by some editors of current journals. I remain genuinely disappointed with the continuing lack of attention to human interpretation and the necessity for value assessments and judgments. Meanwhile, for empiricists and their positivistic brothers the current journalistic *Zeitgeist* is favorable and the planetary orbits are in proper conjunction.

Naturally many behavioral studies do little more than confirm what professional leaders learned long ago through simple intelligent observation. Still some studies have broken new ground and the multitude of small advances and confirmations combine to advance professional knowledge. An immediate advantage has been increased interdisciplinary contacts with psychologists, statisticians, sociologists and the like. These interactions are to be encouraged even at the expense of some valuable accounting training. The need to devote serious study to statistics, probability and mathematics, even though one cannot hope to become competent, means that there is simply not enough time to understand adequately the possible limitations inherent in their application, but an important by-product of the interdisciplinary movement is that some high-class prospects have been attracted to the accounting field. Unfortunately this force works in reverse, for clearly a number of good analytical accounting prospects have been drawn away by the appeal of more glamorous interdisciplinary areas.

VALUES AND ETHICS—EDUCATION

My interest in values and their place in research activity came early. Undergraduate work at a Christian-oriented, liberal-arts college convinced me that values *must* be adopted either consciously or by default. It was also clear that those who oppose the teaching of values in universities are in deep trouble for it is obvious that professors cannot avoid teaching values. Of course their attempts to avoid imparting values may be a conscious decision to let other forces shape the ethical character of society. But even so the fact that a professor displays interest in scholarship and intellectual activity broadcasts that he values these objectives highly and hopes to transmit them to students.

Universities in the thirties placed tolerance for diverse views as a top intellectual value. This value often encouraged pacifism and weak political leadership but with the rise of Hitler, Stalin, and their ilk many realized that different situations call for different priorities even within a rigid value structure and that tolerance, free speech and privacy are not absolute values that are never to be compromised or modified.

It is often argued that universities should be neutral with regard to values and let other institutions, e.g., churches and families, carry the burden of social ethics. This position is of course impossible. Many argue that the highest university value must be respect for intellectual activity—the product that they are supposed to be producing. This view is not shared by all, and some church colleges feel that their priorities are headed by the need to disseminate Christian or other doctrines. Perhaps this is the chief reason why church colleges have not been leaders in research and intellectual activity except in church-related fields.[9]

There have been serious challenges to placing respect for learning at the top of the priority heap. Dewey was interested in problem solving (intellectualism at its best), but he also emphasized indoctrination in the techniques of social democratic living and encouraged schools to widen their responsibilities and take over some traditional family duties in both ethical and practical areas. These later objectives may or may not be desirable in given situations, but it should be observed that such duties compete with the objective of developing intellectual powers. Many state-supported institutions place the need to improve the quality of life through instruction in agriculture, business and community service above the older intellectual view. Teaching basket weaving to disadvantaged indian tribes (as recommended by a highly-rated Canadian administrator) may indeed be praiseworthy but it is not clear that universities are the proper institutions to undertake the task.

Perhaps the most startling shift in values in recent years results from the present emphasis on semi-professional (perhaps fully professional) sports at many American Universities. The Greeks held that a part of education (at some level) should be devoted to building strong bodies and learning behaviors to keep them strong, and in the *Republic* Plato emphasized that intense physical education was especially important to soldiers and artisans. The need for strong bodies is clearly more important in primitive and war-like societies. This association of strong bodies with strong minds may sometimes be justified, but the historical evidence in the Western World hardly supports the thesis, and it may be argued that the time necessary to build and maintain such bodies competes for the limited time available to develop intellects. In any case recruiting and pampering individuals who can scarcely read or write tends to make heroes of the wrong people and to retard genuine intellectual activity.

Even if it is granted that universities should teach all sorts of values, it is still not clear exactly how these values should be ordered and advocated. Some universities try to preserve their presumed neutrality by hiring professors with different views and encourage advocacy even though some advocates are so anti-intellectual that they belittle the very product that universities are designed to produce. While most serious educators value highly the opportunity for students to examine all sides of arguments, it does not seem essential for each to be subjected to rabid advocacy of all positions. This approach does have some merit and appeals to those who feel that human beings as individuals can be trusted to make their decisions and that the aggregate of these decisions will lead to commendable social values.

Sometimes the antineutrality theme is carried to fantastic lengths. In my own experience I have heard speakers argue that American sociologists cannot possibly teach Canadian sociology; that white professors cannot impart an authentic feel for African cultures; that women students (in accounting) should have textbooks written by women who understand the female condition; that only seasoned politicians and businessmen should be permitted to teach politics and business; that only practicing accountants with CPA certificates are able to establish acceptable accounting curricula at the university level. So far I have *not* heard the pluralistic extreme where everyone ends up teaching only himself.

Turn now to the inescapable necessity to teach values to accountants. The virtues of accuracy, for example, are accepted by all accounting students for otherwise they are quickly weeded from the field. Neatness, precision and care for details also have their own rewards, and respect for them is developed rapidly on pain of disapproval.

Respect for the business community and its functions is usually encouraged indirectly by implicit acceptance of business goals. A few teachers have incorporated exercises that involve cooperatives, labor unions, and other non-business hosts. Governmental agencies are often used for classroom material, but such materials are often used to establish conformance to business ethos rather than to further the functions of the agencies. In my own case the depression was indeed a depressing occasion. The psychological deterioration of competent human beings unable to provide for their families was a terrifying experience. (Compare the current urban black-youth experience!) The result was my association of guilt with bankers and businessmen and a turn toward Fabian socialism and later to the Keynesian alternative. In any case I had trouble internalizing accounting values that are tied exclusively to controlled self interest. On the other hand I was repelled by the vicious conflictual sociology of Marx and his communist followers.

Respect for truthfulness and honesty is clearly a requirement for the auditing community. Accounting to conceal rather than to reveal requires a choice between insiders and outsiders. This value choice is related to the hoary ethical dilemma that arises when the interests of an immediate group (landsmen) conflict with the needs of more remote groups. One task of an auditing instructor is to emphasize the values of those beyond the immediate entity.

Somewhere accounting students should learn that misrepresentation by failing to construct an effective overall message (gestalt) by omission or misplaced emphasis is more difficult to detect than specific misrepresentation in the component statements that make up the message. In this area my respect for Theo Limperg has endured through the years. His auditing emphasis was on creating "proper" expectations in the minds of users. He selected his own host group (businessmen) and insisted that proper expectations are those that further "good business administration." This expression is taken as an undefined term in his system, and society's commission to auditors is to present and interpret financial operations in terms of effective administration, and effective administration is a major social goal. Once this social responsibility is accepted, auditing procedures and principles (and presumably ethics) are no longer a choice open to the accounting profession. The relationship of accounting to psychology is nowhere more obvious, and Limperg's association with the business community is equally clear.

In a broad pluralistic society honesty (however defined) is not a clearcut universal objective for all. Interest groups must be traded off against one another and it is impossible to proceed without making choices among them. What may seem honest to one group may seem highly dishonest (and unjust) to others. At lower practitioner levels honesty may be a convenient symbol to further professional unity, but at higher levels it is often more important to recognize the necessary value tradeoffs and to make choices among them. Through the years I have remained suspicious of arguments grounded on honesty, justice, fairness and the like.

The cognition that auditing independence is a poorly defined concept came with an understanding of the sociology of knowledge. With this orientation it becomes obvious that independence in any fundamental sense is a childish chimera. As a result it is necessary for the profession to select a practical definition that can be understood and implemented as a useful construct.

My own approach to ethics has been a relative one, even though I must acknowledge the utility of absolute values—when firmly shared—as stabilizers in a social order. Clearly the values held in the open individualistic society of late twentieth-century America are not identical with those who place group needs above individual needs. Certainly I have never been an individualistic hedonist doing my own thing as if I were disconnected completely from my communities. Unfortunately, those who disregard social controls and assert their right to unfettered freedom are often quick to ask society for help when the dysfunctional consequences of choices become apparent.

On the other side, it is clear that an ideal world does not necessarily follow the concerted will of a dominant group. It is evident that individuals are interdependent and that groups must be granted the right to guide some actions of their members. This is not a currently fashionable position, but I have always held that a society *can* set up its own definitions of such concepts as obscenity. To hold otherwise is to deny support for most concepts defined and communicated within the civilized world. Clearly societies must (implicitly or explicitly) accept these definitions, for only with no dissidents will there be complete satisfaction with decisions by the majority or by any other power group. Charges that it is *impossible* to define such concepts are sheer nonsense. By refusing to accept a common definition society is letting individual actions establish their definitions and determine acceptable behaviors. Since my first exposure to political science, I have held that the First Amendment is one of mankind's really great statements. Yet in late years I have been appalled by those who assert that individual rights are absolute and leave *no* area for group control.

Some positivists and naturalists have argued that ethics should be defined entirely in the rudimentary sense of following rules that are in accord with biological needs for propagation and survival.

These positivists have felt that ethics can be reduced without remainder to naturalistic or biologic foundations. I have never accepted this view although it is clear that many ethical traditions and moral laws do have their roots in the need to preserve the species. The argument is simple to the extreme. Survival is taken as the ultimate value. Science is recognized as the appropriate agency for studying nature and the conditions necessary for survival. It is then argued that ethical problems may be reduced to meeting the observed conditions of nature and *are* therefore subject to study by scientific methods alone. In this horribly simplified conception of human relations much of the richness of human feelings is lost and the necessity to weigh, compare, decide and tradeoff values at the cognitive level is given little attention. I have always recognized the usefulness of this simplification and on occasion have used it to support some tenuous arguments, but I have never admitted that such reductions can account for the entire fabric of interpersonal relations. On the other hand, I have never felt at home with those to ground their arguments in some sort of assumed "human condition." Far too often the human condition is a thinly disguised attempt to expand the accepted concepts of nature to an assumed natural man. Again, argumentation is easy among friends who share the same groundings. It is more difficult to be somewhere near the center with extremists who have dogmatic beliefs barking from all sides.

Many decades ago I was horrified to see the following from highly respected Perry Mason:

> Is there any *accounting* reason why adjustments of paid-in capital can not be made in any way desired by the stockholders as long as legal requirements are met and full disclosure is made of the facts? . . . . Why is this an *accounting* matter?[10]

Mason's position is common among politicians and businessmen who feel that they can discharge their ethical responsibilities by taking lawful actions. This view places all ethical responsibilities on law makers and assumes that public laws express sufficiently the ethics and mores of society itself. Such a view is operational but it abdicates completely all *professional* responsibilities and assumes that the tenuous threads of interpersonal behavior can be completely covered by other institutions. This is strange doctrine for a profession with its own sanctions and responsibilities!

More recently the concept of ethics as lawful behavior has been expanded. Several influential accountants (e.g., Chambers and the positivists) seem to argue that market activities in free-market economies automatically settle problems of business ethics. Again the task of law makers apparently is to see that free markets do in fact result in equitable interpersonal relationships. Markets certainly expedite certain types of business transactions, but I have remained uncomfortable with their self-interest operations as exemplars of desirable ethical behavior.

More recently some theorists have expanded their paradigms into a more general contractual-agential format. Delegation presumably leads to agency relationships, and agency relationships in turn are associated with contracts—express and implied. Such contracts may be the result of market actions or of bargaining arrangements that make use of similar behavioral assumptions. Presumably accountants and their professional leaders have no ethical responsibilities other than to follow the dictates of such agential market relations. For better or for worse, my own view of such a "profession" is clear.

DISAPPOINTMENTS AND INADEQUACIES

The chief disappointment of my intellectual life has resulted from an incipient idealism that owes something to Plato and to Bishop Berkeley. Many times it has seemed that someone should be able to understand and organize the idealistic concepts that make up our discipline. Clearly such understanding and revelation has not come about. Unfortunately similar frustrating failures have occurred in other endeavors. Early musical training led only to translating musical symbols into simplistic melodies with unsatisfactory harmonies and few rich symphonic sounds. In mathematics the technical operations were easy enough to understand, but a satisfactory understanding of the rich logical and physical implications never seemed to actualize. In a similar way listening to foreign languages sometimes yielded sketchy understanding, but somehow meager understanding never bloomed into the richness of meaningful discourse. The language problem has been compounded in the area of poetry. It always seemed that my responses to rhythm, rhyme and the like were limited and piecemeal and that essential emotional experiences were too often beyond my understanding.

It is no doubt childish to hope for a grand denouement of existence, being and a full understanding of the human condition. In any case my experiences with religious and ceremonial rites have not been a grand revelation. The Bible has been interesting primarily in its King James Version with its occasional poetic stretches and moving philosophical passages. The characters never did engage my empathy though it was clear that the religious experience can be deeply moving and a lonesome feeling of missing something of vital importance remains. At one time the oriental religions (especially Buddhism) seemed to offer an avenue for expanding my senses, but Western rationality already was too strong and I simply am unable to understand systems that seem clear to millions of human beings. Their cousins, the phenomenologists and existentialists (Camus, Sartre, Husserl, Heidegger, etc.) offered little help although they appeal to many fellow subjectivists.

As a result of my own condition I have seldom been antagonized by the beliefs of others and seldom tried to convince anyone of the superiority of my own views. This general attitude has carried over into the little pocket of reality known as accounting, where some critics have pointed out that I have failed to delineate and defend my *own* accounting theory. Certainly I admire Chambers and Mattessich for their unrelenting support for the hypothetico-deductive methodology. It is sometimes difficult to resist the persuasion to accept current exit costs (Chambers and Sterling) or discounted expectations (Nelson, Canning, Fisher) or historical costs (Littleton, Kohler and disciples Cooper and Ijiri).

My own failure to find a general theory of accounting has been especially depressing since exciting things were happening in related fields during my formative years. Paton had suggested the desirability of postulating the broad accounting area, and others (e.g., J. H. Woodger) were doing so in biology. A former colleague, Norton Long (1940), was worrying about a Keynesian-like general approach to political science and Easton, Lasswell and Simon were already working in this direction.

In specific areas I vacillated from the Fisher idea of discounting expectations to current entrance costs and to historical costs that feed acquisition gains (subjective values and traditional holding gains) into income as the resources are used. My chief hangup in early years was the inability of the profession to report how managers are doing in terms of alternatives available. The attempt to deal with this impossible task led to my subsequent interest in cost accounting. Hopes in this direction soon turned to ashes, and I was forced to settle for the division of accounting into the routine of more or less continuous reporting and special *ad hoc* studies that are best undertaken when the need for specialized information arises. The necessary tradeoff of better focused periodic statements for less generality was so obvious that I never really followed those who trash the income concept in favor of specificity for every situation. The management science (Churchman) ideal was especially ambivalent with its interest both in specificity and at the same time in models that cover numerous situations. Any type of intellectual activity requires accepting the obvious fact that all situations are different and still recognizing that individual instances must be grouped according to their commonalities rather than their uniqueness.

A most vexing feature of accounting relates to the discounting process. The normative model for capital budgeting and for financial managers usually is a discounting framework, yet accountants have rarely been able to monitor and report success or failure along these dimensions. It does seem that if investors plan and make their decisions by this process then accountants should be able to monitor the process and report *ex post* outcomes. This possibility fails due to the conjointness of all collaborating efforts and perhaps to the need for a budgeting process that allows for changed initial conditions from acceptance of prior proposals.

The failure to construct a better concept of well-offness was among my disappointments. The Chamberlin-Robinson revolution in imperfect competition was presaged by a decade by the less precise but more realistic arguments of J. M. Clark. My own disillusionment began with a chance encounter with the works of Evans (a Berkeley mathematician) who pointed out the inadequacies of two-dimensional presentations that neglected the temporal interdependence of both demand and cost surfaces. The P. M. Sweezy kinked demand curve and earlier works on duopoly and oligopoly cast further doubt on simple MC = MR guidelines and turned my attention to job pricing. Certainly the widely accepted guideline to stop production when MR = MC was (and remains) a ridiculous decision rule.

My relatively unsuccessful effort in costing did give rise to an interest in the ethics of pricing and to the work of DR Scott. This derived interest in ethics and to the social requirements for accounting led to a belated interest in auditing and its function in society. Attention to auditing became associated with the bases for belief, communication reliability, and a return to my earlier interest in semantics. Interest in accounting as a language developed into an interest in psychology and behavioral studies. Unfortunately my own contributions in this area have been meager but perhaps I have provided minor support for hermeneuts, deconstructionists and subjectivists generally in their valiant struggle to refine the grossness of unrestrained scientific methods.

NOTES

[1] My thinking in this area has been influenced greatly by Susanne K. Langer: " 'Fact' is not a simple notion. It is that which we conceive to be the source and context of signs to which we react successfully. . . . 'A world without minds is a world without structure, without relations and qualities, *without facts.*' " *Philosophy in a New Key* (Cambridge: Harvard University Press, 1942), pp. 267-8. The last sentence of her quotation is from Karl Britton, *Communication: A Philosophical Study of Language* (London: Kegan Paul, Trench, Trubner & Co., Ltd., 1939), p. 206. The source and context of value expectations are imputations and not necessarily physical or objective phenomena.

[2] Engineers may indeed be interested primarily in the *physical* properties of things. Accountants are interested in *values,* and values are based on expectations that are related to objectives.

[3] For a semi-understandable exposition see Philip E. Lewis: "Chomsky contends that the grammar of a given language is essentially a theory of that language and determines that the essential criterion of grammaticality is independent of any semantic basis. . . . Chomsky avers that grammar can be defined without reference to meaning, Merleau-Ponty affirms that meaning can be defined without reference to grammar." "Merleau-Ponty and the Phenomenology of Language," in *Structuralism,* Jacques Ehrmann, ed. (Garden City: Anchor Books, Doubleday & Company, Inc., 1970), p. 23. Apparently structural linguistics can be traced to Leonard Bloomfield, *Language* (New York: Holt, Rinehart and Winston, Inc., 1933). For comments see Max Black, *The Labyrinth of Language* (New York: Frederick A. Praeger, Inc., 1968).

[4] This quotation is included in n. 6, below.

[5] P. W. Bridgman, *The Logic of Modern Physics* (New York: The Macmillan Co., 1927).

[6] Arrington's characterization of my wandering from belief in science to partial rejection is essentially correct, but may be slightly over-simplified. After all, the first essay of Volume I begins with the following quotation: "the problem of the philosopher is not about the *world* but about *experience.*" Hector Hawton, *Philosophy for Pleasure* (London: Watts & Co., 1949), p. 197. While Volume V is much less scientific (perhaps downright antagonistic), I still stoutly assert that there are enough commonalities in the human condition to merit classification and common responses to such classes.

[7] I have pointed out to untold number of students that a receiving report is *objective* evidence (more or less) for the existence of a piece of paper with some symbolic items on the surface. How strongly does it speak that specific goods were received? Is the evidence objective or inferential? Is it external? External to

what? Precisely in what ways are the stable experiences that make up the concept of paper objective?

[8] Fortunately many of these practical observations were shrewd and astute. A similar example of empirical shrewdness can be found among practical blackjack and poker players, e.g., Scarne, whose strategies were remarkably close to the odds calculated later with the aid of powerful computers. (Editor's Note: For more information on his strategies, see: John Scarne, *Scarne's Complete Guide to Gambling* [New York: Simon and Schuster, Inc., 1961]).

[9] Many church-related colleges and universities sponsor schools of business administration. Aside from money-raising potential, the chief justification for such sponsorship is to improve the ethical character of business and develop business practices that are consistent with religious commitment. The Roman Catholic Church especially has taken strong stands on usury, just prices and certain kinds of profits. Most religious schools apparently agree that improvement in production and distribution of material well being is sufficient to justify business instruction. Unfortunately so far few practical suggestions for improving business ethics have come from either group.

[10] Perry Mason, "The 1948 Statement of Concepts and Standards," *The Accounting Review*, April 1950, pp. 137-8 (emphasis in the original). His selection of the single class of stockholders as his host group is clear. Moreover he seems to be comfortable with the concept of *full* disclosure without indicating disclosure of what or why. In response to whose needs?

Hermeneutics, Exegesis, and Deconstruction

A fable from the Andy Paton collection:

A fundamentalist preacher was asserting that the world is flat when a brash young college student sought to display his own scientific ability.

Q. If the world is flat, what is holding it up?
A. Posts, brother, sturdy oak posts at each corner of the earth.
Q. How far down, sir, do these sturdy posts go?
A. How far down? I'll tell you, Sonny, how far down. These posts go *all* the way down!

Comment: Nowadays these posts reach down to quark-levels, black holes, big bangs, little bangs, and to symmetries of exquisite beauty. Faith, brother, faith!

Recently there has been some interest in possible applications of hermeneutic principles to theoretical accounting. Some accountants have had difficulty making the extension, but the importance of the area deserves serious attention.

Traditionally hermeneutics has been associated with religious studies and the *interpretation* of scriptural texts. In general hermeneutics is said to apply to the assumptions and framework of principles used, exegesis is used more often to cover the application of these principles to practical cases, and homiletics refers to the methods of persuasive organization in the proselyting and teaching that are known as preaching.[1] According to the *Britannica,* the hermeneutic framework is sometimes:

(1) a literal interpretation depending on a narrow meaning of words, which may lead to rigid codification and to authoritarian belief; (2) a spiritual context that governs the actual wording; (3) the well known hermeneutic principle known as the "rule of faith"; (4) a socio-historical hermeneutic that requires adjustment of Biblical statements to conditions and changing times—"a dialogue between Christian theology and the history of culture" (p. 949); and (5) a more generalized view of the scriptures as allegorical in which words and "facts" are taken not literally but as metaphors with spiritual content. In fact it may be argued that "a 'spiritual' hermeneutic for the Old Testament *require*[*s*] the allegorization of its narratives . . ." (p. 950, emphasis added).

In religious matters external evidence beyond the texts is difficult to establish, because secular historians have written very few relevant texts and archaeologists have uncovered limited support for integrating physical conditions. Thus the interrogating of religious texts usually rests on the consistency of statements (a modified linguistic coherence theory of truth) or on inner individualistic feelings that arise from faith. Incidentally even the most positivistic positivists must finally fall back on *unswerving* faith to support factual beliefs.

In nonreligious matters interpretations also guide actions through beliefs in the efficacy of interpretations and in this area they again agree with pragmatists. The latter group worries about the effective fit of individual situations to the classes necessary for communication and their interpretations also are concerned with the "closeness of fit" of various symbolic analogs. Pragmatists interrogate their hypotheses for "functional fitness and ground their decisions in whether the theory works. In both cases the criteria necessary to find whether a theory works or whether an interpretation merits human action are delightfully vague, but neither group accepts the narrow criteria common to positivism and empiricism. It is clear that both must employ a system of values to order competing hermeneutical understandings and the efficiency of various "workings." Both place high value on individual human beings, are sensitive to specific situations, and strangely join the empiricists in their reluctance to generalize and form broad inclusive natural (or unnatural) laws. Ironically leaders of both movements often hold liberal social values that are based on sweeping generalizations about the needs of the human condition.[2]

A common command in hermeneutics is to "interrogate the texts" whereas the equivalent command for empiricists is to interrogate the external world. How precisely does an inquirer go about interrogating texts? And what exactly constitutes a text?

Clearly the transmission of knowledge from a religious source and a believer is not a monologue. There is something "alien" about the relationship so that an *understanding* must be worked out through a dialogue that requires interpretation and some degree of consensus about the meanings that are "created."[3] Presumably supreme beings know what the messages are supposed to mean, but they are transmitted by human carriers for human usage and therefore require the creation of hermeneutic meaning. Texts in this situation are sometimes obscure but they are even more obscure in more worldly dialogues that are also designed to persuade. In modern hermeneutics one party attempts to "objectivize" some aspects of his personal condition in symbols of ordinary language. Additional parties try to *create* meanings that meet tests of consensuality even though they must be interpreted by aliens who operate in different situations with different contextual overtones. In this regard hermeneuts are at home with pragmatists who also argue that communication requires *some* agreement about the meaning of symbols.

Turn now to the more obvious uses of hermeneutics in the sphere of accounting. First, a secular allegorical framework is more appropriate if not a necessity. Accounting reports, like the scriptures, are attempting to convey semi-intelligible messages that are not obvious in the literal or usual meaning of words. Certainly businesses, like hermeneutic scholars, must take accounting reports and interpret them in terms of their own understanding and needs. For examples, businessman interpret the term net income in a framework of accomplishment and well-offness, and for the devout Christian the verbal symbol "kingdom of God" is given meaning in terms of expectations about conditions and rewards for following one's faith.

There are however some important differences and necessary modifications. Accounting reports hope to use stable symbols with provision for changes in magnitudes and sometimes for changes in non-quantitative content. The scriptures are said by some to be stable and unchanging throughout eternity. It may be that the words remain unchanged, but most semanticists emphasize shifts in the meanings of words as social conditions change. This consideration permits new interpretations to meet different social conditions by retaining the symbolic structure and changing the meanings attached to the symbols.[4] To some extent accountants too follow this path. Within our time the term "asset" has been broadened to include new items (like tax credits) that did not exist in an earlier business climate, and the term "liability" now includes some items, e.g., longterm leases and postretirement benefits that were not included in earlier definitions.

Yet there is a very important difference. In religious matters the scriptures are static (except for new translations) and only the interpretations are changed. In this way the original words may not be changed but are given new meanings to fit new influences and conform to new objectives. Accounting *principles* are more like direct propositional functions in which the structure and grammar remain relatively stable while quantities are expected to reflect changing conditions. Accounting objectives, such as well-offness (income), like the desire for a happy present and after life, remain reasonably stable. Of course accounting measures of progress and success may change systematically over time through flexible designing of the system. Overall religious objectives too remain reasonably stable but the relative influences of the words and historical categories are permitted to change through prophetic interpretation.[5]

In summary it is difficult to incorporate hermeneutics and exegesis directly into accounting although there are obvious similarities. The word-body to be interpreted is stable except in some marginal analytical areas and the main problems revolve around appropriate interpretations for current living. The case for accounting is somewhat different. First, the original words (principles) are not written in stone so that the accounting "texts" themselves may change.[6] Second, accounting rules provide for the incorporation of new changes in a dynamic way. Thus accountants may also change the rules in addition to the specific events recorded in the system itself. In religious matters exegetes have some power to change interpretations of the language symbols to meet new social conditions, and in a broad sense changing the interpretation of language symbols is equivalent to changing the rules themselves. Return now to the allegorical dimension. Certainly the *writers* of the scriptures had some freedom to select the parables and stories used as the basis for allegorical interpretations. Their freedom may have been channeled by inspiration from above, and those who accept the inspired nature of the texts are reluctant to reject them. Some changes have been introduced by tinkering with translations. Translation changes are of course interpretations but they tend to preserve the sanctity of the absolute and place the onus for change on human interpreters. In short, translations open the way for new interpretations without disturbing the feeling of absolute truth that is said to be embodied in the inspired originals. There is a broader field for interpretation, however, for the very nature of fables, allegories, parables and the like includes a measure of ambiguity and lends itself to different interpretations. Moreover it is likely that these interpretations will change as cultural patterns and man's conceptions of *self* and *being* change.

In closing this digression note some similarities between accounting as a normative information system and some aspects of Christian theology. One school of accountants apparently takes a literal attitude and insists that only factual statements should be encoded and that users should be required to make only minimal inferences. Accounting reports are in language form (words and numbers) so that there always is a semantic problem, i.e., the task of interpretation. Factual accountants *ground* their beliefs in substantive matters and on observations.

In a similar way liberal accountants who look on their problem as identifying events and constructing categories to combine and preserve useful information have their counterpart in spiritual hermeneutics. In the latter case biblical stories are selected for their ability to encourage desired spiritual responses. In a similar way accountants select events, decide what aspects of these events should be classified and combined in order to facilitate an interpretation useful to people in search of wealth.

Finally there are a few highly subjective accountants who treat physical facts as more or less incidental and look upon the profession as a vehicle for creating useful metaphors—secular allegories. Their objectives certainly are not limited to furthering economic welfare in the ordinary sense. Goals require constant reinterpretation in order to further the coming of the City of God or a City of Wealth on earth or elsewhere.

HOMILETICS AND PERSUASION

The field of homiletics deals with preaching, as specialized teaching, and therefore deals with persuasion in a religious context. In church work it is distinguished from exegesis by emphasis on the *mechanics* of persuasion rather than on logical arguments (deductions) derived from the broader organizing themes of hermeneutics. Instruction in homiletics usually deals with the organization and presentation of sermons, i.e., the selection of biblical texts, explication of textual meaning, expansion of the theme for congregational relevance, arrangement of statements for emotional impact and coercive influence. In revivals added emphasis is placed on immediate persuasion.

The relationship of modern hermeneutics to homiletics is an interesting one. In one sense they seem to border on the incompatible. A chief function of a preacher (teacher) is to *persuade* his parishioners to follow a common path and to teach them the behaviors necessary to do so. In this aspect homiletics abandons the individualistic contextual commitment so common in hermeneutics. In practice some denominations are more decentralized than others, but the usual interposition of an intermediary whose duty is to explicate proper interpretations seems oddly out of place for advocates of situational analysis and the rejection of broad generalizations. Of course such a commitment cannot be complete for it is well known that some grouping of individual instances and dealing with them as unified classes is simply unavoidable for any type of conceptual thinking.

Yet in an important sense the two are consistent and compatible. Both are interested in some degree of consensus as the grounding for their intellectual endeavors and in directing actions according to ethical standards. The principal criterion for belief is not a comparison of predictions with sense-based empirical outcomes but some consensual agreement about the appropriate roles to be accepted by individual participants in specific situations. Habermas is concerned with such belief controls; he states:

> The hermeneutic interrogation of texts has one thing in common with the "interrogation of nature in the experiment." Both require duly acquired skill that proceeds according to general rules. . . . [T]he hermeneutic art remains tied to "personal virtuosity" to a greater measure than does the mastery of operations of measurement. . . . Whereas empirical-analytic methods aim at disclosing and comprehending reality under the transcendental viewpoint of possible technical control, hermeneutic methods aim at maintaining the intersubjectivity of mutual understanding in ordinary-language communication and in action according to common norms.[7]

It is not likely that accountants will be preaching many sermons to their clients or even to their own employees. Yet effective persuasion is an important part of all professions, and some influential accounting professors can compete with the very best evangelicals. Fellow members of the profession must be indoctrinated to accept professional roles, clients must be convinced that the services are worthwhile, and public agencies that represent various public segments must be constantly reassured that the accounting profession really does fulfill its needs and protect public interests. In fact the concepts of objectivity and even true-false (logically and empirically) are based on agreement, and agreement in turn is always related to persuasion. Persuasion enters into the formation of beliefs about reality and helps shape world views. Ministers have long known the importance of effective persuasion and their education includes some training in the art. Politicians, trial lawyers and salesmen understand the importance of the area. Accountants, sad to say, have lagged and often remained wedded to simplistic views of physical reality and the mystique of input-output and double entry. Far too often the most effective persuasive tools have been authoritative pronouncements from associations, successful practitioners and dominant personalities.

The fantastic scope of persuasion should be emphasized. Often scientists and scholars underestimate the importance of persuasion and relate it to sophistry, con-man techniques and debating strategy. Many are aware that argumentation in the hands of experts can trivialize discussion and interfere with inquiry. Argumentation (like democratic government) requires agreement on *some* rules and *some* values and expert sophists can defeat the best persuasive methods by simply refusing to accept any premises, any assumptions or any of the accepted rules of logic. Logic itself requires mutual acceptance of its rules. Moreover *applications* of logic require agreement about its legitimacy as a model for exploring the sensible world. There should be some agreement that logical classes can represent empirical entities, that deductions from such classes have useful applications, that the degree of support can lead to warranted conclusions and therefore support a determination of relative truth or falsity. Obviously all of these facets require at least some prior persuasion.

At one time I believed that the positivists were on an effective track by distinguishing between propositions that claim truth and simple preference statements. The latter statements were said to be neither true nor false although clearly they are not meaningless. Unfortunately positivists did not realize that, in the absence of rigid stipulation, empirical operations and judgments are necessary to determine the probable truth of any proposition. How then does one determine truth or falsity? He must have been *persuaded* that his criteria are correct and that he *should* follow them. Metaphysicians and religious leaders have simply not been persuaded that the scientific criteria for truth apply to their important conclusions, and modern empiricists seldom accept the deterministic go-no-go orientation of traditional logic.

Return now to the importance of persuasion in interpersonal human affairs. Preaching may indeed be teaching with added emphasis on pros-elyting, but teaching too seeks to persuade students to accept the goals of education itself. Scientific teaching is almost fanatical in seeking support for the importance of knowledge and for furthering its own kind of knowledge. Thus it is not too great a simplification to claim that all teaching is a form of indoctrination. In trade schools and in many more prestigious fields, the objectives are immediate and are constantly before the student. In the humanities and the arts, the objectives may be more ambiguous (e.g., the better life, being an aware human); but they are present and with a little effort can be identified. Even in the religious realm, the objectives of the indoctrination process are not always clear. For example, to fundamentalists the end may be a felicitous after life. For others the goals may be for a community of well adjusted human beings with emphasis on the therapeutics necessary for bringing about such a state. For still others, a major objective may be to convince individuals to accept specific social conditions—an exercise in social control.

Even in logic the everyday tasks of persuasion are of prime importance. A logical person has been indoctrinated to accept the methodology of logic and to ground his belief in logical proofs. He has been trained to accept and feel comfortable only with valid conclusions, and has been indoctrinated to form his beliefs and therefore his judgments by applying the rules of logic to the situations at hand. Thus the determination of true and false is based on judgment, and belief follows the valid application of logical rules to acceptable premises.

The need for persuasion in science is well known and deserves little further comment here. Scientific emphasis on observation, physical models, substance and *things* generally has biased older scientists in favor of physical anchoring. Only within the last century have scientists generally abandoned such nonsense and emphasized a different faith based on the understanding and shareability of experiences. The evidence for such concepts as reality and existence has changed drastically and belief now depends on far more than passive observation. Science has become more metaphysical, and like religion, now depends primarily on the much maligned concept of faith. Yet one cannot stop inquiry here for there must be reasons for holding the beliefs that are held. Scientists are quick to change their conclusions, but throughout history they have maintained faith in their methods. Today however there is a tendency for scientists to abandon closure around *the* scientific method and to expand the ways of understanding and of knowing.

HERMENEUTICS AND INTERPRETATION OF TEXTS

My own reaction to the introduction of hermeneutics to accounting has been mixed. My first response to the concept related it primarily to interpretation as used by positivists and simple semanticists to indicate rules of correspondence that would relate syntactical models to the experiential world. Certainly a careful study of the pitfalls found in constructing rules of correspondence merits the attention of our best philosophers and is past due for discussion and analysis. Mathematicians have pointed out some aspects of mapping experiences into symbols and *vice versa*. Management scientists have admitted that states of nature not represented by the symbols of their models simply do not exist. Some philosophers, including Wittgenstein, have insisted that the "world" be defined to include only aspects of our experiences that can be communicated. Foucault wonders whether the world and all reality are *created* by words, while many have pointed out that the texture of our observations and experiences are limited or bounded by the symbolic representations of our languages.[8]

Phillips has emphasized that there are many levels of interpretation even within the syntactical model, and that even a formal model must be interpreted with respect to the rules that are permissible within the symbolic structure.[9]

Arrington and some of his associates have argued that the relevant domain for hermeneutics is an expanded field of pragmatics. Pragmatics had been partially abandoned by linguists and left for psychologists who were expected to deal with the influence of interpreted symbols on human beings. Interpersonal persuasion is vital for fixing belief, and belief is clearly a key to human activity. Thus sociologists were brought into the picture and ideology, belief systems and social values became key concepts.[10]

The hermeneutical approach clearly places language at the center of knowing and understanding. Hermeneuts seek a more active role for value systems, communication signals and actions that further objectives. Arrington and Francis state:

> Teleological action requires hermeneutical discernment of the *good* of an action and this hermeneutical discernment determines *how* action proceeds. . . . Functional action is involuntary and non-teleological—it does not involve hermeneutical work.[11]

Hermeneutics in this sense is related to (but goes beyond) pragmatics and includes the judgments necessary to assess various language symbols in terms of their fitness to convey social values as well as to accomplish individual objectives. In this it is closely related to pragmatism. For Dewey fitting conjectures to the requirements of the ends in view is the dominant feature of reasoning. In religious matters and in Greek philosophy, ends in view (objectives) have received wide acceptance and are often sanctified under some abstraction such as *the good* or *God's will*. We are not concerned here with whether objectives are primarily employed to focus argumentation or are treated as universal moral imperatives, but it is clear that the concept of economic good is far too narrow to satisfy the needs of those with a broader world view. Fantastic simplification is necessary for the most elementary economic discourse and in some situations the values omitted may be far more important than the objectives retained.

Arrington and his associates go further. They wish to set forth guidelines (principles) for effective hermeneutics. For example, they are definitely against giving preference (priority) to physical grounding and to the grouping of individuals into broad categories.[12] In the interpretation of texts the hermeneut is asked to consider the ends (objectives) of individuals (or very small groups) and to judge the signals (make interpretations) that are pertinent to their restricted ends. Interpretation is highly subjective and must consider the probable consequences for others, and thus returns to interpersonal comparisons and judgments about relative importance.

In an important way taking language as problematic and making interpretations about objectives is similar to Dewey's structure. Dewey saw individuals as confronted with thwarted ends-in-view and possessed of previous knowledge that might or might not be relevant to the relief of the strain. Dewey's *reasoning* is largely concerned with trying to fit this received knowledge into the present situation. The reasoner selects hypotheses (that arise from analogies) and applies them to the relief of the tension. In the hermeneutic sense he is assessing the evidence (texts) and making interpretations.

Dewey too has the familiar "unit" problem. In general he (like many other modern philosophers) considered the individual as the unit and applied his machinery of means, ends in view, functional fitness, etc., to the individual's area of tension. Yet he emphasized the social context, and progressive education is concerned most of all with training the individual to get along in social environments and the democratic institutions that Dewey favored. These interpersonal effects are treated by Dewey through his concept of problematic situations that always include the individual, the social setting (the culture), the brute facts, *facts of the situation,* and the pertinent value systems.[13]

From the social religious values of many hermeneuts, Dewey's process may be flawed and his grouping may become too broad for the objective of education which is oriented toward social living—the socialization of the individual. In this manner he selected his group values (democratic ideals) and treated the task of education as smoothing the adjustment of the individual to harmonious relations with his preferred social group. Dewey was consistent and adamant about his own ends, but the tactics of education could vary to suit the environmental and the social situation. Meanwhile his guiding beacon (grounding?) is the concept of progress and progress itself becomes an important end. (Compare the hermeneutic faith in discourse.) It is obvious that progress without a directional vector (being in "good hands") reduces to embracing the concept of change, and at least some philosophers and educators do defend the concept of generalized change as their ultimate value. Moreover, some businessmen have taken related positions and have asserted that a business cannot stand still and consequently must change or die. They clearly forget that it is impossible for any business or anything else to stand still and that therefore the statement requires extravagant interpretation to merit serious consideration. Certainly to Dewey, cooperating individuals well coached in cooperative behavior will lead to a progress vector that generally (if not inevitably) leads to a better world. The unfolding to Dewey is in good hands.

Scientists, religious leaders, philosophers, auditors, and common folk *must* rest their philosophies on grounded beliefs. The grounds give them confidence and are therefore inevitably privileged, i.e., accorded superior status. Unfortunately "groundings" may have little in common. Positivists and scientists tend to accept certain evidence (usually reports from the senses), while religious leaders and idealists put more weight on non-empirical evidences, e.g., emotional experiences, soul stirrings, authoritative pronouncements, dreams and visions. Belief may indeed be a treacherous foundation, but unfortunately it is the only foundation available and ultimately at some level all belief rests on faith alone.

PROBLEMATIC LANGUAGE

In some ways the rediscovery (in the late fifties) that information is not free has resulted in an abortive revolution. At that time mathematics, computer technology and probability theory were in-disciplines, and the information movement turned to Shannon and his kindred souls for its structure. Economists and accountants then added some rigid behavioral assumptions such as utility maximization, rationality, ability to change probability beliefs in response to inputs, reactions to "shock" and the like and developed the largely abstract model into a partial theory of business and personal behavior. With these specified conditions the application of mathematics and probability theory resulted in impressive information structures by Butterworth, Feltham, Demski, Dopuch and a host of others.

This discussion is not to deny the elegance and possible usefulness of such studies. But it should be pointed out that such theories are limited in scope and fail to include many alternate possibilities. They are, for example, based on standard economic models with the overly-restricted behavioral assumptions of "rational" economic persons trained to react to information in an extreme pattern of self-interest and controlled greed.[14]

In many ways the recent shift to interpretative sociology has been a more interesting development.[15] The primary position is that language in sociology should be taken as problematic, i.e., that language is itself an important variable in all investigations and in all communication processes. This emphasis in itself is not world shaking and standing alone indicates only that the models selected often need adjustment for language effects during the process of interpretation. But clearly in this orientation the model itself (like a simple hypothesis or a simple question) limits the experiences that are relevant and influences some of the experiences that take place. In the broadest case the model is redefined until it either becomes reality itself or greatly influences what the subject considers to be reality. Many positivists and management scientists are aware that their models limit the scope of their investigations and the experiences that are relevant. Many it seems are not aware that language itself performs a similar function and that experiences that cannot be communicated in some language can hardly exist in the positivist world. Many subjectivists think otherwise.[16]

This view of reality is interesting for there are numerous "realities" and for pragmatists (see James, *Supra*) monism and dualism give way to multidimensional realities that emerge in response to different situations. In general this interpretative view frees thought from the necessity to anchor reality, existence, being and the like to some physical base. This freedom comes none too soon, for physicists long ago abandoned or severely modified such concepts as substance, objects and things and turned to substitute concepts based on the stability of observation reports and identifiable (understandable) nodes in *integrated* theoretical structures.

It should be obvious that responses to symbols are highly variable. In fact pragmatists are fond of pointing out that meaning is largely dependent on "habits to respond" and clearly both habits and individuals vary widely over social orders and over intervals with different and changing value systems. According to Carnap and other logical positivists one knows the meaning of a symbolic expression when he knows the conditions for which it is appropriate and which not. (Without values how does he know what is appropriate?) To a hermeneut the meanings of the "texts" are variable and highly subjective but finally must be interpreted and adapted to objectives—ends in view. In any case more explanation of these "habits," standards for "appropriateness" and hermeneutic "understanding" would be useful.

The modern interpretative view is especially concerned with the polysemic characteristics of symbols. Apparently there are differences as to whether it is preferable to have many interpretations (meanings) for each symbol or to have rigorous singular meanings for each. Positivists filter various meanings and usually opt for closure around those that meet their observational tests. Hermeneuts tend to construct meanings that are more situational and relevant to individual objectives. The pragmatist may be somewhere between and he is more likely to emphasize meanings as simple habits if they lead to important individual consequences.

Some polysemy clearly is necessary in any language, for it is impossible to have each symbol refer only to singular experiences in some rigorous one-one relation. At the extreme this situation leaves no room for class formation or for aggregation or abstraction. Apparently Ricoeur[17] feels that there is some optimum filtering that is unique for each interpreter. With no ideal (unique) set of interpretations he must construct criteria for finding optima for each interpreter for each situation.

There are important antecedents for the polysemy controversy. Russell and fellow logicians desire precision in definitions and unambiguous meanings and therefore defend a formal logic that is partially divorced from psychological overtones. In this desire they oppose the "common-language" philosophers and hermeneutic understanding. The latter groups are not concerned with precise definitions, and many question a rigorous concept of language separate from discourse. Certainly the symbolic logicians want their models to be precise and rigorous even to the creation of a special logical law of identity ("All a is a") and thus remove by stipulation the obvious truism that everything is different and unique and that nothing in nature is identical. Wittgenstein, in his rebirth, retained his dualism but retreated to pictures, resemblances and analogies generally. However, logicians in the main still try to banish ambiguity to the interpretative stage—to semantics and pragmatics.[18]

While not many scholars hope for unambiguous models of any type, much less the general models of logic and strict linguistic structures, some feel that an optimum precision exists—an optimum polysemy. This objective is of course both gratuitous and Platonic, for there is certainly no reason to believe that a generalized optimal flexibility will be appropriate for all diverse situations. The other extreme is to retreat until there are no general meanings and all signals are specific to the situation—a condition of chaos. Such a position is anti-intellectual and defies any attempt to get communicable knowledge. Where can one stop between these limits? A common stopping place with some practical support is to rest at the common-language level. This anchoring lacks precision but it has the advantage of using existing conditions and loose but common understandings. It does select a widespread group for its reference class without retreating to the anarchy of specific solutions for each situation.

Turn now to Ricoeur and his sharp distinction between language and discourse and his position that language itself does "Not care how it is used." Somehow the *structure* of the language with its mysterious inner dynamics becomes a useful framework for understanding mankind's troubles and predicaments. In its simplest form his distinction between language and discourse is similar to the well-known distinctions between syntax and semantics, pure mathematics and the assignment of values to variables, models and their interpretations and a host of other dichotomies. A close relative is found in the "new" criticism in poetry (Warren, Brooks, Ransom, etc.) where one is able somehow to criticize a literary production with little or no reference to its pragmatic import other than its structure as poetry itself. In a similar way formal logicians are able to judge an argument with no meanings other than those stipulated in logic. A *good* poem and a *good* argument are brothers!

An obvious assumption of early semanticists, positivists and their relatives was a dualistic world in which the mapping of symbols into referents (or vice versa) was necessary. Stuart Chase (an early CPA) for example was adamant about the need to find real-world referents and felt most comfortable when his referents could be reduced to shareable experiences that can be further reduced to physical things. There is of course no reason to require a single grounding for all interpretations, mappings, correspondences, etc., and in fact this assumption can be mischievous. Observe some mathematical applications to psychology, sociology, and (especially) economics for evidence that physical grounding is not essential for establishing useful referents.

What then are the differences between structuralism and other approaches? It is worth emphasizing that structuralism at its best could represent a shift of emphasis from objective to subjective and a turn from the importance of getting a good fit of the language to some hypothesized objective world to one in which language itself influences how one observes and describes the world—a shift from *abstracting* from a myriad of impressions to *constructing* a coherent structure from these impressions—from the task of observing responses to stimuli to the task of constructing patterns of reality. Structuralist literature hardly reaches this ideal!

There is little that is new in this orientation. Intellectual cliches in related areas are numerous: "The hypotheses determine the facts that are relevant," "The world is all that is the case," "The model *is* the world." "The world is not out there—the world is here," "The past is I." Yet the change in emphasis is important. Whorf represented a stepping stone for his pragmatic view of languages as developing from the needs of the social order and for his realization that language in turn influences social reality. In accounting this orientation views assets as *constructed* entities related primarily to service expectations and only rarely as substantive things. Cost is a sacrifice and unfortunately the expenditure event may become the reality instead of a surrogate. Income as value added (in someone's subjective eyes) may be subordinated to changes in more objective market values.

Accountants are interested in the tradition view of hermeneutics as interpretation of symbols (texts) but they are interested also in the generation of such texts. Messages are related to the selection of the host group, for it is impossible to embrace all mankind. User interpretations, their habits to respond to existing symbols and their probable responses to accounting messages must be considered and modified to conform to the representations that accountants are able to transmit. Unfortunately in practical affairs there are many groups with claims on accounting information and rigid adherence to a single host group may be mischievous. Different users mean different interpretations and changes in the discourses that result.

It is clear that Ricoeur's discourse is similar to the older views of semantics and pragmatics. Interpreters have the task of selecting and structuring messages to fit their objectives. In this respect Ricoeur is also near traditional pragmatists and his spiritual inheritance from hermeneutics is more or less compatible with pragmatic concern with individuals and personal problems arising from specific problematic situations.

Producers of texts too have received indirect help from pragmatists. The Dewey tradition makes use of a complex, muddled problematic situation that involves the individual, his storage bins of ideas, his ability to produce conjectures, his need to relieve the stress and finally his cultural and general environment. Dewey too gave attention to "helpers" to aid the individual reduce his stress and reach some measure of "docility toward ends." In the Dewey case the helpers are educators who help students interpret situations and reach a democratic consensus through useful discourse. Both texts and interpretations may be able to modify response behaviors and entire value systems. James was perhaps nearer to hermeneutics; he was not only highly subjective, but also had a deep commitment to religious forces and constructive interpretations. Furthermore through his own discursive essays and felicitous style, James displayed his interest in homiletics—the art of presenting information and encouraging consensus among those who interpret.

Apparently some modern accounting theorists see the accounting profession much like Dewey regarded the teaching profession. Accountants are constantly producing informational texts that need to be interpreted. Dewey promoted cooperative living and democratic institutions so that the ends to which his efforts are directed are clear. For many newer accounting theorists their profession has not done so well. Accounting leaders have often selected the most reactionary groups and has devoted professional efforts to furthering their values. While the promotion of greed and self-interest may have been aggrandized far beyond the point necessary to carry on the world's work and accountants may have contributed significantly to this aggrandizement, such attitudes are not a necessary part of accounting theory or of hermeneutical understanding. Unfortunately traditional accountants may be turned away from a consensual attitude by the strident arguments and shrill rhetoric of some current theorists—especially those with unreconstructed Marxist views or those filled with New-Left despair.

My own discomfort with the accounting profession is more moderate but no less shrill. A system that neglects all values not related to scarcity is badly in need of help from both humanists and religious leaders. The judgment that only financial equity holders can become acceptable host groups is monstrous. Unbridled concern with the accountants' "bottom line" is simply obscene. (Certainly followers of Martin Luther may well wonder whether bottom-line figures are effective measures of God's approval and grace.) Welfare leaders have shown concern over failure of enterprise costs to coincide with social costs, over the rights of workers, suppliers and customers to useful information, and even greater concern over environmental reports that fail to develop measures of inter-generational conflicts and transfers.

A reorientation also is necessary for the assignment of credit for even these narrow value increases. The traditional assumption that cost factors contribute only to the extent of their historical cost is gratuitous at best. What about contributions from favorable climate? Clean air? Stable government? Willing workers? In short why is all the added value allocated entirely to owners or to the organization? What about involuntary contributions from customers who were misled by unscrupulous advertising claims or were given shoddy merchandise? Populist themes at last have reached the peaceful shores of accounting.

A further suggestion for major reform in accounting follows from the Husband recommendation that the entity be expanded to incorporate more interests and reflect wider responsibilities. In the Husband recommendation, retained earnings are treated as an undivided interest for all organizational participants. A slight extension treats the proprietary section as a social interest, and a thorough-going revision calls for a complete reinterpretation of the right side of the financial statement. For example, the equity section might show the accumulated interests of workers, suppliers, customers, environmentalists, and the general public as well as legal claimants narrowly defined including rights of future generations.

This restructuring of the equities may have little effect unless the social institutions also are drastically changed. Acceptance of equities without legal sanction may be difficult to bring about. So far the simple classification of equities has been difficult to change, and accountants still insist on showing contributed capital to the organization with contributions kept on the books decades after the contributors cease to have any interest in the concern.

Attitudes toward assets also must be changed. Requiring an expenditure to support an asset has little to recommend it and is a candidate for extinction. It is suggested that any differential advantage made available to the entity is a better basis for definition. Original or even current market "values" certainly need reconsideration and different rules for treating changes in subjective values merit attention. The privilege to utilize resources usually implies a responsibility to maintain them. Agreement about specific values may be impossible, but agreement on responsible action is not an impossible task.

The insistence that corporations be held responsible for maintaining important facets of nature is no great innovation. The corporation ordinarily maintains its capital items by taking them to expense and indirectly charging customers for them. In effect such charges are little more than indirect transfer payments since the firm collects from customers and acts as a clearing house for further distribution. There is little that is new here. Most firms make a return (profit) on such collections, and a fee for this chore is not to be censured. What has been lacking are penalties for firms that fail to maintain society's contributions.

NOTES

[1] This section owes a heavy debt to Jaroslav Jan Pelikan, "Exegesis and Hermeneutics, Biblical," *Encyclopaedia Britannica,* 14th Edition, Macropaedia, Vol. 8 (Chicago: 1973), pp. 949–54; and to Jürgen Habermas, *Knowledge and Human Interests* (Boston: Beacon Press, 1971). I am indebted to C. Edward Arrington and to Carol Pollard for interest in this area. They suggest for greater depth: John D. Caputo, *Radical Hermeneutics: Repetition, Deconstruction and the Hermeneutic Project* (Bloomington: Indiana University Press, 1987); Paul Ricoeur, *Hermeneutics and the Human Sciences: Essays on Language, Action, and Interpretation,* John B. Thompson, ed. & trans. (Cambridge: Cambridge University Press, 1981); Don Ihde, *Hermeneutic Phenomenology: The Philosophy of Paul Ricoeur* (Evanston: Northwestern University Press, 1971); David E. Klemm, *The Hermeneutical Theory of Paul Ricoeur: A Constructive Analysis* (Lewisburg: Bucknell University Press, 1983); John B. Thompson, *Critical Hermeneutics: A Study in the Thought of Paul Ricoeur and Jürgen Habermas* (Cambridge: Cambridge University Press, 1981); Richard J. Boland, Jr., "The Coming Hermeneutic Turn in Accounting Research," *Methodology and Accounting Research: Does the Past Have a Future?—Proceedings of the 8th Annual Big Ten Accounting Doctoral Consortium, May 6-8, 1987,* Orace Johnson, ed. (Urbana-Champaign: University of Illinois, 1989); Jonathan D. Culler, *On Deconstruction: Theory and Criticism After Structuralism* (Ithaca: Cornell University Press, 1982).

[2] Among pragmatists William James is closest to the hermeneutic position. He was a stout believer in the individuality of the religious experience and supported a wide variety of such experiences. His criteria for determining whether a theory works is less empirically based than those employed by Dewey and certainly less than Peirce's empirical-analytic view. The hermeneutical emphasis on (and faith in) discourse is more closely related to the dialectic of Hegel but neither group requires every event to be subsumed under or grounded in a hierarchy of deductive nomological explanations. See William James, *Essays in Pragmatism,* Alburey Castell, ed. (New York: Hafner Publishing Co., 1948).

[3] Even an individual engaged in a monologue has a related problem. Habermas states: "Experimentally produced phenomena are based on the suppression of all aspects of life experience in favor of a general effect, i.e., one that can be randomly repeated. . . . For hermeneutic understanding the problem is reversed.

It grasps individual life experience in its entire breadth but has to adapt a set of intentions centered around an individual ego to the general categories of language" (*op. cit.,* p. 162).

⁴ A recent interpretation of Biblical prophets is that they were never seers or clairvoyants. Instead they are said to be "shortrun" interpreters who helped fit the unchanging word of God to local social conditions. They perform the function of reinterpreting the rigid scriptures on a more "situational basis." Thus they add official sanction to the polysemy of the original words.

⁵ The constitution of the United States offers interesting comparisons. This document allows for new interpretations of the words used by the founding fathers to fit changing conditions, but it also allows for changing the words themselves through amendments. It permits some changes to be made rapidly while other changes are permitted only with great reluctance and overwhelming consensus. In the meantime, a faster dynamic is added through the body of legal decisions that is built up around its interpretations. While not quantitative, this body of decisions does resemble the body of accounting information built up in the accounts and in its guidelines (principles).

⁶ In some important ways the interpretation problem in hermeneutics is similar to the interpretation problem in positivism and in Russell-like mathematical models. In the latter cases the symbols need not be burdened with previous rules of correspondence but the whole task of application to the sensory world amounts to interpretation.

⁷ Jürgen Habermas, *op. cit.,* pp. 175-6.

⁸ See Michel Foucault, *The Order of Things: An Archaeology of the Human Sciences,* a translation of *Les Mots et les Choses* (New York: Pantheon Books, 1970). In a general way hermeneutics is related to idealistic philosophies that emphasize internal states and look to external representation through symbols. Yet there is a difference. Habermas states that the "critique of psychologism is based on the insight that experience itself is organized by symbolic structures. An experience is not a subjective process of becoming conscious of fundamental organic states. Instead it is relative to *intentions* and is always mediated by an act of *understanding meaning.* . . . [P]urposes, values, and meanings represent a structure of signification that can be apprehended and analyzed independently of actual life processes, that is apart from organic, psychic, historical, and social developments. . . . Every experience of any cognitive significance is poetic . . . " (*op. cit.,* p. 147, italics in original).

⁹ See John N. Phillips, "Degrees of Interpretation," *Philosophy of Science,* September 1972, pp. 315–21.

¹⁰ The term ideology has received a bad rap in Western thought. Clearly the term applies to a set of structured beliefs and therefore is a belief system. In a

broad sense political activity, if not life itself, is rescued from chaos by ideological thinking.

[11] The likely source of this quotation is the following paper (which has not been found): "Accounting and the Labor of Text Production: Some Thoughts on the Hermeneutics of Paul Ricoeur," Working Paper (University of Iowa, 1989); this paper was revised and published as: "Giving Economic Accounts: Accounting as Cultural Practice," *Accounting, Organizations and Society*, 2/3, 1993, pp. 107–24.

[12] In his deconstruction analyses Arrington himself "privileges" the dynamics of linguistic structure and discourse and "grounds" his value system in a compassionate assessment of the individual human condition—a pragmatic base.

[13] In the related but more structured program of Kurt Lewin, the Deweyian situation is introduced through the concept of *field* with its valences of difficulties and possibilities. Other individuals influence the psychological space and are therefore a part of the process. Hermeneuts seem to be near to William James, who argued that reality was an attribute of the situation and changed as the individual and other parts of the situation change. Thus James was neither a monist nor a dualist. Perhaps he might be characterized as a simple situationalist.

[14] I have long been disturbed by the claims of some investigators that such models are "total" or "general" theories. Certainly they lack generality in their inability to cover actors with diverse value systems or with non-maximizing objectives and in not providing for decision makers who react to new information in unspecified ways. Also missing is an explanation of the extent to which the models themselves influence any investigator who applies them to empirical data. These models are in effect specialized languages that are themselves problematic; thus they influence observations and help to establish the "reality" of their universe.

[15] I for one have never been intrigued with the asserted impossibility of counter-factuals in logical analysis, e.g., unicorns and the like, and have more or less accepted the viewpoint expressed by Wilbur Marshall Urban: "The condition of the meaningfulness of an assertion is not that certain entities about which the assertions are made 'exist'—in the sense of being empirically observable—but that the universe of discourse in which these entities have their existence is *mutually acknowledged*." *Language and Reality: The Philosophy of Language and the Principles of Symbolism* (New York: The Macmillan Company, 1939), p. 227. (Emphasis added.)

[16] Wai Fong Chua comes down solidly on the side of hermeneuts and the "interpretation alternative." She states: "Social reality is emergent, subjectively created, and objectified through human interaction." "Radical Developments in Accounting Thought," *The Accounting Review*, October 1986, p. 615. She would

favor Philipp Frank from an earlier generation: "The question is not: 'Is that thus or so?' It is rather: 'Can we paint the picture in this or in that style, or in both?' " Philipp Frank, *Modern Science and Its Philosophy* (New York: George Braziller, 1949), p. 60. It also may be useful to quote E. R. F. W. Crossman: "Instead of a *stimulus* causing a *reaction* when the *threshold* is exceeded, we now think rather in terms of a *signal* which may be obscured by *noise,* providing the *information* needed to *select* a response." "The Measurement of Discriminability," *Quarterly Journal of Experimental Psychology,* 1955, pp. 179. (Also quoted by F. C. Frick in "Information Theory," Sigmund Koch, ed., *Psychology: A Study of Science,* Vol. 2 [New York: McGraw-Hill Book Company, Inc., 1959], p. 630.)

[17] Paul Ricoeur, *Lectures on Ideology and Utopia,* George H. Taylor, ed. (New York: Columbia University Press, 1986). My own knowledge of Ricoeur comes primarily from the Arrington and Francis Working Paper (1989): "Accounting and the Labor of Text Production: Some thoughts on the Hermeneutics of Paul Ricoeur," *op. cit.*

[18] That they were not able to do so satisfactorily is reflected in logical controversies over the desirability of the exclusive either-or, the acceptance of differentiated types, the need for descriptive translations, and the recognition of various antimonies.

Part I: Modernism, Privilege, and the Absurd

A recent article by Arrington and Francis brings to the accounting profession some faults of modernism and the advantages of deconstructionism along with some of the finest criticism of the decade.[1] An explanation of the terms used may be desirable.

Most scientists will agree with Arrington and Francis that naive modernism as a methodological framework will no longer do as a philosophical basis for scientific inquiry. The simplistic distinction between facts and value judgments is no longer tenable with the realization that facts too are constructions that require judgments. Sharp distinctions between true and false or objective and subjective also must be abandoned, for it is clear that problems of knowledge cannot be resolved through methodologies alone—value judgments are needed. The now fashionable process of deconstruction was developed in recognition of such inadequacies.

> Post modern thought in general and deconstruction in particular demand self-reflection and abandon any desire to somehow "ground" knowledge in an external and transcendental metaphysic like the positivist's faith in observation or the Marxist's faith in historical determinism. Deconstruction . . . works from within a research paper (text), taking an author's *own criteria* for privileging his or her work, and then de-constructs the text by pointing out how the author violates his or her own system of privilege.[2]

There is no doubt that the Arrington-Francis criticism of Jensen and of Watts-Zimmerman is first-rate and responds to a job that badly needed doing. These innovators are bright and clever people but they are not philosophers and considerable portions of their work are essentially philosophical musings and assertions about the human condition. Much of their methodology is nineteenth century science, and like early scientists they must make naturalistic assumptions and other stipulations and remove much of accounting theory from fruitful discussion. Some restrictions are necessary for any inquiry and should be discussed freely. Certainly they should not be dismissed as mere tautologies. It is true that all statements—even their atomic-like sentences—possess some generality and thus positivist accountants often end up with complicated inferential structures to further their investigations and ground their conclusions. The Arrington-Francis criticism is leveled at several facets but their main thrust is directed at the *privilege* such positivists make for their own methods and procedures. The positivist privilege is clearly in the direction of observations that requires a sharp distinction between observer and observed and, sad to say, tries to neutralize the observer or eliminate him altogether. Precisely how they are able to observe an external world by observing what are clearly impressions in the mind of the observer is not entirely clear. Bertrand Russell, long ago, pointed out that the psychological aspect of observation cannot be neglected but may sometimes be disregarded or treated as constant during a particular inquiry or over a limited range. Hermeneuts, like Arrington-Francis, are quick to point out that the term observation is restricted primarily to sense data and that *understanding* may be a more useful term. Understanding, in turn, depends on interpretations of the observational data and the situational constructs that result.

It is clear that accounting positivists privilege observation and employ methods that depend on observation to legitimize their arguments. What is not so obvious is that all argument and therefore persuasion requires some form of legitimization—some sort of grounding—and therefore *must* privilege something. This necessity must be emphasized in any discussion of epistemology, where the discussants are trying to agree on what can be known and how it can be known. Privileging becomes a term to emphasize that some hierarchy of values *must* be established to legitimize the beliefs that support any argument. The traditional justification for grounding an argument does not ordinarily carry the semantic overtones that suggest privilege as an unwarranted arrogation of power. Being able to unearth implicit groundings and point to the value hierarchies that support arguments (conclusions) is a required ability for those who wish to engage in serious intellectual pursuits.

It is clear therefore that all deconstructionists, hermeneuts and post-modernists (including Arrington) must ground their arguments in convincing soil and at some point claim privilege for their own positions and arguments. Consider now the basis for the Arrington-Francis criticism of Jensen, accounting positivists and ultimately all practitioners of early science and its methods.[3]

Arrington-Francis perform a useful service in pointing out that a method of inquiry that depends largely on the possibility of contradiction for its accept-reject norm is *prima facie* suspect, and therefore a mathematical model that neglects all modes except true-false is inappropriate for the complexities of human affairs. In a similar way an accounting framework that catches only two dimensions of events that happen to have scarcity value fails to catch many important facets in its simplistic "double-entry net." Furthermore a grounding in external *things* and market-determined *values* seems pathetic to philosophers with respect for the richer texture of human existence.

Turn now to the task of critiquing a paper by the author's own criteria. This statement implies that if the author uses physical criteria, the reviewers will criticize by physical standards, and, if the original criterion is historical necessity, presumably it will be reviewed in light of historical necessities. But there is still a further problem: Precisely how can one determine whether a writer "violates" his own privilege? Finally if it is the "texts" that are being reviewed, the criticism must be about the author's arguments and his grounding. Presumably "violations" are indicated by logical inconsistencies (by mathematical contradictions) or by improper linguistic procedures. Clearly the reviewer must be permitted to point out that conclusions do not agree with empirical evidence, with sensible data, with historical evidence or with pragmatic and psychological values.

Nevertheless the primary basis for criticism seems to reside in linguistic forms. Bertrand Russell, as a young philosopher, the logical empiricists and the British analytic philosophers held similar views. The privileged grounding in these cases is found in the conventions of language and in its logic subdivision. In intellectual parlor jousting the speaker ordinarily has the right to privilege anything whatsoever; although at the limit, this permission may reduce argumentation to trivial opinions and vacuous expressions. The linguistic conventions of common language may be more ambiguous than logical forms and thus may permit more "violations" than formal logic. In any case this approach to epistemology is related to the older coherence theory of knowledge that is grounded in the consistency (in a broad sense) of propositions that make up the system of inquiry. Adoption of a coherence approach is the chief alternative for those who refuse to ground their theory of knowledge on language symbols that represent aspects of an external world. In science modern physicists usually adopt a coherence theory but they must attempt (sooner or later) to tie their systems to some sort of common experience. This commonality of experience is communicated through language so that physicists too must engage in deconstruction. While they may not hold a strict representation theory they do not deny the possibility of some sort of correlation.

A PRIORI RESEARCH

Some time ago Carl Nelson characterized the pre-1960's research as *a priori* as opposed to the behavioral and market oriented inquiries of later years.[4] The use of *a priori* in this connection is somewhat unusual and may merit further discussion.

My own interpretation of the change in emphasis from the sixties is primarily in the kinds of assumptions that are made. Thus the "tautologies" of the positivists are assumptions that the reader is asked to accept for the argument at hand. These may not be "true" for every conceivable condition but the reader is asked not to question their immediate validity. Interpreters of market studies are asked to avoid questions (and doubts) about conditions behind market forces and the ability of market movements to act as surrogates for the social forces they are alleged to represent. Information economics is based on various technical models that are similar to those employed by Chambers, Mattessich and others in that they must be fleshed out with "tautological" human creatures who employ rationality, greed, knowledge of probabilities, conditional values and a host of similar abilities. Thus they base their finished structures on a myriad of assumptions about the nature of human beings and their values, and apparently these assumptions are based on observations of some kind. To equate these assumptions to *a priori* stipulations is to use the term in its later Kantian sense.[5]

A priori may be used in another sense to indicate that the propositions are basic insights inherent in the human condition or even worse that such insights can be derived by deductive reasoning alone. This view is essentially that of rationalism and at the extreme reduces empirical evidence to a minor position.

Nelson was using the term in the latter sense, and it is true that the official view of the Institute[6] (non-philosophers at best) indicated that a shrewd inquirer should be able to develop by rational means all accounting rules and guidelines. Somehow, somewhere there exist a *few basic* (fundamental) propositions upon which all of accounting practice and theory rests, and the theorist's task is to conduct a Diogenesian search for these fundamental kernels of truth. Moonitz tried to follow such an impossible methodology in ARS 1, but quickly abandoned it in ARS 3[7]. Others have tried to observe events and identify, in some undisclosed manner, those that are *critical* and should be carriers of transactions. Chambers was able to identify neutral accounting rules and relate them to exit values, Mattessich could recognize fundamental flows. Littleton somehow deduced that progress vectors staked out by practitioners were in good hands. With this usage of *a priori* Nelson was correct in his characterization of much pre-sixties research.

Much early research however can hardly be classified as *a priori* except in the former sense. Many efforts were devoted primarily to finding the *consequences* of alternative processing rules, e.g., studies of LIFO, depreciation, equity dilution. Many of these studies offered implicit ethical evaluations of superiority with unstipulated actors, while a few actually specified their host groups or their assessment standards. Paton, for example, ordinarily issued a general statement setting forth those who merited support. Yet much of his theory appears as *dicta* because he often failed to repeat his grounding and point out specific users, emphasize their objectives and show how the consequences of a particular recommendation would help them.

It seems that the later research differed from earlier research primarily in the assumptions that readers were asked to accept. Behavioralists concentrated on clarifying certain assumptions that had previously been accepted as *a priori's,* and researchers of the sixties did ask readers to accept the assumptions inherent in scientific and statistical procedures. In a similar fashion information theorists and model makers generally asked their audiences to accept all sorts of philosophical assumptions and maintain confidence in the methods of mathematics and logic with their required dependence on such simplifications as two-valued logic and the fear of contradiction. Deconstructionists too must "ground" their arguments and "privilege" their values and (yes) their assumptions. This necessity is itself grounded in the interpersonal aspect of the human condition. Whether post-modern privileging is or is not acceptable rhetoric must be left to the reader.

In view of the previous discussion it is clear that all research has an element of *a prioriness* and Nelson's classification of post-1960 research as opposed somehow to *a priori* research has serious defects. Nor is a distinction based on values accepted and values released a useful division.

Little of the post-1960 research has been devoted to the discovery of values although considerable attention has been devoted to theoretical models of choice under uncertainty. Information theorists have more or less stalled on models showing how the process of information choice *ought* to be made if actors already have a well formulated system of values. The Chicago stock-market theorists have prided themselves on being in the Littleton empirical tradition with faith in careful *observation* of facts from limited kinds of market operations. These studies too are not directly concerned with values but concentrate on the actions of reified markets to various inputs. The agential-contractual group accepts (more or less *a priori*) the values of market oriented economists and permits these actions to choose accounting rules and act as surrogates for implied value systems.

In pluralistic social orders with conflicting values such conflicts are automatically "settled" by market operations and political power plays, and following the Chamberian tradition little is gained by direct consideration of value systems. *A priori* markets and contracts are satisfactory representatives of preferences and hence of values. To more recent theorists such representatives are (*a priori*) *inadequate* surrogates. In any case Nelson's characterization is flawed.

Part II: Dissident Literature and the Absurd

A decade or so ago Carol Pollard (a doctoral student) suggested that the literature of the absurd might provide a framework for examining the accounting profession and that dissertations in accounting might sometimes be composed of meaningful impressionistic pieces rather than applications of elementary statistics and mathematics to information problems. This literature is essentially deconstructionist and is concerned—largely in a negative way—with social value systems and modes of communication. These writers also *ground* their arguments, *privilege* their beliefs, *interpret* behavioral texts and construct metaphors. To this point I have failed to do justice to her interesting suggestions.

The conclusion of this essay is that in spite of similarities and close analogies, the attitudes of absurdists are not entirely appropriate for representing dissident voices in the accounting profession. It is true that both accounting and general world views were in deep despair during the depression and early war years. The main difference is that absurd writers offer no solution for their meaningless existence while dissident accounting writers usually start with harsh criticism of the profession (or some part of it) and end with suggestions for solutions. Most early theorists were normative in that they wished to improve the social usefulness of accounting work. Stubborn positivists and empiricists may not express direct interest in the ethical content of accounting but most of them feel that something good results from the accumulation of knowledge about specifics that emerge from their dust-bowl efforts.

It may appear that accounting positivists are following the lead of pure scientists and are pursuing their studies for the sheer love of knowledge. Yet such certainly is not the case. Pure scientists may indeed pursue their studies for the love of *understanding* (knowledge in an expanded form) along with desires for adequate grants and usual markers of prestige and honor. Yet they are in many ways opposed to positivists and empiricists. As a rule pure scientists attempt to integrate the factual environment and—more importantly—impose an *explanatory* structure on such experiences and express the results of their labors in a discourse that is rich in possibilities for understanding and expansion.

It may be useful to point out the aspects of the absurd literature that seem relevant to accounting.[8] The concern here is not with the absurd presentation of human sexuality and professional frustrations that may be associated with it or directly with the God-is-dead theme—(lack of myths, principles and legitimacy). Clearly however the lack of effective leadership and abandonment of philosophical absolutes has led to disorganization, lack of purpose, general frustration and angst. The failure of the absolute led rapidly to serious doubts about the nature of objectivity, independence and reality itself. These intellectual doubts had been expressed by the absurdists at least two decades before being seriously questioned by professional accountants. We *are* concerned here with problems of communication and the necessity for some sort of common (acknowledged) discourse before discussion can become meaningful.

Consider first the concept of reality:

> [T]he man . . . dreamed he was a butterfly and, when he awoke, didn't know whether he was man dreaming he was a butterfly or a butterfly dreaming he was a man.[9]

The concept of reality, like the idea of objectivity, is ambiguous and not a dependable cornerstone for building an accounting structure. The usual definition of both is in terms of consensus of an elite group with the ability to experience the events and interpret them uniformly. Yet dreams are real enough to dreamers. A particular dream by one person may never exactly be shared by others but his reports are believable because others have had similar (analogous) experiences. Clearly a bumbling distinction between some *real* reality and thoughts *about* reality is no improvement over the related distinction between object and observer of object.

The case of mirages is slightly different. For example, desert travelers often have a consensus about the presence of a particular mirage and all may agree that the mirage itself (as an observable phenomenon) is real. What then is unreal about it? The unreality appears because expec-

tations do not agree with the outcomes to be expected from an event defined as real; i.e., the outcomes do not fit into a coherent pattern of expectations of other consequences that define the concept of reality. Even
here the case is not clear, for some elements of a mirage are indeed consistent with acknowledged characteristics of the behavior of light. Thus a
mirage is real in some aspects and by some definitions while being unreal in a host of others.

However there is a more serious objection to the consensual definition of reality. Absurd writers are concerned that the necessity for consensus may destroy the very situational properties that make an
experience unique—and real. Killinger states:

> [W]e suppose that what is verifiable in the experience of the group and
> explainable by the logic of the group is what is truly real. Actually, it
> may be the other way around. It is entirely possible that public agree-
> ment, by its very necessity of achieving common denominators of the
> lowest value, requires the diminution of the very object about which
> consensus was sought, an unconscious and unwitting dilution of the
> very reality it had hoped to fix and permanentize.[10]

Many accountants apparently have taken the view that the individual
event itself is the reality and that the grouping and classifications of
events are constructions that are unreal. Many Americans are nearer to
Plato and feel that the constructions (the secondary characteristics such
as blue, big, etc.) are real and that individual instances are products of
our lower senses. Thus the concept of blueness is often thought to be
more real than various approximations that exist in our experience and
the concepts of line and point in geometry are more real than drawn lines
and points that differ with the individuals making or observing them.
This view is most prevalent in religious and mystical areas where the
name is more permanent than personal manifestations that change over
the years and the *soul* is more important (if not more real) than physical
manifestations of being.[11]

The lesson for accountants is an old one that still needs emphasis.
The old distinction between real and nominal accounts has already all
but disappeared. Assets are now related to expected benefits and there is
little reason to give preference to those potentials that meet tests for
physical presence, objectivity, reality or tangibility. The more important
consideration is the expectation—belief—and how the expectation relates to a particular sensual organ is a subsidiary matter. In a similar way

the alleged unreality of such "mere bookkeeping entries" as depreciation is not an argument of great consequence. Such entries, like others, deal with judgments about values. How such judgments are reached and how they may be audited by others are of course important considerations, and auditors must be concerned with problems of belief and judgment.

THE ABSURD: ALIENATION AND ANGST

Turn now to some better known features of the absurd literature. The prototype exemplar was the pathetic plight of Joseph K in Kafka's *Trial*. He was arrested and tried in a hopeless and nightmarish situation. He is unable to find out why he has been arrested or to ascertain the charges. The accusers are vague and sinister, lack identity and are never revealed as individuals. Joseph can get no relevant information and therefore cannot plan his campaign for acquittal. All sorts of attempts to find anything pertinent lead to endless and hopeless mazes so that in the end he merely gives up and encourages an early conviction.

The theme of human beings embroiled in a hopeless situation with vague goals, no knowledge, no understanding, no compassion, no point to existence and condemned to endless repetitions of their frustrations is common in absurd literature. Vague fears, bottomless despair, undiscernible guidelines, and no one who cares are parts of a formless world where rational logic is absent and aimless wondering with no exits and no human understanding are the rule. It should be noted that this abysmal condition of man often is due to vague operations of an indomitable and intractable universe rather than to inhuman treatment by other human beings. The human contribution is often expressed indirectly by the uncaring lack of compassion shown by those who are not at fault or responsible for the condition.

The old myths that once gave meaning to life are gone and the helpful gods are dead—no longer able to give direction and organization to life through effective myths. Human beings wander along the world's surface without purpose, without direction, alienated from effective human companionship and filled with undescribable anxiety and unbearable angst.[12] Fifty-year-old men talk like babies, old men talk about the past as if it were the present, some talk only in the future tense, a man dies before his fatal accident, etc. The orderly influence of time is abandoned.

Perhaps organizing space-time concepts is in the mind alone and death marks the incapacity to distinguish between space and time so that in this endless morass of despair death becomes a favorable goal where degenerative entropy is stopped and replaced by a more stable state of relief. In some cases there is no recognizable *self* to organize existence and orient an individual to his environment and death becomes a pleasant "wandering home." Sexuality is far too weak to provide a structure for life and without values there is no morality or immorality. Indeed when actions do sometimes seem to have specifiable consequences, these consequences tend to be grotesque and unpredictable.

Time may become meaningless in the absurd world. Clocks strike at irregular intervals and in irregular numbers; "babies act like old men and old men prattle like babies; the past invades the present and becomes the present; events repeat themselves in seemingly endless cycles. . . . Time . . . is no longer predictable and sure."[13] These "endless cycles" are themselves so irregular that the major task of history—and accounting—is no longer relevant. (The accountants' trick of representing balance sheets as timeless snapshots of value potentials has never been quite valid, for the importance of a snapshot of the present has always been to show potential for future advantage.)[14]

Furthermore, writers about the absurd are concerned with language and its divorcement from reality as well as its reification as a *part* of reality. Some absurdists make their point by reducing words to gibberish and nonsense. Others try to reduce the role of words to things in themselves rather than present them as significant symbols. A few feel that words intervene between the individual and reality. Others follow what I believe is an old biblical custom of identifying the word with the event so that words themselves become a reality beyond their own existence. Many absurdists emphasize the power and influence of words by having their characters dominate others by sheer nonsense symbols. Some even feel that words are a means of avoiding communication as if communication in itself is depressing. Others look at language as entertainment that gives release from hopeless angst, and it has been said that Beckett has some of his characters engage in non-stop talking simply to indicate that they truly do exist.

In any case absurdists have been concerned with language and the influence of communication (and non-communication) on interpersonal relations and personal behavior. Attention is given to serious symbolization and interpretation mainly in a negative way by emphasizing its failings rather than its positive (and necessary) function in any social order.

Contributions to professional hopelessness are common to the general social malaise. An absurd dramatist muses about structure and organization. What is the organizing scheme? Who is in control? God? Insiders? Managers? Investors? The long suffering public? It is difficult to be an errand boy for all diverse interests in a pluralistic society. The old idols are falling. Coordinating principles are crumbling. No longer can leaders rely on objective facts, or physical laws, or natural laws to guide their groping hands. There is no *right* way. No *events* are *critical* for all situations. There is no one safe way of confirming, verifying or warranting beliefs. No assurance exists that an accountant, or any other captive of the ideology, can be independent. There is no assurance that independent observers even exist. *Things* are not true or false. Things exist as experiences and result from the ways these experiences are grouped and discussed.

Accountants have trouble handling these rapid changes and defending their traditional turf. This inadequacy extends far beyond accounting and in fact ranges over the entire field of knowledge. Physicists were plagued with indeterminacy and needed a new language to describe their speculations and integrate their findings. Practical logicians found the old true-false dichotomy too simplistic and incorporated some aspects of modern probability theory.

In the social sciences the failure of Marxist economics lessened confidence in the related dogmas of the new left. At the same time sociologists responded by introducing conflictual sociology as a substitute for the more comfortable cooperative assumptions of functional analysis. Psychologists lost faith in the application of simple stimulus-response methods and turned to the organizational powers of observers to bring structure to complicated situations. This change placed more importance on individual interpretations and added diversity. The ability to *construct* became a more important part of reality and reality became more personal.

The field of ethics too has been in turmoil. There was a major decline in faith and acceptance of the eternal verities of the Judeo-Christian religions. Pragmatists emphasized probable truth and situational ethics, and positivists treated abstract ethical systems as nonsense. In America there was ridicule of traditional WASP values and increased support for ethnic diversity. Group goals became subordinated to individual desires and doing "what's right for *me*" became a call to individuality and to self-centered ethical standards. This orientation influenced many religious leaders and encouraged personalistic interpretations. An increasing number now view religion as self-applied therapy instead of a device for controlling individuals in the interest of group values. In political terms the totalitarian structure for getting conformance by manipulating individuals toward social norms moved to the liberal position of letting the individual go his way and manipulating the environment to let him do so.

GENERAL TURMOIL AND ACCOUNTING DESPAIR

It is difficult for modern students to comprehend the turmoil in the accounting profession between the world wars. The age of authority was over so that it no longer was possible to gain respect by imperious demeanor and pompous appeals to tradition. Intimidating throat clearing and withering glances plus hints of arcane secrets from ancient sources no longer sufficed. Trust in elementary arithmetic and the magic of balancing double-entry no longer could be associated with some assumed natural order or with immutable laws of nature. No longer was the public in awe of esoteric scribes who could use a kind of alchemy to provide permanent records by simply being able to write and attest to agreements. Consider now some environmental changes that might have led to this turbulence and to some of the rebellious literature of the period.

The tremendous inflationary period after the first war undermined respect for the accountants' traditional measure of well-offness—income. Measuring this concept from a basis composed of original cost made no sense whatever when inflation was running at 500 percent and the basest peasant could see that he was suffering fantastic losses by holding cash items while accountants were reporting tremendous profits—fool's profits.[15]

Fritz Schmidt suggested that accounting rules for reporting paper profits slowly on the upswing and dumping "losses" rapidly on the downswing tended to accentuate the business cycle itself. Accountants thus became villains in a morality play with millions caught in the relentless clutches of the resulting depression. The victims were in a hopeless position beyond their own control and accountants were given the role usually accorded a merciless physical world in absurd literature.

While DR Scott showed faith in the ability of cost accountants and statisticians to correct some major deficiencies in the economic system, not all cost accountants were so sanguine. Cost accountants were slow to heed the consequences of higher fixed costs with the coming of industrialization and even slower to incorporate the newer economics of imperfect competition. These newer economists had not succumbed to complete despair except perhaps in limited cases of indeterminate marginal functions. Such discontinuities were worrisome but could be handled by way of matching and the use of simplifications such as relative ranges.

The greatest area of confusion and loss of self-image for cost accountants involved the allocation of fixed costs and the charge that they were changing fixed into variable costs at will. Hatfield scolded accountants for their methods of allocating depreciation (capital consumption) but he was convinced that he had found a solution in the world of compound interest. Greer was an articulate critic and acerbic ridiculer of joint cost allocation. He seemed to be willing to abandon this part of cost accounting and to substitute sales prices less some sort of overall deduction for expenses and profit for inventory valuation and periodic income. Many others have long advocated this abandonment, and recently the chorus was joined by various linear programmers. The latter group has given intellectual support to those who advocate situational computations and condemn general-purpose guidelines.[16]

The revolt against assigning fixed costs to periods has many supporters. Arthur Thomas in his earlier works could see no good whatever from such allocations although he softened slightly in later years. This attack later broadened to include the entire concept of periodic income itself. Many accountants (led by Vatter and Solomons) decried the income concept and wished to return to the more primitive fund-flow analysis. However the entire concept of periodic reporting of progress has never been abandoned completely. The net effect of early fund-flow criticisms was to retain the periodic income report but let the allocations be made by default—usually letting the period in which funds were disbursed become the timing mechanism for capital consumption. Modern funds-flow apostles did not return to retirement-replacement depreciation with traditional adjustment for lags and leads between expenditures and expenses. Instead they succeeded in retaining the standard income statement and adding complicated fund-flow statements. This latter requirement appears strange in light of the weird fund statements produced for some conglomerates and the relatively simple back-of-envelope adjustments required for major items.

It is clear that if a periodic concept of any kind is to be retained, there must be some method for allocation of common costs and revenues to periods. It may well be that such a concept should be abandoned, but if it is retained there must be some form of allocation. This allocation can be done by depreciation and accrual allocations or it can be done by default by letting some unspecified process such as time of expenditure make the assignments. Finally anti-allocators should observe that thinking itself is impossible without allocation and that such common places as causation, responsibility and accountability are meaningless without allocations. Again there was not helpless despair, for a return to simple fund flow techniques was supposed to eliminate the need for explicit allocations! Strange doctrine.

DR Scott was among the first to sound a broader alarm and emphasize the breakdown of the entire market system as a device for directing production and allocating distributive shares in an acceptable ethical manner. Accounting itself was not the direct villain, but it was clear that accounting must change. In fact he doubted whether the accounting profession was flexible enough to meet these needs and speculated about joining forces with the field of statistics. The economy was in chaos and (to Scott) reliance on the market system was no longer justified. Yet Scott saw hope in the future through restructuring the accounting profession and thus he cannot be considered a card-carrying absurdist. Although Scott's works generally must be classified as a dissident influence, he followed in the footsteps of his mentor, Veblen, and offered a solution that was short of abandoning the entire social order. Scott moreover expressed an underlying faith in natural law and felt that professionalism would come to accounting through the social need for ethical guidelines in accordance with the old-fashioned, idealized concepts of justice, fairness and honesty.

Public distress with the profession reached a high with the crash of twenty-nine. The profession did not give up completely and adopt an absurdist stance, but the establishment of the Securities and Exchange Commission must have been both a relief and a tremendous blow to professional egos. Apparently leaders of the New Deal abandoned the possibility of internal reform within the profession. They gladly accepted the advice of professional leaders (especially from the stock exchanges), but the result was, at best, a rousing vote of no confidence. In summary, governmental intervention was a recognition of the chaos in the area and also was an affirmation of the positive hope that governmental intervention could reverse the isolation and restore professionalism. While small investors remained alienated from markets for decades, this government activity with full cooperation from professional leaders did much to shore up the respectability of professional accounting.

The controversy over income and its measures had broader implications. It became obvious in the twenties that accountants and auditors had little or no control over corporate shenanigans that were commonplace. Holding companies became so intricate that profits and assets could be concealed and made to appear at will when and where insiders wished. For example consider the Kreuger match empire and Midwest Utilities, where hundreds of accountants and lawyers after years of work were unable to determine the interest of equity holders and finally recommended a return to relative positions at an earlier date. Some firms were showing acceptable profits in their income reports, but were concealing even larger unfavorable results through backdoor charges to retained earnings.

This despair over effective progress and status reports, especially for complicated corporate structures, carried over into the auditing function. The functions of auditing are mainly twofold: to add confidence in reports made by insiders and to give some assurance that the organizational rules for handling assets are being followed. Clearly there is no way that any group can guarantee such results, but professional performance had often failed to engender confidence and sometimes led to sneering remarks about twenty-five cent audits and tic-and-holler experts. Such responsibilities are never solved in any ideal sense even if society is willing to fund 100 percent investigations. Furthermore, the auditor has been in an extremely difficult ethical position because in some matters he is an advocate for his client while in others he functions as a representative of the public interest. This situation is analogous to combining the functions of lawyers with those of judges—an impossible ethical responsibility.

A few leaders, like Churchman, are not mollified by suggested modifications and insist that the concept of accounting income is simply wrong and that basing decisions on it is dysfunctional and misleading. The Churchman suggestions for improvement are not entirely clear, but he keeps returning to the impossible (and non-operational) task of trying to measure income from what would have happened if decision makers had followed all sorts of alternatives that were available but not taken. This view could lead to an absurdist position with no solution available or even conceivable. Furthermore his recommendation to measure the "size" of an asset by its potential for opening more options hardly helps the hopeless plight.

An offshoot of the Churchman position turns in the direction of no general-purpose surrogates with specially designed calculations and reports for every decision. This *ad hoc* replacement of more general aggregated reports reached its apex with the work of Demski and Feltham in 1976, when they embraced the every-situation-is unique argument without reserve and apparently believed that these situational calculations would solve accounting problems.[17]

Meanwhile environmentalists were disturbed about the failure of accounting enterprise costs to equal social costs, and certain humanists became disturbed about the failure to record human resources and costs. Both are genuine problems with no acceptable solutions in sight and with only the crudest of suggestions available.

A further dissatisfaction with the accounting process came in its methodology. At about the time of World War II there was great interest in the methodology of the physical sciences and attempts were made to bring these procedures to the social sciences. Guilford, Lewin and Thurstone in psychology; Hull and Lundberg in sociology and Lasswell and Simon in political science were among the leaders. Philosophical grounding was provided by Comte, a straight positivist, the logical positivists and the British empiricists. It is ironical that the hard sciences at the time were moving into a more metaphysical (even literary) mode and that the social sciences were belatedly advocating an outmoded orientation. The grounding of arguments in observation or historical necessity "privileged" such arguments over rival patterns of discourse and was at best an unwarranted arrogation of power.

It was not long before accountants, dissatisfied with some medieval practices and arguments, joined the scientific and mathematical bandwagon. Chambers emphasized the deductive side of scientific methods and brought rigor and model making to the accounting profession. Apparently he was interested in logical formulation, but his attempts to get formal guidelines from his foundational postulates have not been successful. Yet Chamber's contribution led to excitement among accounting theorists and to renewed attention to foundations. Meanwhile Mattessich, independently, was trying to fit accounting into the larger realm of scientific inquiry. And he too stressed formal postulates and the need for logical deduction. In addition Mattessich was interested in scientific philosophy, the sister sciences and the mechanics of the computer revolution. At the same time he remained loyal to traditional economics and the need for surrogates to represent the value systems that must guide activities. Chambers too realized the need for values, but he seems to have been satisfied with his unbounded faith in markets as ideal surrogates for the myriad of individualistic values, decisions and actions that lie behind the market system.

Among the most vocal critics of accounting have been the active advocates of efficient markets who sometimes have been unwilling to admit that there is anything in accounting worth saving. At the turn of the century Rhea and the founders of the Dow Theory argued that markets incorporate new information into their values rapidly and efficiently.

They posited a group of analysts whose primary duty is to consider influences not covered by formal accounting reports (or those covered at later dates), e.g., rumors of wars, deaths of officers, innovations, entrance of new competition. Accountants, in time, do report the influences of such environmental events by showing lower sales, higher costs and the like; but they are tied to past events of a particular kind and someone else is required to incorporate the expected results of these non-accounting events into security values without delay. Thus one function of market analysts is to consider the probable influences of events that are not immediately recordable in the accounting records. This division of labor permits accountants to stick to reasonably "objective" events and analysts to supplement accounting reports with their own individual estimates of anticipated events.

While these early market commentators did not seriously consider abandoning the usual accounting function, efficient marketers of the second half of the century often felt that accounting is so muddled that it should be abandoned. One view of this position is the belief that analysts should do the entire job and not be confused by rigid accounting regulations. This hypothesis calls for investigation and may well be true. If so, accountants should begin immediately to find the skills and techniques used by successful analysts and incorporate them into the principles of accounting. Until such time, a division of labor no doubt will remain between the professional groups. It should be clear that market technicians have some need for accounting information. Few however have taken the actively negative position of many advocates of efficient market analysis. Apparently the latter trust their risk measures and risk-yield relationships more than they trust accounting narratives about past events. In any case many of the newer portfolio analysts have little use for accounting reports and consider most of accounting to be a prime example of the absurd.

LANGUAGE, MUSIC AND DANCE: A DIGRESSION

The stylized social correctness of classical (and rock) music audiences is sometimes less boring than long discussions about the proper proportioning of improvisation and the obligation to follow written scores. Some conductors pride themselves on being faithful to the written music while others are equally proud of their individual interpretations and variations. Presumably the first group feels that all rights to originality belong to composers, and the conductor's function is limited to coordinating the efforts of members. Due to the necessary polysemy of musical language, such an extreme is impossible. The other extreme is found in late twentieth century progressive jazz in which the ideal often is to escape any written or traditional restriction. Conductors in this milieu act primarily as traffic directors to insure that each artist has a chance to exhibit his ability and to see that he is geared to common objectives.

The scores of music compositions are based on a highly developed language that contains information about such attributes as harmony, counterpoint, orchestration, emphasis, rhythm and the like. Yet musical symbols like ordinary language symbols can be ambiguous and are open to interpretations that may vary widely. Similar specialized languages are used in ballet and more recently in modern computer assisted dance patterns although the room for interpretation to accommodate individual interpreters may be slightly wider here. Chess notation is definite as to the reality created by actual and permissible moves, but is less clear about the situational advantages and sequences that may arise. Counterpoint may be lacking but in the literature of model openings, end games and the like something comparable is available.

The languages and metalanguages of poetry are closely related. Although early rules were rigid, poetry like music has become more flexible and now allows for interpretations that at one time were unacceptable. Mathematics and physics have specialized languages designed to reduce ambiguity and design new terms to replace the polysematic expressions of common language.

There are limits to what even a rich language can express, and it is obvious that the entire realm of reality may be limited by what can be expressed in the language. A composer may have been deeply disturbed by his inability to express what he wished to express and depressed by the inadequate tools of expression. Yet the limitations of musical language may have inhibited many composers from even sensing the richness of feeling that they might have experienced. (Whitehead has mused that geometry is not the whole of reality and that "colors too are relevant," and Ashley has emphasized that accountants capture only bits of reality in their "precious double-entry stuff.") In any case after the performing days of the composer his compositions are at the mercy of interpreters of his musical symbols, and in time even the symbols themselves may be drastically reinterpreted.

Some linguists support a rigid relationship between language and reality, but ambiguity does exist and polysemy clearly is unavoidable. For example if diverse responses to music symbols were absent, the criteria for judging the quality of conductors would be limited primarily to their ability to evoke efficient performances from members.

In summary the written language of music is rich and complex with symbols to represent and evoke responses in many areas, but there are limits to the richness of written expressions and rigid conformance to the language can inhibit free expression. With some polysemy and diverse musical attitudes, conductors do have some ability to improvise and it is ridiculous to say that they follow only the written composition or the original intent of the composer. For comparison observe courts trying to be faithful to the language of the constitution and the intentions of the founders. Even the most acute philologists and etymologists cannot remove the ambiguities that exist in a language system itself. Clearly what conductors or jurists add or take away is limited by their training, and their training has been influenced (constrained and restrained) by the limitations of their languages.

In musical matters the listener too makes interpretations. Presumably he feels the vibrations and is influenced by them. His interpretations are situational and unique, but he also is restricted in his independence. Although he may have no knowledge of written musical languages, he is a product of his social and esthetical environment and the impulses to which he responds are related to such languages and to his personal history. Even with no written composition there still is a composer, and most of the polysemical overtones, interpretations, responses and the related accouterments of communication systems remain.

It has been pointed out that western culture has been concerned primarily with harmonies and only incidentally with rhythms. This concern with harmonies has become so specialized that many combinations simply are rejected as non-music. Some twentieth-century composers have brought respectability to some new combinations that were once thought to be unpleasant discords, but even today many fail to enjoy the treasured combinations that form the bases of oriental harmony. At least some of these new twentieth-century combinations can be captured by the written language of music, but many may remain obscure because traditional language has been so dominant that listeners do not recognize them as more than unrelated sounds.

It is clear that musicians often are not aware of many harmonic overtones, but the situation in the area of rhythm is worse. It is doubtful that present musical notations can catch the seven (or more) simultaneous rhythms of Segovia. Some African musicians have been dismayed at the simplistic rhythms of Bach and other western greats. It is highly doubtful that western musical symbols are rich enough to capture many rhythms of African music, and it also is doubtful whether non-African musicians actually feel many subtle sequences.

SOME POSSIBLE READINGS

It must be emphasized that dissident literature need not be absurdist. In most cases a beacon of hope is held forth as a possibility and the feeling of complete hopelessness is not stressed. Also the anti-hero (survivalist) literature seldom qualifies as absurd, e.g., the comic Charlie Brown, who doesn't win but always manages to survive with touching dignity. Consider also the Charlie Chaplin and Buster Keaton characterizations.

SOME EARLY ABSURDIST LITERATURE
(Adapted from Killinger, *op. cit.*)

Arthur Adamov
  Paolo Paoli
  Le Ping-Pong
  Professor Taranne
Edward Albee
  Who's Afraid of Virginia Woolf?
Fernando Arrabal
  The Architect and the Emperor of Assyria
  The Car Cemetery
Samuel Beckett
  Waiting for Godot
  Endgame
Jack Gelber
  The Connection
  Square in the Eye
Jean Genet
  The Balcony
Eugene Ionesco
  Rhinoceros
  Notes and Counter Notes

Franz Kafka

Metamorphosis

The Trial

Harold Pinter

The Caretaker

The Homecoming

Landscape and Silence

Marcel Proust

A la recherche du temps perdu

Jean-Paul Sartre

Being and Nothingness

Nausea

N. F. Simpson

A Resounding Tinkle

Tom Stoppard

Rosencrantz and Guildenstern are Dead

NOTES

[1] C. Edward Arrington and Jere R. Francis, "Letting the Chat out of the Bag: Deconstruction, Privilege and Accounting Research," *Accounting, Organizations and Society* (1/2), 1989, pp. 1–28. This superb criticism is directed toward Michael C. Jensen, "Organization Theory and Methodology," *The Accounting Review,* April 1983, pp. 319–339; and to a lesser degree toward the Watts-Zimmerman version of positivism.

For further examples of Arrington's deconstructionistic criticism see: Arrington and William Schweiker, "The Rhetoric and Rationality of Accounting Research," *Accounting, Organizations and Society* (6), 1992, pp. 511–533; and for hermeneutical background, see Arrington and Francis, "Accounting and the Labor of Text Production: Some Thoughts on the Hermeneutics of Paul Ricoeur," Working Paper (University of Iowa, 1989) that was revised and published as: "Giving Economic Accounts: Accounting as Cultural Practice," *Accounting, Organizations and Society* (2/3), 1993, pp. 107–124. For Habermas-based criticism see Arrington and Anthony G. Puxty, "Accounting, Interests, and Rationality: A Communicative Relation," *Critical Perspectives on Accounting* (1), 1991, pp. 31–58.

[2] Arrington and Francis, "Letting the Chat out . . . ," *op. cit.,* Abstract, p. 1. Also: "the 'empirical era' ushered in a new style of writing, not a superior way of knowing" (p. 22). And: "Deconstruction . . . [emphasizes] proliferation around knowledge rather than closure around truth" (p. 8). Also: "the validity of an empirical claim . . . is grounded in *understanding* rather than observation" (this quotation not found in the published article).

[3] Arrington and Francis, "Letting the Chat out . . . ," *op. cit.* These authors also are favorably disposed toward Saussure and his structural movement and with Foucault's loose semi-Marxist structures. Personally I have had difficulty with both of these writers and am unable to assess their impact. Foucault seems to combine the multi-antecedent approach of historians with ordinary field techniques and with genealogy as a useful grounding base. Archeologist Saussure clearly performed a useful service by criticizing the oversimplifications of a semantics that posits a one-one relation between words and specific referents. His grounding of symbols in a bootstrap web of other symbols seems less relevant in spite of Chomsky's metaphysics of linguistics and the deconstructionist's grounding in the texts themselves. The reader may be interested in Michel Foucault, *The Order of Things: An Archaeology of the Human Sciences,* a translation of *Les Mots et les Choses* (New York: Pantheon Books, 1970); and Ferdinand de Saussure, *Course in General Linguistics* (New York: Philosophical Library, 1959).

[4] Carl L. Nelson "*A Priori* Research in Accounting," in Nicholas Dopuch and Lawrence Revsine, eds., *Accounting Research 1960–1970: A Critical Evaluation,* (Urbana: Center for International Education and Research in Accounting, 1973), pp. 3–19.

[5] Mattessich denies the *a priori* nature of his own foundations and asserts that they were arrived at by observation of economic and accounting models. Just how he was able to adopt these models for his own *general* model without adopting their more specific behavioral assumptions until later is not clear. Apparently he felt that his empirical observations were adequate to support a "gross" model but more observations were necessary for the fine-tuning process. He states:

> The basic assumptions of my general framework are derived *inductive-empirically* from the many extant micro- and macro-accounting systems. . . . My theory, unlike the *a priori* theories of Chambers, Ijiri, Moonitz, etc., is based on the idea that the specific hypotheses (i.e., the '*fine* structure' of an accounting system, in contrast to the '*gross* structure') is to be inferred from the pertinent *information purpose,* instead of being imposed upon the user in an *a priori* fashion (p. 40, n. 24).

> I have been concerned with a problem neglected by those theoreticians. . . . This is the problem of (1) *separating the general theory* (uninterpreted or semi-interpreted calculus) *from its interpretations,* and

of (2) *creating the foundation of such a general theory* as an indispensable prerequisite for attaining a common denominator for feasible interpretations. In this way it becomes possible to construct under a single theory various interpretations on the basis of different information objectives. . . . I introduced a *general* valuation assumption, thus *tolerating all specific valuation hypotheses* . . . (p. 34).

The basic assumptions were gained inductively by examining a large number of micro- and macro-accounting systems (p. 32).

Richard Mattessich, "On the Evolution of Theory Construction in Accounting: A Personal Account," *Modern Accounting Research: History, Survey, and Guide,* Research Monograph 7 (Vancouver: The Canadian Certified General Accountants' Research Foundation, 1984), pp. 27–45. (Italics in original.)

While Mattessich wishes to ground his constructions on economic observations, most deconstructionists will be impressed with the tenacity with which he continues to privilege deductive rules and mathematical manipulations. So far as I can see no mention is made in this modern survey (1984) of modernism, structuralism, Foucauldism, historicism, hermeneutics and other recent developments. Pragmatists will be puzzled with his ability to select a general empirical-inductive set of assumptions without some guidance from stipulated or implicit objectives. Perhaps the idealistic goal of a *general* theoretical model itself may be sufficient to guide empirical observations and to support his inductive selections of data to observe.

[6] The American Institute of CPAs.

[7] Maurice Moonitz, *The Basic Postulates of Accounting,* Accounting Research Study No. 1 (New York: AICPA, 1961); and Robert T. Sprouse and Maurice Moonitz, *A Tentative Set of Broad Accounting Principles for Business Enterprises,* Accounting Research Study No. 3 (New York: AICPA, 1962).

[8] I have leaned heavily on John Killinger, *World in Collapse: The Vision of Absurd Drama* (New York: Dell Publishing Co., Inc., 1971). As a theologian, Killinger is more interested in theological themes than in mundane accounting affairs.

[9] This is paraphrased from Tom Stoppard who has character, Guil, attribute a similar statement to a Chinese philosopher of the T'ang Dynasty in *Rosencrantz and Guildenstern are Dead* (London: Faber and Faber, 1967), p. 44. See Killinger, *op. cit.,* p. 63 for the source of this quotation.

[10] Killinger, *op. cit.,* p. 160. Guil again: "reality, the name we give to the common experience." Stoppard, p. 15; Killinger, p. 159.

[11] Consider the concept of absurdity constructed from instances and manifestations of absurd actions. (Does absurdity thereby become an actuality and qualify as real?) Compare Saint Anselm's support for the existence of God by

pointing to the beliefs and actions that take account of his existence. These beliefs and actions may constitute the reality. Compare also the prevailing pragmatic doctrine that truth is realized expectations and that concepts should be related to their effects and not to their sources.

[12] According to Richard Gilman: "for a play to be absurdist it must, minimally, exhibit the overthrow of naturalism, the abandonment of straightforward narrative, a lack of interest in psychology and an abstract or fragmented conception of character. . . . [T]o distinguish . . . the absurd from the merely foolish— there are certain positive characteristics. . . . [T]hey include . . . a pressure of ideas behind the language. . . . And finally, there must be a sense that experience is not reducible to our formulas, [and] resists our logic and patterns of conscious meaning. . . ." The Absurd and the Foolish," *Commonweal,* April 6, 1962, p. 40; Killinger, op.cit., p. 14.

[13] Killinger, *op. cit.,* p. 118.

[14] Proust, some absurdists and others have wondered whether history is to be defined as a series of events or as a series of statements about events or perhaps reactions to them. Accounting history is composed of statements about the effects of certain past events that may recur in similar form. Thus accounting statements attempt to explain the origins of present potential and to show the magnitude of this potential with future environmental conditions more or less specified. It is not quite correct to state that such conditions are held constant, for some changes in expectations may be included in the estimates of potentials for future benefits.

[15] Arundel Cotter published *Fools' Profits,* a strong argument for LIFO and current costs (New York: Barron's Publishing Company, Inc., 1940). An example of the gallows (absurdist) humor popular in Germany concerned the wealthy merchant who thought he was making a profit on each transaction but finally ended up by trading the last of his profits for a nail from which to hang himself.

[16] Apparently there is a limited return of support for the assignment of fixed costs to products and to periods. The argument turns on the use of these allocations as surrogates for opportunity costs and as signaling devices to indicate that operations are not going according to plans. Jeremiah Lockwood had earlier emphasized the motivational possibilities of fixed-cost allocations.

[17] See Joel S. Demski and Gerald A. Feltham, *Cost Determination: A Conceptual Approach* (Ames: The Iowa State University Press, 1976), especially Chapters 1 and 2.

Part I: What Can a Positivist Say?

*A strict positivist, seeing a black sheep on a
meadow . . . could only say, "I see a sheep,
one side of which is black."*[1]

A friend reviewing a parade with Calvin Coolidge observed that a pass-
ing street car had been repainted. Calvin is reported to have replied "On
one side anyway." Presumably President Coolidge was a genuine positivist who generalized with caution. In the business of ordinary living,
human beings must make all sorts of generalizations without conscious
thought. Even the belief that the streetcar exists when the observer looks
away is a mental construction and a generalization. Presumably a *strict*
positivist should make this extension with care and try to restrict himself
to "Here, now, see, one side, street car."

Carrying arguments to extreme limits so that they fit into a true-false
logic is not likely to further intelligent inquiry, but the above illustrations
point up the dangers awaiting naive positivists and empiricists who insist
that they deal *only* with facts. It is an elementary tenet of most philosophers that events must be symbolized (and perhaps verbalized) before
they can enter the reasoning process. Furthermore it is recognized that
any generalization requires substitutions and analogies, and that substitutions and analogies in turn depend on beliefs about similarities among
the events. Surrogates (and proxies) are of course types of substitutions.
One criticism of current accounting positivists is that they are precise
about relationships among certain bunches of inferential data (facts) and
are outrageously loose about the adequacy of their surrogates, i.e., their
substitutions and generalizations.

The objective of this essay is to demonstrate that adherence to a
strict factual framework is not only undesirable but is next to impossible.
Positivists, like empiricists and phenomenalists (but unlike phenomenol-

ogists), sometimes abandon their strict factual grounding by simply enlarging their definition of facts and reality. The result is that many of these broad definitions differ little from hypothetico-deductive statements. Others in search of surrogates that meet their rigid factual conditions have greatly weakened general confidence in the adequacy of all proxies to represent variables of concern. From a pragmatic viewpoint there has been some interesting intuitive scrambling to find usable surrogates for ordinary activities. A positivist might be expected to make an association of accounting rules with the size of the organization for these variates are to some degree factual, but it is less certain that positivists should employ size as a surrogate for political activity. Clearly there are "*facts*" and "*facts,*" but to argue that certain clusters of impressions are identical or are acceptable substitutes requires a delicate evaluation.

POSITIVISTS ARE NOT HOMOGENEOUS

Positivists, like empiricists, cover a wide range of attitudes and use widely different methods. It is true that they express a commitment to limiting their research methods to facts, but there are escape routes that permit them to expand their definitions of facts (and their efforts) into the domain of traditional hypothetico-deductive scientists. The definition of "fact" is open-ended and at bottom is based on interpersonal agreement about highly personal sensations experienced by individuals. Facts, in short, are grouped interpretations of individual experiences that have a degree of shareability among those using the concept.[2]

Theories sometimes are distinguished from facts by asserting that theories are associations among facts—the threads that permit one to develop expectations and make predictions. It is clear that this view is vastly oversimplified for theories too have grounding in reality and themselves qualify as broadly defined facts. Facts may be defined to include all sorts of relationships and associations among their components so that facts may be said to include relationships among facts. It is to meet this condition that led Russell and some logical positivists to distinguish between atomic and molecular facts and develop the concept of reduction to physical and chemical elements—physicalism. In view of the belief that facts are interpretations it may be interesting to return to the positivist emphasis on them. Clearly some facts are more obvious than others and meet definitional tests that others are unable to meet. At one extreme are such entities as dreams and hallucinations, which clearly are facts from many points of view but are suspect from others. Most researchers will admit that dreams qualify as facts, but the contents of a particular dream are facts relevant only to a particular situation. The consensus for hallucinations may be less solid because some individuals have never encountered them.

Positivists and empiricists make clear that they have research preferences for those facts that are subject to wide and firm inter-personal consensus. In this sense they are brothers of those scientists who still wish to be objective and require physical evidence from an external world. This research bias may curtail much wild speculation and reduce some fruitless endeavors, yet it may also restrain intuition and interfere with the imaginative process that is the basis for scientific progress. Ordinary scientists and even deconstructionists also ground their arguments on consensus although the scope and nature of the consensus required may differ widely.

Finally positivists may argue that they are concerned not with the facts themselves but only with associations among them, i.e., traditional theories. In this regard their research objectives are similar to those of non-positivists and their commitment to facts is little more than a preference for shareable experiences and confident predictions.

The modern *accounting* positivist's desire to find *whys* is much more difficult to understand, for it obviously is inconsistent with the traditional positivist approach. Karl Pearson, one of the founders of modern positivism, was interested primarily in the *hows* of association and looked at speculation about *whys* only as inspiration for uncovering further hypotheses. Clearly all researchers need the ability to intuit or deduce or somehow stumble upon useful hypotheses, and in this sense positivists are no different from anyone else. To cite a current research effort it may be that the hypothesis associating political activity with accounting-rule selection may have been formulated first. In the effort to make research activity operational the tenuous association of size and political activity probably came much later and was viewed as a practical compromise (a substitution). The association between alternate accounting rules and this intervening variable (size) may be calculated with some precision, but the adequacy of corporate size as a surrogate for political activity often is speculation. Thus the *conclusion* about political activity and accounting rule selection must leave room for considerable speculation. There is nothing fundamentally wrong with substitutions or proxies of this kind. The objection here is that the precision of the statistics at the intervening stage somehow appears to be precise support for the loose association of the primary variables. At best this presentation is misleading.

It is clear that the term fact need not be limited to the physical domain. Demand, for example, is a legitimate economic fact, and role is an acknowledged sociological fact. The logical positivists along with ordinary positivists seem to feel that substantive facts are more neutral and objective than sensations, experiences and the like. The opposing view may be even more persuasive. Russell and others pointed out that observations are operations in the mind of the observer and can not be ascribed entirely to something in the environment, and at the limit solipsists conclude that all knowledge is in the mind of the observer and consequently no warrant exists to say anything about things-in-themselves or the nature of external stimuli.

The intellectual parents of positivism generally are considered to be Ernst Mach and Karl Pearson. Mach, for our simplified purposes, held generally that nature consists of individual instances and that natural laws are creations of the human mind. The sensa that form the basis for the creation of laws are individual instances. Neither Mach nor Pearson gave much consideration to speculation about the real nature of things out in the world. But just what are these instances that Mach sought to describe and correlate by scientific laws? And just what entities are to be described so that their persistence can be inferred and used to support predictions of future correlations? Precisely what is it that is described?

It has been pointed out that positivists cannot depend heavily on the concept of facts, for facts too are interpretations and are mental constructions. It is just as clear that facts do not and cannot speak for themselves. Presumably the *instances* of nature are associated by some "natural" law when stable relationships are found. These associations become *laws* of nature and form the basis for belief and prediction. These associations must have enough consistency to warrant belief, and to have this degree of consistency the sensations themselves must be stable enough to be shared by others. Unfortunately there has been some tendency to base belief on observed predictability, transform this statistical regularity into some natural law and then convince oneself that belief is grounded in this natural law. Belief then is based on the uniformity of sensations and recognition that a particular sensation is a member of the uniform group.

The positivist mind must possess the ability to intuit and establish the necessary associations and find functional (causal) relationships among them. This search for associations is similar to the search by pragmatists for functional fitness and for hypotheses of merit. The determination of functional fitness reduces to the task of finding analogs that promise to aid the association of instances. Positivists establish some sort of association between two sets of events (or conditions to be described) and determine whether the association exists. A pragmatist does essentially the same thing. He stores the specific association in his ideational storage bin and keeps it available for new problematic situations. In the new situation he finds some unsettled features, and, unless he comes to a dead end, he also finds that other aspects of the situation are already known (settled). These settled portions come from knowledge of past associations and from analogous situations. It is to the credit of pragmatists that they bring into the open the necessity for employing analogies and introducing "reasoning" as the process of finding the functional fitness of conjectures for resolving the tension.

What then can a strict positivist assert? First he may state associations among specific sensations involved in his study. Ordinarily these statements are far less universal than desired. He may assert that his sensa are persistent enough for others to share and promote them to the status of objective facts. He can never be sure that his facts are indeed facts, for ordinarily it is impossible for others to replicate the exact conditions. Moreover, he can never be sure to what extent his specific associations can be generalized to cover similar instances. Similar situations are not exact replications so that all generalizations require some tolerance for ambiguities and respect for analogies. In most cases he retreats to an idealized position and asserts that if the initial conditions and the side conditions are constant, *then* his association of specific instances (events) can be generalized. The evidence may be sufficient to support ordinary scientific belief, but there is a philosophical glitch here. Precisely what is his warrant for assuming that the association in a particular situation can be expected to hold in other instances? Except for truth by stipulation there is no guarantee that the peculiar characteristics that made the specific association work were captured in the original study. There can be no guarantee that the bundle of elements that are associated in the actual instance can ever be reproduced or even stipulated unambiguously. Facts, in short, can never be identical.

The positivist often acknowledges his dependence on stipulation by recommending an "if-then" format. This formula states simply that *if* the exact conditions of the known instance can be reproduced in all relevant aspects, *then* the researcher may expect the stated outcome. What is important is the *faith* that the new experiment is close enough to the original so that we can *believe* that the association will hold. The equivalent stipulation in logic is simple: A implies B, A' is equivalent to A, therefore B.

In more practical affairs. A implies B, A' is *substantially* equal to A and therefore A' gives substantial reason to expect B.

In summary the touted precision of positivism is highly suspect from a broad philosophical view. First, there is a lack of precision about the nature of facts. Then unavoidably there is some looseness (slack) that arises from the necessity to *interpret* intersubjective facts. While we may believe that the sensations of others more or less correspond to our own experiences, the belief that they are *identical* has much less support and indeed is akin to the difficulties of replicating exact initial and side conditions. Thus even when there is homogeneity among researchers there always is the additional problem of being sure that the surrounding environmental conditions are similar. Inasmuch as a prime objective of positivist inquiry is to provide a basis for prediction, the investigator must assure himself that the side conditions are similar enough to warrant application of the association (law) to the new case. In applied science it is not sufficient to specify that *if* certain conditions are met, certain expectations are in order. Instead the reader needs to believe that these conditions are actually met. Thus there is looseness in the estimation of the original conditions, further looseness in the results registered, still further imprecision about the association rule, and finally all sorts of indecision about whether the conditions of the expected case are similar enough to warrant application of the rule.

The limitations of the preceding paragraph are common to all sorts of inquiry and are by no means peculiar to positivism. Yet positivism has invited criticism through followers with supreme confidence in the precision of the process and its secure foundation.

It is possible to limit the definition and not permit a positivist to generalize beyond the particular instance under investigation. Presumably some one else—a nonpositivist—would make more comprehensive generalizations. The important interest is *not* in the outcome of particular instances. Extension to *similar* instances is the objective of predictive research. Traditionally positivists have been interested in predictions, and there is little reason for refusing to make them. At this stage positivists are similar to other researchers. What then *are* the distinctions and why are they made?

Differences between positivists and others are largely matters of degree. Positivists do not emphasize the part played by the individual in structuring reality and tend to accept a dualistic paradigm in which the world is independent of the observer and waiting to be described. The positivist has great faith in his ability to observe and arrange sensations into *factual* groupings that are shareable and also well grounded in an independent world. Finally a positivist probably generalizes with more caution than other researchers, although with the development of modern statistical methods all researchers tend to follow similar patterns. Why positivists *wish* to disassociate themselves from other investigators is not clear. Evidently they wish to identify more closely with the nineteenth-century scientific establishment and withdraw more sharply from speculative philosophers.

In its most restricted form positivism may be equated to dust-bowl empiricism in which the ideal is to have *no* hypotheses to guide research efforts. The result of this untenable course is little more than aimless conjectures or chance associations. The normal extension of this view is that there can be no valid generalization of the results so that the results speak only for themselves. In short the message is a simple description of a single event (instance) in an independent world. Clearly no one subscribes wholeheartedly to this extreme view.

Certainly everyone should be allowed to make conjectures (form hypotheses) about possible associations and outcomes. These hypotheses are guides to expectations and reduce the impossible task of trying all sorts of associations in an aimless fashion. When hypotheses are presented, researchers judge whether or not (or to what extent) their expectations are confirmed. They are permitted to select and circumscribe their research projects and to assess the validity of particular outcomes.

One interesting point here is that all sorts of judgments are required. To philosophers these judgments are straight forward value assessments that judge whether the results are close enough to some standard to permit a comfortable opinion. Even in the most limited case some judgment is required before a statement of simple association is warranted. These judgments are in addition to those required to decide whether the elements of the association meet the general definition of facts.

Confidence in an association often is increased when there are repetitions of similar cases. Numerous instances of accurate prediction build confidence in the derived law and in its applicability to *similar* situations. Such discriminations are possible, and the required identification of similar situations is within the ability of able researchers. What about prediction in less similar situations? Is a law granted superiority if it works in different kinds of experiences? Modern accountants seem to feel that general laws are preferred over predictions with a more limited scope. Clearly this superior value rating is not applicable if the conditions move beyond the borders of relevance, and it is not inevitable that general-purpose rules are more desirable than precise rules covering more limited events. Events, are not equally important, and it may be that the loss in precision from general application is greater than any possible gain from having a broad general-purpose scanner.

In any event the distinction between the above cases is not entirely clear. Since no two cases are identical, the application of any rule gives rise to some ambiguity. Confidence may indeed be higher if the situations are similar and the initial and side conditions can be compared directly for then there is more interpersonal agreement about sensations and about the *facts* of the situation. Incidentally, when predictions are applied to expected future situations, similarities must be assessed in this context. Of course expectations too are facts but they are not precisely the kind of facts required for the original association. In any case new judgments are required to extend a rule from actual to expected situations.

SOME POSITIVISTIC VALUE JUDGMENTS

Consider now the types of value judgment found in investigative work. What precisely is the difference between the value judgment that accurate prediction itself is good and the judgment that a particular outcome is preferred? What kind of judgment privileges interpersonal agreement and objectivity over subjective commitments? The judgment that higher *economic* income is preferred over lower well being? More directly, the attachment of a high value to scientific knowledge differs in what way from the personal judgment that study of the classics is desirable?

It is common knowledge that rational policy decisions require knowledge of antecedent-consequence relations. It also is commonplace that the ends in view shape the search for antecedents and consequences and the facts that are relevant to the inquiry. Another common conclusion is that all evidence requires weighing and evaluating and thus in an important sense requires value comparisons. Judgments without values (standards)—irrationality—is not considered at this point. The practical task is to distinguish various judgments and to assign their execution to specific decision makers. The theoretical task is to consider the place of evidence and belief in judgment formation.

In positivist economics *policy* makers decide what overall values are to be emphasized and positive economists—armed with objectives from policy makers—find the consequences of available alternatives so that selections can be made by rule-makers, e.g., legislators. The intuitive search for possible alternatives could in principle be made by either group, but their narrow training hardly qualifies positivists for the intuitive and highly subjective task of finding alternative conjectures (possibilities). What judgments remain for the positive researcher? Clearly he is permitted to make *some* decisions even if the objectives of the study and available alternatives are given. At the accounting level these positivists argue that the objectives and broad principles of accounting are determined through the market mechanism or by non-accounting bargaining groups. Judgments and decisions remaining for the accounting profession are limited essentially to bookkeeping and calculating details. Yet even bookkeepers may have limited freedom and be able to make some low-level judgments.

In the same general way policy makers and the research establishment can stipulate their overall objectives along with the kinds of studies deemed relevant for meeting them. At times the Institute[3] has sponsored precise studies and specified (at least suggested) how they are to be conducted. Standards (values) for accuracy, parsimony, elegance and generality may be set by scientific policy makers and sent down to those who make the inquiries. Various degrees of decentralization are found, but it is not the objective here to discuss desirable levels of decentralization. It is clear however that some problems of decentralization are to be found in bookkeeping, practical in-the-field auditing and indeed in the entire field of human relations.

To summarize it is argued here that even in the most centralized research organizations, decisions always need to be made and they require judgments based on standards and objectives. Such judgments are needed even at the lowest levels of discrimination and cognition, and also are needed to judge whether or not the standards from above (or from the environment) have been met with the desired degree of conformance. Thus the most demeaned positivist researcher must take certain responsibilities and make necessary judgments about them. To be sure his actions no doubt will be reviewed, but even here the low-level researcher must make value judgments involving reprimands and penalties for not meeting the standards. He not only judges whether the standards have been met, but he also weighs the tradeoffs necessary between competent results and the penalties for incompetent work.

Finally, just what can a strict low-level positivist say? Certainly not very much! More than a computer?[4] He does relate phenomena in ways that are considered to be relevant. He works with his own sensa and relates them to an interpersonal construction known as facts. At all levels he judges whether his sensa are shared sufficiently to qualify as facts. He may discard all sensations that do not meet his definitions, and defiantly claim that he deals *only* with facts. To the degree that he can shift *all* responsibility for judgments he may claim that his research is value free and accept his role as an automaton.

SOME HISTORICAL BACKGROUND

Modern positivists and empiricists certainly are not the first to have their activities constrained (controlled?) by the available facts rather than by broader more nebulous models and theories. Certainly they do more than "peek at the data" before applying for grants. Many have faith that working the data will lead to conclusions automatically so that decision making becomes a mechanical operation and selecting from alternative proposals more or less automatic.[5]

While the phrase "peeking at the data" may be comparatively new the idea is an old one. No one, so far as I know, ever denied that fact patterns may suggest possible associations among them. The importance of this insight was emphasized in sociology and economics early in the twentieth century.

Thurstone, an outstanding Chicago psychologist and psychometrician, states:

> If no promising hypothesis is available, one can represent the domain as adequately as possible in terms of a set of measurements or numerical indices. . . . [W]e start with no [?] hypothesis, but we proceed, instead, with a set of measurements or indices that cover the domain, hoping to discover in the factorial analysis the nature of the underlying order. . . . [T]his . . . is sometimes referred to as an attempt to lift ourselves by our own boot straps. . . .[6]

This approach involves far more than a quick scan of the data and may have been an important influence on Friedman and later on the Chicago accounting empiricists. (Billy Goetz, a Chicago product, also recommended "fumbling" with the data until some order appears.)

The University of Chicago's place in this development has been important. Early giants such as Dewey, Mead and Knight certainly were not in the empirical tradition, and the business school in its prewar years was known primarily for its sophisticated economic approach to management accounting. However many early Chicago sociologists were empirically oriented and considered themselves to be social *scientists*. Friedman may have been impressed by these social-worker-scientists, but it also is likely that his interest in statistics brought him under the influence of Karl Pearson, the arch positivist.

The growing popularity of the behavioral sciences (at Chicago and elsewhere) in the early post-war years was surprising in view of the growing unpopularity of Watson's behavioral psychology. (My own behavioral approach to accounting was more pragmatic and tried to avoid this anomaly by combining behavioral techniques with gestalt psychology and metaphoric interpretations.) Chicago accountants (*circa* 1960) seemed to be sympathetic to a behavioral framework but opted for a straight-forward empirical foundation. This term fitted better their emphasis on efficient markets, and their market research is in the area of group actions with little interest in individual actors and their motivations. "Empirical" therefore is a term that permits a wide research latitude and fits well with the seemingly endless streams of market information. The change at Chicago from empirical to positivist is not so obvious. The early logical positivists later played down the name positivist and adopted logical empiricism. Not only is there a longer more illustrious philosophical background for empiricism (e.g., Aristotle, Locke, Hume and even Kant), but the term itself suggests experience and is more subjective and less dependent on an external world to which models, mathematical expression, and linguistic symbols must be fitted.

Finally accounting positivists apparently have avoided their cousins, the legal positivists. Yet both have an interest in things and relationships as they exist rather than in abstract justice, natural law and other areas of metaphysics.

Wesley C. Mitchell, a Chicago Ph.D. and a Columbia institutional economist, believed that he had established a new economics by grounding his research in statistical manipulation of economic data. Institutionalists generally and the National Bureau of Economic Research in particular have followed Mitchell's lead and often have applied methodological techniques to data with the hope that theoretical associations will become obvious.[7] The tradition of Thurstone and Mitchell dies hard.

In the rigorous sciences ordinary observation is supplemented by all sorts of supports such as microscopes, spectrometers, accelerators and the like. Clearly social scientists may improve their observations and intuitions by using the very best statistical and mathematical techniques available. The facts of the case *may* be decided early in the research effort rather than in response to deductive hypotheses or (in the pragmatic case) from settled portions of a problematic situation. This type of investigation may or may not be as efficient as the usual hypothico-deductive or the pragmatic process of inquiry. The objective here is not to criticize the selections of statistical tools used by empiricists or to object to their failure to make preliminary screenings of the data. Some generalization from derived associations among the piles of data is necessary for useful research and is necessary even in the most rigorous sciences. After all Thurstone's decision that a preliminary screening of the data may lead to useful scientific information is itself a hypothesis.

Part II: The Accounting Positivists

The remaining portion of this essay will examine the methodological positions of modern accounting positivists, especially those in contracting and agency research. The preceding portions present some serious misgivings about positivism in general despite its welcome restraint on wild generalizations and nonoperational models. The current Chicago-Rochester researchers can hardly be called positivists under a strict interpretation of the term. They are to be commended for using some of the most sophisticated statistical techniques now available for finding associations among different data sets. Unfortunately their loose substitution of fact sets as surrogates and intervening variables for actual variables of concern is supported only by the weakest verbal support. They also retain some unacceptable attitudes (and jargon) of the positivists on the objectivity of facts, the unimportance of interpretation and the faith that methodology can be substituted for value judgments. Finally they seem to forget that confidence in their conclusions depends on the weakest link in the chain of support—not the strongest. Observations and statistical sophistication need to be supplemented by interpretation before they can qualify as understanding.

PROFESSIONALIZATION: ACCOUNTING OR ABOUT ACCOUNTING?

The traditional view is that accountants select host groups and accept their objectives as legitimate and worthy of support. Accountants then forge rules to furnish information to further these goals. One result of this condition is that accountants may accept conflicting host groups. In this sense it can be argued that accounting principles are determined exogenously. The result may be greater diffusion of responsibility and acquiescence to outsider demands and monetary incentives. Presumably those who pay for tailored information services can get them while users with insufficient funds or without the necessary organization are left without. These unfortunates may get ill-fitting, special-purpose information from others, or they must be well enough informed to modify and utilize these reports. Some simplification and codification of rules becomes desirable, although complete uniformity is seldom desirable when there are diverse user needs.

The accounting profession must select its host group, but exactly how this process operates is a matter of contention. Accounting positivists emphasize the importance of users competing in free markets on the basis of entrepreneurial self-interest. Non-positivists emphasize the limitations of such markets and the importance of broad social needs and the desirability of professional codes of ethics to ameliorate the harsh self-interest of market forces. In effect professionalism is designed to contravene certain market forces and positivists might do well to include professional attitudes among their market determinants.

The transformation of a group of individual accountants with diverse objectives into an accounting profession requires consolidation of objectives and accordingly some consolidation of accounting rules. In the process a profession acquires dynamics of its own with its own professional objectives, responsibilities and authority. The profession is required to make choices and exercise its own value judgments about the consequences of alternative rules in which user needs are important and must be satisfied. More importantly the imposition and acceptance of responsibilities means that some authority (and the required power) must be granted to the profession. This authority enables the profession to influence accounting measuring and reporting rules.

Churchman, Chambers and to some extent Mattessich have suggested that the goals of an organization and the objectives of accounting are exogenous to the field of accounting, and Chambers especially has emphasized the importance of market allocations. Accountants need not concern themselves directly with making their own value tradeoffs, for they can accept the prevailing hierarchy of values from these outsiders. Unfortunately the need to evaluate simply returns when accountants decide which outsiders (users) they are going to serve. Market determinations privilege the squeak of the money wheel. In the Chambers case it is assumed that the numbers produced in markets are useful to all relevant exogenous users and can serve as proxies for *all* individual values and rankings. Other cases may be more complicated. If accountants select insurance policy holders as their host group, the protection of insurees becomes more important than measuring income for the owners. Accountants for tax evaders may feel that their clients' desires are more important than a tax structure that represents public values. In short, who are these exogenous people? Laborers? Residual equity holders? Managers? National income computers? Social welfare economists? Creditors? Prospective investors? Some impersonal fund or entity? If all are important enough for consideration and there is conflict, who decides whose interests shall prevail? Is there any wonder that many accountants have decided these matters by listening to the cash register and market quotations?

Thus professional accounting choices are more complicated than simply choosing a host group and adopting its objectives. All sorts of value tradeoffs become necessary, and the resulting choices, while *influenced* by outsiders, must be made by the accounting profession. From a conceptual viewpoint, it is the requirement to make these decisions that gives accounting the right to call itself a profession.[8]

The diversity of user needs means that some looseness in accounting rules may be desirable, i.e., the value tradeoffs indicate that choice of accounting rules is influenced by pressure groups operating in their own self interest. The practical outcome is that users must conform to a limited number of rules. The accounting profession (with its limited power to force conformance) may insist on a specific method for handling financial leases but may permit a multitude of acceptable inventory and depreciation formulas. Modern accounting positivists have concentrated largely on what sets of conditions lead to the market selection of certain alternatives. This research is interesting in itself, but it omits entirely the body of accounting doctrine that deals with consequences, value assignments, guidelines and possible alternatives that influence markets indirectly or limit their scope.

Now alternative sets of accounting rules do not constitute an endless smorgasbord of possibilities and much accounting effort has been expended to develop acceptable alternatives. The ethical judgments—the normative aspects—of the profession require research devoted to consequences and it is these consequences that must be evaluated. Current positivist research is devoted to the market mechanics for selecting alternatives by non-accountants who participate in the mechanical process.

SOCIOLOGY OR ACCOUNTING?

Consider now the charge that positivist accounting is concerned with the sociology of accounting and not with accounting itself. In general this criticism has been misplaced and indeed it can be a source of strength for the positivists. They are concerned with the actual adoption of accounting rules, they do consider the milieu in which accounting operates and they *sometimes* concentrate on factors that influence market choices. The traditional approach to accounting research concentrates first on the accounting rules by relating probable consequences to the needs of identified users. This process is normative although some researchers try to avoid normative conclusions and express their output in the form of "if . . . , then . . ." implications. Observe that the latter approach deals primarily with finding certain kinds of consequences from accounting actions, but it omits one very important set of consequences—the effects on user desires and behavior.[9]

At the lowest level non-normative accountants can merely catalog the various accounting alternatives, i.e., the various measurement rules that are considered to be a part of accounting. These inventory lists could constitute their entire research. The next step includes those who are concerned with the consequences of listed alternatives. Normative accountants must decide which of the alternative lists are superior for the amalgam of users they are attempting to serve. These decisions require a hierarchy of values that must be attached to parties of interest. Normative accountants also require some knowledge of the consequences of using alternative lists and of the necessary machinery for reconciling conflicting values. Sterling and Chambers, for example, are confident that the consequences of using current exit values are preferable for the parties they wish to serve. Presumably they have identified the available alternative lists, traced expected consequences, selected users, arrayed them according to relative importance and concluded that current exit values are superior to all known alternatives.

The *accounting* positivist tries to position himself securely between the extremes of list making and rendering final approval. At their best the Chicago-Rochester positivists are showing *how* certain recognizable conditions influence actual accounting rule selection. They try to describe how rules are actually selected and are not concerned directly with preferences. While positivists may not need to render normative judgments at this level, they do encounter difficulties in hypothetical alternatives that have not yet achieved the status of traditional facts.

Positivist accountants may consider various organizational structures and try to predict the consequences of such structures in terms of accounting rule selection. Organizational structures and certain aspects of the environment do influence the selection of accounting methods. There may be enough *uniformity* to generalize widely and there may be enough *stability* to predict usefully. There also may be enough of both to *explain* satisfactorily, but the explanatory chasm often is considered to be beyond the generalizing abilities of positivists and simplistic empiricists. Preferences of outsiders for accounting alternatives is a study of users (non-accountants); these parties make up a part of the environment of accounting and also are relevant to the sociology of accounting. In any case an accounting positivist is able to say that some population of users did actually select certain accounting rules. However it is quite an inferential leap to conclude that these users *preferred* the alternatives actually selected, and it is a wilder leap to conclude that users *should* have made the selections they did. To their credit accounting positivists make few such leaps.

Consider now the Christenson statement: "Chemical theory consists of propositions about the behavior of chemical entities (molecules and atoms) not about the behavior of chemists."[10] This analogy is interesting but it is not quite on target. Watts-Zimmerman *et al.* do *not* study the behavior of accountants as accountants or the sociology *of* the profession, e.g., how accountants treat their associates (juniors), how they organize their work, how they elect their officers, how they react with clients, how they preserve their independence. Yet their research is *not* historical, i.e., about accounting rules and how they have developed. Little is said about the consequences of accounting methods other than lags and leads in reporting income and some elementary concepts of debt and equity relations.

Chemists do indeed deal with valences, ions and similar chemical constructions. Accountants deal with wealth potentials, restrictions, adverse interests and changes in them. Both construct metaphors (consider the poolroom molecular model) and hope that they will be useful for explaining phenomena. Both have guidelines (rules, principles) for observing, analyzing and relating their data. Chemists attempt to *predict the behavior of chemical entities* under stated conditions and accountants hope to predict the reactions of human entities to accounting reports about wealth. Watts-Zimmerman go beyond naive positivism, generalize their individual cases, predict which accounting methods will be selected and (they say) *explain* some aspects of the selection process.

Chemists seldom assay the near impossible task of explaining *why* their entities behave as they do. Lower order associations may be simple enough, e.g., positive and negative charges attract, reaction valences must be equal, but higher order explanations become an infinite regress and it becomes impossible to explain in any fundamental sense precisely why any relationship exists. Until recently accountants have not been deeply concerned with *why* human entities react to their reports but it is time that simple research at lower explanatory levels gets more attention. Accounting positivists too have extended their domain and have tried to isolate explanatory strains that might account for the selection of alternative accounting methods that affect shortrun-longrun changes in reported wealth. Estimating the consequences of organizational structure and action is in keeping with the chemists's task of finding the consequences of various combinations of atoms and other entities. Since it is impossible to specify and report all consequences of organizational (or chemical behavior) some criteria for relevancy are needed.

A further analogy between accounting and chemistry is available. The accounting positivist attempts to relate the organizational structure to the selection of accounting rules. The chemistry analogy seeks to find the selection of alternative chemical investigations made by the industrial-military-scholarly complex that uses the output of the chemical profession. An appropriate chemical analogy is to seek conditions that exist in the industrial structure that lead to the selection of chemical investigations (research).

It is tempting to downgrade or even reject the agency-contracting movement for the wrong reasons. In summary it appears that none of these negative criticisms are fatal so that attention may be devoted to possible positive contributions. In the favorable area it is argued that the agency-contracting orientation makes a substantial contribution to the theory of organizations and is an improvement over the so-called entity theory, or the simplistic view that all corporate managers are working furiously to maximize shareholder value.

It is clear that accounting positivists are far from being naive positivists and certainly are not logical positivists of the Vienna School.[11] They are far too interested in explanations to fit into the strict Pearsonian school, which holds that science is a description of the past with faith in continuity. They may or may not agree with Mach that scientific *laws* are creations of the human mind and that only *instances* belong to the external world. Accounting positivists do place value on intuiting new hypotheses and the use of surrogates—even outrageous ones. They recognize the weaknesses of their proxies. Understandably positivists soft pedal the necessity to have accepted *values* for grounding the legitimacy of their conclusions. As a rule they accept the usual definitions of facts and depend largely on statistical methodology to support their conclusions.

Their position on values is typical of positivists generally and follows the dogmatic footsteps of Milton Friedman. They realize that value judgments are necessary for the most simple positivist investigations, and they prefer to emphasize *political* methods for those who apply value systems. In short they wish to separate *investigatory* values and choices from social welfare values and political concerns. The format is traditional positivist and leads to the more usual "if . . . , then . . ." format. Only the most naive positivists can believe that they are presenting value-free facts without value components. Most rely on accepted methodologies and political incentives as proxies for their research judgments and present their *own* research judgments as a basis for additional choices by those sanctioned by the political and economic establishment.[12]

Consider now the criticism by Tinker and others that positivistic research depends on market economics and neglects underlying Marxist class struggles.[13] The separation of value judgments to be made by different groups does create different roles for these groups. With these differences in roles comes differences in prestige, power and the like; and in all societies the ability to control the policy decisions is associated with authority and the power to dominate. Ordinary usage associates power with the ability to enforce values on others, and associates authority with the legitimacy to exercise such power.

In a well-working society, politicians are given authority to make certain group judgments. Scientists control value judgments associated with their own methodologies and their applications. Individuals exercise value decisions about their own persons so long as there are no over-riding conflicts with group values. In the latter case a new value-authority center is created to work with interpersonal value conflicts at various levels, e.g., families, counties, cities, states, sovereign countries.

Members of any social group may disagree with the distribution of power and class struggles, group conflicts, and individual confrontations clearly follow. Such conflicts are not peculiar to capitalistic structures in Western societies. Various Czars and later soviet leaders have encountered power-class disagreements, often with violent reactions. In principle capitalist accountants need not reject the amalgamation of value judgments by way of markets although they may disagree with particular distributions.

Consider now the criticism of Christenson and others that positivism is an "obsolete methodology."[14] These criticisms arise from the charge that positivists do not give proper consideration to the ability of the mind to help construct the world and more specifically that they place the importance of observational verification above the mental function of formulating hypotheses and theories. Certainly there are naive positivists who wish to reduce all concepts to *things* that can be grounded in reports from the senses and fail to recognize that things are labels attached to reasonably stable and shareable mental constructs.

No one, so far as I know, denies that important scientific discoveries have been made by methods that are essentially positivist. Many modern physicists carry on their work fruitfully by assuming that such constructions as quarks exist independently of the observer and direct their research activities to establishing the conditions that might account for them and their behavior. Moreover investigators in all sciences now feel comfortable with structures based on mental constructs that are systems oriented and systems correlated with sensations from an external world. In the social sciences physical (external) grounding is difficult to conceive and doubly difficult to construct, so that such constructs as roles, groups, statuses, wants, etc., require supporting evidence of a different sort.

Most researchers feel that the older attitudes toward falsification and verification of hypotheses are no longer applicable and that positivists too need to reorient their thinking. No one in a probabilistic world thinks seriously that hypotheses can be so rigorous that one negative instance requires complete abandonment of the conjecture. Likewise no one expects to *prove* (verify) a proposition beyond the possibility of negative instances. Modern statistics has done its work well and few serious scientists depend on deterministic go-no-go logic as the basic criterion for scientific belief.

SPECIFIC PROXIES AND SURROGATES

Despite their factual orientation, positivist accountants have encountered severe criticism for their selection of surrogates to represent variables of accounting concern. Consider first that *all* investigation is carried on by using analogies, surrogates, proxies and the like. For example temperature changes are measured by expansion of liquids or metals; well-offness by national income indexes; value added by receipt and expenditure allocations; general adaptability by intelligence tests.

It is not the substitution of proxies for variables that is the basis of criticism. It is the specific surrogates selected that draw critical fire. For example to find whether managers operate "opportunistically," bonuses are used as an intervening variable along with an assumed preference for immediate income. It is the choice of income timing that is measured and the measurements are permitted to speak for the degree of opportunism. This is quite an extension for positivists who are grounded firmly in facts.

Consider debt-equity (leverage) investigations. The judgment to be made is whether managers in high risk situations tend to use accounting methods that favor near-term income reporting. Leverage becomes a proxy for risk. Cost reducing outcomes are surrogates for managerial behavior. Then it is assumed that the higher the debt/equity ratio, the nearer the covenant restraints; the nearer the constraints, the nearer bankruptcy proceedings; and the nearer bankruptcy, the higher the expected values of the costs involved. The *positive* part of this research is limited to the association of debt-equity ratios to accounting choices. While the research is loosely grounded in facts, the conclusions are far removed from their factual grounding and require at least three inferences along the way. The inferences themselves often are interesting and creative and serve as convenient linkages between the facts and the conclusions reached. A popular non-positivist paradigm might consider these linkages to be interpretations of the outcomes (in terms of accounting rules) from the leverage hypothesis. One conclusion is clear: Current accounting positivists are not reluctant to make wide generalizations from their "factual" structures.

Consider finally the political hypothesis that the need to lobby and incur regulatory costs affects the selection of accounting rules. If a marginal economist establishes that managers wish to optimize income and that political action influences income, he may argue that political expenditures (like expenditures for other purposes) should be carried on until marginal cost equals marginal revenue. Clearly the selection of an appropriate accounting system may be a factor both in decreasing marginal costs and increasing marginal revenues. Presumably a positivist should investigate actual cases to find if *in fact* such political costs are incurred and to confirm a correlation between their incurrence and the actual accounting rules selected.

Accounting positivists could undertake to find if political activity is associated with the selection of alternative accounting methods. Presumably in practice they wish to correlate—in an economic cost-benefit relation—the amounts of incremental lobbying and related expenses with incremental savings from using a particular accounting method. A strict positivist normally would make an actual comparison of several firms and let others generalize and suggest subsequent studies. In the field of accounting they have followed an unusually complicated series of surrogates and inferences. For example, it is assumed that large firms are more vulnerable to political attention and therefore are more likely to select accounting rules that reduce current reported income. Previous research on consequences has indicated that certain accounting methods will reduce current reported income. With the granting of these hypotheses profit-maximizing and informed managers from large firms may be more likely than managers from small ones to seek profit-reducing accounting procedures in the short term. In any case, accounting positivists use size as a proxy for governmental pressure.[15]

SOME COMMENTS: MOSTLY FAVORABLE

From one view it seems that accounting positivists do not need to determine the objectives of an organization or to evaluate whether the objectives ought to be furthered or condemned. Whoever makes the choices makes them, and it need not be assumed that they prefer the consequences. It is not even necessary to identify the actual decision makers or to find some sort of organizational *will*. Whoever made the choices has the power to do so and does so. Finally it is not necessary to decide who counts and arrays them in some hierarchy of importance. Whoever makes the decisions does the necessary weighing so that it is possible to conduct positivist research with irrational organizations. Such research simply is not concerned with the decision-making process.

In the past similar attempts to escape responsibility for deciding and evaluating have not been entirely satisfactory especially when these efforts are devoted to finding explanations. These attempts reduce to letting surrogates or institutions do the deciding without regard for the process of decision-making. Several attempts have been made to let the *events* speak for themselves when they become critical enough for accounting recognition. At least one highly original writer has postulated a series of *flows* of inputs and outputs, and these flows somehow separate themselves into those that are carriers of transactions and those that require no accounting recognition. Rational men, scientific men, economic men and self-maximizing businessmen have been postulated and presumed to make decisions. Entrance markets, exit markets, natural forces and God's will have sometimes been observed (or constructed) and their outcomes allowed to represent the necessary choice-decisions.

With the positivist-contracting approach it is not necessary to select an entity orientation or to assure that the value of the interests of certain participants should be maximized, minimized or obliterated. For a strictly positivist approach it is not necessary to identify the influential parties who select individual accounting alternatives other than to assume that, whoever they are, they influence bargaining in market-type operations. Whether the choices are made by personnel who are authorized by corporate rules and are operating with ethical conventions is not an immediate concern. Thus for this kind of research it is *not necessary* to construct a selfish, grasping, greedy set of individuals with little or no identification with the organization—in short there is no need to assume an agency-contracting *man* to go with all the other men who have been postulated throughout social and religious history. Nor is it necessary to assume an accounting profession with an ethical code designed to soften some of the harsher effects of market-bargaining. Research—positivist research—has not been (but could be) directed to finding out whether contracting parties do behave in this assumed fashion. At present it seems that a self-maximizing assumption does little more than simplify the model and the arithmetic.

The methodology of contracting-agency accountants is simple enough. The attitudes of the contracting parties are held constant as one of the stipulated side conditions so that research can be narrowed to relationships of such variables as size, bonus contracts and bond covenants to accounting rule selection. This procedure is common to all research and is necessary to limit the universe. (A critic might speculate about differences if the methodology were applied with the stipulation that the contracting folks were born again Christians agape and filled with concern for some group rather than individual members.) Is there any reason why the methodology cannot be applied to any mixture of greedy and compassionate people?

For the accounting positivists this selfish donnybrook (or cooperative venture) gives rise to an unspecified leadership with authority distributed to all agents who have the ability to contract. In orthodox organization theory some residuum of an authority remains with each participating party so that all members (whether cooperating or competing) have some limited ability to contract. With such splintered leadership it becomes difficult to be normative unless objectives are coordinated.

It may be that accounting-positive restrictions are selected not to carry on positivist research but to *explain* the results. Yet historically explanation has not been an important part of positivist theology. In fact it may be argued that when positivists leave their area of "dust bowl" empiricism and start explaining, they are no longer positivists.

From the historical point of view accounting positivists superimpose a C. Wright Mills conflict model (as opposed to a functional model) over an organization structure suggested by Commons and Simon. Commons, two-thirds of a century ago, pointed out that the organization *will* was the "symposium" of settled *working rules* that have been hammered out by compromises among previous and existing power centers plus all the authority exercised by the pockets of freedom remaining among participants. The policy vectors that result from this symposium framed, for Commons, a working definition of corporate will. As an institutional economist he tried to minimize normative assertions about where the power should reside or who should exercise it.

March and Simon were concerned with organizational will and the exercise of corporate power to make choices. They too wished to reduce normative overtones, describe phenomena and give low-order explanations. Organizational choices in their view are made by all sorts of individuals at many levels under various restraints. March and Simon even comment in broad terms on the choices of accounting methods to support managerial decisions. In general they feel that organizational choices in financial matters are made on the basis of some composite interest and that accounting alternatives then are selected to support and justify the previous choices. In this narrow aspect Carnegie-Mellon may be ancestors of the Rochester positivist-accounting choice framework.

The most important consequence so far from agency-contracting may well be its attraction of some intelligent students to the mundane field of accounting. The combination of upper-division mathematics and statistics with elementary philosophy and sophisticated financial information has proved to be attractive to a goodly number of inquiring scholars.[16] In addition integrated concentration on the forces that influence the actual selection of accounting practices has undoubted merit. Finally the stressing—perhaps overstressing—of positivist methods may reveal to traditional researchers the fantastic number of normative assumptions that ordinarily underlie their work.

Otherwise the results to date of fierce intellectual effort in the contracting sector seem meager. Results seem to confirm what battle-scarred practitioners have suspected for a century or so. All sorts of forces operate to change accounting rules and to create new ones and the profession responds to all sorts of outside pressures from managers and other decision makers. It does not require finely-tuned research technology to convince practitioners that *at least* six contracting variables could be influential in selecting and developing accounting conventions. Consider: "*six variables* . . . have explanatory [*sic*] power. These variables are managerial compensation, leverage, size, risk, interest coverage and dividend constraints."[17] Veteran practitioners as well as intuitive students can have a holiday expanding this list to include such items as ego needs, sociological status levels, power relations and a myriad of widely distributed situational factors.

Possibilities for useful extension of the contracting-agency paradigm are numerous. With the addition of standards (objectives), the entire field of dysfunctional costs may be investigated. Failure to internalize organizational goals clearly involves both costs and benefits from various points of view.[18] An even broader extension can be made to include the costs of pluralism and the resolution of conflict in government. Deconstructionists can point to the costs and benefits of polysemy and to the ambiguous penumbra that surrounds all guidelines, classifications and generalizations.

NOTES

[1] Anatol Rapoport, *Operational Philosophy: Integrating Knowledge and Action* (New York: Harper & Brothers, 1953), p. 74. Apparently even a strict positivist is able to compare his sensations with the defining properties of "black" and "sheep" and to render judgments that the criteria have been met. Value judgments?

[2] I have never been impressed by or interested in the long linguistic and logical debates about counter (contra) factual expressions, e.g., discussions of unicorns and the present king of France. Wilbur Marshall Urban deserves repeating: "The condition of the meaningfulness of an assertion is not that certain entities about which the assertions are made 'exist'—in the sense of being empirically observable—but that the universe of discourse in which these entities have their existence is mutually acknowledged." *Language and Reality: The Philosophy of Language and the Principles of Symbolism* (New York: The Macmillan Company, 1939), p. 227. Strict positivists have difficulty in handling the comparison of alternatives for making decisions. An alternative not taken is a fact only in the sense that someone believed the alternative to be a legitimate option, i.e., consensus about the availability of the option is the pertinent fact—not the details of the proposal. Effective discourse requires that factual domains be related to consistent and relevant concepts of reality. In earlier times this requirement was related to levels of abstraction.

[3] The American Institute of CPAs.

[4] Computer experts are inclined to argue that many decisions can be made on the basis of quantitative rules. Indeed they can, and at many levels. But who makes the rules? Who establishes the variables worthy of being monitored? Who renders decisions of relative importance in case of conflict? Who decides that the numerical assignments represent appropriate tradeoff values?

[5] Some well-known statements may deserve requoting at this point. DR Scott is *not* known as a positivist, but listen: "the fundamental function of accounts and statistics [is] to so analyze and present the facts that the decisions of the management will be automatic. Instead of presenting accounts and statistics as tools through which management controls operations under its authority, this course presents them as means through which the management is itself controlled by the facts." "Unity in Accounting Theory," *The Accounting Review,* June 1931, p. 107. In spite of Dewey's wise council that the settled parts of the problematic situation (in general the hypotheses) divide the data into relevant facts and irrelevant information, his more practical successors at Chicago tended to follow a more inflexible factual path. Consider the following statements: "George [Schultz] used to talk about the little bits of evidence—accumulating them, letting them pile up until decisions were easy. . . . [O]ften the facts will seek you out. If all the evidence is not yet in, we [Chicago Business School Researchers] do not publish. . . . [I]f the supporting evidence is present, the conclusion becomes redundant." Sidney Davidson, "Where is the Evidence?" *Issues and Ideas,* Spring 1971, pp. 29–30.

[6] Louis Leon Thurstone, *Multiple-Factor Analysis: A Development and Expansion of The Vectors of Mind* (Chicago: The University of Chicago Press, 1947), pp. 55-6. (This quotation from Chapter I, "The Factor Problem," is reprinted in *Readings in Philosophy of Science,* Philip P. Wiener, ed. [New York: Charles Scribner's Sons, 1953], p. 197.)

[7] Allan G. Gruchy states: "by pouring the voluminous data of business cycle history through the narrow sieve of statistical analysis, Mitchell endeavors 'to create order amidst the confused facts of observation'. . . . Mitchell came to regard his studies of price phenomena and the business cycle not as an extension of the work of the orthodox economists but as an introduction to a new type of economic theory." *Modern Economic Thought: The American Contribution* (New York: Prentice-Hall, Inc., 1947), pp. 269, 251.

[8] To some extent professions have acted as centers for countervailing power opposed to the forces that follow the harnessing of greed to fuel economic activity in a market economy. Powerful interests certainly exert a major force on the rules of a profession and on the behavior of its members. Nevertheless small unorganized interests *are* heard and *do* influence professional rules and the alterna-

tives provided. The rise of corporate takeovers and buyouts of the eighties is evidence that business management does not merit serious consideration as a profession. Widespread abandonment of professional responsibilities in favor of personal gain also has lessened respect for business schools and made some business professors ashamed of their affiliations. So far the accounting profession has fared better, but recent experiences with banks, real estate clients and savings and loan operations raise serious doubts.

[9] This is not to deny that many academic researchers end their investigations with definite normative recommendations. Early accounting research was almost entirely of the normative type. I have never been happy with those who feel that factual studies (and the sociologists of accounting) are just "talking about accounting" while normative recommendations constitute *real* accounting. I have been even less happy with those who claim that only the structure is *real* accounting and that normative conclusions are *mere* ethical preferences.

[10] Charles Christenson, "The Methodology of Positive Accounting," *The Accounting Review,* January 1983, p. 6.

[11] The present discussion owes much to Ross L. Watts and Jerold L. Zimmerman, "Positive Accounting Theory: A Ten-Year Perspective," *The Accounting Review,* January 1990, pp. 131–156. Consider the following statements: " 'The program of the Rochester School is concerned with describing, predicting, and explaining the behavior of accountants and managers, not that of accounting entities' " (p. 147, quoted from Christenson, op. cit., p. 5). Even more interesting: "when accounting choice is cast as part of the efficient contracting technology, variables often used to explain and predict accounting choice are endogenous" (p. 152). Incidentally Watts and Zimmerman are in line to become the Milton Friedmans of the accounting establishment. See also their "Towards a Positive Theory of the Determination of Accounting Standards," *The Accounting Review,* January 1978, pp. 112–34; "The Demand for and Supply of Accounting Theories: The Market for Excuses," *The Accounting Review,* April 1979, pp. 273–305; and an expanded effort: *Positive Accounting Theory* (Englewood Cliffs: Prentice-Hall, Inc., 1986).

[12] In this area they are more or less in agreement with my own traditional view. I have never objected to *attempts* to separate value judgments and assign their execution to different individuals and groups. For example, I am quite willing to let scientists investigate the ozone layers with their own judgments, values and methods, and to let politicians decide public policy in this area. I do resent strenuously those who somehow feel that the myriad of small value judgments made by scientists and other research scholars are somehow not value judgments or choices at all. Often unfortunately only the policy applications are considered to be value judgments.

[13] See Anthony M. Tinker, Barbara D. Merino, and Marilyn Dale Neimark, "The Normative Origins of Positive Theories: Ideology and Accounting," *Accounting, Organizations and Society* (2), 1982, pp. 167–200.

[14] Charles Christenson, *op. cit.,* p. 19. Christenson comes through as something of a deconstructionist and a mild supporter of hermeneutics.

[15] Surely Watts and Zimmerman go too far: "Presently, there is no alternative theory for the empirical regularity between firm size and accounting choice other than the political cost hypothesis" *op. cit.,* p. 140. Students take over!

[16] The importance of this facet should not be underestimated. Recently the need for accounting professors seemed to be without end, and the need to open new areas for dissertations, theses and faculty research was obvious. In the 1920's, and even later, Berkeley, Michigan, Minnesota and some other great universities had only one full professor of accounting, and the quality of doctoral students in accounting, to be charitable, was below the level expected in economics and the sciences.

The traditional ideas for accounting research were well worked over by World War II and the pressing need for new areas was obvious. In 1945 the Wharton authorities were uncertain whether portions of philosophy, semantics, mathematics, sociology, literature, psychology and tax matters were appropriate research topics for accounting. Fortunately Penn was committed to encouraging interdisciplinary scholars and providing competent faculty members to lead and advise them. Yet it was approximately another decade before candidates could choose accounting for their doctoral concentration.

[17] Watts and Zimmerman, *op. cit.,* p.140.

[18] Calculation of the costs of dysfunction in organizations is especially troublesome. It is necessary to specify the viewpoint from which these sacrifices are observed. What is a cost to one set of contracting agents may be a benefit to others. This difficulty is found in all cost-benefit analyses where some parties are subject to the costs and others receive the benefits.

Persuasion, Opinion, and Belief—General Considerations

Turn now to an area of tremendous importance to accountants and auditors—the fixation of belief. This area relates questions of evidence and methods of persuasion, and clearly is influenced by cultural and social attitudes that include prevailing ideologies.

This essay is devoted primarily to general aspects of evidence and support for beliefs, while the next essay is concerned primarily (but not entirely) with applications to accounting. The present essay begins with a general discussion of the area, follows with a detailed outline of the methods and persuasive influences often used to fix belief and formulate opinions. Attention then is directed to a discussion of some facets of the correspondence and coherence theories that usually support opinions about truth. Unfortunately less attention is devoted to religious and historical supports for belief, and very little attention is given to such influences as intimidation, hero worship and authority generally. But some attention is given to the related hermeneutic concept of understanding as a substitute for more dogmatic concepts of truth.[1]

It has been pointed out that the usual true-false dichotomy is a specification of *extremes* that coincide with feelings of certainty one way or the other, and for this reason has little practical value for empiricists. Furthermore this grouping can be used even in logic only by stipulation. Thus logic gives only vague limiting guidelines for the pursuit of empirical knowledge which is based primarily on beliefs that vary more or less between the extremes of certainty and uncertainty.

We have pointed out the psychological element in determining truth, falsity, warranted assertability, mathematical proof, informal proof and belief. We now expand this discussion to give more attention to the part persuasion plays in this seemingly rigorous area. As soon as empiricists admit that these concepts have important psychological components, the rigid true-false division reduces to a Platonic ideal that may help them cling to absolutes and stable entities in a sea of uncertainty.

Abandonment of true-false as an absolute is difficult. There is something appealing, austere and even beautiful about the truths of formal mathematics and logic, and it takes some conditioning to replace this austerity with such mundane elements as rhetoric, persuasion and ordinary salesmanship. The purity of stipulated reasoning with such axioms as "$p \rightarrow p$" so that p always is exactly the same in all uses and the assumption that to be equal means equal in every aspect is difficult to abandon and doubly difficult to replace with a pedestrian framework that often is associated with sophistry, debate-coach techniques and con-man methods of persuasion. Even worse, persuasion opens the door for influences such as strong-arm techniques, fear, intimidation, domination and related atrocities. However, it also does bring to the fore the overriding importance of ideology and the influence of shared beliefs, social pressures and the over-riding importance of culture in the area of belief and truth.

The contention of this paper is that beliefs are closely related to expectations and that a study of expectations and their causes is a fruitful way to approach problems of belief. In general a belief is a psychological conviction about consequences and values, and is related to the tenacity with which one holds his bits of knowledge and his values. Some investigators feel that an expectation is situational and specific, whereas belief is reserved to indicate general support for the anticipation. This relationship also is present in explanation, where prediction is considered to be specific to the anticipation, and explanation is used to set forth reasons for the anticipation.

The recommendation here is that belief be treated as identical with opinion and that both be related to their psychological supports. Attention is directed to the factors that lead to the formation of psychological sets that help form opinions and beliefs. At the professional level accountants and auditors are busy not only *giving* opinions about various matters, but they also have a more important function: *creating* beliefs and opinions in others—specifically among those who count—the dominant reference groups.

At the general level one's disposition to hold beliefs may be influenced by inherited traits and by the prevailing ideology. Inherited traits may be important to biologists and sociobiologists, but are of concern here only insofar as they provide models for inquiry. Culture has been defined as the man-made portion of the environment and influences beliefs traditionally through the concept of ideology. Weber, Mannheim and a host of sociologists have emphasized features that shape ideology: the cultural features that influence the concept. Marx was a leader in using the ideology concept to influence others and to support his own persuasive rhetoric, and he did in fact look behind the concept at its socio-economic determinants.[2] The more immediate problem here is to find what experiences count for or against a belief.

Scientists are reluctant to accept nonsensory evidence without shareability, and for better or worse they consider shareable sensory evidence to be more stable and convincing than fantasies, dreams and images. Sensory evidence apparently affords more convincing support than bursts of emotion. Phenomenologists, existentialists and idealists generally are willing to be convinced by other than *objective* evidence and to consider all sorts of subjective supports that are not shareable in ordinary ways. The reader must be careful here about the opposition of subjective and objective and the opposition of reality and fantasy. It is obvious that dreams, fantasies, images and religious stirrings are *real* to many persons, e.g., psychologists, psychiatrists, preachers and to the individuals themselves.[3] The concept of reality therefore is an illusive construction with widely differing interpretations. The subjective-objective division also rests on a shaky foundation. Both require recognition of similarities between present and past experiences and the ability to recognize the stability of sensations.

It is clear that belief is related to expectations and that expectations that actualize are related to knowledge. Sometimes knowledge is defined to be identical with belief, but more often it is considered to be supported by belief and on occasion to be justified by belief."[4] Lucky guesses may well lead to knowledge but they hardly qualify as effective support, and a scientist must find some way to distinguish between "accidents" and the operation of his laws.

SELF-EVIDENT TRUTHS

Among the most primitive explanations is that beliefs are self-evident. This explanation is strange for it is difficult to understand how a *belief* can be *self* evident. This view ordinarily indicates that the support is so overwhelming that belief simply cannot be resisted and doubt is immediately resolved. This question-begging position may be convincing in some situations and to certain groups. Religious adherents may hold that God's design can be sensed correctly, incorporated in individual consciousness and used to form community consensus. Natural law adherents (including our founding fathers) expected our rational propensities to recognize relevant evidence and our democratic foundations assume that enough beliefs are held in common to sustain widely divergent and pluralistic organizations. Existentialists and related subjectivists often take a similar view. Sartre, for example, feels that a sincere individual can neither be deceived nor deceive himself. Anarchists, along with many devotees of the new left, feel that the individual can sort out and organize important aspects of his life without coercion or advice from others acting as individuals or in concert. Exactly what kinds of influences are important to these groups is not clear, and in the case of nihilists and related extremists the situation is even less clear.

A slight variation of self-evident support moves toward experience and usually is presented as "immediate experiences." Clearly "experience" of some sort must be used to support belief, but just as clearly all experience can not be pertinent. The usual meaning of *immediate* presumably is direct sensations that are more or less diverse.

In religious matters the questions of evidence and belief have led to what seems to be a greater and greater polarization of Christian faiths. At one extreme are those who base their faith and beliefs on the authority of sacred writings and the authority of designated church people who help interpret the scriptures and thus clarify the message for those less able to comprehend the doctrines.

At what seems to be the other extreme are Christians who take an individualistic approach that is essentially existentialist. These religious leaders feel that a sincere individual's own conscience cannot be deceived and will lead to acceptable beliefs. Others wonder what exactly in the human condition leads to this unique ability. Clearly humans and their beliefs are conditioned by all sorts of environmental and social influences, and the mystery is how these influences converge to an acceptable body of knowledge. The literature of internalization and identification may be relevant with all sorts of cultures and subcultures serving as role shapers. Sometimes identification is with mankind in its entirety and becomes the basis for humanism. Libertarians have also concentrated on the individual and have faith that following one's desires will lead to acceptable behavior.

Most accountants are more or less practicing naturalists without a great deal of philosophical sophistication. In general they feel that the world is out there and exists independently of human experience and human interpretation. Thus *things* are assumed to "exist in themselves" and the testimony of our senses is sufficient to recognize, correlate and accommodate many of their features. The influence of the individual in organizing the data (conceptualism and gestaltism) must be of some concern to naturalists, but the extreme views of solipsists and the dangers of the egocentric predicament are more or less neglected. In fact most business people may see little difference between the idealist view and the naturalist position. The former assumes some sort of idealized (perfect) conception to which the images of our senses can only imperfectly aspire. For organizing some types of thought such an assumption may be useful, but the naturalist usually is content to assume that what is out there exists and that our senses can comprehend some part of it. Whether one can *catch all of it* in an intellectual net supported by only five senses is highly questionable and relatively unimportant for the business of living.

Consider some common influences at work to generate and support belief.

PARTIAL OUTLINE: SUPPORTS FOR BELIEF

I. Authority and authority figures.
  A. Respect for authoritarian figures—the strongman in government.
  B. The hero in history.
  C. Religion—transcendental authority from above.
  D. Magic and myth—to undermine belief in natural laws and an orderly universe.
  E. Rigid role-and-status commitments.
  F. Authority through:
    1. Fear and anxiety—brutality, intimidation, ridicule, domination, generalized anxiety
    2. Love—largely emotional resulting from nearness and appreciation of others—*agape*
    3. Faith—largely will to believe with little support from alternative foundations.
  G. Examples from accounting—AICPA releases, handbooks, textbooks, heroes: (Schmalenbach, Limperg, Paton, Dicksee, May), senior-junior status, mystique of double-entry, early scribes as semi-holy men.

II. Analogies and historical evidence.
   A. Evidence through analogies—no two things identical except by stipulation (if p, then p); for pragmatists, analogies are problematic not stipulations.
   B. Measures—to indicate closeness of analogies, their relevance, goodness of fit.
   C. Analogies—by way of models, scenarios, paradigms, parables, metaphors, historical analogs.
   D. Historical evidence:
      1. Special importance of tradition
      2. Patterns of development as models
      3. Initial conditions—and developmental influences stable enough for transfer
      4. Degree of transfer—influenced by habitual interpretations from stable customs and usages
      5. Assumed patterns—cyclical, progressive, will of God, pendulum, economic and technological arrangements, semi-randomness.

III. Correspondence Theories (Realists and Naive Naturalists).
   A. Objectivity, referents, real world *out there* includes most positivists, semanticists, scientists, management scientists, accountants.
   B. Correspondence with what?
      1. Physical models—balances, stocks, flows, fundamental measurements, capacities, hydraulic and electrical analogs
      2. Biological models—instincts, traits, group will, survival, grow or die, needs, biological organisms
      3. Biological-psychological—utility, stress, rationality, irrationality, greed, internal controls, conservatism, user needs
      4. Physical-biological models—total systems, synergism, control devices, feedback
      5. Communication models—switches, synapses, noise, patterned signals, mechanical error
      6. Sociological-psychological models:
         a. Functional models—coordination, cooperation, integration, managers as coordinators
         b. Conflictual models—buying conformance, resolution of conflict, maximizing residual interests, insider-outsider framework, agency assumptions.

IV. Coherence Theories.
   A. Statement true when *related* propositions are true.
   B. Systems oriented—truth criteria applied to entire models and broad theories not individual propositions, complex laws of physics.
   C. Logical arguments—conclusions supported by logical system, relations among propositions, consistency.
   D. Rhetorical arguments—persuasion, sophistry.
   E. Discourse—hermeneutic understanding, expansion of semantics, dialectic.
   F. Consistency with statements from other disciplines:
      1. Economics—income, wealth, maximization, values, markets
      2. Pure mathematics, theoretical engineering
      3. Statistics—correspondence with abstract probability, chance, risk, uncertainty
      4. Behavioral—consistency with statements from biology, sociology, psychology
      5. Aesthetics—beauty, simplicity, elegance, precision.

This essay is not concerned directly with fear, intimidation and the like as possible persuaders. Only brief attention is given to some leaders in accounting. Even less attention is directed to the hero-in-history thesis and to the relative importance of individual leaders when compared to the *Zeitgeist*—the general spirit of the times.

While using authority as the basis for belief seems to be simple, the problem of selecting among possible authorities remains a vexing social problem. Commons states:

> [I]n warlike and feudal times . . . only the wills of martial heroes were deemed worth while; then [the will] was extended to unwarlike merchants . . . ; then to serfs and peasants; then to the most timid of people. . . .[5]

In democracies authority has been broadened and refined until it emerges as "the voice of the people." Good democrats are said to listen when the people speak, accept the results and believe in the wisdom of the evaluations. Voting becomes the accepted method for gauging the degree of social consensus. Even here some practical ambiguities remain for certain groups may be excluded from the process. At various times women, children, criminals, slaves and others have been excluded and their opinions considered to be unworthy to support either argument or belief. In modern accounting research market operations have more or less replaced the professional voting process. Markets exclude those without funds or particular interests. Professions exclude those without accepted professional credentials.

BELIEF GENERATION: INFORMATION AND RHETORIC

Turn now to some influential factors in the fixing of belief and consider terror and coercion as instruments. A portion of a population tends to be rebellious when confronted with discipline of any sort, and these along with other types may react negatively to coercion in any form. More generally terroristic methods and conspirational responses may prove to be exciting and lead to negative reactions and disbelief. Hatred generated by oppression may well lead to an automatic questioning of all pronouncements from those in power and thus reduce the effectiveness of authority.

There also is a tendency to believe statements of one's own subculture and to assume that messages from other power structures are entirely manipulative and generally false. This tendency is especially strong in the current rebellious youth who follow the ideology of the recent student left. In general they simply ignore traditional informational sources and depend entirely on the garbled and vitriolic (and sometimes astute) reports of their own underground presses. (Republican papers for Republicans, Democratic papers for Democrats and radical papers for radicals!) The values and goals of the subculture are internalized to the extent that nothing whatever advocated by the dominating group (or competing subcultures) is believed. For a historical case consider Marx and his vituperative responses to Feuerbach, Dürhing and utopian socialists who were bullied, terrorized and manipulated beyond traditional limits. It is highly doubtful whether Marx changed the beliefs of these leaders greatly, but he may have influenced many others to accept his beliefs.

We are at an interesting juncture here: To what extent do currently held beliefs tend to support similar views and reject dissident ones? On the face of it, construct reinforcement should solidify value bases, and frequent subjection to differing views may weaken attachments. Dictators have long suppressed competing views and the reports of many oppressed under Hitler and Stalin testify to the cumulative influence of continuous barrages of one-sided reports even when these statements are clearly antithetical to the well being of the receivers.[6]

Some interesting studies have considered the tenacity of belief and the desire of subjects to maintain a consistent and undisturbed pattern of beliefs. Apparently individuals can be induced to make sharp changes in their belief patterns by sufficient peer pressure. In some cases they simply have been unwilling to accept the testimony of their senses and have restructured or even reversed their beliefs to be consistent with the most ridiculous peer positions. Attempts by scientists and others to incorporate new information with the least disturbance of existing beliefs are well known. In general the inertial effects of such entrenched beliefs have been widely discussed and well documented.

At one time rhetoric may have been limited to the use of persuasion to convince popular audiences and may have been crafted to supplement logic, which apparently was used to convince more intellectual audiences by moving from premises to conclusions and following accepted rules. Plato certainly was an enemy of Sophists and their supposed tendency to trivialize argument by a nominalistic approach to truth and logic.[7] John Stuart Mill apparently considered logic to be the strategy of thought with rhetoric as the means of reporting and adding commentary. Aristotle, and later Cicero, were more favorably disposed. Aristotle divided the task of persuasion into several parts. Invention, for example, denoted supporting arguments with *extrinsic* arguments coming from documents, testimony, eyewitnesses, etc. Certainly science has depended heavily on extrinsic items, and accountants have deep faith in externally generated documents and evidence. As Young and Becker state:

> We have become much more interested in techniques for discovering what is unknown than in techniques for bringing old beliefs to bear on new problems. Thus the classical art of invention has diminished in importance while the modern art of experimental inquiry has expanded immensely.[8]

In this connection consider briefly the process of hermeneutic understanding. These folks abandon dependence on crude observation that is somehow to be applied in a naive objective manner without subjective involvement. Instead of the dualistic subject-object separation, they offer the concept of understanding where a consensual meaning can be arrived at through "objectivizing" the senders intentions and "interpreting" the signals so that meaningful communication can be conducted.

They depend heavily on *discourse*—primarily linguistic give and take among interested parties—to further the process of understanding.

In the process of discoursing, precise definitions may give way to more amorphous explications, and persuasiveness along with collateral explanatory statements become important elements in creating understanding. In an important way alternatives (theories?) may be reduced to various ways of "saying" (describing). No attempt is made either to develop some idealized concept of understanding or to obscure the need to have accept values for selecting preferable ways of presenting narratives (arguments).[9]

Discourse differs from traditional semantics in several ways. Most early semanticists were dualists who divided the world into grammar (syntax) and some sort of real world referents which individuals coordinated by rules of correspondence. These coordinations were known as assigning values to the variables in mathematics and interpretations in logic and much scientific work. Presumably the symbols and the symbolic structure along with the referents belonged to some hypothesized *real* world. Traditional semantic interpretation then constituted the chief subjective element and consisted primarily of finding relationships among facets of an objective world. Finally human effects were largely relegated to the field of pragmatics, although a subdivision known as general semantics combined semantic and pragmatic aspects. In practice the details of pragmatics were turned over to psychologists or in the case of Korzybski and his followers to a hybrid psychiatrist *cum* linguist.

Discourse depends more on interaction with less emphasis on objective referents and one-one relationships between symbols and referents. In psychological movements the older view is more stimulus-response oriented, while the latter depends on a gestaltistic framework in which meaning is *constructed* through mutual understanding.

Accountants should be interested in the long rhetorical disputes over the separability of style and substance of what *is* reported as opposed to *how* it is reported. This division has been of concern to rhetoricists and to poets as well. Whether these elements can be separated enough to satisfy analytical standards is not a concern here although accountants and others often tried to separate them. Clearly the more sophisticated view is that the usual sharp distinction between style and substance has been overdrawn. Those who emphasize this distinction tend to be naive realists who believe in objective entities that make up the substance and feel that *style* is independent of these substantive entities.

These stylists sometimes are user oriented but some seem to disregard user interpretations and concentrate on abstract canons for language. The more modern framework takes a dim view of substantive things that exist independently of observation and concentrate on *interpretations* of signals and *construction* of meaning from style, substance and all other facets that can be invented or sensed. Rhetoricians have a responsibility to be convincing, and many feel that arguments are more convincing when they include some *evidence* that is more general than the particular argument and thus is more likely to be accepted. They therefore create substance from data that are widely shared and accepted. The persuasive task then is to present data in a style that will show their *relevance* to the problem at hand. Dewey has his investigator search for "settled" aspects of a problematic situation so that analogies may be marshalled to support hypotheses that alleviate the stress or relieve the strain. But for Dewey these settled aspects of the situation are by no means confined to substantive matters. The persuader at least hopes that his evidence will be accepted and its relevancy admitted. Often the arguer hopes to find some persuasive foundation in addition to verbal support. Observe that relevance does not speak for itself or manifest itself in some undeniable nexus and that further steps may be necessary to convince the subject—perhaps by logic, or causative association.

The rules of logic often are employed in cases where acceptance of both the evidence (premises) and the rules of logic make it embarrassing to deny the conclusion. There is little new in logical persuasion. The advocate keeps trying until he finds some statements (premises) with which the subject agrees. Then if he is subject to persuasion by logical processes, he is led to conclusions that he can accept. The agreed premises and the accepted rules of logical transformation provide the necessary foundation blocks, and persuasion from logical arguments comes from accepting the preliminary statements—the axioms, postulates, premises—and the from intuition that the rules of two-valued logic apply. Incidentally Nihilists survive by denying the existence or relevance of premises and thus are able to reject the conclusions. A more common approach, used successfully by the student new left, is to be selective and deny all disagreeable premises while concealing their own implicit assumptions. Zen too is a useful refuge for those who do not wish to be persuaded. The Zen doctrine, as I understand it, emphasizes raw experience and refuses to look for or accept causal and related relationships among the experiences.

Often persuasion to accept premises begins with analogies that form stepping stones. Past experience may have been so compelling that it is aggregated and accepted as a scientific law, a natural law, a commission from God, etc. In these cases belief is encouraged by faith that the accepted *law* applies to the extended case. Persuasion here takes the logical form of convincing the subject that some more general relationship applies to the particular case—that the present case is a member of the class of cases covered by the generalization.

Accountants are well aware that they must use *style* to present their own combination of expectations and judgments that may vary from simple factual inferences to complex constructions. They also are aware of the need to arrange, package and report these beliefs in a convincing manner—convincing enough to justify their claim on the social dividend and justify their fees. All sorts of manipulations make up this segment of *form,* and it is far too simple to hold that form is applicable only at the word and sentence level. To an important degree it is the entire gestalt that conveys the message.

It is evident that some titles may be more moving, more attention getting and more convincing than others, and intuitive and artistic elements also are involved. In music melodies, rhythms, harmonies, counterpoints and the rest are important components of the message and in poetry similar factors are at work. The accountant—in the name of form—can vary titles, degrees of aggregation, arrangements, ordering, proximity, location and a host of related variables. Printing emphasis may substitute for intonation. Brevity, organization and structure may be manipulated for emphasis and to convince the reader of the importance and relevance of more traditional numerical statements.

CORRESPONDENCE

The traditional philosophical base for accounting and its practitioners has been naive realism. Thankfully they have never been so naive as to argue that objects and events themselves are entered in their books, and most have been too sophisticated to accept crude forms of representative realism in which the words *represent* their physical counterparts. Yet the feeling that their entries represent *something* about external events served the early profession reasonably well.

It is clear that accountants must retrieve something from memory storage and encode something about the situation into verbal form. These verbal forms may be thought of as pictures or representations of some separate realities. Early pragmatists, for example, thought of meaning as habits to respond to symbols as if they were some separate and outside reality. Carnap, among logical positivists, defined meaning in pragmatic terms as knowing when (in particular instances) to use symbols and when not. Semanticists were fond of using an analogy in which the symbols were maps of the *real* territory. Their admonition to those who would understand language was to find the referent.

Accountants long have been aware of the need to limit the reality that forms the basis for their records. The usual limiting rule is to consider only realities that result in transactions. This recognition is most important for it isolates a part of reality that merits accounting recognition. Unfortunately, the operational rules for defining transactions and making the necessary division have not always been clear, but this rough guideline has served with fair success for several centuries. Generally transactions have been defined as changes in economic values over a limited area—an entity. To the credit of early double-entry theorists, the changes in wealth were recorded so that *potentials* for future changes in wealth could also be disclosed along with certain claims on such potentials. In fact, except for error-disclosing potential, this feature may be the only original contribution of double-entry bookkeeping.

Observe that accountants have never been so naive that they relied completely on physical reality (things). In fact their emphasis on events and change fits well with the view of modern theoretical physicists. Why then did accountants emphasize tangibles and other aspects of physical things and abhor intangible assets? This attachment may arise because it was easier for businessmen to allocate values to tangible sources or because it was less difficult to audit tangible sources of value. Unfortunately some teachers have forgotten that accountants are concerned primarily with values and that physical inventory movements, etc., are of little importance except to serve as easily recognizable nodes for value assignment. The little importance that physical realities do have comes from their usefulness in helping to understand the underlying mechanisms for value changes and the levels of value potential.[10]

COHERENCE

Strangely, coherence theory seems to be out of style among phenomenologists, existentialists and defenders of the new left. This organizing structure for supporting belief usually is used to portray truth as consistent with related propositions. The current distrust for this view is especially difficult to understand in light of the popularity of "holistic" methods and the widespread acceptance of systems theory. It may be related to the current distrust of logic and its methods.

The coherence approach need not be oriented primarily to particular linguistic forms, e.g., related propositions, but this association usually is made to distinguish coherence from correspondence. If linguistic relationships are associated with the senses, they are usually treated as correspondences; while, if they are related to other propositions in a structured system, they establish the coherence position. A little reflection will show that the senses also are involved in trying to determine the truth, falsity or consistency of related propositions. Even if these analogs are propositions or some type of sensual entity, they must be appraised in terms of their connectedness. In fact it may be argued that all these related experiences need to be verbalized and stated in proposition form before they can be used even as supporting analogies. The opposite view is that one is able to sense such relationships in an immediate visceral way with little or no help from language and its symbols.

In any case the coherence theory of deciding warrantedness for tentative belief (truth) is closely related to systems thinking. Belief is systems supported in the sense that relevance of the analogies is established by a constructed system of relationships.

It is difficult to understand the current disrepute of coherence theories. Physics would be dead without such devices because complicated theoretical constructions simply are not testable as simple facts in isolation, and their truthfulness, relevance or verification is determined largely by whether they mediate successfully between interrelated expressions of observable conditions *and* constitutive relations.

It may be argued that the scientific emphasis on coherent structures is precisely what turns off modern existentialists. Some may refuse to admit specific determinants for immediate perceptions, e.g., a perceptive person simply cannot deceive himself. Apparently this ability is assumed to be a part of the human condition. The problem is not entirely subjective-objective, although many readers will agree that the truth conditions of propositional systems may have some claim to objectivity. Subjectivists will emphasize that sensing the relevance of any system of propositions or experiences is a subjective matter. Inferences may be systems supported or they may be isolated and lonely.[11]

The modern version of coherence also is related to mathematical thinking. Pure mathematicians are accustomed to look for coherent relationships, and they feel comfortable when each of their statements (propositions) is consistent with other accepted statements. Coherence in the mathematical sense means that the new statement relates to others in ways that meet the conditions set forth by the rules of the mathematical system. Presumably proof is acknowledged when there is mathematical coherence with postulates, previous theorems and prescribed axioms.

A noticeable difference exists between the personal requirements for the coherence and correspondence approaches. The coherence framework is based on the assumption that an individual has a high level of cognitive ability and considerable knowledge about the truth and falsity of related propositions. Moreover he must make the judgment that his present proposition follows established rules and is consistent with other propositions whose truth or falsity already has been judged. Reliance on senses still remains, for the individual must be able to structure individual propositions before making the vital comparison to establish consistency or inconsistency with the system. Moreover, there must be some ability to compare these inputs and outputs for relative congruence with accepted true statements in order to judge warrantedness (correspondence).

At first glance, correspondence theory seems to require less intellectual effort for all sorts of naturalistic analogies may be offered. For some the mind produces "pictures" of some presumed reality. The term "resemblances" has been bandied about by some very subtle observers, and the assumption of some sort of *ideal* concept that can only be approximated by ordinary minds and sensory equipment still is widely held. In any case the use of physical, biological and related models requires judgments about the adequacy of rules of correspondence among elements of the specific situation and elements of the model. The real world itself may be considered to be a model constructed from various sensations and resemblances, but the problem of assessing similarities and differences still remains.

DIGRESSION ON PROPOSITIONS AND BELIEFS

Consider again the use of truth and its derivatives in the field of communication and logic. We argue that any truth structure is subject to systems analysis and can be approached at different levels. It is sometimes argued that facts cannot be true or false and subjected to tests for warrantedness. But there is no way *objects* themselves can be true or false. The case is similar for those who hold that facts are constructed by the observer from sense impressions from sensa. Although truth or falsity are not assigned to the sensations, there may be doubt as to whether the sensations meet the criteria used to determine existence.[12]

The usual questions about brute-level facts are related to beliefs about existence. Determining the existence of a string of relatively stable sensations certainly is different from determining validity in rhetoric and logic. The judgment of existence requires a decision as to whether a given sensation meets (to the required degree) the defining properties for inclusion in the stipulated category. Definitions usually are not considered to be true or false, but similar judgments about them are required before they can be used effectively.

Turn once more to beliefs and their near relatives, expectations. Many wish to treat beliefs and expectations as identical, while other investigators feel there are important psychological differences. One may believe for example that human beings are inherently good and at the same time expect them to be bad in special situations. This divergence may be discussed in terms of probabilities, individual instances, class definitions or membership differences, but may not be discussed further.[13] In short, it is possible to believe in a relationship with little expectation of finding examples to support the belief.

The usual approach is to argue that it is expectations that are true or false—justified or not justified. An individual forms an expectation on some basis or other, and erects criteria to decide whether the expectation is warranted. Application of appropriate criteria then may lead to a subsequent belief about the warrantedness of the first anticipation.

Chemistry students may believe that hydrogen and oxygen under specified conditions will form water, and a million elementary students have transformed these expectations into firm beliefs. Even more millions of children have turned their heads from their favorite toys with the expectation that the playthings will still be there when they return. In a like manner common folks along with applied mathematicians and theoretical physicists expect certain relations to remain invariant after spatial and temporal displacement. Finally religious persons believe that God exists as an important force in their lives and according to their own individual criteria (soul stirrings, personal testimony, rational argument, scriptural evidence); their expectation may be warranted and verified. Their expectations are supported by *their own criteria,* and the support may be sufficient to justify their beliefs.

Consider now propositions and the widespread view that truth is something that attaches to propositions alone, i.e., to verbal statements that assert a relationship of some sort.[14] Consider first the relationship of verbal expressions to expectations (anticipations) in a psychological sense. A proposition makes an assertion and in some situations creates an expectation and serves as an hypothesis to be investigated. Notice however that the inquirer may or may not *believe* the statement so that it is not accurate to assume a stable relationship between statements and beliefs. Moreover, some non-propositional expressions, especially emotive signs, can generate expectations even when they are not verbalized in a formal manner. The point here is that propositions have only a tenuous relationship with expectations, and it is expectations that need to be verified. A proposition is designed to express an expectation. A test of the expectation may lead to the belief that the proposition is or is not accurate, and this belief may be called true or false.

We are arguing here that it may be useful to apply verification, warrantedness and confirmation to expectations, and reserve different words to describe the decision about verbal expressions. Some pragmatists (especially William James) favor the expectational approach with truth being defined as successful efforts, and success expressed as congruence between the expectations created by propositions and the actual outcomes.[15] In any case the proposition *may* be a verbal expression of an expectation so that the warrantedness of the expectation may be applied to the proposition that created the expectation.

A very simple belief is that a proposition, when tested in acceptable ways, can be justified and this approach may help with the distinction between hypotheses and conclusions. Readers should be familiar with the argument that a conclusion is itself a confirmed hypothesis. How then is it different from earlier hypotheses (conjectures) that led to the test and its subsequent transformation into a conclusion? The difference seemingly is due to intensity of belief. Yet here too there is trouble for different people often are involved and the intensities of their beliefs are likely to vary and be difficult to assess. Ideology, education and indoctrination are relevant but it is clear that facts are hypotheses and that theories too are hypotheses—perhaps broader ones or ones that are held with belief structures that are weaker than facts.

PEIRCE AND BECKER

One of the more interesting and ingenious approaches to belief is that of Charles Sanders Peirce.[16] Peirce (pre-Dewey) contrasts belief with doubt, which is seen as an irritation that leads to a struggle known as "inquiry" in the hope of resolving the irritation and arriving at some state of belief. Thus, "Doubt is an uneasy and dissatisfied state from which we struggle to free ourselves and pass into the state of belief."[17]

Perhaps the most interesting of Peirce's conclusions is that belief is a habit. Logic results from the successful application of habits and is itself a product of natural selection, *ala* Darwin. Belief may be "of the nature of a habit" but what decides which habits survive and therefore what beliefs survive? Clearly an important element is faith in a religious or secular sense, but Peirce wryly comments: "immovable faith yields great peace of mind. It may . . . give rise to inconveniences, as if a man should resolutely continue to believe that fire would not burn him. . . ."[18]

Peirce is not concerned with individuals who stubbornly persist in their beliefs, and points out that social pressures are likely to be against them. The discovery that other folks may have beliefs equivalent to his own means that social interaction must be considered (the fixation of belief becomes a community affair) and that institutions will arise to find and perpetuate "correct doctrines." This process he terms the method of authority and finds it held in higher esteem than the tenacity of individual belief.

From the community approach and its resulting ideology Peirce considers how individuals influence one another. Some doubt will remain about most beliefs, and in the absence of brute force some congenial method of convincing others must be devised. He argues that the concept of nature (and by indirection objects) has been widely used and has led to the feeling that beliefs are in accordance with the natural order—natural laws—and the structure of a rational world. But beliefs acceptable to reason are related to those induced by more mundane affairs and some force toward uniformity is desirable.

One method of procuring a degree of uniformity is to assume that beliefs are influenced by some permanent outside grounding: "something upon which our thinking has no effect."[19] He then moves to the arguments of science. Unfortunately science requires some concept of reality and thus the basis for belief is shifted to consideration of what is or is not real. It may indeed be easier to agree on the defining properties and relations necessary for reality, but as C. I. Lewis and a host of others have pointed out, agreement on objectivity and reality is difficult indeed.[20] Clearly there is no final solution in this direction.

The disposition to believe, to make judgments of true-false, confirmed-nonconfirmed, beautiful-ugly, right-wrong, etc., are largely culturally determined and therefore are classic examples of ideology in operation.[21] Carl Lotus Becker, following Whitehead and some philosophers of the seventeenth century, applies the term "climate of opinion" to emphasize the influence of ideology on belief and the need to use historical techniques to understand customs and beliefs. He argues that the statements of Dante and Thomas Aquinas are simply unreadable unless they are considered from an historical viewpoint; yet

> if their arguments are unintelligible to us[,] the fact cannot be attributed to lack of intelligence in them. . . . Life on earth was but a means . . . for the testing of God's children. . . . Existence was thus re-

garded . . . as a cosmic drama, composed by the master dramatist according to a central theme. . . . The duty of man was to accept the drama as written. . . . The function of intelligence was therefore to demonstrate the truth of revealed knowledge. . . .[22]

The recent anguish of existentialists over existence and man's predicament apparently was not a problem in those times.

In the Becker account of this drama the acceptance of other-worldly evidence as set forth by the religious leaders and supported by sheer faith was already being undermined by the time of Dante. God had given man a rational mind but for what use in such a deterministic world? What better use than to rationalize rules from the "Heavenly City" with the pragmatic and generally untidy world of human existence. It was only later that Voltaire and others demonstrated that reason could be employed to undermine faith, and later still that St. Thomas, a man of unshakable faith, employed it to support faith as well as to destroy it.[23]

In later years the arguments of St. Thomas' *Summa* were treated by positivists as pseudo arguments (meaningless). Becker continues: "Its conclusions seem to us neither true nor false, but only irrelevant. . . ."[24] Argument does become trivial when one or both sides do not accept either the premises or the logical machinery for moving acceptably from propositions to other propositions.

Some modern philosophers have made a complete historical turn with no faith in teleology and with full faith that man is a bewildered, alienated entity aimlessly wandering through the gloomy interstices of space-time without guidance and without objectives. In Becker's words:

> What is man that the electron should be mindful of him! Man is but a foundling in the cosmos, abandoned by the forces that created him. Unparented, unassisted and undirected . . . , he must fend for himself. . . . Whirl is king, having deposed Zeus. . . . [W]e look about in vain for any semblance of the old authority. . . . [W]e may still believe in Zeus. . . . [Still] [n]o serious scholar would now postulate the existence and goodness of God . . . for explaining the quantum theory or the French Revolution. . . . The fact is that we have no first premise. . . . Our supreme object is to measure and master the world rather than to understand it.[25]

Yet the rise of facts as the primary basis for belief has not completely prevailed and science has not removed the mysteries of the world by declaring them meaningless. Again Becker states:

Physics, which it was thought had dispensed with the need of metaphysics, has been transformed by its own proper researches into the most metaphysical of discipline(s). . . . We now suspect that [logic] is something the mind has created to conceal its timidity and keep up its courage, a hocus-pocus designed to give formal validity to conclusions we are willing to accept. . . . When sufficiently hard pressed, therefore, the physicist solves his difficulties by turning mathematician. . . . [O]ur world can be computed even if it doesn't exist.[26]

WILLIAM JAMES-CASH VALUES AND PAYOFF MATRICES

Previously I have mentioned the possibility that James' cash value of truth and his general approach to philosophy were at least consistent with modern decision theory.[27] The reader may be familiar with his use of theories as instruments and his use of truth as a guide for expectations. These ideas are simple enough and it is difficult to understand the ridicule they have engendered.[28] It is understandable that Singer's instrumentalist followers were leaders in developing the payoff matrix and probabilistic decision theory, but it is unusual that none of James' direct disciples (except Singer) have taken an active part in this development.

James was familiar with Pascal's argument that belief in God is a game of chance in which the penalty for failure to believe when he exists makes belief a statistical necessity. In fact James expanded Pascal's argument so that only an infinitesimal chance that God exists (with payoff stakes so great) makes it irrational to disbelieve; he stated: "what have you to lose?"[29]

We consider now some of James' arguments. He held that an hypothesis is a proposal presented for our judgment and belief, and he makes an immediate distinction between those that strike the reader as non-possibilities (dead) and those that seem to pose an actual possibility. (The former are more or less nonsense—the wrong questions—the *Mic* of Zen advocates.) Live hypotheses offer an option for belief or disbelief and are designated as "living" options. James states:

> He who refuses to embrace a unique opportunity loses the prize as surely as if he tried and failed. *Per Contra,* the option is trivial when the opportunity is not unique, when the stake is insignificant, or when the decision is reversible if it later proves unwise.[30]

In this vein he argues that to a confirmed atheist the Christian proposal "is a dead hypothesis from the start" and "that the empiricist tendency has largely prevailed in science, while in philosophy the absolutist tendency has had everything its own way."[31]

Yet "living options never seem absurdities to him who has them to consider" and "we have the right to believe at our own risk any hypothesis that is live enough to tempt our will."[32]

The step from such probability assessments to decision theory is a small one. James is even aware of the values that must be associated with alternatives and only fell short by failing to develop a specific framework. No doubt he considered the greatest benefit from this line of reasoning to be the substitution of "success probabilities" for the completely true or completely false of traditional logic.

NOTES

[1] "The irritation of doubt leads to the struggle to attain belief. The end of this inquiry, which aims to dispel doubt, is knowledge." Harold H. Titus, *Living Issues in Philosophy,* 5th ed. (New York: Van Nostrand Reinhold Company, 1970), p. 260. "Acceptance or rejection of a proposition is called a *judgment;* it is always an individual act. . . . The psychological disposition to make judgments which assert a proposition may be called *belief. . . .*" A. P. Ushenko, *The Theory of Logic* (New York: Harper & Brothers Publishers, 1936), p. 27.

[2] Weber, Mannheim, Pareto, Schumpeter, along with numerous theologians have not been willing to accept Marx's materialistic explanation that depends entirely on narrow economic matters. Moreover some have not been pleased by his definition of exploitation in terms of laborers only. Physiocrats argue that anything above keeping the non-agrarian population alive constitutes exploitation of the rentier class. In a similar manner capitalists might argue that giving anything more to labors, managers or rentiers than is necessary to get them to perform and reproduce constitutes exploitation of the entrepreneurial group. A modern return to physiocratic ethics is evident in the expropriation of oil developments with the implied conclusion that *all* the property value belongs to the country claiming the territory (land) and none to the capitalists who furnished the facilities or to the brain trust that knew where to drill and how to extract the contents.

[3] William James, the most existentialistic (and gestaltistic) of pragmatists, has dealt with this area in some detail:

> The . . . contents themselves are not true, they simply *come* and *are.* Truth is *what we say about* them. . . . Purely objective truth . . . is nowhere to be found (Lecture II, "What Pragmatism Means," pp. 62, 64).

> She [pragmatism] has in fact . . . no rigid canons of what shall count as proof. . . . She will count mystical experiences if they have practical consequences (*ibid.,* pp. 79–80).

[On the representative theory of truth:] Where our ideas cannot copy definitely their object, what does agreement with that object mean? (Lecture VI, "Pragmatism's Conception of Truth," p. 199).

Behind the bare phenomenal facts . . . there is *nothing* (Lecture VII, "Pragmatism and Humanism," p. 263).

[Consider also his gestaltist orientation:] [E]ven in the field of sensation, our minds exert a certain arbitrary [?] choice. By our inclusions and omissions we trace the field's extent; by our emphasis we mark its foreground and its background. . . . We receive in short the block of marble, but we carve the statue ourselves (ibid., p. 247). The three lectures cited above are in William James, *Pragmatism: A New Name for Some Old Ways of Thinking* (New York: Longmans, Green, and Co., 1907). (Editor's Note: Lectures II and VI also appear in William James, *Essays in Pragmatism,* Alburey Castell, ed. [New York: Hafner Publishing Co., Inc., 1948]; the quotations from them are on pp. 149–50, 157, 160.)

It is clear that James, like other pragmatists privileges "practical consequences"—a delightfully vague concept.

[4] See "Knowledge and Belief," *Encyclopedia of Philosophy,* Volume 4 (New York: The Macmillan Company and the Free Press, 1967), p. 345.

[5] John R. Commons, "Institutional Economics," *The American Economic Review,* March 1936, p. 245, n. 11. Apparently I am among the few who consider Commons to be among the leading social scientists of the early 20th century. See *Essays,* Vol. IV, pp. 101–127.

[6] Dictators are not the only ones who are aware of the devastating effects of counter information and influences. Pimps also try to remove their charges from standard cultural values and encourage their association with others sharing their values. Labor unions have the task of weaning workers from owners and managers and furnishing their own propaganda to promote cohesion and hasten the internalization of union goals.

[7] "Platonic anti-rhetoric . . . stresses not the art of writing but the quality of the writer in his adherence to truth and virtue: a good writer is a good man writing." Richard E. Young and Alton L. Becker, "Toward a Modern Theory of Rhetoric: A Tagmemic Contribution," in *New Rhetorics,* Martin Steinmann, Jr., ed. (New York: Charles Scribner's Sons, 1967), p. 79. Other contributions from this uneven volume have improved this discussion.

[8] *Ibid.,* p. 82.

[9] There is a long tradition of privileging discussion in philosophy and in practical affairs. The senate of the United States is a handy example, and the newly independent Indonesia placed great faith in *Gotong-Royong* until the for-

mal assembly was dissolved because the politicians were forever talking and never acting.

[10] The dualistic philosophy behind this view is clear to all. My own appreciation of the importance of language in accounting first came in the thirties from teaching elementary courses. For a college student to solve an accounting problem it is necessary to interpret the words of the exercise to arrive at an estimate of the events that transpired. These projected events are analyzed in terms of changes in wealth categories and the changes then are translated into accounting syntax. At the time it was obvious that at least two languages were interacting, but it took at least another decade to recognize that a further translation was required, i.e., an interpretation of the accounting language for user needs.

[11] Alan R. White emphasized that: "Any attempt to change the meaning of 'coherence' from coherence with other statements to coherence with facts (or reality or experience) is to abandon the theory." "Coherence Theory of Truth," *Encyclopedia of Philosophy* (*op. cit.*), Volume 2, pp. 132-3. He also wonders about the adoption of this essentially "idealistic" concept by some logical positivists and to some extent by the young Bertrand Russell. A. N. Pryor emphasized that the main thrust of Russell's truth is toward a correspondence concept; he quotes from Russell: "truth consists in some form of correspondence between belief and fact." See "Correspondence Theory of Truth," *ibid.*, p. 223.

[12] Dewey apparently was thinking at this level when he characterized some phenomena as "brute facts" that are simply *there*. Susanne Langer can argue that facts are assumed sources of sensations to which we react successfully, but she (like Cohen) is already on a level that requires a broader system. Those who consider facts to be "true sentences" (mainly logical positivists) still are on a different systems wave length. Percy S. Cohen relates facts to beliefs: "Facts are nothing more than statements which we believe to be true about particular events. . . ." *Modern Social Theory* (New York: Basic Books, Inc., 1968), p. 1.

[13] Examples also are found outside the ethical field. One may believe in witches and not expect to encounter them. Astronomers may believe in black holes or weak and strong forces without expecting to find examples. The process also may run in the opposite direction: Experiences may lead to expectations, and expectations may harden into beliefs.

[14] Logical positivists use this approach. They tend to emphasize language: propositions become sentences, science becomes the language of science, and *sentences* are true or false or nonsensical. The nonsense statements include all declarative sentences whose truth or falsity cannot be established or refuted according to the stipulated criteria. Interestingly, an extreme mystic might believe that statements confirmed by positivist criteria are foolish, although they would not use the term "nonsense," for nonsense usually indicates propositions that are not verifiable by sense criteria.

[15] Consider the following pragmatic approach by non-pragmatist R. G. Collingwood: "no one can even try to define a term until he has settled in his own mind a definite usage of it: no one can define a term in common use until he has satisfied himself that his personal usage of it harmonizes with the common usage. . . . [Some] think that in order to construct a definition or (what is the same thing) a 'theory' of something, it is enough to have a clear idea of that one thing. That is absurd. Having a clear idea of the thing enables them to recognize it when they see it, . . . but defining the thing is like explaining [it]. . . ." *The Principles of Art* (London: Oxford University Press, 1938), p. 2.

[16] "The Fixation of Belief," *Popular Science Monthly,* November 1877, pp. 1–15; reprinted with some later amendments in *Classic American Philosophers,* Max H. Fisch, ed. (New York: Appleton-Century-Crofts, Inc., 1951), pp. 54–70. Peirce's better known, "How to Make Our Ideas Clear," also is reprinted in this volume, pp. 70–87. (Page numbers of future references are from the reprint.)

[17] *Ibid.,* p. 59. Apparently Peirce felt that true conclusions required true premises and thus would disagree with Whitehead and many others (*ibid.,* p. 57). He also was interested in setting forth some preconditions for logical reasoning: "a variety of facts are already assumed when the logical question is first asked. It is implied . . . that there are such states of mind as doubt and belief—that a passage from one to the other is possible, the object of thought remaining the same, and that this transition is subject to some rules which all minds are alike bound by" (*ibid,* p. 58).

[18] *Ibid.,* p. 62.

[19] *Ibid.,* p. 66.

[20] Peirce's conception of science may be too Newtonian to suit modern philosophers: "Its [science's] fundamental hypothesis . . . is this: There are real things, whose characters are entirely independent of our opinions about them; those realities affect our senses according to regular laws, and, though our sensations are as different as our relations to the objects, yet, by taking advantage of the laws of perception, we can ascertain by reasoning how things really are, and any man, if he have sufficient experience and reason enough about it, will be led to the one true conclusion. The new conception here involved is that of reality. . . . The test of whether I am truly following the method is not an immediate appeal to my feelings and purposes, but, on the contrary, itself involves the application of the method" (*Ibid.,* pp. 66-8).

[21] We neglect here those who argue that we are born with drives and related yens that can be taken as given and that ethics, esthetics and values generally result from traits of this sort. The extreme extension of this thinking is that ethics, esthetics, etc., can be studied scientifically as manifestations of these drives so that much current work in these fields simply is speculative philosophy.

[22] Carl L. Becker, *The Heavenly City of the Eighteenth-Century Philosophers* (New Haven: Yale University Press, 1932), pp. 5-7.

[23] "Most men . . . feel the need of good and sufficient reasons for their faith. . . . This is perhaps one of the reasons why the thought of Dante's time was so remorselessly rationalistic. The faith was still intact, surely; but it was just ceasing to be instinctively held . . ." *Ibid.*, pp. 8-9.

[24] *Ibid.*, p. 12.

[25] *Ibid.*, pp. 15–17.

[26] *Ibid.*, pp. 24-5, 27. Also "[W]e must cling to the ascertainable facts though they slay us" (p. 26). At this point, we neglect further discussion of the religious aspects of belief. For an excellent and careful discussion of these aspects see Martin E. Marty, *Varieties of Unbelief* (New York: Holt, Rinehart and Winston, 1964). Marty is not greatly impressed with an assumed "God of explanation" or with the philosophical counterpart outlined by Etienne Borne as "In the Beginning Was Hegel" (pp. 124, 134n).

[27] See *Essays,* Vol. V, p. 59.

[28] The influence of James on future "instrumentalists," especially on Edgar A. Singer, Jr., might best be left to Singer disciples Cowan, Churchman and Ackoff. Singer introduced probability concepts to define his concept of *truth* to go along with his highly idealized Platonic *answers* that were valid and useful in all cases. His probabilistic notions warned him that one or a few negative instances could never "disprove" an answer, but he seemed unable to retreat from a more absolute construction that could countenance no negation. See E. A. Singer, Jr., *Experience and Reflection,* C. West Churchman, ed. (Philadelphia: University of Pennsylvania Press, 1959).

[29] From an address, "The Will To Believe," to the Philosophical Clubs of Yale and Brown Universities. Published in the *New World,* June 1896. Included in William James, *Essays in Pragmatism, op. cit.,* pp. 88–109. Apparently James anticipated Bertrand Russell's similar argument that God may place highest praise on those who make rational decisions and rest their honest beliefs on traditional evidence. God may abhor safety plays and fail-safe decisions that border on dishonesty. To Russell unrestrained faith may not be the bargain that some fundamentalists suggest.

[30] *Ibid.*, p. 90.

[31] *Ibid.*, pp. 96-7.

[32] *Ibid.*, pp. 107-8.

Accounting Belief

> *. . . professional sociologists [accountants]*
> *were more concerned with establishing their*
> *discipline as an objective science and institu-*
> *tionalizing it in universities than they were*
> *with saying something important. . . .*[1]

The objective of this essay is to discuss the formation of opinion and be-lief in accounting from a semi-historical and personalistic view. In an im-precise way the discussion covers the early part of the twentieth century and the later search for principles and guidelines, the use of mathemati-cal models, the drive to become scientific, the emphasis on statistical (behavioral) studies, the fascination with markets as surrogates for val-ues, the use of agency (bargaining) models for rule selection and for as-sessing the costs of failures to internalize dominant values and finally the belated concern with ethics in a profession that depends on integrity and acceptable judgments for its very existence. In the same imprecise way attention is given to the prevailing support for opinion formation—tradi-tion, authority (heroes), successful practice, mathematics, logic, scien-tific methods, data from related fields and physical models. To some extent the discussion has been organized around individual accountants and their struggles to find support for their own beliefs and value systems.

Early accounting in the United States clearly had a strong depen-dence on authority. The accounting profession also established a hierar-chy of authorities whose duties include inducing compliance along with belief and respect. The well-established legal profession had a well-de-fined system for selecting and ordering authorities. For the lower courts the evidence and basis for belief is the authority of higher courts. The supreme court departs from its own previously established authoritative positions with reluctance and only when its majority is convinced that social needs call for substantial change. Even here the constitution serves as a stabilizing feature that stands between the possible vacillations of public opinion and a stable base for judicial judgments. The constitution serves to remind jurists and legislators that some values are to be traded off with extreme reluctance.

A profession seeks knowledge about the values of a broader society to find the extent of its commission and sanction. As social relations change, the borders of professional responsibility change; this makes it necessary for leaders to keep in touch with the desires and needs of their constituencies. Adherence to tradition is one way of structuring (and controlling) responses to changing social conditions. Respect for tradition (e.g., *stare decisis*) is a retarding influence on vacillating changes in the social order and interpretations of such changes. This adherence tends to smooth and stabilize possible fluctuations in beliefs and helps to reduce the turmoil of rapid changes. But it also has an economic cost in the form of slow professional responses to user needs, and in a rational economy these costs presumably are compared with the probable benefits from stability. In such cases it is unlikely that a profession will ever be out front in accepting responsibilities. It is interesting to note that a similar defense is used for adherence to income smoothing techniques, to secret reserves and to conservatism generally.

In summary, it may be argued that historical tradition is seldom a strong basis for supporting opinion and belief, but instead must itself be defended by reference to opinions and beliefs derived from other sources. It is a pleasure to report that modern accounting historians have turned away from exposing the antecedents of bookkeeping techniques such as work sheets, journals, day books, trial balances and are now emphasizing the broader aspects of accounting as they relate to historical changes in economic and social attitudes.

ACCOUNTING AUTHORITY

Substituting authority for knowledge to support belief is found in most developing areas. New professions like accounting do not have many candidates for heroic models. Historians recall attempts of early independent Americans to create new heroes to replace previous ones from the British tradition and to establish their own instant traditions. Various new sub-cultures in the world are actively following this procedure. Communist states were reasonably successful at creating their own heroes and their successors now are busily at work creating a new group to replace them. Statues of Lenin and Stalin are rapidly coming down and no doubt new ones will be going up. Afro-Americans and perhaps other ethnic-Americans are vigorously promoting hero status for many of their meritorious compatriots.

Human beings have a need for strong leadership and bigger-than-life heroes to support their values and aspirations. Yet there is fierce controversy over the importance of heroes as promoters of social changes or as firm foundations for grounding belief.[2] For example it is argued that such individuals often are pushed by the climate of the times and that the importance of leadership and personality has been greatly over-estimated. In accounting it is probably true that the legitimacy of its procedures in early years came largely from successful practice and that some individuals (e.g., Pacioli) became important leaders because of their association with successful practice or through their forceful presentation of its techniques.

Commercial bookkeeping has a long tradition with a chain of received doctrine supported by the greatest authority figure of them all (Pacioli) and extends far beyond to the high status of scribes in the Near and Far East. The cost accounting tradition is much shorter and its appeal to authorities is much less obvious, but recent knowledge of the Soho Foundry (and similar historical discoveries) raises doubts about the newness of many cost concepts. Some engineers were used as authorities in setting and disclosing standards, and some pioneers commanded respect. J. M. Clark rightly became a hero because of his profound understanding of economic costs and because he offered a bridge to the more prestigious field of economic theory. Eric Camman for a decade or two also was something of a heroic figure, but his authoritative luster diminished as the popularity of basic standard concepts and techniques diminished.[3] McKinsey, Schlatter, Vatter along with Van der Schroeff became leaders if not authority figures in the field.

J. M. Clark is an especially interesting case for he is certainly an authority in accounting without formally being an accountant. Clark himself had considerable standing in his own field, economics, through his own efforts and through his famous father. It is even possible that the younger Clark may enjoy a greater reputation in accounting than in economics. Certainly he combined the best of industrial engineering and economics and combined relevant portions for accountants.[4]

Vatter has been most successful in adapting Clark's ideas to accounting, although Vatter himself made little use of either authoritative reasoning or professional practice to support his positions. Vatter came out of the costing environment of the University of Chicago which had been established by McKinsey and was oriented to industrial engineering and consulting. This combination along with high-level theoretical education in accounting and economics at Chicago fashioned this outstanding theorist's view. Yet his best known contribution—the fund paradigm—was based directly on governmental accounting and was in fact a restricted application of the existing entity approach. His strong anti-income stance may have developed from governmental accounts. His effort to reduce personalistic overtones is more difficult to understand in view of his recognition that objectivity is essentially interpersonal agreement and that measures of responsibilities accepted and discharged can be designed even for governmental operations.

American handbooks of accounting are an interesting case. Saliers, in the first Ronald edition, was a known figure and he selected well-known figures to furnish various sections of the work, e.g., Irving Fisher for the section on economics. He also displayed the names of his editors prominently to enhance the authoritative image. Paton's successor volumes relied heavily on the authority figure of Paton himself and downplayed contributors. An authoritative flavor was supported by numerous references, but these references often included second-rate scholars who happened to have popular texts or readily available expositions. One criterion for these citations was no doubt the recency of the publications and recency itself may have added an authoritative touch and an up-to-date image. Interestingly, this concern with recency has been adopted by many current research scholars who more or less disregard the history of ideas, quote only recent references, and throw away all journals of the previous decade.

Early texts in general accounting gave few credits to authoritative figures, but instead set down principles as if they were immutable doctrines without serious alternatives or rivals. As a result some of these writers became well known and were themselves cited as authorities even though their contribution often was to compile and present current practice. Many of these early writers were involved with self-help and correspondence courses, and Walton, Finney and Saliers were noted for expressing clearly at least one acceptable way of handling most accounting problems without introducing controversies and possible alternatives. There were exceptions. Kester gave semi-rigorous logical arguments to support many of his positions and sometimes introduced alternatives. Cole, Hatfield and Sprague actively defended their positions and were forerunners of Paton and his argumentative presentations based on logic and rigorous economic theory. These writers and others have become authoritative figures in accounting. Paton has been honored as the accountant of the twentieth century. Sprague is an important early figure and Hatfield only slightly less so. Littleton, May, Scott, Esquerré, Gilman and a host of others are quoted by numerous graduate students and are referenced in untold dissertations.

In Germany, Schmalenbach was a monumental authoritative figure, although many others such as Schär and Schmidt later developed well-known strains of thought. In the Netherlands, Limperg was equally prestigious with Meij and Polak and others sharing some professional authority.

All over the world there are occasional authoritative folks in academe. At present their prestige often is associated with the sophistication of their statistical research and only incidentally with substantive accounting. In the early days the Interstate Commerce Commission and state insurance regulators forced compliance but gave little opinion on theoretical matters. In the twenties the Committee on Stock List of the New York Stock Exchange had important authoritative stature and some teeth for coercive effect. The Securities and Exchange Commission adopted relatively unchanged many of the Committee's views and quickly became the leading authoritative force outside the profession. Its rapid rise in prestige may have depended to some degree on its power to force compliance, but its first Chief Accountant (Carman Blough) was a scholar in his own right and insisted on careful discussion before issuing directives. On balance, the SEC probably made use of logical arguments more effectively than other agencies, except rare public utility commissions that sometimes employed expert witnesses who were in fact expert.

The concept of authoritative support is messy at the practical level. It is not necessary that authorities come from the accounting field. The prestige of cognate fields and professions may be accepted as authoritative role models. Bankers, economists, engineers, sociologists, psychologists, philosophers, poets, statisticians, historians, mathematicians and even early scribes have at times served as role leaders for the accounting profession. The fact that leaders from these areas employ specialized concepts and techniques has been used to support assertions that similar concepts are appropriate for accountants.

THE INSTITUTE AND GAAP

The American Institute of Certified Public Accountants (AICPA) offers an interesting study. Its prestige grew in the early thirties through its consolidation with a rival professional organization and active cooperation with the Securities and Exchange Commission. To a large extent it became the liaison vehicle and sounding board for SEC proposals as well as a source for suggesting change. Further power came with control of the professional examination. This control permitted the Institute to become more influential in setting collegiate curricula and influencing what is known as accounting theory. Many weaker universities adopted AICPA statements as their bible for structuring theory courses. An unbiased assessment of this condition cannot possibly be positive even though uniform structures offer obvious advantages.

Negative considerations are numerous. First, the AICPA is a practitioner's forum with emphasis on the how-to-do it and not on fitting accounting into the larger scheme of intellectual endeavors. Second, releases too often were in the form of dicta rather than arguments acceptable to academics. The statements often were issued to meet specific problems in the well-known brush-fire approach. The advances and possible usefulness of mathematics, statistics and behavior sciences were all but neglected except in the area of elementary sampling. Finally the people who selected the problems, advanced acceptable solutions and wrote the releases, were busy men without rigorous philosophical training. The results often were effective procedural handbooks rather than theoretical discussions. Some alternatives were presented for preliminary discussion and possible consequences sometimes were set forth. Unfortunately this research was carried on within a narrow business context with virtually no discussion of alternative value systems and broad social consequences.

It is true that limited attempts were made to bring academic theorists into the process. How much influence these minority members exercised still is open to question. The Institute apparently recognized its lack of a *general* theory sometime in the late fifties. Some first-class academics were enlisted to produce monographs on selected topics. In some cases the recommendations of these writers were partially adopted and in other cases they were rejected practically out of hand. A cautious generalization is that acceptance depended primarily on consistency with what was actually being done so that the traditional body of rules was disturbed the least.

The views of the leadership as expressed through the Institute are best contained in its commitment to generally accepted accounting principles. It is by examining this commitment that the *basis* for the beliefs is uncovered. In its starkest interpretation "generally accepted" reduces to little more than supporting what is being done (accepted) as the *basis* for what *should* be done and reduces to a sketchy list of what in fact is being done. From this viewpoint the profession has advanced very little. In the early years, professional leaders inventoried what practitioners were doing and prepared lists for the education of all members. Leaders from time to time reexamined the lists to decide which practices still were in use, which had been discontinued and which had been added. To outsiders it looked as if these examiners were *creating* principles (guidelines). These men certainly did not need to be heroic theorists, although they did need some knowledge of prevailing practices, and some ability to decide when new practices merit recognition. At this level the foundation for acceptance and belief is nothing more than what is being done—an unsophisticated basis for deciding the value system of a profession.

Clearly GAAP is meant to be more than a simple report on the degree of acceptance of common accounting practices. More clearly GAAP is meant to be a set of directives and thus to be a statement of preferred procedures. This identification of fact with value is an old tenet that has long been discredited. Even its extension to Social Darwinism is of only heuristic value since user needs that once justified the practice may no longer be present.

It is obvious that the generally-accepted doctrine reduces to little more than an instruction to observe and accept practice as the standard, but there is a sense in which this attitude may be commended. This doctrine is a significant advance from the previous *authoritative* statements. The change in name indicates an important shift from principles based on authority to principles based on generality of usage. Democratic citizens are not likely to be impressed by authoritative pronouncements from self-constituted authoritative groups. The generally-accepted approach is more likely to hit a responsive chord in a pluralistic society. Moreover the change fits better with democratic values and with the currently popular scientific approach based on consensus and with tentative verification rather than absolute truth.

A simple reading of the GAAP literature indicates that professional leaders are far too sophisticated to limit themselves to tabulating practices or to represent themselves as authorities whose opinions automatically become authoritative. Their criteria for superiority may not always be clear, but there is evidence that they do consider the need to identify a host group, trace the consequences of alternative procedures, and evaluate expected consequences in terms of the values of the host system. The point here is that they should emphasize their selection criteria and stop the naive implication that what is accepted forms the proper basis for determining what ought to be done. In the meantime scholars feel that the movement from authority figures to observation of practice is something of an improvement.

MOONITZ' BASIC POSTULATES

It is more difficult to uncover Moonitz' philosophical basis for belief, for he was severely restrained by work at the Institute prior to his arrival. Nevertheless some respect for professional authority is evident in the very fact that he followed in the earlier footsteps of the profession and discarded the axiomatic approach of Chambers and Mattessich as well as the ethical-sociological orientation of DR Scott.[5]

Based on its study, a Committee of the Institute insisted in its report (without argument and support) that "postulates are few in number," are "basic assumptions" (and on a more hopeful note) "are derived from the economic and political environment. . . ."[6] Moreover these postulates must serve as "a meaningful foundation for the formulation of principles and the development of rules" (*Ibid.*) Principles are also guidelines for action and form a "settled ground or basis of conduct or practice."[7] So far as I know, no one would object seriously to this characterization, but many may feel uneasy with the following: "after postulates so derived have proved useful, they become accepted as principles of accounting" (*Ibid.,* par. 17). This relationship between postulates and principles parallels the traditional distinction between hypotheses and theories, but to my knowledge no scientist suggests the use of the term postulate in this manner.

Before going into the details of Moonitz' articles of faith it may be observed that his approach is **essentially positivist in orientation**. His faith in observation and methodology is essentially the faith of empiricists everywhere, although none of his excellent publications have been empirical studies. In fact most of his work has been essentially deductive and he has not fallen into the empiricist's trap of holding that if one observes steadfastly and accumulates sufficient data the *right* decisions will be more or less automatic (e.g., DR Scott, George Schultz, Sidney Davidson). To arrive at the policy guidelines outlined in Sprouse-Moonitz it is necessary *to observe* and *order* conflicting value systems. This task requires more than analytic tracing of antecedents-consequences unless one is committed to the rigid belief that what *is* done is what ought to be done. No one could accuse Moonitz of holding this naive belief, but he seems to follow Littleton and the Institute in this direction.

Moonitz recognizes alternatives to his approach, but displays sufficient confidence in his methodology to support some firm opinions and some rigid professional guidelines. His first step is to identify accountants. (Members of the AICPA?) The second operation is to observe what these identified folks actually do. (Clearly their accounting activities must be separated from activities as husbands, civic members, etc.). The third step requires an inference from what accountants *do* to what constitutes accounting *problems*. This step requires moving from actions to possible strains these actions might relieve—the problematic situation. Incidentally an assumption of rationality is necessary at this point to correlate problems and appropriate actions.

A further inference might locate those who have the problems—the sufferers who count. In this manner the problems may be partially bounded, limits defined and the situations partially clarified. Discussions with these groups may lead to a further inference of importance—insights into their objectives. Inasmuch as problems arise from thwarted goals, it may be possible to infer objectives from analyses of the problems.

What about alternatives available but not taken? Such situations clearly cannot be observed directly. As in the Littleton program, there simply is no way that observation of practice can disclose and evaluate these opportunities. This failure is not unique to Moonitz (or Littleton) but underlies scientific methods generally. Even the experimental method does not apply (except through tenuous analogy) to alternatives not considered in the experiments, while the important job of finding new hypotheses is beyond the boundaries of science itself. Most investigators—except perhaps extreme positivists—do not limit their belief systems completely to scientifically supported information. Beauty and ethics too are pertinent.

Although a rigorous antecedent-consequent approach is not fully developed in either monograph, there is sufficient evidence of its use to satisfy most academic critics including hard-core pragmatists. Certainly the rejection of the monographs by the profession did not stem from pragmatic criticism, for the original charge to the authors was in the long tradition of *finding the fundamental* bedrock foundations of the profession—certainly not a pragmatic or behavioral objective. It is my guess that much (certainly not all) of the furor that finally killed active support came primarily from the Sprouse-Moonitz practical extension to specific accounting guidelines. In this extension specific recommendations for the conduct of practice were set forth clearly and with some pragmatic support. In retrospect the mistake of the authors may have been that their recommendations were not in substantial agreement with what the profession was then doing. Observation of practice in 1960 simply did not square with the recommendations of ARS 3. This deficiency was an affront to the dominant traditionalists in the profession and to some sympathetic academics. The inconsistency consisted in asserting that the basis for the investigation and the foundation for the recommendations rest on what accountants were actually doing and then recommending procedures that the profession certainly was not doing or (as it turned out) wanted to do. It is as if the authors observed what the profession was doing and on the basis of other (undisclosed) criteria rejected it.

COHERENCE AND CORRESPONDENCE IN ACCOUNTING

Detailed attention to the coherence and correspondence approaches to truth and belief may seem far from the practical field of accounting but such is not the case. Consider first the coherence framework where one's belief in the truth of a proposition (or in the efficacy of a mental construction) is based on the conclusion that a broader enclosing system has explanatory power.[8] Modern physics is no longer based on simple cause and effect and many concepts are not susceptible to verification except in relation to some broad theory of which they are a part. They are accepted—treated as reality—because their behavior is consistent with that of related theoretical systems. Often there simply is no hope of verification through *correspondence* with particular aspects of reality or with non-system statements about a substantive universe.

Consider also the field of psychology—a discipline nearer to accounting. Parts are related not only to one another but to wholes and explained or even defined in terms of their contribution to the performance of broader explanatory systems. As in physics the system of inquiry is broadened to include observers and their structuring abilities. Organization theorists have adopted similar views and argue that at least some specifications of a *part* must be in terms of the *whole* (the organization) and that certain aspects of the organization cannot be explained entirely in terms of its components.

Accountants too are systems oriented and use many concepts that correspond to independent reality only through surrogates derived from consistency with broader operations and theories. Costs expire through a complicated network of technical requirements that are related to sacrifices, benefits, service expectations, matching and finally to income. Income in turn is an operationalized definition of value added in liquid form and a system to measure well-offness and efficiency of operations.

Review again some elementary aspects of the *correspondence* theory as applied in accounting. This theory is represented best by those interested in semantics who treat truth as being a relationship among language symbols and external facts. The facts supposedly are derived from some outside reality. In philosophy this view is held by realists and naturalists who feel that the world is out there and that the job of the scientist is to *discover* the laws that govern its operations. An analysis of this approach requires examination of the semantic rules for assignment, i.e., the rules of correspondence or (in mathematical terms) finding values for the variables. These rules specify what symbols attach to what external facts and in what ways.

Perhaps the most telling criticism of this scheme is that it completely neglects the part played by the inquirer in structuring the *Gestalten* and the parts both the inquirer and the language play in determining the reality that governs particular investigations. The discussion here is limited to pointing out the wide use of an objective record among scientists and positive researchers who attempt to avoid value judgments. Unfortunately physical models and *things* also are widely used as supports for accounting beliefs. The correspondence approach relates the abstract concepts and statements of accounting to physical things or (better) to events that users can recognize as substantial elements in their own existence. While physical correlations to accounting concepts may firm up belief and acceptance, very few accounting concepts are related directly to ordinary physical reality. As discussed elsewhere, physical characteristics play no important part in accounting and they acquire importance only as anchoring points for reaching value judgments and engendering confidence in expectations and opinions.

Accountants do deal with physical inventories but their statements essentially are about inventory values. With regard to buildings they are interested in shelter, protection, upkeep, tax advantages, beneficial life and are interested in physical features only as supports for making these judgments. Certainly they are not interested in the color of the paint, the excellence of the housekeeping, the beautiful vistas except in so far as they impinge on values—efficiency, sales promotion and probable maintenance expenses. It follows that the usual distinction between tangible and intangible is of little concern. This distinction probably is related to confidence in the required judgments about values rather than the corporeal nature of the *thing* that seems to be the source of the expected benefits.

The case for physical support generally is better in the case of assets and worse for historical accounts. However, it should be remembered that the concept of asset is one of the most abstract in any field. To arrive at the concept of asset the accountant abstracts from all facets except expectations of certain benefits and then constructs rules to find value assignments for them. The revenue concept is on the same level of abstraction. The equivalent economic concept is gross value added, but accounting simplifications often reduce the operational content to the process of aggregating sales. At this point evidential support comes to depend largely on overt actions. It may be useful to call them events and tie the recognition of events to some kind of actions—physical or otherwise—that are discernible and common to aware observers who have been trained to interpret them in similar ways. The concept of income as the net increase in wealth from certain sources requires a similar degree of abstraction and construction. Simplifications that are substituted for well-offness have no close physical counterpart, and like so many concepts found in the field of physics are pure constructions. How then does one "verify" the income figure? Clearly he does not look for physical existences that somehow determine their own amounts and present them to the accounting community. Verification in this case is a process of determining whether the event-recognition and value-assessment rules for recognizing and measuring income have been followed. A more serious question is whether the income as measured by the conventional rules is an adequate surrogate for the related concept of well-offness or its simplification—net value added. The latter is the heart of accounting theory, and the theorist is completely in the land of accounting metaphors. Correspondence is now between accounting statements and a reality far different from that composed of physical things.

To summarize, accountants from the beginning have taken a naturalistic view of the universe and in later years have received massive support from those interested in semantics. It is a commonplace that accountants view their field as a language—in a vast simplification—*the* language of business. Certainly one of the primary chores in beginning accounting is to help students understand the necessary tools of the trade. First, the process requires translating the words of the exercise into business events. Second, the influence of the inferred events must be translated into their effects on matters of concern as represented by the accounts. The relevant influences shown in the accounts are then arranged and rearranged into configurations that are thought to be useful for judgments and future actions. The user then combines these reports with other information, makes judgments and formulates policies. Thus, in a sense there is a translation of certain aspects of textbook language into events, then a translation of the inferred events into accounting language, and finally a translation of the accounting language into expectations and policy judgments.

To semanticists meaningful sentences must have identifiable referents in some sort of hypothesized world, and popularizers have been fond of the analogy with maps. Clearly maps may be poor representations, out-of-date or simply inadequate, and thus lead to all sorts of unrealized expectations. My own view of accounting is that it can still use the techniques of semantics with some modification. The positivistic and scientific dogma that the symbols must be related to physical concepts must be abandoned. The accounting symbols must be attached to mental constructions (concepts) and become metaphors for creating expectations. Crude observation clearly is inadequate. Hermeneutic understanding may not be too sophisticated.

A. C. LITTLETON

Littleton has been characterized as an historian, an evolutionist and most of all a Dewey-type pragmatist, yet in important ways his world view is closely related to that of the Institute and in a different way his influence can be seen in the Moonitz of Accounting Research Study No. 1. In the latter cases pragmatism (user orientation) is present only in the background and is less dominant than in genuinely pragmatic structures. Littleton had an abiding faith in the place of practice in forming normative rules and therefore was comfortable with Dewey's reassurance that theory cannot be separated from practice.

The basis for Littleton's belief rests on an early scientific methodology that somehow assures him that progress in practical affairs always is directed toward preferred states. Philosophically this attitude is that of naturalism and the technique most trusted is that of observation. His trust in the goodness of progress may have come from acceptance of a form of social Darwinism, which holds that successful practices and actions tend to survive.

It has been fashionable to classify Littleton as an evolutionist, and in some ways this assessment is accurate. In support of his belief that the profession is progressing toward higher levels, he looked to the past and in scanning the past he became interested in some historical aspects of accounting. Much of his historical interest centered around the techniques of accounting, and he indicated little interest in observing and reporting theoretical features of the profession. It may be inevitable that one who bases his methodology (and his theories) primarily on observations also develops an interest in history as a record of such observations. Interestingly there was little concern with accounting as a type of historical analysis, although his interest in the changing techniques of recording may have indicated some attention in this direction. (Could his unswerving commitment to historical costs have been an indirect result of his general interest in history?)

Acceptance of the good-hands philosophy does not ordinarily emphasize decision making and the conflict of values that makes all decisions problematic. In fact one wonders how observation, even in its more complex forms, can lead to choices involving hypothetical courses that might become available. Observation of past regularities may suggest inferences about future events and consequences and records of the past may help preserve memories of analogous situations. But even here the emphasis is ordinarily on the inductive process rather than on historical aspects. Littleton to his credit did not neglect these aspects and in fact usually is classified as an inductivist.

Accountants normally try to analyze actions in terms of their ability to accomplish objectives. Explanations for a service activity are in terms of functions and rest on a teleological imperative to further accepted ends in view. The point here is that Littleton did not place primary emphasis on the need to coordinate practices into theoretical constructs that lead to desirable behavior.[9] It is obvious that he holds an instrumentalist philosophy, but his accounting theories are based primarily on typologies that only indirectly are concerned with user ends. Furthermore, from the viewpoint of social interactionism (philosophical conceptualism) he fails to highlight the part of the theorist himself in *constructing* theories that explain mundane practices.

Littleton was interested in the historical aspects of accounting, but there is little evidence that he used evolutionary *methods* to support his beliefs and to influence his theory formation. In one sense an observer views the immediate past when he observes current practices, but Littleton was not effective in using evolutionary patterns to justify his positions. Specifically he was not interested in relating past practices to past economic conditions and developing predictive machinery that would help forecast accounting changes to meet *new* social conditions. Finally, as I understand his position, Littleton did not defend his opinions (and beliefs) by reference to recurring patterns in traditional practices. Even *Stare decisis* was not an important factor except in the elementary sense of practice exists and is therefore important in some unspecified way.

In summary the Littleton technique is to look at practice and to treat theory as descriptions (generalizations?) of the practical activities that make up the profession. Observation of practice may be similar to observation of social roles, but in all such cases theory should coordinate general *relationships* among the observed (or inferred) entities. Notice that physical grounding is not necessary, and the correspondence in service professions is between the observed world of practice and the statements of the theory that mediate among practices and values. His objective may be to explain practices in some coordinated manner, but Littleton never seemed to address the problem of explaining why some practices are, or should be, preferred over others. The objective of molecular theory may be to predict what molecules will do with specifiable side conditions, but the objective of accounting theory must be more than prediction of what accounting practitioners will do under stated conditions.[10]

Some might say that accounting theorists *explain* rather than predict accounting practices. Except for a time perspective there is no methodological difference between the two. Explain in terms of what? Some investigators have reached the end of their explanatory abilities by stating that something simply exists or somehow responds in a predictable fashion to a given stimulus. These end-products may be sufficient for practitioners, but they will not satisfy serious investigators and they hardly qualify as explanations much less theories until value assessments are included in the explanatory system.

W. A. PATON—HEROES AND COHERENCE

We turn now to Paton's foundations for belief and the values that support his faith.

Paton's family were school teachers who encouraged wide reading, rational conversation and a deep respect for scholarship and genuine intellectual effort. William Andrew, with two well known physicists in his immediate family, was at home with scientists and with scholars generally, yet he remained fairly narrow in his outlook and world view. Certainly he did not parade his knowledge of science and scientific methodology, although his early interest in accounting postulates and general interest in theory indicates solid training in logic and an interest in getting a coherent structure. An interest in logic might have led to an interest in the related field of mathematics but apparently such was not the case. While he was rigorous in argument and in handling simple calculations, he indicated no interest in calculus or with formal probability theory even though his incisive writing style is a model of mathematical precision combined with an uncommon flair for rhetoric.

It is also strange that Paton's models did not include engineers.

Engineers were extremely active in cost accounting (especially in connection with standards) and engineering was better established than business in academic circles. Engineering also was more rigorous and had much in common with physics, which next to mathematics still is the most prestigious academic study. The fact is that Paton indicated little interest in engineering—even engineering economics—and almost none in formal cost accounting.

A further curious fact is that Paton indicated little interest in either sociology or psychology. At the turn of the century, Michigan was especially strong in sociology (Mead, Angel, Cooley) and had some exposure to Dewey and his followers in psychology. Moreover, Paton displayed little interest in history and its application to economics, business or accounting. He seldom referred to DR Scott and simply ignored Sombart and the broader aspects of accounting and the social order. Fortunately he was consistent and did not burden his students with a mass of detail about early day books, journals and useless fragments from Pacioli.

Formal philosophers apparently acted neither as his heroes nor his role models. There is little evidence in Paton's writings to indicate strong leanings to individual philosophers or to philosophical schools. He was convinced that the business world is out there and contains economic entities and accounting transactions. He considered accounting to be a practical study and looked to results rather than to origins. His interest in accounting principles may be interpreted as a pragmatic interest in creating a more useful profession rather than as an attempt to find any underlying basis for its structure. On rare occasions he became carried away with "basic" and "true" and such semantic constructions, but these lapses did not seriously affect his outlook and he must be treated as a practicing pragmatist. Certainly he was far from an existentialist. He was little concerned with such entities as being, existence, self and the like yet he apparently did not realize that his discussions of entities were similar to arguments for the social determination of self and the enigmas of identities and collective wills. Finally Paton did not feel comfortable with modern accounting empiricists. Current research in behavioral and empirical areas was considered to be belaboring the obvious and exhibiting virtuosity in numerical (statistical) manipulation. Deserving theorists should be concerned with structure and consequences.

Paton's intellectual love—economics—not only furnished the structure for his accounting theory but it also furnished his heroes, his role models and the values to be internalized. In short Paton's foundation for belief and his faith underlying his accounting rules is rooted in economics and developed through logic. He exhibited deep faith in the logical development of arguments and the need to identify antecedents and trace consequences. The tenets of neo-classical market economics furnished the values and processes that *ought* to be followed. Thus his basis for criticism is whether accounting practices are logically and ethically consistent with the principles of pre-Keynesian economics. His fundamental faith thus is consistent with the value systems of protestant religious leaders, especially Calvin, but his disinterest in such developments as the Sombart thesis remains a mystery.

The source of Paton's actual beliefs are a little more difficult to understand. Certainly he did not look for support from authoritative figures in the accounting profession. He was not a quoter and seldom referred to authorities in either accounting or economics.[11] Nor did Paton look to practice for his beliefs although he had respect for Andersen and May. Certainly he was not sympathetic to those who viewed their function as describing practice.

Clearly Paton considered accounting to be functional and therefore normative and teleological and he displayed interest in logical coherence. He was impressed with the necessity for coherence in his accounting structure. His models usually were from economics rather than from the physical sciences or biology. His beliefs therefore require help from the behavioral sciences, yet he devoted little attention to psychological and sociological matters and was satisfied to accept the conclusions of these disciplines only after they were filtered through neo-classical market economics. His ethics too were derived from conservative economic sources that are supported by a strong Calvinistic moral code.

In summary Paton was a typical deductive logician who attempted to deduce normative accounting principles from propositions found in capitalistic economics. The objectives for accounting were to further the activities of worthy people operating in the financial-economic world. His logical grounding and a shrewd seat-of-the-pants feeling for user psychology encouraged attention to the consequences of alternative accounting actions and supported his conclusions. With respect to the more theoretical aspects of his work, Paton was an exemplar of the coherence approach to truth and belief. His occasional attempts to support his conclusions by correspondence with physical referents were on the whole unsuccessful. His advocacy of a physical-unit approach rather than the pool approach to inventories and fixed assets may not have been an outright disaster, but it inhibited his consideration of expectations. Unfortunately expectations form the basis for economic value.

Paton's familiarity with logic and scientific procedures is illustrated in his serious attempt to set forth some postulates for developing accounting theory, but my present assessment is that his under-played behavioral approach has been more important than his logical postulates.[12]

In fact the following quotations from Paton's discussion of postulates indicate his strong underlying behavioral orientation.

> Accounting is a highly purposive field and any assumption, principle, or procedure is accordingly justified if it adequately serves the end in view. . . (p. 472).

> [The] enterprise . . . constitutes a real institution. . . . It is "the business" whose financial history the bookkeeper and accountant are trying to record and analyze. . . (p. 473). [But] human beings are the immediate means by which the affairs of a business institution are conducted and . . . it may be necessary to focus attention directly and exclusively upon the individual owners and managers and their acts (p. 476).

> A balance-sheet statement of asset values is really only provisional; it depends upon the future for its validation (p. 486).

> [T]he accountant, like the economist, postulates a world full of rational business men (p. 489).

While Paton made unmistakable behavioral comments and assumptions and was emphatic about his preferred user groups, there is little or no evidence that he tested his recommendations by appropriate scientific methods. His propositions in this area must have seemed obvious or were deduced from his theoretical structure. Most of these propositions could have been tested by appropriate experimental methods and the usual scientific paraphernalia, but it is evident that he did not attempt to do so.

His refusal to treat purchase discounts as income is a typical example. From the theoretical side, his definitions would not permit him to consider discounts offered either taken or neglected as *costs of product,* and without costs there could be no assets or expenses. Moreover without realized value increases, there could be no income. In his structure discounts offered and taken simply did not constitute a separate recordable transaction except perhaps in the form of a memo. On the other hand discounts offered and not taken were a cost and represented a lapse of management rationality that called for disclosure. His own defense is more simple: It makes more sense to reprimand the treasurer for losing discounts than to compliment him for taking them. His motivational vector is thus a reversal of traditional wisdom and points in the direction of organizational goals.[13]

R. R. STERLING: FAILED PHYSICALISM

The patient reader will now be convinced of my strong subjectivist attitudes in which the objective world is an inference from impressions made in the mind of the observer and that observation, far from a simple sense impression, is a complicated integrating process that should lead to understanding. In this view meaning is created by human consensus—by understanding.

In view of this attitude it is a disappointment that some of my most competent students and colleagues have taken a simplistic physical road. Both Don Vickrey and Robert Sterling have certainly understood my own subjective framework, and Vickrey in his dissertation constructed a competent assessment of it. Both have to some extent fallen under the eloquent spell of Chambers and have become active advocates of current exit costs along with cash equivalents and related paraphernalia. I have been a mild to active supporter of current entrance costs for a half century or so, but in view of the covariance, I have sometimes accepted exit values as surrogates for current entrance values. Exit values, even without the Chamberian revival, have had a respected history in limited areas such as estate accounting, realization and liquidation reports, and as a basis for dated "net worth" summaries for finding periodic income from single-entry records.

In my opinion Sterling's early contributions (as outstanding as they have been) were hindered rather than enhanced by his reliance on physical models and analogs. Apparently he has accepted the view that accounting is composed of measurement rules, but he seems to have been slow to accept accounting as a set of behavioral assumptions focussed on behavior and not on physical constructions. Sterling's innovative year at Yale with Margenau and his colleagues may have developed his interest in substantive external reality in spite of the fact that modern physicists (including Margenau) have consistently moved further and further away from substantive realities.[14] In any case Sterling's considerable interest in scientific methods must have been enhanced, for of all the sciences physics is most concerned with constitutive systems that can be expressed with mathematical precision and on occasion subjected to empirical verification.

It is therefore no surprise that Sterling's dissertation employed a framework that concentrates first on the physical level of output and units of physical output (CAPS) and later moves to problems of accounting interest—valuations (VALS). In some ways this methodology is similar to that of the early Mattessich, where input-output and flows become the basis for his accounting theory. From my own viewpoint this procedure is precisely reversed, for there are no guidelines for selecting and evaluating the physical analogs until needs and objectives are specified. A subjectivist starts with objectives and value systems as expressions of human concern. Thus values are derived from felt needs and human desires. Much further down the line accountants may or may not become interested in analogs such as physical facts, units of capacity and the like.

Sterling long since has moved to a strong normative stance, but has not entirely abandoned his commitment to the importance of physical analogs. Consider the questions he asked physicists about various inventory methods. From a subjectivist view one wonders what could possibly be gained by asking physics students about accounting allocations and accounting valuations. Certainly to ask any group—educated or not— about the relation of behavioral factors with which they are not familiar is destined to be fruitless. It is no wonder that physicists (or any other elite specialized group subjected to such questions) reached the conclusion that accounting is a pseudo profession and its practitioners charlatans of the first order.[15]

As an alternative suppose that his questions and instructions had been presented in the following way:

1. State first the objectives of the process. In the case of inventories the goal is to help provide a measure of well-offness (income) and *potential for further augmentation of wealth.*

2. Explain that some effort must be exerted to accomplish the objective of wealth creation, i.e., that sacrifices (costs) must be made and it is necessary to forego some possible advantages to achieve others.

3. Emphasize the need for rules to recognize new values added and values sacrificed in order to approximate net value added, i.e., that some sort of matching is necessary and related to time intervals, decisions and actions.

4. Point out that these success reports are made on a periodic basis and that aggregation is necessary.

5. Emphasize that human minds need to isolate events that can be used as critical points and as carriers of relevant changes in the

accepted measures of well-offness, i.e., that human minds need patterns of experience that can be shared and can act as surrogates for the constructions desired.

6. Show that the rules for recognition of new values added may sometimes be related to physical units of inventory that pass some critical point, say delivery.

7. Highlight the practical problem: What recognizable clues might be appropriate for a useful measure of benefit and sacrifice.

Once objectives are specified, matching simply is a problem of attribution and finding cognitive nodes to which returns and sacrifices may be related. The general point here is that "object" classification of expenditures is seldom decision-relevant for managers or owners except perhaps construction and maintenance engineers. Often object classification can be omitted without great loss and carried on entirely on a functional basis. In fact this switch is in keeping with the usual concept of value. The value of inventories inheres *not* in the physical units but in the ability to raise revenues and (as a rule) value is an expectation of benefits rather than some physical presence.

Physicists certainly are not interested in income measures and the detailed arguments over their adequacy to measure general well-offness, but they do have a general objective of fitting together certain concepts for broad explanatory systems with acceptable predicting power. In electricity, for example they are interested in potential, resistance, flows and the like as components of an integrated explanatory system. It is not necessary that they assign a high priority to human welfare resulting from electric power, cheap power plants, efficient transmission systems, profitable utilization and increased national product, but they do have a well defined objective to find a more general and more precise understanding of certain experiences. They have their own criteria for values: precision of prediction, breadth of explanatory power, generality, and sometimes parsimony or even elegance. Thus theoretical scientists have objectives, hierarchies of values and criteria for judgment and these objectives may indeed rank above the crass pursuit of wealth or social well being.

Present-day researchers in accounting might argue that empirical studies in physics must be confined to what physicists do and how their procedures are selected. Such studies in accounting or in physics may be worth doing, but they are by no means free of value judgments. More generally positivists have asserted that they are not able to judge the superiority of one value system over another in some abstract moral climate. Clearly some independent standard is necessary along with some method for isolating and evaluating deviations from the standard. The positivist answer is to assume that market determinations and bargaining contracts are the appropriate relationships (climates) instead of the factors that determine market prices and motivate contractual bargainers. By some legerdemain this decision is not a value judgment! Sterling is clearly no positivist and he does not shirk from taking normative stands. Most criticism comes from those who disagree with his choice of surrogates.

It may be inevitable that pragmatists must be normative theorists, for they consider ends-in-view (objectives) to be a part of the problematic situation and must look for possible behavioral reactions before selecting their conjectures and assessing the relevancy of analogies to serve as "settled" portions of their inquires. In a similar way all normative accountants also must be practicing pragmatists. They must agree on the ends-in-view before making an assertion that one resolution is more desirable than other explored alternatives.

In this context Sterling recognizes the problematic situation and (on balance) accepts business oriented ends-in-view. Apparently he concludes that the use of current exit values is the preferred resolution. How he reached this conclusion is not at all obvious. His magnificent analytical and synthetic work is not directly related to his being a successful or "failed" empiricist and there is less empirical support for his CCE stance than one might expect. Fortunately he remains adamantly committed to a normative approach even though he still retains a lingering desire to ground accounting concepts in physical terms.

E. O. EDWARDS AND P. W. BELL

It is only fair to say that I have never been greatly impressed with the Edwards and Bell effort even though I have admired Edwards' earlier accounting works. The grounding for their assumptions offers no great problem because their framework is essentially that of traditional economics with emphasis on economic men striving to better their financial positions. Little specific attention is given to explicit behavioral consequences of various accounting alternatives. Even less attention is given to modern information economics or to the current expansion of observation to include discourse and hermeneutic understanding. The result is an interesting discussion of some of the relationships that are relevant to the accounting process in terms of traditional economic values. The conclusions are without empirical support; therefore this effort is a clearcut example of what Nelson termed *a priori* accounting.[16] This uneven exposition contains some interesting observations, but unfortunately the terminology and exposition are far from being clear and often are downright confusing for accountants. There is emphasis on economic expectations and the subjective aspects of income, but there also is enthusiastic rediscovery of some well-established accounting ideas.

They begin their exposition as good disciples of Fisher and the discounting of expectations, but like all practical economists they soon abandon the idealized Fisherene concept except for shortrun guidance. For longer term accomplishment they opt for more traditional income concepts based on current entrance values and the separation of gains into operating profits and holding (acquiring?) gains.

The most interesting portion of this highly regarded volume is in the area of excess subjective values—a variation of the old consumers' surplus presented as "subjective" goodwill. In my own early days of teaching, it was common to justify the traditional recording of accounting transactions as exchanges of equal values. In the late thirties an economics student (James Dusenberry) objected to this characterization, and my eyes were opened to the obvious motivational fact that each transaction should yield some increase in expectations—some "excess" present value. Throughout the remainder of my teaching career, the income problem was approached as an exercise in deciding how to distribute this increase in expectations over time and to possible sources so as to provide useful information.

In any case Edwards and Bell dealt with the recognition of such subjective values in a detailed manner. From a modern non-positivist viewpoint their methodology leans heavily on external "realization" of such values as if the realization comes automatically through market operations. They also resurrected and expanded the division of gains into those attributed to operations and those that resulted from shrewd acquiring and holding of resources. In spite of Gaffikin's indirect admiration of their methodology, the process here is the time-honored method of attributing admitted consequences to possible antecedent (causative) factors.[17]

NOTES

[1] Bennett M. Berger, "Model of a Man Engagé," Book Review of *Power, Politics and People: The Collected Essays of C. Wright Mills,* Irving L. Horowitz, ed., *The New York Times Book Review,* April 28, 1963, pp. 3, 50.

[2] Thomas Carlyle was a leading defender of the hero thesis and Sidney Hook was an able opponent. See Thomas Carlyle, *On Heroes, Hero-Worship, and the Heroic in History,* Carl Niemeyer, ed. (Lincoln: University of Nebraska Press, 1966); Sidney Hook, *The Hero in History: A Study in Limitation and Possibility* (New York: The John Day Co., 1943); or, for a more balanced treatment, Eric Bentley, *A Century of Hero-Worship: A Study of the Idea of Heroism in Carlyle and Nietzsche* (Philadelphia: J. B. Lippincott Co., 1944).

[3] At one time Camman was one of my own personal heroes, although my first interest in basic standards came through Jeremiah Lockwood of the Wharton School. The practicality and usefulness of isolating a technological variance that discloses the cost of using antiquated equipment has always been appealing. Furthermore a system of accounts that can kick out proportional changes as well as absolute amounts as a routine part of its output has some appeal.

[4] John Maurice Clark, *Studies in the Economics of Overhead Costs* (Chicago: The University of Chicago Press, 1923).

[5] Maurice Moonitz, *The Basic Postulates of Accounting,* Accounting Research Study (ARS) No. 1 (New York: AICPA, 1961). Present comments apply in part to his joint effort with Robert T. Sprouse, *A Tentative Set of Broad Accounting Principles for Business Enterprises,* ARS 3, (1962). The identification of ethical with sociological is criticized elsewhere. Incidentally the recommendations of ARS 3 afford unmistakable evidence that the joint authors are independent spirits and far from meek followers of professional authority.

[6] "Report to Council of the Special Committee on Research Program," *Journal of Accountancy,* December 1958, p. 63.

[7] *Accounting Terminology Bulletin No. 1: Review and Resume* (New York: AICPA, 1953), par. 16.

[8] It is necessary to reach a prior decision that the broader system is working. The criteria for reaching this decision may require observation of related entities, and this assessment requires elements of a correspondence theory. Some philosophers have tried to avoid the distinction. The situation is similar to finding whether the rules of logic have been followed without using empirical methods. For this reason the distinction between analytic and synthetic also is suspect.

[9] Littleton's "Choice among Alternatives" suggests such an approach but fails to place value systems as the dominant consideration. *The Accounting Review,* July 1956, pp. 363–370.

[10] The modern positivist movement in accounting theory seems to have returned to this structure, i.e., the objective of accounting theory is to predict what accounting rules will be selected under the assumptions that a free market exists for alternative rules and that the accounting profession and ethical matters are passive factors.

[11] Little attention is given to H. C. Adams and Durward Springer, his teachers at Michigan. He discarded the work of Saliers in the first edition of *The Accountants' Handbook* including the excellent section by Irving Fisher on economics. An informal count of his citations in *Accounting Theory* shows four references to Sprague, two to Hatfield and no more than one each to a half-dozen others.

[12] Due to Paton's form of exposition, it is difficult to determine precisely what does constitute his postulates. Herbert F. Taggart prepared a careful list of Paton's general assumptions (postulates): "Foreword to the Reissue," William Andrew Paton, *Accounting Theory, With Special Reference to the Corporate Enterprise* (Houston: Scholars Book Company, 1973), p. ix. (In the 1962 republication [Chicago: Accounting Studies Press, Ltd.], this was included after the "Publisher's Preface" in "Remarks on the Republicaton of Paton's *Accounting Theory*," pp. 5-6.)

[13] In the same vein, he tended to agree that standard costs are the cost of product and that excess variance costs are the cost of something else—perhaps management blunders. Thus he advocated *prudent cost ceilings* to the amounts that should be capitalized for assets, and in the tradition of Marx decreed that excess (socially unnecessary costs) do not add value and should be taken as immediate losses. Obviously the accountant performs a watch-dog function, and hopefully his disclosures of dysfunctional actions will deter stupid managerial behavior.

[14] See for example Henry Margenau's outstanding volume, *The Nature of Physical Reality, A Philosophy of Modern Physics* (New York: McGraw-Hill Book Company, Inc., 1950).

[15] There is satisfying evidence that Sterling has substantially changed his position, for he now maintains that accounting numerals seldom represent phenomena in any way. See Robert R. Sterling, "Confessions of a Failed Empiricist," in *Advances in Accounting,* Volume 6 (JAI Press Inc., 1988), pp. 3–36.

[16] M. J. R. Gaffikin wonders about the reverential respect that accountants have for economists, but states: "Edwards and Bell held an advantage over other accounting writers/researchers. They were economists and thus were trained in a field of study held to be far more methodologically 'advanced' at that time: they were missionaries from a more sophisticated society." "Legacy of the Golden Age: Recent Developments in the Methodology of Accounting," *Abacus,* March 1988, p. 20. More advanced "methodology" it may be, but there is little evidence of it in Edgar O. Edwards and Philip W. Bell, *The Theory and Measurement of Business Income* (Berkeley and Los Angeles: University of California Press, 1961).

[17] Richard Mattessich has added his scholarship to those of us who have long felt that Edwards and Bell failed to give full credit to the much earlier con-

tributions of Fritz Schmidt and others; see "On the Evolution of Theory Construction in Accounting: A Personal Account," *Modern Accounting Research: History, Survey, and Guide,* Research Monograph 7 (Vancouver: The Canadian Certified General Accountants' Research Foundation, 1984), p. 39, n. 4. Incidentally the separation of gains into operating and other functions has a well-known history that includes the work of Clarence Nickerson and Willard Graham in the thirties. Paton and Stevenson (1918) discussed the matter and concluded that the attribution problem was too complicated to expect of accountants; see Chapter XX, "The Basis for Revaluation," *Principles of Accounting,* (New York: The Macmillan Company, 1918), pp. 451–469. Also see Paton, "The Significance of Treatment of Appreciation in the Accounts," *Twentieth Annual Report of the Michigan Academy of Science* (1918), pp. 35–49; reprinted in *Paton on Accounting: Selected Writings of W. A. Paton,* Herbert F. Taggart, ed. (Ann Arbor: Bureau of Business Research, Graduate School of Business Administration, The University of Michigan, 1964), pp. 21–35. (Editor's Note: In the article, Paton explores the complexities of separating operating and appreciation gains/losses and seems a bit less pessimistic than the conclusion that Carl draws from the Chapter XX discussion. He states: "the recognition of *all* value changes in the accounts does not mean that no differentiation is possible between the results of actual operation and [appreciation]. . . . It is quite possible in most cases to organize the accounts and statements . . . to reveal both . . . [income] from operation . . . and total net [income]. . . . But I think . . . there is not a single case in which . . . [income from operation] as presented by the accountant is restricted to the results of technical operation alone. . . ." [p. 28].)

Auditing—A Belief System

It has been said that all belief rests on faith, and religious leaders some-times use this statement to emphasize that science too rests on faith. This attitude may serve a useful purpose in emphasizing that everyone (even extreme Zenists and expert Sophists) must finally ground their beliefs in faith. Unfortunately it tends to obscure the important question: Precisely what is it that encourages faith and serves as the necessary grounding?

This section is concerned primarily with auditors, whose livelihood depends on their ability to sell their expert opinions. Auditing opinions are expected to present a unified picture that (taken as a whole) represents fairly the financial position and results of operations. Two preliminary points must be emphasized. First, leaders in the profession must make judgments about the interpretations that users are likely to make. Moreover, they must form opinions about user needs and which interpretations are likely to further user objectives. Second, the overall master representation that emerges must be composed of smaller tasks that can be performed by practitioners on the job. The *leaders* assume responsibility that the particularized representations—individually in association and in total—present an acceptable basis for drawing conclusions about important financial and operating dimensions of the entity.

In summary, leaders in the profession must *believe* that the representations will help accomplish preferred objectives and they also must *believe* that the individual representations when taken in conjunction will result in creating the overall metaphors that are desired. Lower level practitioners too have their own belief systems. On each specific representation, they are asked to perform sufficient inquiry to justify a firm opinion. Presumably practitioners specify these subsidiary investigations so that the sum of the particular representations will convey an acceptable synergetic picture.

Finally it often is said that managers—not auditors—are responsible for the representations. But wait a minute! Auditors attest to managements' particular representations and they do more: They assert that the sum of the selected representations presents an adequate financial picture of the concern being audited. To limit auditing responsibility only to explicit managerial representations without maintaining control over management's obligation to disclose important information does not satisfy the profession's commission.

Auditing has at least three serious problem areas. The first is the impossible ethical load that results from being an advocate in some situations and being independent in others. We have discussed this problem area before (*Essays,* Vol. I, pp. 45–55) and now wish only to emphasize that the legal profession has been careful to separate lawyers as advocates and judges as independent public servants so that the ethical ambiguity is greatly reduced.

The second problem area is concerned with the ability of auditors to give opinions on managerial representations about financial and operating affairs without themselves being valuers, experts on materials and (supposedly) other assets as well. The profession has real trouble here, for operations are concerned with values acquired, values disposed of and values added, and assets too are potentials for adding value.

This essay is concerned with the third problem area—the broader problem of setting guidelines for giving judgments on other peoples' representations about their intentions and expectations. An important early question is: Precisely what is the difference between having the auditor himself make the representation and having the auditor give an opinion that managerial representations are acceptable? More directly, can an auditor give an opinion on someone else's opinion without accepting responsibility for both that opinion and his own?

Now opinions require judgments, and judgments require comparisons and comparisons require standards. Divergences from standards must be determined and *evaluated* so that an opinion of adequacy, relevance, materiality or warrantedness can be rendered. From whence come these norms and this ability to weigh relative importance? Can auditors *create* these norms without being experts in assessing expectations and judging values? Normally a sequence of judgments is required. First, the profession must decide which set of possible norms will be taken as the standard. This task in practice has been taken over by the Institute and various professional associations. Second, someone must observe specific situations and compare the events with the representations made by management. Thus, two related sets of opinions are involved: first, whether the norms (when adequately followed) fairly represent what society wants represented and, second, whether in fact managements' expressions are sufficiently in accordance with the norms. Presumably the latter duty is performed by individual auditing houses, but is it necessary to state specifically in each opinion that the norms have been followed and that the outcomes fairly represent financial conditions and the results of operations?

SUPPORT STRUCTURE

The auditor's basis for belief is somewhat complicated. First, he usually accepts the assumption that the world of events exists more or less independently of his own behavior. In philosophical terms he is a natural realist who believes in an external world with events that have consequences that impinge on his responsibility. The general accountant's task is to abstract from many aspects of these events and to construct an appropriate language system into which relevant aspects can be translated. Making bookkeeping entries then becomes the routine task of mapping certain consequences into the appropriate language categories. The task of the general accountant is to decide which events are to be carriers of recordable information (transactions) and which consequences merit preservation. General accountants have the task of *constructing* accounting concepts and in so doing they must consider user needs, costs of providing information, etc. In addition they must consider possible interpretations of the language symbols and thus become low-level employers of symbolic interactionism and its related concepts.[1]

The auditor's position is clearly related. It is a commonplace that he performs a social function by increasing confidence in accounting reports by compressing user probability distributions that proper events have been specified and their relevant consequences adequately recorded.[2] Clearly auditors cannot recreate the events themselves in order to verify them. Yet only the most naive realists deny the possibility of a reconstruction of the event pattern. The point here is that auditors seldom are able to fortify their opinions by replicating past events, but they must be able to reconstruct a plausible probabilistic model of their structure.

This is the heart of the matter—the need for auditors to draw inferences and to depend on these *inferences* to support their beliefs. Faith in these inferences becomes the basis for judgment and belief. A receiving report *is evidence* and speaks in relatively soft tones that goods were received. The auditor reconstructs from the report and supporting evidential influences a model that suggests the goods were in fact received. The point here is that opinion is supported by a system (network) of inferences that suggest a probabilistic coherence theory of truth. The later presence of similar goods may provide further evidence. An inventory of finished stock that requires such materials might act as further support. Thus the receiving report is a partial basis for the general *inference* that the materials were received.

All are familiar with the concept of objectivity in a subjective agreement among competent parties. Belief is fostered when others agree. What others? Presumably the people who agree must have some abilities in common, e.g., *scientific* observers, *aware* human beings, *economic* men, other accountants. Thus auditors feel comfortable with inferential beliefs when other auditors interpret outcomes similarly. The power of ideology is important here and the inevitable indoctrination of the training and educational process is at work to create homogeneous conclusions. Auditors are *taught* by professors and supervisors to look for certain types of evidence. Auditors are taught to weigh these fragments in similar ways. Auditors are instructed to accept analogies and draw inferences in customary ways. Thus belief and opinion formation are socially determined, and to the extent that these social prescriptions are internalized each auditor is committed to such beliefs and opinions. It is not surprising then that the Institute has emphasized GAAS (Generally Accepted Auditing Standards). What is not so clear is why it has sometimes emphasized "authoritative" releases. Unfortunately this authoritative posture has resulted in attempts to influence curriculum planning, course structure and other interferences with the educational responsibilities traditionally borne by universities.[3]

Reliance on an adequate system of internal controls adds confidence that the inferential correspondences between documents and events are warranted. In a similar way a system of sharp internal controls serves as a substitute for replication and the inability to recreate accounting events. Thus confidence arises from coordination and coherence rather than from direct correspondence with the events themselves, and in a broad philosophical sense dependence on an integrated system is an application of the coherence theory for establishing truth and supporting warranted representations.

Yet support from coherence is not the entire story. It is also desirable to establish some degree of correspondence between the documents and the accounting facts in a more direct relationship. In practice correspondence becomes an end-product and its accomplishment is primarily through a network of coherent structures. The concept of an accounting fact can not be identified solely with sense organs or with observations of shareable sense impressions classified as physical objects. Transactions are accounting facts in the modern scientific view. The transaction is a fact in the sense that it belongs to a class of events that can be isolated by their consequences in accounting variables such as assets, equities, revenues, etc. Incidentally non-accounting effects (attributes) of an event are omitted even though they may be relevant facts for many other investigations. The accounting fact is only that aspect of an event that is related to value and wealth—exchanges, potentials and quantitative changes.

The possible uses of the correspondence theory of warranted representations is now obvious. How does an auditor assure himself that the language symbols and their expected interpretations result from inferences that correspond with the accounting facts? The *coherence* of his system variables become the warrant for accepting the *correspondence* of the representations to the facts that have an impact on the firm.

This discussion neglects the function of auditors as discoverers of dysfunctional operations such as carelessness, embezzlement, fraud and the like. These operations are concerned with the efficient creation of wealth and the possible decrease in values through dysfunction. Clearly this element is important but is does not concern us at this point.

AUDITING OPINIONS—SOME PRACTICAL QUESTIONS

Recently banks and other financial institutions have had an interesting language inversion in the area of public reporting. In this fantastic world it often seems that events in the outside world do not happen unless statements certify that they transpired. It is as if there are no losses until the statements report them.

It should be clear that *accounting* losses occur when accountants say they occur and they say they occur when it serves professional objectives to do so. Yet something is inconsistent with a service activity that denies an occurrence that everyone else acknowledges as an accounting event. Specifically it is strange for a service activity that deals with changing wealth potentials to adopt rules contrary to the usual concepts of wealth.

At best this procedure violates any *coherence* theory of truth and even fails to meet the standards for *correspondence* of symbols with events.

Sometimes it is argued that refusal to recognize what others would call losses is essential to keep orderly financial markets. The criticism here is not to deny that rules are sometimes selected over alternative possibilities because they help someone avoid stupid decisions, e.g., the maintaining of secret reserves. Yet by most norms many current bank losses already have occurred, and to an outsider it is not a legitimate function of accounting to suggest that a savings institution meets its legal capital requirements when in fact it does not. It is of course possible that future conditions will show that the losses have been recovered, but even in this case it seems more reasonable to change the regulatory laws than to corrupt the accounting process.

Consider in more detail bank loans to third-world countries. Assume for the moment that such loans will require further loans for meeting interest obligations and that such loans are worth perhaps thirty cents on a dollar when assessed realistically. Assume further that public accountants are recompensed by society for providing unbiased opinions on the financial and operating affairs of their clients. Clearly existing loss reserves are grossly inadequate to register the agreed amount of capital deterioration. Finally assume that all requirements of RAP (Regulatory Accounting Principles) and related pronouncements have been met. In such a case, what is it that a public accountant following GAAP (Generally Accepted Accounting Principles) can say? And what does his opinion add to the knowledge already available from conformance with RAP?

In short, what is it that a public accountant following GAAP adds? Perhaps the most important disclosure is precisely what he does *not* say—that the regulatory requirements are designed to protect (?) depositors and are simply inadequate to serve investors and that RAP requirements often are distortions of the primary functions of accountants elsewhere. Some financial institutions may have the choice of using RAP and RAP-like regulations or adopting GAAP and other industries may have specialized requirements that cannot be adequately met by general accounting guidelines, e.g., the high priority that insurance regulators give to protecting policy holders. Certainly private and agency accountants should at least give notice that the institutions have or have not followed RAP and GAAP guidelines. Assuming that GAAP recommendations are worth following and that their provisions are not covered by RAP, it seems that auditors should be required to follow both or at the very least disclose relevant differences.

Clearly an opinion from a public practitioner that financial institutions have followed RAP is of little or no consequence if there is faith in accountants and auditors employed directly by the regulatory commissions. Public practitioners should at the very least confirm that RAP has been followed and in addition they must decide whether general GAAP (when appropriate) has been followed. It may be too much to ask society to pay for an additional independent opinion that the agency auditor's opinion about RAP is adequate unless something from GAAP is added. If the objective is to check on the work of agency auditors, the task may be in the wrong venue. Normally the agency's own hierarchy of auditors (who are external to the institution) should perform this function and help to provide needed assurances.

It is clear that market participants often see through shoddy and transparent accounting policies. A few years ago security prices for certain big city banks went up in response to serious writedowns for loan losses that all competent investors knew had already occurred and had not been previously revealed in the accounts. It may be that investors were relieved because the writedowns may not have been as great as they expected. Yet in view of the previous disregard for *values,* there should be little reason to believe that these belated writedowns would be adequate. Could it have been that investors appreciated even slight movements toward honesty in financial reporting?

In the case of banks with large third-world loans, there has been a major trend toward using accounting reports to conceal rather than to reveal prevailing situations. The reason is primarily legalistic and the twisting of accounting guidelines is condoned so that these financial firms can escape onerous legal controls. Unfortunately these controls often are oriented towards statements rather than to the facts. To write down these investment loans adequately often would lead to embarrassing problems with capital safeguards legally designed to protect the public. Apparently whether the losses in fact exist or whether they are known to exist is irrelevant so long as legalistic realities are met.[4] The control operates through reported numbers with little reference to underlying conditions.

An obvious "solution" is for the auditing firm to render a qualified opinion. What does such a report imply for financial institutions? It may for example assure readers that RAP has been followed, but that GAAP has not been met. In the case of loan writeoffs, it may imply that GAAP has been followed but that the magnitudes are not sufficient to meet the auditor's standards for acceptable financial and operating statements.

The latter condition is a possibility in all lines of auditing work and cannot be escaped. The individual auditing firm must render its own opinion on financial matters, and to follow to the letter the procedures indicated by GAAS is not sufficient. These guidelines must not only be followed; they must be followed judiciously and effectively so that the entire financial position is fairly represented.

It is clear then that following GAAP and GAAS do not inevitably assure the public that the results fairly represent financial and operating conditions. The judgments of the individual auditing firm may be faulty so that neither GAAS nor any other set of guidelines can assure the reader of adequate measurement and disclosure. The point here is that it simply is not sufficient for an auditor to certify that GAAP and GAAS have been followed. He needs to assure the reader that these guidelines have been followed *adequately* and that the statements reflect the entire financial situation fairly.

The last condition is one of discipline over practitioners and control over their education and practices. The public is confronted with a dual problem. First, are GAAS guidelines adequate—when properly implemented—to assure adequate reports. Second, has the individual firm exercised mature and expert judgment in applying the guidelines so that the reported numbers create appropriate expectations? GAAS indicates what should be done—the steps to be taken. Individual firms apply the rules and render judgments. Some of the judgments relate to whether the representations are consistent with the guidelines. Yet the important judgment is whether or not the representations in the minds of interpreters fairly represent the conditions. Observe that the second judgment is that of the individual auditing firm and apparently a necessary precondition is that the general guidelines of GAAP and GAAS have been followed.[5]

It may be argued that practitioners audit the past (and the recent past known as the present), i.e., the facts and actual events. It is the interpreter's task to relate them to the future and to form expectations. In this division of labor the Institute is asked to set forth a set of GAAS that can be followed by practitioners and can also facilitate the transition necessary for interpreters to move from opinions of the past to expectations about the future. This may look like an impossible task, but the past facts selected for audit are selected because of their potential for recurring in the future. To facilitate this extrapolation is precisely the work of accounting.

What is to be done? The individual practitioner may give his opinion that GAAP and GAAS have been followed but that the numbers are not acceptable. Yet the public is not primarily interested in whether GAAP and GAAS have been followed. It wishes an opinion that financial conditions are fairly represented in all important aspects. With this standard (in the tradition of Limperg) there would be no qualified opinions. That is, an assertion that conditions are well represented in certain areas and not fairly represented in others is scarcely acceptable. This deficiency may be ameliorated by showing alternate figures that result from the auditor's own judgment, or the statements may be composed of the auditor's judgments with supplementary notes indicating the importance of deviations from management's opinion. This shift in emphasis (intonation) is *not* likely to happen so long as GAAS makers insist that representations in the statements are entirely those of management.

Suppose for argument that the representations are those of management and that the representations by auditors are confined entirely to opinions about them. Suppose further that auditors are required to state the differences in and the importance of all divergences. The interpreter can then read the statements and the opinion as a single unit and reach his own judgments. Yet he has a further problem. He still must decide which set of representations to accept (if either) and apply his own judgments that include material from a broader environment. Of course he must make his own judgments in any event, and no doubt he will soon learn to recognize differences in optimism (and rigor) displayed by different auditing houses, and, unless they "speak with one voice," among various supervisors and partners within each firm.

Return now to an opinion that states that RAP but not GAAP has been followed and gives no idea as to the importance of the deficiencies. Such an opinion is clearly inadequate for modern business. Investors must have their own reliable conversion factors. Here again they may not be sure that the individual auditor's judgments are worthy of consideration even if GAAP and GAAS have been followed. For example, investors must trust their own judgments about appropriate writedowns of third-world debt rather than the judgments of bank managers or agency auditors even if they are supported by opinions from reputable independent auditing firms.

AUDITING—SOME FURTHER PROBLEMS

The modern audit often covers many subsidiaries and associated firms, and several houses may be involved in auditing the various components. Many interesting questions can be raised about the nature of such relationships among professionals. The chief question concerns the assurance that the public should have in the competence of such conglomerate audits.

Several partial solutions are available for multi-house audits but few are entirely satisfactory. In this country the public has rejected the concept of direct governmental control over auditing activities, and in any case governmental direction of multi-national conglomerate audits must wait for major improvements in international cooperation.

Perhaps, as a compromise measure, concerned governments could require that all phases of an audit be done by one private firm. Clearly such a policy is not appropriate for a pluralistic society. It would require that firms have numerous branch offices or require enormous travel time. Small local or regional firms could service only smaller clients with larger jobs automatically going to large international auditing houses. The result is a movement in the direction of oligopoly and concentration of auditing power in even fewer firms.

A more realistic alternative for America might be to approach the problem through the more general concept of delegation. Firms already have solid experience with assignment of tasks and responsibilities so that delegation should not be a great extension. Delegation of some responsibilities to appraisers and valuers by auditing houses is an established practice. What is new here is the relationship among professionals who are in other respects in direct competition. It is true that competing businesses may make all sorts of cooperating agreements and there are some precedents for this among competing professionals. General medical practitioners cooperate with specialists in forming opinions although they are not in direct competition. Law firms often cooperate in the preparation of complicated legal documents. Some of these situations may be applicable and the usual superior-inferior relationship certainly is not a necessary condition for delegation.

In subcontracting relationships the results to be followed are set down by the prime contractors along with the power to reject if their conditions are not met. It is as if the hierarchical chain is simply extended to cover entities that are not normally a part of the authority-responsibility chain. This relationship sometimes is emphasized by taxing authorities through their distinction between employees and independent contractors. This distinction is unavoidably vague, but the distinguishing feature usually is determining which party has the authority to specify the methods for doing the work.

It seems that a revised relationship is appropriate for auditing houses that combine to do the work needed for professional opinions. The relationship is among professionals so that it should have few or no features of the traditional superior-inferior structure. In a sense the audit arrangement is a cooperation of equals who are actually independent except for the common bonds of professionalism and the acceptance of a common code of ethics. But such is not entirely the case.

The relationship among the cooperating firms is not quite symmetrical. The dominant member of the conglomerate is asked to give an opinion even though much of the evidence may be furnished by auditors handling affiliates. But the latter render their professional opinions without comparable dependence on the former. In practice this asymmetry may encourage the ability of the former to specify work patterns to be used. It is true that both are independent contractors, but the risks and possible liabilities from poor work run first to the house giving the overall opinion. In most cases the house doing the work on the affiliate also issues an opinion, and sooner or later it too must accept responsibility for its own more limited scope. In practice this effect may turn out to be relatively unimportant, but the power of the firm giving the broader opinion to reject the work of the other would seem to indicate the existence of some hierarchical effect.

It now is fashionable for auditing houses to audit the work of others. This practice is on the whole salutary and probably should be encouraged.[6] Certainly the necessity for one firm to risk its professional reputation on the work of others encourages this practice. Moreover it is more discreet to carry on this general search for quality than to exert direct pressure on cooperating firms during particular engagements or in response to specific complaints. This development also could lead to cooperation among top level personnel and ultimately to the development of super-managers who may be only loosely attached to a particular auditing firm. At the very least it should result in more uniformity among firms and closer adherence to professional associations that develop uniform guidelines and set minimum standards for work. Another effect might be that the profession becomes segmented with tiers of firms as well as levels of practitioners within each firm.

Major accounting firms have made practical arrangements to meet these problems. The difficulty is that little information on the topic has reached the general public. The widespread cliché that there must be cooperation among equals, but one is more equal than others may express some of the dilemma but does not afford a solution. The usual opinion statement discloses the dependence and admits responsibility, but does little to explain the mechanics of the relationship. The following Arthur Andersen statement in its report ("To the Shareholders and Board of Directors of Teledyne Inc." that was included in the Annual Report for 1989) is typical:

> We did not audit the consolidated financial statements of. . . . Those statements were audited by other auditors whose reports have been furnished to us and our opinion . . . is based on the reports of other auditors . . . (p. 18).[7]

MANAGEMENT REPRESENTATIONS

Turn now to another important problem for the profession: To what extent, if any, does the auditor's opinion extend beyond management's representations and assure the reader that important aspects of the business have not been omitted from the managerial statements. It is clear that opinions on the statements that *management does make* is not sufficient, for management may simply fail to make important statements and relieve the auditor of his responsibility and the public of its essential information. This possible failure simply is an extension of the nagging uneasiness of all auditors about possible failure to uncover essential information.

It should be obvious that some limits must be placed on management's freedom to withhold or conceal information. It simply is not enough for the auditor to limit his assurances to the accuracy and relevance of the statements that *are* given. Clearly the range of items that might be omitted by an uncooperative management is wide and there is no guarantee that even good auditors can find and disclose all of them. Yet the auditor earns his share of the social output by decreasing uncertainty, and adding confidence about the representations that actually are made. It also is clear that there is no way that *all* uncertainty can be removed by expert auditing review or by any other means, and that users must accept uncertainty with every decision. An auditing opinion definitely is not an insurance policy even though commonalities abound.

The point here is that an opinion on management's representations alone does not satisfy what society needs and expects from independent auditors. It may be that the Dutch standard of "creating proper expectations" is too idealized, but it may be argued that the information needed for such expectations ought to be provided.

Despite exorbitant legal fees and inefficient legal processes, this is a period of contention and extensive litigation. Is it possible to avoid liability for an inaccurate overall presentation by restricting the opinion to specific representations presented by management? Is it possible that each individual managerial *representation* is correct and that the overall picture presented by the accounting *statements* is inadequate or incorrect? In short is the opinion about overall financial conditions or about accounting *statements* and their components? Apparently this distinction is not sharply drawn, but most opinions aver that at least they cover management's actual statements.

Arthur Andersen (in the 1989 Teledyne Annual Report) accepts a broader responsibility in addition to careful mention of auditing and accounting standards; it states:

> These financial *statements* are the responsibility of the company's management. Our responsibility is to express *an* opinion on these financial statements *based on our audits.* . . . Those [generally accepted] standards require that we plan and perform the audit to obtain reasonable assurance about whether the financial *statements* are free of material *misstatement.* An audit includes examining, on a test basis, evidence supporting the amounts and disclosures on the financial statements. An audit also includes assessing the accounting principles used and significant estimates made by management, as well as evaluating the *overall* financial statement presentation. . . . In our opinion . . . the financial statements referred to above present fairly, in all material respects, the consolidated financial position . . . and the results of their operations and their cash flows . . . in conformity with generally accepted accounting principles (p. 18, emphasis added).[8]

Observe that acceptance of responsibility for disclosing non-representations is implied: "An audit also includes assessing [and] . . . evaluating the overall financial statements." The report states that an *audit* does these things, and since the firm conducted an *audit* it accepts such responsibilities. Some ambiguity remains in the last sentence, for the opinion states that the financial statements *fairly* state important aspects of the business, but (only?) "in conformity with generally accepted accounting principles." The last expression seems to imply that the firm's responsibility has been discharged by an opinion based on conformity to professional standards. This statement is in a standardized form, yet it does not clarify *what* is in conformity with generally accepted accounting principles. Could it mean that the statements are fair only to the extent that following generally accepted principles makes them fair? Does the firm's responsibility and liability end with its conformity to accounting and auditing standards?

Turn now to the kinds of evidence that auditing houses use to form beliefs and to support opinions. One may wonder why auditing firms find it necessary to assure the reader that they performed their duties properly and in accordance with professional requirements. This claim may increase the confidence of users who are more familiar with the professional association than with the individual firm, but the objective may be to diffuse responsibility and direct possible liability from the individual firm audit to the broader association. This shift of course is one of the primary reasons for advocating uniform methods in any profession and, by itself, is not to be condemned.

Opinions are based on (derived from) audits and apparently the audits are those performed in conformity with standards set down by appropriate ruling associations. It is admitted that acceptable audits are on a test basis, and it is asserted that the audits as conducted do "provide a reasonable basis for our opinion." Finally an adequate audit includes in its procedures appropriate methods to yield evidence for "assessing accounting principles used and significant estimates made by management, as well as evaluating the overall financial statement presentation." Unfortunately it is not always clear how the auditing procedures actually used are able to yield sufficient evidence for these beliefs. Obviously such detailed explanations have no place in each auditing report. Supposedly auditing courses and auditing on-the-job training provide adequate explanations. Some critics are not so sure.

Yet "We believe that our audits provide a reasonable basis for our opinion," is a salutary general statement. It asserts that there is a basis for the opinion and that this basis is reasonable. Some leeway is provided by the adjective reasonable. Some doubt *may* remain, but for such doubt to actualize some *unreasonable* feature must come to the surface. The burden comes to rest on the interpretation of the term "reasonable."

Precisely how does a firm arrive at belief on a *reasonable* basis and to a *reasonable* degree? The profession addresses this question in three ways:

1. "[O]ur audits [are] in accordance with generally accepted auditing standards." We are to infer that following accepted auditing standards constitutes sufficient evidence for an accept-reject decision.

2. "An audit includes examining, on a test basis, evidence supporting the amounts and disclosures in the financial statements." We
are to assume that the test basis is sanctioned and in the particular case is sufficient evidence to support the disclosures actually
made in the financial statements.
3. "An audit also includes assessing the accounting procedures and
significant estimates made by managers, as well as evaluating
the overall financial statement presentation." Contentious parties
may wonder precisely how these *judgments* are reached.

We conclude this section by inquiring again about the possible difference between an auditor's giving his opinion directly on the financial
facts of the firm and giving an opinion on management's representation
of these facts. Management may of course knowingly make false representations that need to be set right, but the more interesting case is when
management makes representations that it thinks are correct but do *not*
express the auditor's beliefs.

Sometimes there will be direct conflict between management's and
the auditor's beliefs even though common indoctrination may encourage
a measure of consistency. When they do agree, the consensus forms an
embryonic example of objectivity, where objectivity is defined in terms
of social consensus among trained observers.

However questions remain. In cases of conflict whose opinions shall
prevail? In what circumstances and to what extent do managers persuade
individual auditors to change their beliefs? Does the auditor need to form
his *own* opinions on the facts before he can give an opinion on representations about them? If this is the situation, what advantage results from
insisting that the reports are representations by management? Escape
from possible liability? Why should the auditor be allowed to escape full
responsibility? Perhaps such a process encourages management to be
more serious and responsible about making statements. Do managers
and auditors now share legal responsibility?

This is not the place for a detailed discussion of the alternatives
available when managers and auditors disagree. When persuasive techniques fail, management may seek more congenial auditors. Clearly
homogeneity of beliefs is important to assure some semblance of professionalism, and the Institute accordingly works toward uniformity and
conformance. Managers have some constraints for they must present audited reports to the public. Thus consensus and uniformity in the profession exerts tremendous pressure on managers to accept and follow the

rules suggested by the accounting profession. Managers, working in concert, may try to change accounting and auditing guidelines, but as individuals they often are limited to techniques of persuasion and to the selection of alternative auditors who may be more favorably disposed to their views. We neglect here the modern positivist view that the market mechanism selects accounting and auditing principles with the influence and ethics of the profession entering only as minor forces in the market process. Incidentally this is a researchable topic and can be approached by empirical methods.

CONFRONTATION AUDITING: A DIGRESSION

Many have noted the rise of confrontational sociology as an alternative for the more cooperative functional orientation. There are discussions in earlier essays of the adversarial framework found in the operation of courts, the political system and market economics generally. This change in emphasis in organization theory means that an organization is viewed more as a device for resolving conflict and less as an arrangement for coordinating diverse forces. In the functional approach an organization is viewed primarily as a cooperative venture and research is directed first to the behaviors that are consistent with the accomplishment of unified goals and consistent ends-in-view. Research in either case takes the form of finding dysfunctional activities, non-consistent goals and the costs of non-conformance. From a confrontational basis research could proceed in a similar fashion and attempt to measure the advantages of cooperation, goal congruence and solidarity (lack of pluralism).

While American social scientists may be moving toward models based on conflict, the Japanese view of management has lately renewed interest in a cooperative functional framework. In the United States the conflict approach gained emphasis when early politicians de-emphasized efforts to reduce the power of monopolistic owners and gave labor organizations more effective weapons to attain a balance of power. The management philosophy of the Roosevelt years (at least until the wartime necessity of cooperative effort) accepted the permanence of labor-management conflict and rejected the more cooperative approach that is at the heart of socialist ideology. Seemingly the rationale was taken from the popular balance-of-power doctrine among sovereign states. Such a balance, even though precarious, restricts extremists on all sides so that solutions tend to be near the center. Of course it has been an unstated assumption that the middle is somehow the most desirable path even though extremists from all sides would hardly agree.[9]

It is interesting to note that from the viewpoint of a psychologist the New Deal's balancing act also reinforced a sharp shift in worker loyalties. It is necessary for any successful union leader in a confrontational atmosphere to redirect the loyalty of individual workers from management or owners to the union. In short, to be successful the union must shift worker identification from the owner-manager-firm entity to a feeling of brotherhood for the union group. Thus sneering references to paternalistic managers are understandable for it certainly is less difficult to alienate workers from greedy owners and non-caring managers.[10]

It is difficult to explain the belated appearance of confrontational research methods in view of the long established tradition for competition and conflict in both the economic and political structures of the Western World. Research from this vantage point departs from the assumption of continual cooperation and concentrates on identifying the conflicting groups and attempting to specify their conflicting goal patterns—their objectives. These goal patterns are related to the bonding process that leads to group cohesion. Finally, much of the resulting research then is directed to conflict resolution as a major social necessity rather than to occasional studies of dysfunction in the functionalist tradition.[11]

Consider now the position of an auditor. His relationship may be adversarial to those who record, operate, control, summarize and report. In other respects he may share goals with stockholders and those who stand to gain by adherence to policy rules, e.g., with those having responsibility for the performance of others. It is interesting that some aspects of the auditor's role are similar to those of law officers in the broader social body. Policemen too are friends of those who wish to see the laws obeyed and often are seen as enemies by those who wish to subvert them. Enforcement sanctions differ of course, but both hope to act as deterrents to those interested in dysfunctional activities and also as supporters of those who wish to see the organization function in the interests of its objectives.

As a brief review consider the social duties and roles of those in the auditing arm of the profession. First their function is to see that organizational rules are consistent with the objectives of dominant groups who are permitted to set the rules for the organization. The auditing role is one of cooperation with the power structure and adversarial to others. This function requires reviewing the accounting system to assess its adequacy and disclose the features essential for accomplishing goals. Yet before this decision can be made, it is necessary to decide which individuals (or subgroups) count, determine their objectives and somehow weigh their importance. Auditors must make provision for resolving conflicting goals and then assess the operating, recording and reporting rules to find if in fact they are acceptable procedures. In practice auditors perform some of these functions by reviewing the system. One may question the adequacy and competence of many professional reviews of this sort, but it is clear that the auditing supervisor can approach it in a functional (cooperative) way or as a problem in adversarial relations and conflict resolution.

Second, the auditing profession has accepted the task of deciding whether the operating rules are in fact being followed by all groups subject to the restraints imposed. This function too usually is fulfilled by the auditing supervisor in his overall review of the system, but unavoidably some details remain to be decided at the operational level. In one sense the auditor is in conflict with operating personnel, recording personnel and with some levels of management. Auditors by their very presence broadcast that rule-conformance is expected and is being monitored.

These relationships may be modeled as a complicated game with conflict as the prevailing force, yet the game is by no means a zero-sum game and it is possible that an audit will benefit all parties. Certainly benefits may accrue to members of the monitored groups themselves, for honest members may benefit by being removed from possible suspicion. There is no reason to believe that the benefits lost by dissenters will inevitably be equal to the benefits gained by others. The usual approach is to take an organization-wide view and model the problem in some cost-benefit format. The costs to the organization are composed primarily of auditing and system compliance costs while the benefits usually are in the form of a reduction in dysfunctional activities. Thus, auditing and related controls can be viewed as activities designed to reduce dysfunction and the cost of inconsistent goal structures (or pluralism) in the organization.

The latter facet can be extended to conflicts among various non-auditing groups and the possible costs of having an organization with inconsistent objectives. Overall objectives of any organization must be subdivided into various subgoals and in turn these must be related to activities and responsibilities of subordinates. This task of dividing broad objectives into consistent implementing actions and standards often is a monumental task. There also is potential for inconsistency in the goals themselves as well as conflicts among all subordinates who have some freedom to alter activities or reports about them.

The recent emphasis on contracting and agency relations is clearly related to possible costs of dysfunction: the costs of inconsistent goal structures, the lack of goal congruence, the costs of political pluralism and the costs of delegation in an organization. This concept is far from new in the field, although careful specification and the sophistication of the mathematics have added novelty. Before the turn of the century managers often were wary of piece-rate methods with their emphasis on worker bonuses and neglect of quality and longterm welfare of the firm. At a different level Berle and Means, in the depression years, pointed out many important consequences of differing objectives for owners and managers. Early organization (and entity) theorists emphasized the need to buy conformance from employees at all levels (including managers). The sophistication was low-level and there is little evidence that trade-offs or cost-benefit calculations related such sacrifices to the costs of dysfunction. Economists in this area probably assumed that entrepreneurs would reach economic (tradeoff) decisions on conformance payments and costs of inconsistent objectives. However, lack of attention to the cost of information may have been common among those who allocated funds on a marginal basis.

One may wonder why sociologists have failed to give guidance in the area of dysfunction. Parsons and others have studied institutions as complexes "of institutionalized role integrates" and stressed "role-expectations and . . . corresponding sanctions." Parsons' concept of anomie is developed to cover certain ambiguous role expectations that can lead to "[t]he polar antithesis of full institutionalization . . . , the complete breakdown of normative order. . . ."[12] Apparently he wished to encompass more than a simple mathematical model of contracting and agency by including the ambiguous and confused relations that make up anomie and producing a model to include these confusions.

It is clear that sociologists are more advanced than accountants in the area of methodology and therefore might have given rigorous attention to the costs of anomie. Yet few if any operating models have been presented, and cost-benefit studies of related concepts, e.g., alienation, have been rare in both economics and sociology.

NOTES

[1] "The term 'symbolic interactionism' is a somewhat barbaric neologism that I coined in an offhand way . . . [and it] rests . . . on three simple premises. The first premise is that human beings act toward things on the basis of the meanings that the things have for them. . . . The second premise is that the meaning of such things is derived from, or arises out of, the social interaction that one has

with one's fellows. The third premise if that these meanings are handled in, and modified through, an interpretative process . . ." Herbert Blumer, *Symbolic Interactionism: Perspective and Method* (Englewood Cliffs: Prentice-Hall, Inc., 1969), pp. 1,2. This popular sociological approach is practically identical with conceptualism in philosophy and is closely related to hermeneutics in religious discussions.

[2] It is tempting to say that auditors' opinions decrease uncertainty. They do decrease uncertainty about the veracity of the representations, but they may increase uncertainty about other important aspects of the situation. We neglect here the broader aspects of auditing, e.g., evaluating the adequacy of the system itself and assessing management's job of managing.

[3] In general first-rate universities have not known quite how to handle the emergence of accounting in the academic arena. While university leaders were debating the academic respectability of public accounting, the Institute moved in on the more *service* oriented universities and encouraged special schools of accounting with, what seems to traditional academics, some unfortunate course and curriculum recommendations.

[4] This criticism is not to deny the tradition for emphasizing language and the part played by social scientists (and the courts) in creating social facts and social reality. See for example George Ritzer's discussion of symbolic interactionism and related topics. *Sociology: A Multiple Paradigm Science* (Boston: Allyn and Bacon, Inc., 1975), pp. 141–185. He states: "man is an active creator of his own social reality. . . . [T]hey [social interactionists] go further and deny the existence of any social reality beyond that created by man at the moment" (p. 89). In philosophy the conceptualists emphasize man's active part in creating *all* reality.

[5] The recent debacle of Lincoln Savings & Loan Association and Arthur Young & Co. (now Ernst & Young) is regrettable for all concerned, but it illustrates some points argued throughout these *Essays*. "William Black, a regional general counsel for the Office of Thrift Supervision, said 'Lincoln is proof positive that any thrift in America could obtain a clean audit despite being grossly insolvent.' Regulators say that . . . the thrift was pulling one of the biggest scams on the American public—valuing allegedly worthless desert land owned by the thrift at high prices and bending accounting rules to upgrade worthless assets." Lee Berton, "Spotlight on Arthur Young Is Likely to Intensify As Lincoln Hearings Resume," *The Wall Street Journal,* November 21, 1989, p. A20.

Some observers suspect that the Institute is not entirely blameless and for decades have wondered how auditors can give meaningful opinions on financial conditions and operations without being "valuers." Consider what may happen if the following Arthur Young defense is true. "Arthur Young officials say they are blameless in the matter. Land valuations, for example, are made by third parties *and must be accepted by auditors.* . . . 'All appraisals of land [owned by Lincoln Savings & Loan] were done by appraisers hired by the company, and *we had to rely on them.'*" (*Ibid.*) (Emphasis added to the reported comments of Mr. Gladstone, co-chief executive of Ernst & Young and former chairman of Arthur Young.) On the use of qualified opinions in the troubled thrift industry, consider the following statement from Arthur Young: "[W]e issued a qualified opinion or disclaimed an opinion on the financial statements of 135 of the more than 300 thrift audits we did from 1986 through 1988. . . ." (*Ibid.*)

[6] This practice is common among all professional associations when the actions of a member are suspect. Observe however that these investigations usually are in response to reported wrongdoings and are done to preserve the reputation of the association and its members. A more general application and one more appropriate for the auditing situation is that of a number of Eastern doctoral-granting universities. It once was common practice to have a distinguished member of, say, Columbia's faculty sit in on doctoral examinations and review dissertations of candidates at Johns Hopkins. The effect (other than to enhance various egos) was to assure the public that the requirements of member universities met scholarly standards. Many universities perform a similar internal auditing function by requiring doctoral committees to include at least one member from related departments.

[7] The "Those statements . . ." part of the quotation is same as that given in the standard report format for situations in which the auditor's opinion is based in part on the report of another auditor; see *Reports on audited Financial Statements,* Statements on Auditing Standards 58 (New York: AICPA, April 1988), par 13, pp.12–13.

[8] The content of the excerpts presented here also are the same as those given in the standard form for the independent auditor's standard report on comparative financial statements. *Ibid.,* par. 8, p. 9.

[9] We neglect here the broader behavioral aspects of a balance-of-power approach to international affairs. Presumably it was thought that wars among carefully balanced powers would have a lower probability of coming about and that the greater destruction would be a deterrent. Wars among balanced powers may be *more* prolonged and *horrible* so that the conditional payoff may more than offset the lessened probability of conflict. We also neglect here the possibility that information always is incomplete. Leaders may misevaluate relative military strength, the advantages of surprise, uneven technological advances, irrational reactions and the fearsome possibility that human beings may indeed enjoy such conflict.

[10] We do not intend here to imply that this type of group reorientation is peculiar to unions. Revolutionists also use the technique, and it is not by chance

that Marx and his followers hurled sarcastic barbs at more moderate socialists, liberals and gradual evolutionists. A tactical revolutionary advantage arises from a clearcut delineation of the conflicting groups with sharply focussed enemies and friends and an us-them alienation. For an interesting recent case consider the strategies of the Berkeley revolutionaries, whose interest in anarchism and nihilism led them to oppose all institutions (except their own revolutionary groups) and consider the individual as the unit most worthy of attention. Such examples may convince sociologists that a conflict model is best suited for social study; it certainly provides would-be revolutionaries with ready-made support and effective tactics for conducting their warfare.

[11] Perhaps the most general case of alternative avenues for social study is found in ethics and political theory. Some therapists apparently start with the assumption that humans inherently are good and argue that social institutions should be arranged to enhance individual freedom. Others assume the depravity of the individual and seek to arrange social institutions to coerce, control or reform him along ways more acceptable to prevailing groups. The first amendment sets some guidelines for the individual-versus-his-group conflicts and the courts are constantly at work adjusting the balance. Modern tirades on the right to privacy illustrate an important aspect of the broader problem.

[12] Talcott Parsons, *The Social System* (London: Collier-Macmillan Ltd., 1951), p. 39.

Sociological Analogs—
Viewpoint and Methodology

The objective of this essay is to review some sociological models with the hope of finding useful insights for the accounting profession. The functional approach and confrontational (conflict) models have been discussed earlier and are only mentioned here to point out that both belong to the scientifico-factist group and that neither is strongly behavioral nor interpretative (hermeneutical) nor interactionist in its orientation. Those who look at organizations as instruments for resolving conflict may be comfortable with the confrontational format and emphasize the costs of dysfunction and lack of internal goal congruence. Functional advocates may emphasize savings from cooperation but it is clear that such differences are not likely to bring revolutions in the scientific community.

In this essay consideration is given first to some sociological models in the broad sense. Later attention is directed to the Kuhnian revolutions in science and accounting. Friedrichs, in an important study, divides sociologists into two main groups; the prophetic and the priestly.[1] In simplified terms *prophetic* sociologists are interested primarily in predicting future states of their systems and thus fit in well with scientists everywhere. Their investigations are to find how the sociological complex works and to provide activist members (and others) with useful information for policy formation and planning. Inasmuch as they seldom are activists, and their methods are not revolutionary many have assumed that they stand for the social *status quo* and belong to the conservative wing of the discipline. Clearly they tend to cluster near the objective side of the spectrum with its usual assumptions that objective entities exist and can be classified and treated as things. Thus they are in the camp of semanticists who wish to find referents, to older physicists who wish to observe nature, to operation researchers who wish to find models to represent reality and to accountants who often are frustrated engineers and consider accounting constructs such as assets to be part of a substantive reality and objective phenomena.

According to Friedrichs, *priestly* sociologists are concerned with the interaction of the investigator and his universe. Sociologists are aware that knowledge comes from experience and that to omit the subjective element is to neglect an important resource. This involvement of the researcher is the basis for all interactionist theories and goes back at least to Weber and Marx. Perhaps for this reason, interactionists have been associated with activists who wish to change existing social systems.[2] For the priestly, he states: "Persuasion rather than proof is king" (p. 2). (Is there a difference?) Later he quotes Michael Polanyi: "We must recognize belief . . . as the source of all knowledge" (p. 100). Then Friedrichs paraphrases and quotes Robert Merton, who "argued quite explicitly that scientific activity of necessity involved 'emotional adherence to certain values'" (p. 101). Next he quotes Howard Becker, who feels that scientists too have a priestly aspect: "All value-judgments, other than the supreme value-judgment that prediction is in and of itself worthwhile, are to be set aside . . ." (p. 102).

In accounting there is an ethical or priestly aspect that springs from the need to agree on a group (or groups) whose values are acceptable and whose needs are important. The newer group of accountants are more openly priestly in that they often question the worthiness of traditional host groups or seek to change the responses of those selected. Clearly the interactions of information producers and information users depend on the symbolic overtones of language and the necessity for interpretation.

There is no doubt that early accountants who asked only for the facts were little more than intellectual journeymen pursuing their simple craft. A major intellectual advance came with the realization that facts (or events) do not speak for their own relevancy, but must be selected with full consideration for decisions about the future. (Unfortunately some very good modern accountants sponsor "event" theories that somehow identify *critical* events without making value judgments.) The position of present-day dissidents is that scientific prediction is not sufficient and that accountants must consider language interpretation, social interaction, individual behavior and a host of other sociological and psychological variables. Both intrasubjective and intersubjective attitudes and values are important. In many cases advocates of the priestly paradigm, when free of scientific restraints, tend to reify theories (and language), to employ freely constructed realities and to adopt a set of values that generally are anti-establishment.

RITZER'S TYPOLOGY

For a more detailed summary of sociological paradigms turn to a slightly modified framework provided by Ritzer.[3] His classifications like all others suffers from some overlap that results from the need to classify diverse sociological material into sharply defined paradigms. This essay is concerned not so much with Ritzer's typology as with the accounting applications and the research methods that seem to be most appropriate. In short interest here is in discussing some distinctions that might be made among paradigms, theories, orientations, frameworks and the like. The traditional view is expressed by Kuhn who explains the rise of new paradigms in terms of general anomalies that arise and cannot be explained by existing explanatory structures.[4]

To be successful a new paradigm, according to Kuhn, must exhibit certain characteristics. Certainly it must be able to attract a following, and the attraction for followers usually takes the form of offering acceptable explanations to some anomalies that arise in existing and competing structures. The new explanatory structure must contain some remaining ambiguous areas that give neophytes opportunities for expansion and problem solving. Therefore it must be open ended. Finally new paradigms need not become dominant for rational reasons. Political and public relations techniques often play important roles.

As the basis for further discussion consider the slightly modified summary of paradigms given by Ritzer. This classification may be appropriate for the field of accounting, and may help understand some of the current writings of individuals and groups.

I. Social Facts Paradigm:
   A. Orientation toward facts that are independent of the observer.
   B. Exemplar: Emile Durkheim—"social facts should be treated as real things" (p. 25).
   C. Divisions:
      1. Structural-functional theory—facts interrelated for cohesive structure of society.
      2. Conflict theory—social "order is maintained by coercive forces within society" (p. 26).

    D. Appropriate research methods:
       1. Questionnaires and interviews, comparative and perhaps historical studies.
       2. Social facts are *not* disclosed by introspection.

II. Social Definition Paradigm:
    A. "The subject matter is *not* social facts, but the way in which people define those social facts. . . . [I]f people define things as real, they will be real in their consequences" (p. 27). (Compare Saint Anselm and William James.)
    B. Subjective in areas of both intrasubjectivity and intersubjectivity.
    C. Exemplar: Max Weber.
    D. Divisions:
       1. Action theory of Weber, Parsons and others—"all human behavior . . . takes account of the behavior of others . . . " (p. 85).
       2. Symbolic interpretation (Mead, Blumer)—emphasis is on interpretive understanding (*Verstehen*), construction, empathy, introspection (interpretation mediates between stimulus and response).
       3. Phenomenological (Schutz)—emphasis on subjective consciousness—method of introspective description—"subjective analysis of things in consciousness replaces objective analysis of things in the world" (p. 112).
       4. Ethnomethodology (Garfinkel)—"concerned with the routine activity of everyday life and the modes of consciousness through which it is maintained" (p. 116).
    E. Research methods: Observation, expanded to understanding, case methods, occasionally empirical.

III. Social Behavior Paradigm:
    A. Social definitions and facts are metaphysical—"The behaviorist seeks to understand, predict and even determine the behavior of man" (p. 29).
    B. Exemplar: B. F. Skinner
    C. Theories:
       1. Behavioral sociology—"close to pure psychological behaviorism" (p. 29).
       2. Exchange theory—"psychological variables always intervene between social facts; they are the effective cause of the de-

pendent social fact" (p. 154). "[H]istorical change can be explained only by psychological principles" (p. 157).
3. Research methods—interview, questionnaires and individual case methods. Heavily experimental—behaviorist "uses his description of behaviors to infer things about intrasubjective and intersubjective states of mind" (p. 177).

Accountants may not be concerned with the definition of facts and the arguments about whether some facts are more real than others or are more or less real in different situations. Certainly facts themselves are constructions (interpretations) that depend on experiences stable enough to be usefully classified, and they may be classified in any way that promises to be worthwhile. Experiences may arrive through any of the senses so that pre-factual data may be touched, observed, smelled, etc. Consider further that some experiences may require aids of various sorts, e.g., infrared astronomical mapping, and consider the possibility that an infinite number of possible experiences may escape our five sense organs. Readers may wish to consider in what sense one can *observe* a person or a building or a group. One must be aware that attitudes, integrating inferences, consequences, etc. are necessary for observation. Certainly the important properties of a person (or a machine) are not what is *seen* in any simplistic objective way.

Aside from the philosophical niceties, most accountants are comfortable with the concept of facts as mental constructions. Assets to an accountant probably are as real or as factual as the sociological concepts of groups and roles or the psychological constructions for traits and responses. Engineers often are interested in some physical constructs that also may qualify as assets, but they usually are less interested in the value attributes that accountants consider to be necessary conditions. Accountants must be value oriented and the important defining relationship of an asset is its value in some context and not whether it is a machine or a building or a rectangle or a piece of art or an intangible. Accounting, like physics and biology, does not cover all reality or include all facts or encompass all interpretations.

Factists are naive realists in their philosophical outlook, and believe firmly that the world is independent and that a competent researcher can capture its important aspects in sensory nets. Operations researchers tend to construct models and discuss the isomorphism of the models to supposed *real* states of nature. In one sense they may be considered to be interpretative for they are required to prepare models (language structures with or without mathematical overlays) that represent reality. However most operations researchers and sophisticated management scientists tend to think primarily in terms of fitting models to external data rather than in constructing reality.

Who are the accounting factists? Who are the accountants who are concerned with reality and physical or objective *things*? At the lowest level are those who want "just the facts." Fortunately these accountants can be dismissed readily because they are now of little influence, but unfortunately some exceptionally bright minds are not far away.

Turn now to definition of the symbolic-interpretation paradigm and to its accounting application. The following general discussion follows closely the outline of Ritzer: "In contrast to the social factist, the social definitionist sees man as far more 'voluntaristic,' far less coerced by society, and far more a creator of the society in which he lives."[5] Contrast this position with that of advocates of ideology and the sociology of knowledge. Many have followed Marx and Mannheim and have been sympathetic to the ideological thesis. This doctrine emphasizes societal influences on the thinking and behaviors of individuals. Culture in this sense can be equated to the "man-made" environment and thus is consistent with the tenets of definitionists who subscribe to symbolic interactionism. Certainly man in communicative interaction is responsible for cultural "things." Yet advocates of the sociology of knowledge stress the converse vector, i.e., the reciprocating influence of man's constructed reality on the realities he *creates*. This interaction is not inconsistent with Ritzer's classification. In fact an Hegelian-Marxist might employ this dialectical process to explain changes in cultures and thus provide the dynamics that factist explanations sometimes lack.

We now present a summary of Arnold Rose's assumptions and propositions that form a foundation for symbolic-interactionism theory.[6]

Assumption 1:
> *"Man lives in a symbolic environment as well as a physical environment and can be 'stimulated' to act by symbols . . ."* (p. 5).

Assumption 2:
> *"Through symbols, man has the capacity to stimulate others in ways other than those in which he is himself stimulated"* (p. 7).

Assumption 3:
> *"Through communication of symbols, man can learn huge numbers of meanings and values—and hence ways of acting—from other men. . . .*

General Proposition (Deduction) 1:
Through the learning of a culture . . . , men are able to predict each other's behavior most of the time . . ." (pp. 9–10).

Assumption 4:
"The symbols—and the meanings and values to which they refer—*do not occur only in isolated bits, but often in clusters, sometimes large and complex. . . .*

General Proposition (Deduction) 2:
The individual defines (has a meaning for) himself as well as other objects, actions, and characteristics" (pp.10–11).

Assumption 5:
"Thinking is the process by which possible symbolic solutions and other future courses of action are examined, assessed for their relative advantages and disadvantages in terms of the values of the individual, and one of them chosen for action" (p. 12).

Clearly symbolic interaction has come a long way from Durkheim's view that interpretation is not appropriate for finding social facts and that "One social fact could only be explained by another social fact."[7] This view is quite a way from Bierstedt's position that "Sociology . . . has no primary interest in the individual, nor in his personality, nor in his behavior, but concerns itself rather with the nature of . . . *groups*. . . ."[8] Certainly the blank-paper analogy of Hume does not fit this structure. Interestingly Mach, a strong positivist, might have been sympathetic for he was adamant in holding that nature has only instances and that the laws of nature are human constructions. This view has been amplified by conceptualists who insist that laws are free creations of the human mind. Marx of course reified theories and considered them parts of reality in spite of his otherwise simplistic version of naive realism. Recent communication experts have been highly mechanical with their usage of noise, entropy and the like. They have recognized clearly that symbolic interaction is necessary, but (so far as I know) have not been especially interested in the refined aspects of interpretation.

It should now be clear that the movement toward hermeneutics in economics and accounting is in the area of symbolic interactionism from the sister field of sociology.[9] Emphasis is placed on objectives (values), symbolic representations, interpretations and the development of all sorts of constructed realities to further individual needs.

In accounting the professional task is to select worthy individuals and help them pursue their objectives. Certain means, intermediate objectives and values are necessary. The accountant selects from a wide variety of experiences those that seem important for accomplishment of his goals; then he constructs a symbolic system from these experiences. These systems then are interpreted by users, combined with knowledge from other sources and used as the basis for decision and action. Thus it is clear that accountants must be concerned with the interpretation of their symbols. This concern must include some knowledge of users, their objectives and their ability to make interpretations by attaching predictable meanings to the symbols.

More generally all who treat accounting theory as a problematic language accept the symbolic-interactionist paradigm. Some teachers have introduced semantic differentials into their accounting theory courses. Others have compared accounting to narrative composition and to the writing of poetry. Many have treated accounting concepts as metaphors designed to induce responses for easing user strain and creating desirable states. Clearly the process cannot be represented as naive representationism, for the world to be represented is far from a simple structure made from physical sense impressions. Instead the world that is represented is a system of subjectively constructed relationships. The concept of income, for example, is supposed to represent changes in something that might be called "well-offness." Planning implies a network of relationships that are assumed to be predictable and the related concept of control implies that in some ways this network can be manipulated in accordance with these predictions.

At a more general level the symbolic interactionist orientation is congenial for all who emphasize the subjective aspects of accounting. Accountants who just call for the facts are alienated for they are uncomfortable with applying simple recording rules to complex mental constructions. Physical scientists who search for something *fundamental* to distinguish substance from non-substance also will not feel at home. Measurers who distinguish between fundamental and derived measurements may regard the modern foundations of accounting as flimsy supports. Accountants who make an issue of tangible and intangible feel uncomfortable. Naive realists who feel that the symbols must *represent* some natural substances also will be strangers. All researchers who feel that some *basic* difference exists between the reality of a sensation and the concept of a sensation will be unhappy. Of course there are all sorts of differences among the above concepts. Distinctions are made for different reasons and to accomplish different objectives, but somehow they *must* be made. For the refugee in a desert there are immense differences between a water hole and a mirage. The waterhole may be a *real* waterhole, but the mirage is a *real* mirage, a dream is a *real* dream and the UAW is a *real* organization.

The dimension that accountants are interested in is related to potential for useful service—value. It often is the potential of the entire entity that is important, but entity-wide potential is composed of potentials from many cooperating sources and the accountant is asked to identify and separate the contributions from each. Unfortunately the benefits from synergism and various other valuable arrangements are joint products and specific attribution becomes a hopeless morass if not an impossible task.

The language of accounting sometimes picks up synergistic and neglected value potentials through recognized goodwill calculations and market quotations. Accountants present earnings reports that approximate the accomplishment of objectives over an interval. The interpreter then must assess general business conditions during these past periods, predict future conditions and determine a range of expected values. These assessments are closely related only to facts within the accounting language. It is true that these accounting facts must be expressed and measured in terms of surrogates. Some equities for example are based on legal facts. Revenue is an accounting term, but it is sometimes measured by billings—a more generally recognized fact with broader application. Expense is a specialized accounting construction that is related (though traditional lags and leads) to the more widely accepted concept of expenditure. The concept of markets is a broader based fact (construction) than the accounting concepts it helps to define and measure. In general highly specialized accounting facts invariably are related to more generally accepted concepts that are modified to make them operational in the accounting framework.

It is clear that this wide diversity of facts must be ordered and placed into some hierarchy of relevance and importance. Consider the simple accounting process for inventory writedowns. Remember that changes in values are the prime objective.

Accountants usually admit that physically damaged inventory units merit a writedown (a value transfer) but many are unwilling to accept the inference that a decline in market value (also a fact) is sufficient evidence to support a writedown. To most accountants deterioration of physical units may have relevance to value. Markdowns in department stores also are facts, but often the fact of an outright sale is rated considerably higher than the fact of an authorized markdown. The latter in turn is rated above the fact that the merchandise manager is gloomy and depressed, but has not yet admitted in writing that he will accept less than the original market price. The case of obsolete goods is a little more complicated. The evidence for obsolescence may be in the form of market quotations (facts) or in the form of managerial opinions—facts of lower order. Not only do accountants follow Durkheim's command to treat facts as things, but apparently physical facts (things) are the very best kind. (Compare the early logical positivist emphasis on the desirability of reducing all language to "thing" language and "thing" predicates.)

Further examples may be found in the area of machinery and equipment. Some accountants have suggested different provisions for physical wear and tear and obsolescence. A small group has opposed the writeoff of fixed assets until the machinery has been physically removed and the buildings razed.

The broadest factist orientation is found in the still widespread distinction between tangible and intangible assets. This distinction has been elevated by some to a principle of great importance, but it often obscures the problem at hand—concern with the evidence for value recognition.

Clearly no serious theorist questions the need for discrete identifiable experiences that can be used to help form judgments and set beliefs. Individual judgments often vary widely and this variation can be embarrassing for a profession that bases its opinions primarily on market transactions. Thus it is not surprising that professional leaders are deeply concerned about the need for common grounds to anchor their beliefs. In some cases the language of accounting is simply incapable of expressing a basis for useful interpretation. In other cases the units of accounting language must be combined with other symbolic representations (constructions) before coherent interpretations can be drawn.

Factists associate liabilities with the presence of a legal state—the debtor-creditor relation. This legal state is not exactly a physical presence, but it serves as a more or less objective criterion even though it arises from interpretations of legal language. But what about all sorts of negative forebodings and premonitions that have not yet reached the stage of legal fact? Contingent liabilities are handled poorly in the symbolic system of accounting. The common solution is to expand the nonnumerical part of the system to include non-specific account titles to convey foreboding judgments that have not yet reached an *acceptable* factual basis. (The feelings and the accounts of course are facts in their own contexts.) The accountant often adds side notes and footnotes that use the broader languages of the culture. *Within* accounting language are ways of expressing such possibilities through constructs such as reserves for contingencies and related earnings restrictions. In spite of derisive comments from critics such restrictions provide an important enrichment of the accounting language. Vague titles and rounded amounts may be an unsophisticated form of disclosure but they do help convey probabilistic beliefs. Interpreters would do well to listen.

Return now to Ritzer and consider the research methods that might be appropriate for the three paradigms.

The accounting factist is likely to be a traditional scientist who believes that the world is an external existence and the task of investigators is to discover its laws. Thus observation plays an important part in his research, and the observations can be of physical things, markets, individuals, groups, etc. Ritzer argues that factists tend to reject experimental methods because they are set up artificially and because they are microscopic where (for sociology) more macroscopic entities are desired. They may use interviews and questionnaires, but these methods are individualistic and, according to Ritzer, are seen "through individuals' eyes" (p. 68). In any case they do not emphasize the problematic nature of the questionnaires or the personal interactions that are part of all interviews.

Management scientists should be sympathetic to the factist approach, for they are interested in fitting models to real-state conditions, manipulating the models and predicting outcomes among the realities they attempt to model. Since it is true that a model may be interpreted as a language, some operations researchers also can be included with the symbolic interactionists.

Ritzer points out that questionnaires and interviews are only two of the many possible methods that factists might employ or use with some modifications. He emphasizes contextual analysis (individuals attitudes related to their social positions), pair and triple analysis (generalization from dyads and triads), partitioning (from gross studies to smaller units) historical (longitudinal) models, and comparative (cross cultural) methods.

The behavioralists according to Ritzer have been interested primarily in the methods of psychology. They tend to use observational and experimental methods. Statistical support is required for acceptable generalizations and the formation of proto-theories. Intrapersonal considerations are discounted and interaction with the investigator is all but neglected. The unique fact that the researcher is a part of the experiment and might use this unique relation for better understanding is minimized. Yet it is unfair to say that the problematic nature of language is completely neglected, for the symbols used by individuals are language symbols and always require interpretation by those who react to them.

Turn now to symbolic-interactionism and avoid for the moment the fact that interaction often is associated with strong normative positions advocated by the new left and many Marxists. Tinker is most visible in the Marxist group and some newly launched journals hold vague to rigid leftist positions.[10] These views sometimes are difficult to separate, but in general individualists and libertarians are non-Marxist and anarchists; and syndicalists and nihilists seldom are associated with sociology-of-knowledge advocates or classed with the traditional communist left. Disillusionment with the greed that fuels the motors of western capitalism combined with the horrors of alienation and angst have led both groups to take on a flavor of the absurd. Like Beckett's well known tramps, they view the accounting profession as wandering aimlessly and waiting for the coming of some Godot-like savior. To argue that double-entry bookkeeping inevitably must be a tool of gross capitalism and that its practitioners blindly follow the arcane rites of satanic employers simply is not true. Capitalists have no monopoly on double-entry accounting and controls even though some traditional scholars, e.g., Moonitz and Hutchins, seem to imply a close association between them.

Who are the accounting factists? Who treats social facts as things? Probably most of us at least to some extent. Yet the reverse may be more common, i.e., seeking things to serve as relevant facts. In practice this reversal often takes the form reifying the institutions for group action as things and treating individuals as stereotypical economic or contracting men with assumed characteristics. Chambers and his disciples certainly evaluate group actions in markets above individual preferences, and the mid-west KRISP and COMPUSTAT tape researchers associate great masses of gross market data with possible antecedent causes.

The currently popular agency approach would be included under Ritzer's factist paradigm. Agency advocates adopt a straightforward conflict model with some rigid behavioral assumptions about managerial behavior. This paradigm is in keeping with the attitudes of the sixties and seventies and the resulting "agency man" is an unpleasant subdivision of the tattered economic man: greedy, only marginally interested in his organization or in professional goals, adverse to work, and a prime believer in what's-in-it-for-me ethics. Researchers in this area have not been interested in the behavioral attributes of this creation and thus are not traditional behavioralists. In fact they are interested primarily in a market calculus for deciding which alternative accounting rules will be accepted. Therefore they are related to those who are interested in setting forth probabilistic models for losses and gains from information changes.[11]

The growth in behavioral studies in accounting has been phenomenal, but the value of the results may not be quite commensurate with the effort exerted. For this group belief is supported almost entirely by statistical measures. Their approach has been largely experimental, for it has been comparatively easy to find individuals and groups (college students, for example) to perform the required tasks. Often the sophistication of the methods employed has counted more than the confirmation or rejection of the hypothesis and the outpouring of doctoral dissertations has been limited only by access to market tapes and classroom subjects.[12]

My own orientation always has been with the subjectivists and my primary concern has been with values. This view sometimes has been confused with an outer-directed ethical paradigm, but in few cases have I shown preference for a given set of values. It is true that accountants select their host groups and by so doing express their own value systems. This selection of a host group thus helps direct the processes of the accounting profession. The profession then must face some basic questions. What symbols lead to what interpretations? Which events and which aspects of these events need to be recognized and symbolized? What is it that leads to the consideration of some events as transactions and others as candidates for oblivion? Accounting output—to repeat time and time again—comes in the form of metaphors, and it is the expected interpretation of these metaphors along with the selection of objectives that form the focus of the profession.

STERLING: RECALCULATING THE OUTPUTS

Sterling states:

> With minor exceptions, none of the outputs of an accounting system are *separately* verifiable. . . . Neither "net income" nor "total assets" are observable or separately measurable. . . . The auditing process is not a verification of the outputs; instead it is . . . a *recalculation* of the outputs and an "examination" of the underlying business documents in order to check on the accuracy or verity of the inputs.[13]

The symbolic output of the accounting system is verified through establishing belief that the defining operations for such accounting constructions have been adequately followed. But verifying whether these constructions lead to desirable decisions and actions is a more important matter for professional theorists. From a broad point of view the reactions of users to accounting reports constitutes the output of the accounting system, and it is these outputs that require occasional audit. Even here there are two levels of audit. Theorists are concerned primarily with whether the reified accounting systems are acceptable. Practitioners are concerned with whether the *particular* numbers and disclosures are consistent with the system's guidelines. The interest here is not with Sterling's philosophy (which now includes emphasis on ethics and values), but with his attitudes toward verification. Certainly it is difficult to *see* income or *touch* a liability, *feel* an expense or *hear* the harmony of revenues. It also is difficult to touch a quark or hear a black hole.

Apparently it is not prediction that marks the distinction between science and accounting in Sterling's world. Chemists mix all sorts of acids, bases and the like and predict outcomes. Businessmen mix all sorts of manufacturing and selling skills with various mechanical contrivances and predict outcomes. Accountants combine many kinds of control devices and predict the effects on human behavior. The design of a simple accounting system is based on a host of predictions about the net benefits of account classifications, processing methods, variance reporting, planning standards, etc.

The concern here is with the place of recalculation (and verification) of outputs. While the main task of science is to predict possible states of nature, scientists are also concerned with establishing the reliability of their predictions, and as a part of this task they are interested in the validity of the evidence available to support the predictive apparatus. The usual method of evaluating a predictive formula in science is to establish similar side conditions and replicate the situation. The outcome of these replications help establish confidence in the predictive process. The replications are experimental confirmation of the relationship among inputs and outputs, and often yield side benefits by establishing the scope and range of the predicting formulas.

In a broad sense replications are a form of audit. Presumably the original scientists check their own calculations and laboratory techniques on both inputs and outputs. Third parties may enter the process to check outputs and inputs of colleagues, associates and supervisors. This work is related to bookkeeping, clerical routines and internal auditing supervision. The trouble in auditing (and in some sciences) is that auditors cannot replicate the associations directly. It must be admitted that comparison with similar firms and with the same firm through time is a poor substitute for replication, but the objective is similar. What about outside auditors as recalculators of the outputs? Consider again the two common outputs of the accounting system: the measurement of potential for well-offness (assets) and periodic changes in such potentials (income). Verification in these complex situations may be considered on two levels. It is necessary to verify the particular reported symbols, e.g., amounts and sources of contributions, classes of equity rights, and it also is necessary to assess the adequacy of output symbols to do the job society expects them to do.

If an independent scientist is asked to audit the work of other scientists, he normally tries to replicate the experiment. If he is not able to replicate (as in astronomy), he does what accountant-auditors do. He checks the calculations. He looks for historical precedents and commonalities. Finally just as an auditor assesses the adequacy of particular accounting principles to see whether they are appropriate for user needs, the scientist auditor assesses the scientific methodology, the apparatus and the procedures to judge their adequacy to yield reliable scientific beliefs.

There is an important difference in degree here. A scientist performs a confirmatory experiment that is as near identical in all relevant aspects as can be arranged. Confirmation as in all replications and deductions always depends on analogy and the acceptance of a standard goodness of fit. This dependence on analogy should give pause for all those who feel that there is something exact about science or about the deductive process. The accountant is less fortunate. He tests the responses of his users for stability through repeated presentations (over time) and he sometimes infers their responses by comparing them with those of other individuals and groups. At this point, statistics and probability theory become especially useful.[14]

In summary it should be clear that scientific methods are appropriate for professional leaders to use when constructing principles to guide practitioners. In turn practitioners apply scientific methods when assessing the techniques for internal control and for the general adequacy of the accounting system to satisfy client needs. Clearly the output of the overall accounting process is being tested constantly for the actions it promotes or dissuades. These actions must be investigated for their desirability and this type of investigation requires a definite set of values. Actions in turn are selected by users after evaluating alternatives through their interpretations of accounting symbols and surrounding cues. Professional leaders must consider user actions and interpretations of these cues and symbols. In the longer run interpretation by users can be influenced by "educational" programs but in the shorter view they may be relatively stable. The result may be an uncomfortable professional lag in adopting new ideas.

NOTES

[1] Robert W. Friedrichs, *A Sociology of Sociology* (New York: The Free Press, 1970). This volume is an important contribution by any standard and has had considerable influence on my own thinking. The content is technical and demanding, but the author has kept sociological jargon to a minimum.

[2] Friedrichs' use of prophetic and priestly seems a little strange in view of the fact that old-testament prophets were more than mere seers who tried to foretell the future. They also set forth shortrun guidelines for moral living that were consistent with the broader view of right living with God.

[3] George Ritzer, *Sociology: A Multiple Paradigm Science* (Boston: Allyn and Bacon, Inc., 1975). My discussion throughout this essay owes much to Ritzer although I have found Friedrichs' philosophical grounding more interesting.

[4] Thomas S. Kuhn, *The Structure of Scientific Revolutions,* 2d ed. (Chicago: The University of Chicago Press, 1970).

[5] Ritzer, *op. cit.,* p. 100. Also: "To the social factist, the individual is seen as responding to such external forces as culture, norm, and role. . . . [T]he social behaviorist sees external stimuli determining the behavior of man. The fact that man *creates* his own world is either ignored or denied in both paradigms, but not by the symbolic interactionists" (*ibid.,* p. 101).

[6] Arnold M. Rose, "A Systematic Summary of Symbolic Interaction Theory," *Human Behavior and Social Processes: An Interactionist Approach* (Boston: Houghton Mifflin Company, 1962), pp. 3–19. (The assumptions and propositions given here also are quoted in Ritzer, *op. cit.,* pp 101–105.)

[7] Ritzer, *op. cit.,* p. 40.

[8] Robert Bierstedt, *The Social Order,* 3rd ed. (New York: McGraw-Hill, Inc., 1970), p. 9 (emphasis added). For a similar expression, see: Charles K. Warriner, "Groups are Real: A Reaffirmation," *American Sociological Review,* October 1956, pp. 549–54.

[9] A leader in this field has been Deirdre N. McCloskey. See his *The Rhetoric of Economics,* (Madison: University of Wisconsin Press, 1985). C. Edward Arrington is the most articulate exemplar in the field of accounting.

[10] Anthony M. Tinker. For an early effort, see "Towards a Political Economy of Accounting: An Empirical Illustration of the Cambridge Controversies" (1), 1980, pp. 147–160; and for a later more satiric indictment, see "Panglossian Accounting Theories: The Science of Apologising in Style" (2), 1988, pp. 165–190; both in *Accounting, Organizations and Society*.

[11] It would please me if some agency theorists would research the forces behind the market selection of accounting principles, e.g., the influence of the accounting profession on market participants. After all, professionalism and codes of ethics were developed to combat the immediate self-interest of market operators.

[12] Many recent issues of *The Accounting Review*, for example, contain not even one article without detailed tables of data and the usual paraphernalia of elementary statistics and probability. Much of the data, it should be added, are secondary. The *Journal of Accounting Research* also might qualify as an applied statistical journal with special attention to stock market tapes.

[13] Robert R. Sterling, "On Theory Construction and Verification," *The Accounting Review*, July 1970, pp. 450-1.

[14] The difference here is similar to the gap between relative frequency interpretations and subjective probability. To be useful, relative frequency must accept each event (e.g., toss of dice) as identical in *all pertinent* ways. Clearly, it is impossible to arrange all decision makers in this way so that further refinements are necessary to develop confidence in the assessment of subjective probabilities.

Kuhn: Scientific Accretions— Accounting Paradigms

My poor early assessment of Thomas S. Kuhn's contribution[1] (later sharply reversed) no doubt came from a long commitment to the belief that scientists (and other thinkers) try to incorporate new knowledge with the *least* disturbance to existing beliefs. In effect the incorporating attitude looks at the scientific enterprise as a process of accretion that continually changes but inevitably adds to a corpus of knowledge and in doing so modifies and temporarily corrects the existing body.[2] Humanists and related anti-scientific establishment groups are concerned with the lack of accretion in the humanities and consequently with the failure to sustain an increasing body of knowledge in these areas. Many parlor-jousters have attacked science by belittling the accretion hypothesis, arguing that science too has an aimless element and that accretion itself often is little more than a stockpiling of practical knowledge that soon must be discarded.

My first impression of Kuhn's contribution was that it was a humanist's masterful attempt to develop the thesis that science has no advantage from accumulation and no mystical formula for intellectual progress. Finally the emphasis on quantitative and qualitative situations seemed to be little more than applying Marxist terminology to the usual distinction between minor predictable changes and major breakthroughs that sometimes pop up during inquiry.

Furthermore at that time the then new sociological conflict theory advocated by C. Wright Mills and other followers of Hegel and Marx[3] was advanced as a replacement for the more coordinated functional framework utilized by Talcott Parsons and more traditional social scientists. Yet Social Darwinism and related strictures from Herbert Spencer

195

had emphasized conflict and the economist, Galbraith presented his own variation of the Hegelian dialectic known as countervailing power. Under the influence of William H. Spencer (not Herbert) I came to view the legal system as a device for resolving social conflicts and legal case summaries as histories of social conflicts that were important enough to require formal adjudication.[4]

In economics, the whole utility revolution and the sharp break from cost driven value determination is only three or four generations from the Austrians and Edgeworth. A couple of generations later this revolution was followed by the development of imperfect competition (J. M. Clark, Joan Robinson, Edward Chamberlin) and later by the Keynesian undermining of Say's Law. Later generations have obtained exciting intellectual stimulation from game theory and complex mathematical and computer refinements of existing theory.

Revolutions in related disciplines are numerous. Perhaps they are most obvious in physics with relativity and Kuhn's own template, quantum theory. Some biologists were overwhelmed by advances in molecular biology, and many traditional mathematicians were unable to follow the turns and twists necessary to move from traditional analysis to the newer more prestigious forms such as topology, algebraic geometry, logistics. Many early sociologists and psychologists were unable to move from a speculative framework to operational studies of behavior, to gestaltistic combinations of functionalism, to conflict models and to the application of phenomenology to a new existential sociology.[5]

Philosophers have been notorious for abandoning the old and adopting fresh orientations with all sorts of devious twists and turns. Readers are certainly aware of the deep cleavage between logicians along with positivists, analytical and language philosophers on the one hand the existentialists and phenomenologists and their relatives on the other. Historians must be counted among the foremost in the switching parade. Ranke—just give me the objective facts—still has followers. Toynbee, Spengler and others have opted for grand designs with assumed and actual conflicts working according to some inexorable plan. Croce, Ortega and many followers have emphasized subjective existential aspects and the need for each generation to rewrite its history to fit its own changing attitudes and objectives. Thus sharp breaks in Marxian qualitative patterns and a panorama of changing paradigms also are visible in the field of history.

Similar qualitative breaks in accounting may be less obvious, but they are numerous and may merit a second review. Recently a contingency and agency framework with highly developed techniques has been applied to some well known conflictual concepts. A decade or so ago emphasis shifted quickly to information theory with elegant mathematical and probabilistic models and to efficient market research with all sorts of semi-empirical studies that made use of computerized market data to support an untold number of hypotheses about the effectiveness of accounting data. For a century or so businessmen, accountants and economists were aware that information was not costless (e.g., telephone bills and compliance reports) and that market participants tried to incorporate new information rapidly into their activities. The accompanying emphasis on uncertainty was an expansion of an ancient idea through the application of newer probability and decision techniques.[6]

A decade of so earlier some accounting academicians emphasized that their output should influence real people with specific objectives. This insight encouraged a spate of behavioral studies and a determined search for empirical evidence to support hypotheses and help predict user responses. This development should not have surprised older heads, but the sophistication of the statistical methods left traditional accountants with insufficient technical knowledge to contribute to the movement or even understand its research reports. Meanwhile intellectual developments in the behavioral sciences added prestige and fitted into possible solutions for traditional problems in budgeting, auditing, predictive measures, etc.

The period immediately preceding the behavioral and empirical revolution was marked by a gradual but amazing development of managerial accounting. The newer organization theory emphasized the entity as an organization and accountants turned from the well-established entity accounting of Paton with its emphasis on the equity holders to the need for efficient internal management. In turn more effective management and wider information should aid all cooperating and contending parties. In fact a general business-administration orientation was emphasized by Dutch accountants from early in the century. Included were Limperg and others who based their accounting principles directly on the practices of good business administrators and looked to these practices for legitimacy and support for their professional pronouncements.[7]

It is interesting to note that the Paton version of entity theory was something of a revolution from the then dominant foundations provided by proprietary theorists with their simplistic (later rejuvenated) assumption that management's primary goal is to maximize the value of current residual proprietary interests. The Paton version of entity accounting stresses useful information to all *financial* parties at interest. Managers are to be monitored through various measures (including income reports) and are shifted about, along with all other economic resources through the marginal process. Managers are in effect administrators who coordinate the interests of all equity holders. Accountants listen to managers because management's goals are surrogates that represent the desires of various equity interests in acceptable proportions. Unfortunately it is not obvious that maximizing the present market value of residual (or even all) securities does in fact work to the benefit of *any* (not to mention *all*) parties with equity rights in the organization. It is even less obvious that such a simple maximizing rule benefits outside social groups.

One of the characteristics of such changes is that professional prestige usually is correlated with the acceptance of new scientific and methodological structures. Researchers who use the newer frameworks and techniques become the darlings of prevailing peer groups and new intellectual elites are established. Perhaps the best description of the process is given by Friedrichs in his comments on Kuhn's contribution. Ponder the following extensive quotations in relation to recent revolutions in accounting.

> [The new framework] is typically accompanied by its acquiring a recognized place in the larger scientific [accounting] community and curriculum [by] developing its own journals. . . . [T]he common base is made clear in textbooks, with the history of the substantive area appearing to have led inevitably to the present paradigm. Those few who are unable to accept the consensus thus achieved are written off. . . . The few who would still operate in terms of other paradigms are simply ignored. . . . Such science progresses rapidly because it is not distracted by alternative frames. It narrows the range of meaningful problems. . . . [P]rofessional education takes place, typically, within the confines of a single paradigm. The structures that guide him are simply the way his science *is*. He learns them as he learns his mother language and the norms of his personal life: by internalizing as "real" the "reality" of those about him. The "rules" he lives by are raised to the level of consciousness only if and when the paradigm itself is shaken (p. 5).
>
> [H]e did not originally accept the paradigm on the basis of evidence but rather on the authority of text and teacher. . . . [T]he practicing scientist finds the speculative nature of philosophy of little interest. Those who have dabbled in it . . . almost invariably lose status among their peers . . . (pp. 6, 7).

Not unexpectedly, those who contribute most . . . to the . . . new paradigm are apt to be [the] relatively young . . . whose training and careers to that date have escaped the rigidities that were normal to socialization within the traditional paradigmatic framework. . . . Some will not be converted; they will simply be by-passed. . . . [T]he revolution does not so much seek any direct conversion of the mass membership . . . but rather tries to capture those key figures who are the "gatekeepers" to the texts that guide the younger generation through the discipline's rites of passage. . . . [T]he text plays a role much more equivalent to "holy writ" . . . (p. 7).

Hypotheses that might have been rejected at other times as extravagant are condoned; the air—professional meetings, the journals—is filled with dissent and rancor. . . . Simple "proof" is insufficient because those adhering to the traditional paradigm and those supporting the new one use their separate paradigms in that paradigm's defense. . . . [A}fter a revolutionary episode, the scientist must be re-educated in terms of a new image of the world (pp. 8-9).

[W]hen the textbooks are re-written in terms of the new gestalt, the "history" of the discipline—insofar as it appears in the texts at all—is rewritten as well. There is no partisan interest involved. The writers themselves now see the discipline's history *through* the new paradigm. . . . No wonder, then, that science appears even to those most intimately involved as linear and cumulative. With each revolution the discipline re-draws its family tree (pp. 9–10).[8]

At a later point we will return to the controversy about the cumulative body of scientific knowledge and the wandering quality of humanistic thought. At this point attention is directed to some dominant paradigms in accounting thought. Students in finance, industrial engineering and management should have no difficulty in applying the Kuhn-Friedrichs criteria to their own fields. Scholars who do not adopt efficient market techniques and the capital asset pricing models are simply disregarded. Traditional industrial engineers and production professors found it necessary to adopt the research tools and language of operations research. Traditional management professors were forced to beat the drums for decentralization, bottoms-up organization and the divorcement of top management from functional areas and to adopt the research paradigm of management science.

Attacks on the traditional *income* paradigm derived from the on going and successful revolution in psychology, sociology and philosophy itself—the existential demand for emphasis on specific and contextual explanations and the substitution of individual measures for traditional general-purpose measures. In America the rapid shift from varieties of positivism to the functionalism of systems theory and then to existentialism and phenomenology directed attention away from such broad concepts as income to smaller centers of performance and accountability. In part this movement may have been accelerated by rebellious members of the new left, but there is evidence that its influence is far wider. In religion, for example, there seems to be a definite turning from the concept of community, social control and individual (personal) salvation to the existentialist teachings of Tillich, Buber, and Berdyaev that emphasize the personal therapeutic aspects of the religious experience.[9]

In accounting the renewed interest in the "limited indexical," the situational, the specific, the contextual and the resulting trend toward specialized reports was accelerated by the fantastic development of modern computers. These sophisticated inventions make it possible to provide more detailed contextual information for specific individuals and for specific decisions. While there is no question that many possibilities remain undeveloped, these particularized reports still have not displaced the continued use of the old-fashioned broader measures. Overall income measures still are with us in spite of solemn warnings (from some brilliant people) that income reports would be obsolete by 1980. Average returns on aggregated decisions still are being calculated, and aggregations such as variances, markups and stock-turns still are used to help assess whether overall plans are being followed. Clearly some aggregation is unavoidable, but so far the accounting profession has not established optimum standards for specific activities or criteria for adjusting to dynamic social changes.

Return now to Kuhn's comments on the tendency to "by-pass" scholars who use older paradigms without attempting to convert them. Consider the field of economics. Despite the broad view of Pareto and Austrian attitudes toward general equilibrium, Anglo-Saxon economics took a narrow turn with Marshall and his attempt to save the early English tradition by combining its cost features with marginal utility analysis. American universities of the early twentieth century emphasized marginal utility and (except for Fisher) pretty much neglected the broader features of general equilibrium economics. American institutional economists, following the German Historical School, were tenacious in teaching a broader historical and sociological view, but they too were shunted aside by the newer paradigm of marginal analysis and the economics of the individual firm. Certainly the newer school of micro-economics was more contextual and fitted better into the growing study of business, which by its nature deals in large part with smaller decision making units. The teachings of institutional economists (Veblen, Commons, Ely, Mitchell) were swept aside, and only lately has the empirical aspect been expanded by some able workers; e.g., Kuznets, Katona, Copeland and groups at the National Bureau and the Brookings Institute.

ABORTIVE ACCOUNTING VIEWS

DR Scott was an acknowledged disciple of Veblen and he too was swept away by the views of more technical accountants and the more analytical approach of Paton and others who follow neo-classical economics. So complete was Scott's burial that only a handful of disciples were developed and, most of them earned their livelihood by teaching and researching in traditional universities.[10]

While Scott was an acknowledged disciple of Veblen whose lead he followed in taking a broad sociological view, he also was in the middle of a more comprehensive stream set by John R. Commons with emphasis on the ethical aspects of economics, accounting, social statistics and the legal process. Except for occasional works (notably by Odmark) Scott's emphasis on the ethical dimension of accounting went largely unheeded and no major change of direction emerged. In fact Scott was largely forgotten or pointed out to graduate students as an example of what accountants may become when they dabble in related fields.[11]

Scott and some of his disciples indirectly warned the profession about the unrestrained acceptance of a cooperative functional model. Members of a social organization have both cooperating and conflicting goals, and this pluralism puts pressure on the accounting profession to select and reject various groups and to consider the provision of alternative kinds of information. Like law makers and professional groups elsewhere, their guidelines tend to help certain participants and restrain or actually harm others. The profession thus must decide who is important and accept a functional perspective with regard to them. Excluded groups may see themselves as outsiders and withdraw from the organization; in so doing they make the organization more homogeneous and its goals more consistent. Others may continue in the organization and continue to engender conflict from within. Scott certainly failed to start an interdisciplinary revolution, and he was shunted aside by many who should have adopted his recommendations. Scott had hoped to educate ethical managers who with the help of accounting and statistics would preserve a degree of equity among consumers, owners, creditors, laborers and the general public.[12] A half century later, many management teachers adopted a similar view and advocated a new-age manager to perform these functions. No longer were managers to be preoccupied with maximizing shareholders' interests. Instead they were indoctrinated to preside graciously over extractions from customers through fair pricing and at the same time treat workers as human beings, take care of suppliers, protect the public and preserve the environment.

A second example of an abortive paradigm is found in Vatter's interesting fund theory. The fund approach may have been too similar to the traditional entity theory to constitute a successful revolution. In any case the fund theory with its retreat from personal overtones is directly opposed to the more successful revolution that emphasized behavioral studies of user needs and satisfactions.

Vatter, however, was a member of the more successful anti-income revolution, and his rigid stance influenced enthusiastic followers to assert that the income concept already was obsolete. The shift to a required funds-flow report was a first step in the revolution, but miserable results in the real estate and other fields slowed expansion. The accompanying retreat from working-capital tests for income realization was hardly a revolution for it had been advocated by many economists (Hayek, Hicks) and by some accountants (MacNeal, Sterling, Solomons). These anti-realization authorities insisted that mixing liquidity with what is essentially a concept of value added and dividing the cash flow into return *of* capital and return *on* capital was an unnecessary allocation.

The price-level controversy has been only a mild revolution. Price-level accounting has been a hard-sell in America, where inflation is a worrisome but semi-controlled factor. Clearly the movement had become a bona fide revolution in many countries after the twentieth century wars. In Germany the need was obvious and intellectual momentum developed under the leadership of Fritz Schmidt and many Dutch and French accountants. In America a number of Schmidt's articles were published in early *Accounting Reviews* and the crusade was taken up by George Husband, Henry W. Sweeney and even earlier by Paton. The great depression had settled on America by the time most publications in this area became available and with depressed prices writedowns (not writeups) became popular. Since World War II, however, serious inflation in developed countries along with dramatic movements in Indonesia, Latin America and most third-world nations revived interest and the

American Institute of Certified Public Accountants provided weak guidelines for seriously affected enterprises. (Editor's Note: Later the Financial Accounting Standards Board provided more extensive guidelines that for a time required large companies to give supplementary disclosures on inflation effects and now merely encourages the providing of such data.)

Near and distant cousins of price-level recommendations included arguments for specific replacement costs, current entrance costs and exit values. Many early accountants were influenced by technological changes but only a few wished to abandon historical costs in favor of replacement costs. It was argued that in a fast-moving technical society no businessman replaces his assets in kind and that therefore such costs are not relevant. LIFO was a mildly successful minor revolution, but the possibility of not replacing in kind was a common negative argument. The Dutch accountants created the term "economic replacement" to indicate that it was *economic* capacity rather than physical capacity that should be maintained, and Oscar Nelson pointed out that current entrance values of used assets include estimates of obsolescence. These considerations increased the popularity of current entrance costs, but this variation failed to reach revolutionary proportions.

Those who favored LIFO of course were close kin to advocates of using replacement costs for all assets. Many argued that the worst offenders in times of changing prices were inventories and fixed assets, and actively advocated LIFO to modify inventories and appraisal techniques to keep fixed assets and capital consumption charges in line with current economic conditions. Others felt that such recommendations were makeshift and held out for more complete adjustment through frequent application of various cost indexes. The recommendations of Sprouse and Moonitz helped to clarify this position but they too fell far short of creating a professional revolution.

The Chambers approach is a minor variation of entrance-cost and price-level models, but even the enthusiasm of its founder and an untold number of followers has been unable to elevate the doctrine to revolutionary level. For a time the journals were filled with discussions of exit values and the relevance of CCE's, and traditional entrance-cost contributions were in danger of being ignored. Moreover, as predicted, a new journal (*Abacus*) was founded and for a time was largely devoted to the cause.

The Chamberian doctrine is traditional even though it is unequivocally wedded to the use of markets rather than to more direct entrepreneurial estimates for filtering and incorporating new information. Yet it has been difficult to convince old-timers that exit values are essential parts of the income-determining or decision-making process for concerns with continuing operations. To many the going-concern decision partitions events into these relevant for continued operations and those no longer relevant except when the decision to abandon becomes pertinent. Over-zealous claims that the market-determined CCE's do away with "arbitrary" allocations and are not themselves allocations also failed to convince traditionalists. A belated insight that emphasized the high co-variance between entrance and exit values reduced the revolutionary zeal. Very little empirical or behavioral research actually resulted from the exit paradigm, but some interesting theoretical articles and stirring addresses were produced.

For the accounting profession the recent emphasis on efficient-market studies qualifies as a major revolution, and for some time researchers in other areas of accounting and finance were simply ignored or passed by. Immense prestige passed to the University of Chicago, where the ideas were largely conceived by students of finance. The *Journal of Accounting Research* by concentrating on such studies gained enormous prestige and carried the banner for the new paradigm.

Some accountants—including this one—were at that time interested in developing a behavioral framework for formulating accounting theory. The behavioral recommendation hoped to employ all research strategies common to the broader behavioral sciences, e.g., simple surveys, group dynamics, case studies and of course behavior of people in market contexts. In general these studies are empirical, but early supporters wished to include value systems as well as methods for evaluating systems. Decision theory by necessity includes values and ethical concepts and must be a part of behavioral research. Such comparative studies may not be scientific in the narrow sense, or empirical in the traditional usage, or positivist in any of its numerous forms, but they are certainly operational and worthy of serious intellectual effort. Without a value dimension accountants find it impossible to evaluate an accounting system, recommend a given strategy, or make any decision whatever. By 1985 *The Accounting Review* was concerned primarily with empirical work, and each article now contains numerous statistical tables and copious references to elementary probabilistic concepts. Unfortunately little research has been concerned with values, and some sponsored committee work has been unrewarding at best.

Consider now business and accounting training at some important universities. The Chicago School took a scientific framework and came up with an empirical orientation and a strong positivist base. Unlike Harvard with its amorphous situational case studies with ambiguous and indeterminate outcomes, Chicago professors held consistently that business is grounded in scientific inquiry and that to be worthy of university effort business problems must be amenable to rigorous structuring and reasonably predictable outcomes. Economics became the model for the underlying paradigm, and at one time the business school at Chicago contained within it one of the better economics departments in America. Friedman and Stigler from pure economics were a major influence, and their emphasis on positivist interpretations and structures were adopted. Thurstone and Mead served as convenient cornerstones for emphasis on organizations and behavioral studies. There is an irony here for Friedman: while espousing a narrow positivist view, he has not been at all bashful about policy directives.

Thus Chicago was a prime candidate for emphasis on empirical matters when the newer developments in computer technology and subjective probability arrived. The torrent of market and corporate data was overwhelming and crying for analysis. The data formed a gold mine for accountants who are supposed to "account for" various outcomes in terms of antecedents and causative factors. Conjectures and firm hypotheses followed in droves and *JAR* has been filled with market-computer analyses that attempt to discover and explain connections among events—usually information inputs and market variations.[13]

We are not concerned here that a study of such data might not be empirical in a strict sense. However the usual pattern of empirical research: conjectures → hypotheses → data → data manipulation → conclusion is modified, for the data are available and the research effort often becomes one of finding hypotheses for which the data may be relevant. All sorts of relationships have been suggested, but most of them attempt to relate actual price movements in a causative manner to identified inputs from the accounting domain. The outpouring of these research studies was tremendous and provided bases for dissertations throughout the land. The popularity of this accounting revolution was enhanced by the abundance of data and the obvious lack of previous information in this area. This area had been a veritable wasteland with support for accounting theories coming primarily from speculations about behavior.

One of the more interesting revolutions in accounting has been in the area of information theory and linguistic analysis. Accountants had long been aware that information is not costless and accounting itself, along with legal fees, advertising bills, computers and computer maintenance require substantial resources. Moreover accounting, in the popular cliché, is the "language of business"—the medium through which information normally is transmitted.[14]

The materials for the information revolution had been around for some time and the revolution itself was an extension of the new area of management science. Certainly the need for decision making is no big deal; everyone engages in it on a daily basis. The concept of uncertainty is known to all and probability theory in non-rigorous forms is an important part of all living. The need to find alternatives and to cast about for new possibilities are common features of simple living.[15]

One might have expected the information revolution at some point to take a behavioral or at least an empirical turn, but in fact the development under Butterworth, Feltham, Demski and their followers ran to mathematical model making with modifications to incorporate modern probability theory. In this respect their output has been more in the tradition of early Mattessich with its emphasis on meta-models and abstraction from the particular applications that accountants need to make. This trend is toward an older management science that emphasizes abstraction from the "real" world and the construction of simulated models. This tendency, it should be emphasized, is the very antithesis of the phenomenological and pragmatical emphasis on the contextual and the particular, e.g., deconstructionism.

Businessmen and accountants soon discovered that not all people at all times behave in an idealized rational pattern and that complicated models of human nature often are gratuitous and sometimes useless. This helped to undermine the determinism hidden in some influential and elegant models of behavior and permitted consideration of various kinds of indecision and dysfunction. The older stimulus-response paradigm, even with probabilistic responses, already had been improved by gestaltistic construction from ambiguous signals. The newer informationalists may or may not have improved understanding by "saying it differently": they replaced stimuli with ambiguous messages and treated responses as decisions for selecting possible actions. The phenomenologists were quick to use irrationality as a partial rationale for their indexical procedures that depend more directly on contextual and situational explanations. General models depend on uniformity in the attitudes, values and language habits of their subjects. The usual assumption has been that they are consistently rational in choosing actions that will maximize their feeling of well-being—a non-operational assumption that can be applied to all choices and therefore is an observational [?] tautology. As non-positivists are quick to point out, value systems must be taken as problematical and actions may or may not be consistent with stated or accepted values.

The agency-contract paradigm provides an interesting format for structuring costs of certain organizational conflicts, but the emphasis has not been in this direction. Expositors have devoted attention primarily to the problems of accounting rule selection. The latter emphasis is unfortunate for the relevant theory is reduced to little more than a preference assertion that accounting rules are selected by markets through individual self-interest bargaining. At the extreme this recommendation leaves no room for professional influence (and ethical evaluation) and resolves the important question of "who counts" by simple market or market-like activities carried on by greedy actors.

This set of assumptions about the nature of man and the hidden grace of self-interest has no need for professional ethics, and the accounting profession becomes a spineless creature devoted to the execution of market directives with even less influence than capitalist entrepreneurs who at least have some freedom to accept or reject market directives. These matters are discussed in other essays and the emphasis here is on the costs of pluralism and non-homogeneous organizational objectives.

It is clear that the new agency (contractual) paradigm can be viewed as a problem in costing dysfunctional elements of an organization. Sociologists have long been concerned with the traumatic costs to individuals of social requirements that bring about impossible stress and anomie. Psychiatrists have been more interested in the individual and his own sacrifices than in the costs to society of having untold numbers of social misfits who are simply unable to pursue the objectives that society desires.

Apparently agency theorists are in accord with psychiatrists on the makeup of the agency man. This successor to the economic man apparently feels no guilt about his own greed, his failure to accept group values, his lack of desire to work and his lack of compassion for others. He may indeed be the typical man of the twentieth century, but, so far at least, agency accountants have presented little positive evidence to support this hypothesis.

Psychologists and sociologists have been concerned with social misfits and the crimes and other deviances that arise when individuals fail to internalize the values of their dominant social groups. Political scientists have long commented on the possible costs and inefficiencies of democratic governments when compared with totalitarian regimes. So far no one has conducted detailed studies of the possible costs of pluralism either in small areas or in wide governing bodies. Such studies should be interesting in spite of difficulties such as trying to decide which sets of values are to be used to measure the sacrifices. Certainly there is no reason to feel that the sacrifices of each dissident group should be equal to the sacrifices of society or of any other group.[16]

Many older generation accountants more or less accepted the assumptions of the agency paradigm. Paton and many early organization theorists assumed that the "organization" simply bought and paid for conformance from all members. Those who observed strikes and other facets of labor relations were certainly aware of the cost-benefit balance between the cost of providing better working conditions (including higher wages) and the benefits from having a cooperative and loyal working force. The values of balancing worker morale and cooperative effort are buried in a myriad of other factors but show up in the earnings reports and occasionally in goodwill valuations. In a wider context current Japanese managers are now high-lighting the possible costs of the adversarial framework of labor and management in American business.

Make no mistake, genuine costs are connected with pluralism and dysfunction. Yet there may be advantages that are equally difficult to measure. The benefits to members from having more freedom must be considered even in such prosaic areas as decentralization where the organization also may receive benefits from better goal integration and less diversity cost. At one limit the organization might simply abandon its own goals and accept the unguided goals of its members. The required heterogeneity of constituent goals means that this anarchistic solution seldom is found in a capitalist organization, but cooperatives may have enough goal congruence to encourage this informal approach.

It should be clear that all research structures must contain various assumptions and many unproved relationships. In any case an *avant garde* group should not be criticized because they must accept human limitations and make assumptions about the human *natures* of their actions. Objections already have been raised about some agency assumptions. For example, must all agents be relentlessly selfish self-maximizers? This assumption of unremitting conflict is consistent with the anti-functional (confrontational) attitudes of many sociologists since C. Wright Mills and may be appropriate for all bargaining and market models.

Return now to functionalism and conflictual perspectives and consider the charge that accountants are apologists for the *status quo*. Early sociologists often were considered to be apologists for existing institutions, but later they have been associated more often with protest and anti-establishment views. In terms of the cooperative-conflictive controversy the accounting profession is on the side of functionalism and has recognized the need to reconcile conflicting forces. From a broad point of view any service activity tends to further the *status quo* through the selection of a stable (and often prosperous) host group whose interests it wishes to promote.

Limperg perhaps was the most positive advocate and clearest expositor of the functional nature of accounting. He saw the need for trustworthy information amid a myriad of distracting particulars. His concept of the profession was that of a functional organ of the social order with specific and well-defined duties to perform. Most accountants of the Western World hold similar views and consider organizations as primarily cooperative arrangements set up to accomplish common goals. Major conflicting parties, it is assumed, simply withdraw or resolve their important conflicts in setting up the organization and hiring managers to mold the remaining diverse interests into homogeneous organizations. The accounting function typically has been to furnish information so that managers can operate efficiently in the interests of all equity participants and equity holders in turn can judge the performance of management in directing resources toward objectives.

Return again to the broader question of knowledge accretion in science the arts and accounting. Certainly humanists have not been overwhelmed by the accretion of their own knowledge. Even before Kuhn some historians were not so sure about the cumulative effect of scientific knowledge and felt more comfortable with the weaving around that an intuitive perspective implies. Past centuries have been filled with the ghosts of abandoned scientific theories and all scientists become experts at changing their beliefs. In spite of valiant efforts to integrate the new into the old, few seventeenth-century scientific beliefs remain intact!

It should be obvious that accounting is a *social* activity in that its general concepts and specialized contributions are designed to inform and influence human beings. For practical work the accountant can abandon most physical analogs and models that are removed from human beings in social interaction. Certain non-personal aspects, e.g., arithmetic, recording devices and measuring instruments still remain; but their relevance is more indirect. These non-personal features of course are related to accounting, and must be reviewed from time to time and be treated as problematic. The point here is that simply being a human may provide some insight about the needs and behaviors of other human beings and that an accountant should not be reluctant to take advantage of his human perspectives. In the hard sciences it may be difficult to empathize with neutrons and similar constructions, but it should be less difficult to identify with other human beings and to turn any resulting insights to professional advantage. Humanists follow this path, and like scientists (and everyone else) find it impossible to do otherwise. In any case scientists cannot be certain that only cumulative effects—the accretional residues—lead to stability and to confident prediction.

The case against crude physical models to represent human interaction is not difficult to make. Modern sociologists demand more and are often unhappy as well with biological models for social interaction. Sociologists of the existential persuasion are particularly unhappy with Spencer's biological representation of the social order even though both Darwin and Spencer employ conflict models. What then should be the model of choice? Answers are vague. The *avant garde* stricture to treat *everything* as problematic is useful but not very helpful. The use of language as the model sometimes places the cart at the wrong end, for language itself is the result of needs to communicate in social interaction and to some extent has a physical and biological base. Even Chomsky, who is sometimes advanced as the model for phenomenological linguistics, feels that only a part of language can be explained by the social aspects of human interaction and that a "deeper" need is buried somewhere in the human condition. It certainly is true that man is a social animal, but he also is a biological animal and in part at least a physical creature.

Our superficial survey of some accounting developments does not indicate an overwhelming synergistic explosion from the cumulative effects of knowledge and research. The accounting profession certainly is a humanistic endeavor and the field has broadened to produce a fabric with structure and design. Agency theory examines the intuition that goals need not be consistent much less congruent. Information research expands the older view that the marginal utility of a dollar should be equal in all directions (including expenditures for information) to include probabilistic judgments. Aggregation research has furthered our scanty knowledge that something may be lost and something may be gained by abstraction and by combination. Market studies have reminded us that there are non-accounting and non-managerial sources of information and that markets can provide new information for accounting judgments.

These advances clearly are important accretions but it still is difficult to conclude that they are revolutionary. The band-wagon effect from enthusiastic journal editors and over-zealous researchers often gives the impression of seething revolutions. Remember however that some excellent accounting scholars confidently predicted in the fifties that income accounting would be obsolete in thirty years. At times even the best scholars become poor predictors and succumb to revolutionary zeal.

My own preference throughout the years has been in the direction of functionalism and cooperation rather than dysfunction and conflict. My interest turned first to the legal system as an important institution for resolving interpersonal conflicts and then turned to political institutions as the major process for adjusting contending interests. From this point of view there is no better place to study the conflictual side of social history than through the political process and the decisions of its courts. This attitude certainly did not prevail in the early years for sociologists (and political scientists) often were functionalist and education for the legal profession moved regrettably toward the technical aspects needed for the practice of law. Lawyers dealt daily with specific conflicts and a major objective became consistency in the body of common law—not contributions to abstract theory.

The years of World War II channelled much intellectual effort into conflict situations, and exhaustive study of war games high-lighted the mechanics and processes of goal accomplishment in a context of adverse interests. Morgenstern and Von Neumann started their own revolution by formalizing game theory and emphasizing thinking opponents who respond to competitive strategies. This effort was impressive as well as esoteric. Game theory along with the foundation from duopoly theory provided an important thrust to abandon the cooperative framework that is the basis for functionalism.

On the other side institutional economics provided a strong force in the direction of cooperation. Commons held that a cooperative attitude was more descriptive of social history with competition and conflict being a late and temporary condition that arose primarily from the institution of private property. Moreover in Commons' view, man was considerably more socially conditioned than portrayed by classical economists and indeed was far from the rational decision maker that along with greed have been the chief defining properties of the classical economic man.

The Carnegie group, with a middle-of-the road approach exerted tremendous influence on the development of the new field of organization theory—a study of group behavior in limited contexts—and thus on accounting theory. They argue that generally entirely too much sharing of organizational goals exists for unmodified use of strict conflict and game-theory models. Therefore some emphasis is placed on less aggressive members so that potential conflicts can be headed off or ameliorated by payments and perquisites or by compromising until goals are shared enough to generate some degree of organizational homogeneity. It may be argued that this approach (along with much of modern economics) is indeed a "conflict sociology" that applies to all interpersonal relations. The important practical problem is how to reduce such tensions to the extent necessary to carry on the world's work. An important methodological problem is how best to model social situations that require cooperation even when goals are only partially internalized. There are costs for failure to achieve goal congruence, and modern accounting theory may be able to model such conflicts and reveal such costs.

My own approach has been to emphasize cooperative aspects in the functionalist tradition. No one questions the presence of dysfunction and much auditing attention is designed to reduce such activities. Some degree of homogeneity is attained by many means and buying off dissidents certainly is important. Dissenters may be forced out of the organization by group pressures and through mobility, e.g., selling and buying equity interests. Members coming in tend to share goals. Those going out may have found it difficult to internalize and make necessary compromises. Mobility of this sort tends to reduce pluralism and encourage the use of a cooperative (functional) methodology. Persuasion also is an important tool for inducing homogeneity and untold man hours are devoted to reducing dysfunction by encouraging "team spirit" and deeper feelings of belonging. The success of such programs is itself an interesting subject, and it is beyond understanding that the accounting profession and logical theorists have paid so little attention to the fields of dysfunction, persuasion and opinion. Opinions necessarily involve predictions. Predictions require evaluations. Auditors are not evaluators! Recently they have been paying dearly!

NOTES

[1] *The Structure of Scientific Revolutions,* 2d ed. (Chicago: The University of Chicago Press, 1970).

[2] This attitude is too widespread to require documentation. My own attitude was taken from William James, *Essays in Pragmatism,* ed. Alburey Castell (New York: Hafner Publishing Co., Inc., 1948).), *passim,* esp. "What Pragmatism Means" (pp.141–158); this "essay" is Lecture II in James' earlier *Pragmatism: A*

New Name for Some Old Ways of Thinking (New York: Longmans, Green, and Co., 1907), pp.43–81. Accretion sometimes is ambiguous. Some argue that the humanities only add to their bodies of knowledge while the sciences not only accrete—they develop.

[3] See Mills, *The Sociological Imagination* (New York: Oxford University Press, Inc., 1959); and John Rex, *Key Problems of Sociological Theory* (London: Routledge and Kegan Paul Ltd., 1961).

[4] Even Kuhn's repeated use of the term paradigm added to my negative reaction. While this term may be of limited help to distinguish between physical and conceptual models, this advantage is small indeed in light of the numerous substitutes available, e.g., framework, system, model, perspective, orientation, theory, representation and analogy. To complicate manners the term paradigm had a well established usage in grammar, where its usage is precise. Apparently its use in philosophy can be traced at least as far back as Kant and in religion to models of goodness associated with Jesus.

[5] So far the results of combining sociology with the phenomenology of Husserl, Heidegger, Schutz, Sartre and others seem to be meager, although the discussions now are voluminous. For a detailed and enthusiastic polemic, see Paul Filmer, Michael Phillipson, David Silverman and David Walsh, *New Directions in Sociological Theory* (London: Collier-Macmillan Publishers, 1972), esp. Chapters 5 and 6. Consider also Harold Garfinkel, *Studies in Ethnomethodology* (Englewood Cliffs: Prentice-Hall, Inc., 1967).

[6] The requirements of some models for estimating entire probability distributions doubtless taxes the abilities of businessmen. Consider probable responses to requests for probabilities for "best possible," "worst possible" and "most probable" outcomes. It is difficult to believe that decision scientists would foster such ambiguity. (Incidently Trygve Haavelmo in 1989 received a nobel prize for his 1941 introduction of probabilistic concepts into econometrics.) It probably is safe to say that doctoral candidates in accounting now need far more competence in statistics than in traditional accounting. Some recent dissertations seem to have used no accounting at all except for some borrowed accounting terminology.

[7] Neil H. Jacoby points out that when he first encountered a school of business (1930's) the analytical subject matter was largely economics and accounting. It is my own impression that behavioral science now is a full partner with economics and that probability-statistics can now claim equality with accounting. See Jacoby, *Corporate Power and Social Responsibility* (New York: The Macmillan Publishing Co., Inc., 1973, 1976), p. 61.

[8] Robert W. Friedrichs, *A Sociology of Sociology* (New York: The Free Press, 1970), pages as noted. Many of my generation in accounting became:

"The more mature—although they may [have] contribute[d] significantly to the discovery of the anomalies that set the revolutionary process in motion—have been wed much too successfully and long to the earlier model" (p. 7).

[9] In a simpler time the recognized functions of religion often were classified into several areas with therapy for the individual being only one. The sociological perspective that studied religion as a device for facilitating social living and control still has a large following. Some scholars continue to emphasize fear of death and promises of after life as devices to reinforce social control and help relocate individual priorities.

At times the individual therapeutic aspect of religion seems to conflict with the objective of saving (controlling?) groups but perhaps this difference is a matter of simple tactics. Consider the following comment on psychiatry—a related therapeutic profession. "A . . . 'peculiarity' of psychoanalytic practice is that it has traditionally refused to have anything to do with the welfare of any one else in the patient's milieu. . . . He [the therapist] does not try to represent the interests of his patient and society at . . . the same time. . . . [that] he gains much of his power to help the individual by openly allying himself with the patient as over against the demands of society." David C. McClelland, *The Roots of Consciousness* (Princeton: D. Van Nostrand Company, Inc., 1964), p. 124.

The tremendous surge in popularity of analysis undoubtedly influenced the new left and its compulsive attempts to be non-judgmental no matter how heinous an individual's actions or how deviant his behavior. There is evidence that the Berkeley dissidents of the 60's were influenced by IWW slogans and anarchist propaganda, but it still is my belief that psychiatric attitudes afforded important intellectual support.

[10] Among the more unreconstructed accountants have been Vernon E. Odmark, Lawrence J. Benninger, Orace Johnson, Robert L. Kvam and Robert C. Culpepper.

[11] It is true that some of Scott's publications on technical bookkeeping and accounting were not distinguished and that even his *The Cultural Significance of Accounts* lacked sharp focus. Yet most of his broader work was first rate, his articles in interdisciplinary journals were well received, and his work on accounting principles ("The Tentative Statement of Principles," *The Accounting Review,* September 1937, pp. 296–303) is among the best to date.

[12] By the Eighties, Scott's puritanical views on the profession's ethical duties were treated as historical relics, and were replaced by a positivist contagion that uses self-interest struggles in markets and contract bargaining to settle ethical problems and reduce professional influence to an ethical cipher.

[13] The Rochester variation—again with its own journal—sought to limit an understandable empiricism to a narrow and simplistic version of positivism that also is based on the market-bargaining process.

[14] A study of language, along with its usage and meanings in individual contextual situations is a necessary part of understanding the accountant's "reality." Modern phenomenologists go beyond the traditional study of semantics and syntax and insist that in all social situations (including business organization) the formal and informal languages be treated as problematic and not taken as a structural constant. A problematic treatment of language in a business context clearly includes accounting—its structures, meanings and contextual usage. Emphasis is more on how to express the business *Gestalten* and less on traditional ways of presenting facts. See especially, Paul Filmer, Michael Phillipson, David Silverman and David Walsh, *op. cit.,* pp. 140-7, 232. Problematic language in social research also is given high priority by Ethnomethodologists. See for example Harold Garfinkel, *op. cit.*

It is unfortunate that the concept of noise has not been explicitly expanded into the more general concept of problematic interaction. Advocates of hermeneutic understanding remain uncomfortable with the engineering emphasis on noise and indeed on information itself.

[15] It is true that the new approach makes use of modern techniques, e.g., subjective assessments, certainty equivalents, mathematical programming and computers, but the input factors themselves were well known. How many times must a deserving business student be subjected to the wonders of payoff matrices, inventory models, queuing sequences, learning curves, entropy diffusion measures and zero-sum games? Many graduate courses in management became little more than elementary college mathematics with the examples and problems changed from physics to business situations.

[16] In a similar way accountants have no reason to insist that the cost to one party in a transaction always should equal the benefit to other parties. One of the consequences of a common monetary measure is that for some transactions, e.g., debtor-creditor relations, accountants often do assume that the claim of one party equals the obligation of the other—the debtor-sacrifice is equal to the creditor-benefit. Most philosophers are properly appalled!

Discounted Expectations— Incorporating New Information

This essay started as a discussion of income as discounted expectations in relation to the timing of new information. It remains concerned with the introduction of new information, but it has been expanded to include alternative methods of income definition.

It is clear that defining income as the difference between someone's discounted expectations at two points in time brings new information into the estimates at each statement date. Thus all sorts of conjectures about both internal (transactional) affairs and general business (exogenous) conditions are incorporated periodically in the statements. A major problem remains because the reported income may vary widely when different individuals are asked to make the estimates.[1]

The current entrance values and its cousin, current exit values, also incorporate some new information at the end of each period. General expectations for the entire industry are amalgamated in some manner by traders and incorporated in the new and used market values for assets. Certainly current values for inventories include expectations about disposal prices, and current fixed asset prices are influenced by the profitability expectations of those trading in these markets. In some fashion the market considers the opinions of participating buyers and sellers and these broad amalgamations may be employed instead of the direct estimates of managers (or owners) in the Fisher discounting scheme. Advantage from the resulting objectivity is at least partially offset by the failure of market participants to understand the particular conditions facing specific firms. Thus in Machlupian terms market prices include "industrial rents," but do not include the subjective rents peculiar to the firm and its specific situation.

Historical cost methods—along with hold-to-maturity conventions—are the slowest to react to new expectations. Expectations of market participants at the time of acquisition are considered, but changes in subsequent opinions are recognized only for occasional writedowns for service life adjustments. Acquisition cost seldom is changed over the life of the assets to reflect changes in management's own expectations. In fact most acquisitions are recorded at cost, which always is lower or at least as low as discounted original expectations so that acquisition cost rarely reflects even original value expectations. Excess subjective values simply are neglected in the initial recording process. Historically original-cost accounting does permit the introduction of new management information if it affects service lives or residual values. For inventory items new expectations are not registered until the articles are sold and unrealized positive expectations on unsold articles are simply ignored.[2]

The objective of this essay is to discuss the Irving Fisher concept of income in terms of the admission of new information and to compare it with traditional views.[3] The discussion is comparatively simple for it is obvious that income, measured as the difference between a discounted subjective stream of expectations at two points of time, *must* be due to new information that somehow changed expectations. This incorporation of new information extends to the selection of any new discount rate used, for the appropriate discount rate changes in response to new information that (largely) is about external conditions. Alternative rates are offered by the various markets, but the selection of the one appropriate for the firm's own configuration of resources and risks is a subjective matter that cannot be completely replaced by market surrogates. To some extent changes in discount rates reflect environmental conditions, and changes in specific estimates of benefits and payments reflect conditions within the firm. This generalization may be useful in a heuristic way, but possible interdependence can not be neglected.

An obvious relationship also exists between Fisher's overall income model and the treatment of specific assets and their amortization. Current entrance values for used assets should vary as market expectations respond to price levels, technological improvements and a host of related considerations. In the case of specific items the estimates are made by others, and somehow are incorporated and unified in competitive markets. In the Fisher case, comparable estimates are made by managers or owners in order to get estimates of overall benefits and payments specific to the firm. In the market approximation of the Fisher approach, industry-wide estimates are incorporated through current entrance values rather than through direct managerial estimates.

It is clear that an approximation of Fisher's income measures may result from using changes in market values at two points in time. This surrogate introduces a broad range of new information and outsider investor opinion at the end of each measurement period. Thus the longterm model for market valuation is similar to the model advocated by Fisher. The chief divergence is that different individuals make the judgments and form the necessary expectations. But even this difference may be over-emphasized, for market participants certainly consult with manager-owners and vice-versa, so there is some tendency for the two sets of judgments to converge.

It also should be clear that traditional historical-cost methods and the income realization model generate lags in the introduction and implementation of new judgments. There also are major differences within traditional systems, e.g., between LIFO and FIFO or between replacement and retirement depreciation.

For further discussion consider first the part played by discounted expectations at t_0 when they remain unchanged over the period t_0–t_1. Then consider the influence of *unexpected* events that were *not* included in expectations at the beginning of the income period and remain unchanged except for any reinvested proceeds, i.e., capital available to influence expectations at t_1. Finally consider the influence of new expectations that arise within a period and are expected to continue into future periods. In conclusion compare the Fisher scheme with traditional cost-revenue accounting and with Ijiri's triple-entry concepts of momentum, impulses, trebits and the like.[4]

Fisher is firm in stating that his starting point is expectations and that certain operations on expectations can be used to define periodic income. He is even more clear in stating that resource (asset) *values* are derived from expectations. Thus capital values at various times are determined and then distributed (attributed) to specific sources (potentials) that seem to bear direct (semi-causative) relationships to the stream of expectations. This attribution may be combined with usual accounting procedures to help with liquidity and control problems. Canning apparently tried to articulate sources by using direct and indirect accounts with goodwill acting somehow as an unassigned synergistic valuation account.[5] Yet apparently he was never interested in the usual simplification of modifying the bookkeeping to show system differences between values of the assets and values of securities at the end of each period by adjusting his overall master account for the income reported.

As I understand Fisher, he first considers the potential available in the firm and from the environment and establishes a stream of beneficial expectations for the organization. These estimates along with appraisal of risks result in capital values and differences in capital values that define periodic income. Inasmuch as the series runs into the indefinite future, the discount factor is important primarily to the extent of irregularities from new evaluations and new information in the expectation stream. Income is affected by changes in expectations during the current period about conditional amounts and appropriate risks for the discount rate. Thus income differs from the straight compound-interest accumulation and it differs because of new information introduced during the period. For some economists it is precisely the difference between a compound-interest calculation based on beginning worth and Fisher's calculation that represents entrepreneurial income.

If Fisher's expectation stream meets certain conditions it can be integrated and the integration expresses capital values. Presumably if the stream meets necessary conditions, it can be differentiated, and all sorts of behaviors can be related to its rates of change. There is little evidence that Fisher or Canning were interested in developing second or higher derivatives much less attribute them to impulses of various orders. Less sophisticated forms of summing and differencing were used by cost accountants and most capital budgeteers.

Perhaps one of the reasons for this neglect was a consequence of the differing nature of the curves. The expectation curves are changed at the end of each period so that new expectations can be given consideration. Thus differentiation of the old curves might be of some interest at the end of the period to indicate the momentum from old expectations, but this knowledge hardly seems to be essential. Differences between the derived values from the new curve and the old at the end of the period might indicate the momentum changes introduced by new expectations. In a similar manner the second derivations of the two curves when compared might suggest supplementary forces at work.[6]

However, there is a further difficulty. Discounting the stream of beneficial expectations ordinarily is not the same as discounting an expected income stream. Recall that income is found by taking the difference between the discounted expectations at the beginning and at the end of a period—the difference in capital values. These differences should consist of many components. An important element may be the difference in the discounted values of the old expectation curve at the beginning and its projection at the end. As we have pointed out, this difference for a long continuing stream of expectations is not likely to be significant unless there are important irregularities in the patterning of old expectations or the discount rate has changed.

The more interesting aspects result from new expectations and changes in old expectations that are present in the new function and absent in the old. It is the discounted value of these items that make up an important part of the reported income for the period by influencing the ending value of capital goods. In an indirect way this analysis may be likened to momentum and force, and to some extent it may be possible to "account for" some of the income features by isolating critical actions and judgments.

Some of these changes in expectations may be from environmental or exogenous features (e.g., better business conditions) while other parts of the gross change in capital values (and income) may be internal. In any case they sometimes may be indirectly related to certain budget variances.

Consider for a moment the traditional problem of keeping capital intact in the discounting process. As usual there are no definitive recommendations but the problems are similar to those found in traditional accounting. To subtract the original capital value is more or less equivalent to keeping original expectations intact. A recalculation of the original capital value at later discount rates provides some measure of changes in risks now foreseen. Analysis of the remaining differences helps break out the influence on expectations of new developments during the period. A recalculation of the beginning capital value to include these major changes is similar to adjusting the budget for known changes in expected potential during the period.

Turn now to unchanged expectations over the interval. It is clear that the expectations for the second year will be influenced by reinvested profits of the first and that expectations will be changed thereby. Neglect this aspect for the moment by assuming that such resources are withdrawn immediately. If they are withdrawn later but still before the ending period, only the gain from the reinvestment of the earnings increment will be included in ending expectations. (At this point all such effects are neglected.) It is clear that this is a static situation and that the reported income for the period is simply the expected interest on the original (and final) expectations. This case is of little interest to theorists.[7]

What about events during the period that were unexpected at the beginning, take place completely during the period and thus leave a mark on ending expectations insofar as profits or losses are reinvested or disinvested? Of course the special unexpected event itself is not in either the beginning or ending expectations, but its results (unless withdrawn) would influence ending expectations by changing the resources and therefore the ending expectations by establishing a different potential base and perhaps by changing the overall optimism about future expectations generally.

These windfall items may be accounted for in the traditional accounting format, but precisely how are they handled in the discounting process? Clearly they did *not* enter into early expectations but their effects must enter end-of-period beliefs. (Neglect for the moment the possibility that windfalls may be interdependent and therefore may change beliefs about future patterns.) This outcome is consistent with traditional definitions. Windfalls ordinarily are defined as unplanned events that do not enter into plans and therefore are not conduct determining. If windfalls are not expected to occur again in any discernable pattern, the relevant income consequences are new resource potentials that influence ending expectations. The primary influence on income accordingly is the availability of resources that result from the windfall and are not withdrawn.

Observe that there are no irreconcilable difference here between the results reported by traditional accounting and the discounting process, and that no serious emendations are needed to the income definitions. More flexibility is available for traditional accountants, who sometimes define such windfalls as non-income and record them directly as capital adjustments. These direct adjustments may be a carryover from discounting designed specifically to keep the results of such happenings from influencing future expectations. Such variations are available to both discounters and other accountants. For example, accountants could treat these items as gains or losses and let investors apply their own filters. Or, they could create new classifications, such as "non-recurring income," to warn readers not to change expectation levels but at the same time to show that additional resources are made available by such gains.

One must not forget that the accounting concept of income has all sorts of supplementary defining properties, e.g., realization in working capital terms and support in the evidentiary area. Subjective decisions are necessary in all cases and subjective beliefs may be triggered by the reasonably stable experiences that make up the ordinary definition of objectivity. In practice it may be possible to include such restrictions as ancillary conditions. (In the newer accounting of Ijiri, these results seem to require the attributions needed to assign "impulses." Momentum may be assumed to be more or less instantaneous, but force is no longer present.)

Turn again to events during the interval that directly influence future expectations, but are not considered in beginning estimates. Normally certain events can be associated with such changes, but informational inputs of this type often are highly subjective. Traditionally changes in expectations are classified into two groups. One is concerned with changes in judgment about specific benefits, while the other is concerned with expected changes in appropriate discount rates.

In a broad sense it may be argued that changes in discount rates reflect exogenous (environmental) conditions. To the extent that these rates are reflected in markets, they are more or less objective and they reflect the market's judgment of appropriate rates for various risks. However the *subjective* element returns when attempts are made to select a discount rate that is appropriate for the specific risk for the enterprise. The Fisher approach requires some individual or some mechanism (e.g., the appropriate market) to select, from numerous discount rates that are available for all sorts of risks and external conditions, the one rate that best expresses the conditions that face the particular firm.

It is true that market prices of a specific concern's securities employ risk factors in the discount rates that are implicit in market values. Presumably differences between total market value of the securities and management's estimate of the discounted value of the firm are due to different estimates either for beneficial (cash) throwoffs or for differences in judgments as to the appropriate risk premiums factored into the chosen discount rates. It may be argued that market participants vary widely in optimism and pessimism and that the income of specific firms fluctuate widely from this factor alone. Yet managers may be subject to even wide ranges of optimism and pessimism in their estimates of cash flows or in their selection of appropriate discount rates. The amalgamation of participant judgments through the market process may lead to less volatile periodic income, but the presence of shortterm traders could amplify the variations.

If one accepts the relative efficiency of markets in their ability to select discount rates appropriate for the risks, it may be argued that the variation in discount rates accommodates changes in the environmental risk so that the reported periodic profits incorporate exogenous business conditions. Turned the other way, failure to adjust discount rates at the end of a period and thus reflect new knowledge of environmental conditions leads to seriously misvalued expectations and misstated periodic income. In summary an active and efficient market should incorporate specific events of the period along with new estimates of future events and modify them by applying appropriate risks. In short the discounting method of Fisher, Canning and associates should yield figures similar to those found by comparing the value of a firm's securities at the beginning and end of the period.

Return now to the mechanics of recognizing the advantages of an event that occurs during a period and continues into following periods. This case is similar to taking up expected profits on contracts when the contracts are received, and (through the discounting process) is vaguely similar to taking up profit as a percentage of completion. The advantages from the billed part of the event are shown somewhere among the resources of the firm and can be assessed in the usual way. The unliquidated part of the event should benefit future periods and by assumption has not yet increased accounting assets. In the Fisher structure it is necessary to estimate these unreceived benefits and subject them to a discounting process to get the value of the business at the end of the period. Presumably financial analysts value unfilled orders in a similar fashion although their methods for doing so are not always clear.

The Fisher accountant, like the financial analyst, must go further for he must recognize changes in optimism from the business environment that have not yet led to specific events that influence the firm's prospects. Undoubtedly this dimension of the problem has alienated traditional accountants and has led to the charge that discounting future prospects results in capitalizing optimism and pessimism and reporting such changes as income. In view of this charge, modern discounters have all but abandoned the Fisher model except as an ideal. They have retreated to the more comfortable current market position, where industrial rents are capitalized in current market prices and excess firm expectations are required to wait for more traditional acceptance.

What about the influence of the extra resources already made available by an interim event? The asset base will be greater by virtue of favorable events, and this greater potential will be reflected in the ending asset valuations and therefore in periodic income. What is the function of accounting in such a format? Does it make any difference whether interim entries "articulate" with the estimating base? Is there need for any traditional accounting, except perhaps to keep track of equities and contributions and to show some details about assets?

There may still be a function for bookkeeping and accounting, but it will have little or nothing to do with income determination. Income that results from the discounting process is determined by differencing two discounted streams of expectations. To some extent such expectations will be influenced by the accountant's interim recording of asset (potential) changes. It still is necessary to determine who owes whom and to assist with various controls. Records of sales by lines, territories and salesmen will still be useful. Depreciation and similar records may be needed for tax matters, and thus may influence expectations indirectly. But there is a more direct area in which accounting recognition is needed for such interim events. Suppose, for an example, that benefits are received and withdrawn before the end of the year. Failure to make some sort of entry will mean that earnings withdrawn will not be recognized as earnings. The added resources with their added expectations simply are not there at period's end. Thus to the extent that owners live off the enterprise, the living expenses never show up in income.[8] Clearly gains from specific activities may not be disclosed by the discounting-income process. It is difficult enough to estimate the future benefits of the entire organization for eternity and then select an appropriate discount rate to express the longrun risks. To do so for each line of goods and for each territory also is difficult, but the isolation of each transaction with the usual accounting detail is next to impossible. However it is clear that estimates of future benefits for the firm may be aggregates of expectations for smaller subunits. Certainly details such as replacements, sales levels for goods of various kinds and wage rate changes need to be integrated into the overall estimates.

It is exactly at this point that traditional accounting combined with a measure of income determined by differences in market valuations of the outstanding *securities* becomes interesting. (The bookkeeping entry that takes up excess market values can be added easily by taking the loose debit (or credit) to goodwill or some more aptly named account.) Market values for the securities then are used as surrogates for more subjective discounted expectations. In general this proxy may be preferable for it is less subject to managerial and other insider manipulation. It certainly is more objective. Now objectivity can easily be overvalued and treated as a divine object, but it does make the output of the system easier to check, helps practitioners follow the required procedures and substitutes an outside source for what can easily be a for-interest, insider operation.

Finally, none of the advantages now derived from traditional accounting need be forfeited, and regular accounting with traditional measurements and controls may be carried on as before. In fact if the market approach is combined with current-asset-value accounting (entrance values) the differences between the value of the assets and the value of the business may be isolated. If assets are carried at current exit values, the approximate difference between the value of the firm in immediate liquidation may be compared with value of the business as a going concern. Some accountants are uneasy about the practical problems of computing both immediate command over resources in liquidation and the value of discounted prospects. But human beings—even accountants—must learn to live with ambiguity, and become accustomed to the necessity for surrogates, proxies and analogies.

The traditional discounting process works from expected future benefits (expected cash flows) to capital values and from capital values to income. Clearly irregular expected receipts need individual attention, and poorly behaving patterns may create summation problems that require the most modern mathematical methods. Even so attempts to apply integrating methods to time-placed individual receipts and then aggregate the sums may be less satisfactory than simple spread sheets of periodic projections.

Consider now possible advantages that might result from recognizing new expectations continuously over an interval rather than at the end. If the discounting method of measuring income is combined with traditional double-entry accounting, there does not seem to be much reason for using the continuous approach. Perhaps it is better to make the calculations when they are fresh in mind even though they may need to be modified as new information becomes available at statement dates. The budgeting procedure may be improved and it is conceivable that control might be improved. However it is unlikely that the non-income functions of double entry (e.g., recording cash, inventory or sales for management purposes) will be influenced. Moreover problems of control require application of individual control techniques since application only to overall estimates doubtless is too coarse for even the most aggregative theorists. In any case some attention should be given to the estimators themselves to determine over or under optimism and to reveal those with better foresight.

Turn now to analysis that might be desirable and to reconciliations that might be possible with the discounting concept. The most easily understandable reconciliation might be an analysis that relates calculated income figures to budget estimates. Managers might, for example, look at their estimates of future benefits and a range of estimates might be given with probable influences on income. Disclosure might be made of the differences in estimates for major components. For example, changes in estimates of the profitability of various products, lines and/or territories might be disclosed. Similarly changes in expected expense outlays of various kinds might be made, e.g., replacement of major asset components, payment of liabilities and expectations of earthquakes or other natural disasters.

In a similar way managers should disclose differences in the discount rates used at the beginning and end of accounting periods. While differences here may often be due to the different risks appropriate for the firm, further details might be enlightening. A different rate might be selected to take into account expected differences in environmental conditions and the general business climate. In other instances differences may be due to changes in risk-taking policies adopted by management. Swings in general optimism and pessimism displayed by the managerial estimators may be even more important. It may be useful to disclose how and when each estimator changes his estimates and why he does so. This kind of control reporting might provide a bonus by motivating estimators to be more careful about their projections. Certainly over a longer period such disclosures might help investors evaluate the quality of individual estimators and the consistency of their projections. Market advocates may still feel that market mechanisms may do a better job than company insiders. Insiders may have better information but unfortunately they are also motivated by self interest.

These considerations may be generalized and perhaps related to triple or to n-tuple entry. The job of summation is not simply a function expressing expectations for future cash throwoff multiplied by a constant rate factor. The discount factor is a problematic variable. It makes sense to know its behavior over time and specifically to know its derivatives and the appropriate rates when valuations are made, i.e., the momentum factor or at least its major components. The desirability and relevance of having momentum measures are obvious for those who wish to assess the rapidity of changes in income or wealth or efficiencies.

In the Fisher context markets should present a schedule of rates, and managers and interested investors should select the appropriate rates for individual firms. The instantaneous rates of changes in both these components might be useful but such a procedure requires judgments about appropriate future rates. This calculation becomes complicated for the functions and families of functions that change over time. In any case disclosure of the behavior of such functions and families of functions might be a useful adjunct.

It should be desirable to breakout that part of the calculated income that is due to changes in expectations of beneficial flows and calculations may be directed first in this direction. In any case, traditional accounting tries to measure how well the firm does with actual environmental (business) conditions for each period. In a further set of decisions investors must assess the firm's ability to adapt to different business conditions. The Fisher method incorporates some aspects of budgeting by bringing estimates of future business conditions directly into measures of past income. This incorporation of expected changes in the business climate is made through estimates of future cash throwoffs in a forecasted environment and through the selection of an appropriate discount rate. The two are not independent.

While many consider Fisher's scheme to be grossly aggregative with a single figure for enterprise value, such need not be the case. He could have suggested the breakdowns that balance-sheet and income partitions usually portray. His stream of expectations presumably is built up by aggregating all sorts of interdependent individual estimates. Segregation of individual liabilities should offer less difficulty, for these unfavorable streams are less interdependent. Still some supplement is desirable to keep track of areas as such as cash (for liquidity), amounts owned and owing and inventories (for buying and control). Perhaps this kind of thinking led Canning to distinguish between direct and indirect valuation. Recall that his framework uses direct estimates for separable assets, treats inventories as a hybrid and considers most items that normally would be discounted as valuation accounts—not assets. Valuation accounts presumably come from discounting operations with goodwill becoming the *master* valuation account. Apparently Canning was not willing to take up differences in the market values of securities outstanding as income and make periodic adjustments to his master valuation account. Just why he did not advocate this surrogate for discounted values is not clear. Certainly Paton was aware of this possibility in the early thirties, but rejected the concept as a task to be performed by investment analysts.

Further discussion of the similarities and differences between Fisher's process and traditional accounting may be of interest. First, it should be clear that accountants are concerned with individual assets (resources or potentials) and how they are accounted for, aggregated and presented in financial statements. These potentials may be accounted for as original costs, but over their lives they must be related to expected future benefits and therefore to income. Original costs show the minimum expectations (discounted) at the time of acquisition and current market values express more up-to-date appraisals of general potential. Thus to an accountant it does not seem strange to work from potentials to benefits generated—i.e., from assets (capital) to income instead of from income to capital as in the Fisher process. Rules are established for recognizing new beneficial configurations and for expressing the decline in existing potential. The accounting process then selects certain public events as criteria for recognition. Thus increased expectations are recorded when supported by happenings that can be observed by others and recognized as evidence of the actualization of expectations. In a similar way potentials of various types are reduced and matched with actualized expectations. Meanwhile unrealized expectations are represented by unamortized cost (or market) numbers. The cost-allocation process does not remove the necessity to estimate future expectations, for the usual rules for matching require maintenance of a proportional [?] relationship between benefits expired and total benefits expected.

It is possible to write off all potentials at once and to treat gross expectations as income, but most accountants prefer to keep records of resource potential (values added and available) and periodically to recognize increases and decreases in these potentials.

The Fisher process works entirely from discounted expectations to capital values, and then from differences in capital values to recognized income. Thus capital values are derived from expectations, and income is derived from differences in capital values. This unidirectional view usually needs some modification because causation reduces to joint efforts and interdependent functional relationships. In the Fisher case it is clear that the accumulated potential on hand (the amount of assets, plus nonasset resources) must have some influence on expectations. In one sense the accountant lets costs speak for the potential, and the differences in recognized potential (allowing for investment and disinvestment) are defined as income. It is true that expectations influence the amount of asset potential allowed to remain on the books, but it is equally clear that asset values influence expectations.

Future estimates are needed in both the Fisher and ordinary accounting process, but it is difficult to decide which system is more sensitive to change in expectations and errors in forecasts. For Fisher errors and corrections enter directly into the stream of estimated benefits, but they are influenced by the discount factor. The accountant, working with costs that are themselves residues of previous discounted expectations, also adjusts his cost residuals to corrected estimates. For example if a one-half reduction in benefits is expected, the Fisher operator would simply reduce his expected value by one-half and apply the discount rate to reduce it to present value. The accountant who also foresees the one-half decline presumably would reduce the carrying value of his potential by one-half and neglect the discount factor. Which is preferable in all cases may be difficult to decide. Presumably the accountant has not taken any excess subjective value into consideration, and thus none is included in his writeoff. The Fisher accountant includes the excess subjective value when making his estimates of benefits and then modifies it by way of the discount rate. It may be that increased pessimism will completely wipe out previous optimism and the resulting decrease will be reflected completely in reduced capital values and therefore in reported income. That is, much of the new loss may be a correction of a previously reported gain.

CURRENT AND HISTORICAL COSTS: FURTHER COMMENTS

Return now to the introduction of new information in historical and current cost systems—the chief surrogates for discounted prospects. Current exit costs may be combined with the more interesting concept of current entrance costs; because in most situations where market changes are pertinent, the differences between entrance costs and values will be reduced to approximate amounts for transferring and installing the resources. Current entrance costs are given preference not because the results will be significantly different, but because for a going concern entrance costs are more directly "conduct determining" (the term is Fred M. Taylor's) than exit values and their command over resources in liquidation.

A clearcut advantage of current costs is that they bring new information about asset and liability values on the books at each statement date. It is true that this new information is from external sources and does not necessarily reflect the expectations of the managers or other knowledgeable insiders. But if income is designed to set forth information about managements' ability to utilize the resources entrusted to them, then it may be desirable to replace managements' expectations by the judgments of others not directly influenced by the estimates. Thus it may be argued that the loss from less intimate knowledge is more than offset by the reduction in possible bias and self interest.

Managements' assessments are situational and should consider all sorts of particular conditions, while market estimates are made up of different opinions made by different individuals for different conditions and unified by market prices that in fact may express no one's actual assessment. Unsatisfied suppliers feel that quotations are too low for their conditions and unsatisfied demanders feel that prices are too high to warrant expenditures. These market prices are constructed in a highly specialized manner from expectations held by outsiders and are therefore more "objective" and more amenable to audit. There also is a major advantage for current values: These figures (especially exit amounts) express the approximate value of one possible alternative—immediate liquidation—and signal this alternative at each statement date. This alternative usually is rejected, but a system that signals the value of this option periodically can be condemned only if higher costs cancel any advantages over *ad hoc* studies prepared only as needed. A further advantage of current-exit costs is discussed elsewhere but deserves mention here. It is difficult to find agreement on proper definitions and measures of social costs, but current market price is one simplification that usually can be implemented.

Possible gains from early incorporation of independent information into statements of managerial stewardship may be clear enough, but how does the historical-cost system go about introducing new judgments into the system?

DIGRESSION: HISTORICAL COSTS

Under the historical-cost system, new information about current fixed asset prices are recognized upon replacement of fixed assets. These cycles often are very long, and unless modified, new and pertinent information may be delayed for decades or longer. Changes in judgments about service lives and residual values may of course be introduced as needed by changes in depreciation and amortization rates. Further modifications sometimes are introduced by supplementary notes and comments. Moreover historical bases are modified occasionally by introducing appraisals to give an acceptable accountability base for return on investment and to modify the income measure itself.

Historical cost methods do bring all sorts of current judgments into the records at statement dates. Judgments about supplies and fuel used are routinely brought up to date. Inventory and cost of goods sold require periodic assessments, although there often is controversy over the precise methods. Of course cash, receivables, revenues, labor costs and the like are recorded at frequent intervals and adjusted for end-of-period judgments. In fact most adjusting entries are designed to introduce new information into out-of-date account balances.

Turn again to the old question of whether it is desirable to retain the discount rate at the beginning of the period for discounting ending expectations.[9] It should be clear that a given change in discount rates from t_0 to t_1 is new information that must be included in Fisher's concept of income. It has been suggested in previous essays that this type of information is concerned largely with environmental conditions, but direct estimates of expected fund flows for a particular firm are not free of environmental influences. The point here is that such changes are shifts in beliefs about variables that influence well being and income.

The supposed objectivity of discount rates (especially when compared with direct fund estimates) can easily be over emphasized, for the subjective problem returns when the analyst selects an appropriate rate to express the risk for an individual firm. It may be useful to separate various subjective elements in order to isolate responsibilities and to monitor the effectiveness of operations. A menu of market discount rates may have some objective features, but both selecting a particular menu and deciding on a particular item are highly subjective.

It must be concluded that discounted-receipts income should include differences in the discount rates used. To neglect such new knowledge is to assert that new information about alternative investment opportunities and changes in risk are not relevant to the concept of income. Of course some accountants have assumed a locked-in position and have argued that alternatives foregone simply are not relevant to income measures. Many favor this position (essentially the basis for historical costs) because it clearly is impossible to consider all possible alternatives that must be sacrificed. However the fact that one can never measure or even recognize all opportunities foregone does not justify neglecting those that are available.

FISHER: TAXABLE INCOME

In the Fisher framework taxable income takes an entirely different turn, for Fisher's practical taxable income does not result from discounting estimates of future consumption expenditures at two dates. When *ex post* consumption expenditures become available, their use is recommended rather than results from the discounting process. This is an interesting recommendation, for he neglects possible shifts in expectations about future expenditure and thereby neglects this type of new information. Apparently he is willing to sacrifice some information to get harder *ex post* numbers that are associated with realizable cash that can be verified by tax auditors. In doing so he abandons any attempt to keep capital intact.

It is clear that a modified taxable income defined as discounted estimates of future consumption expenditures is more closely related to Fisher's general concept of income. In fact this process may be a desirable simplification if expected benefits are interpreted simply as expected consumption. Funds deferred for capital investment should finally result, after a technological-financial delay, in consumption. The net effect of the change is to defer taxation until funds are withdrawn from the investment sector and devoted to consumption. Thus for an expanding economy consumption expenditures should increase in the future so that in the expansion years taxable income would be lower and in years of disinvestment the amounts should be greater. For a mature steady-state economy the taxes would be about equal, but there would remain a constant incentive for growth and thus a deterrent to a slowing economy. Lower taxes or expected lower tax rates should stimulate consumption and retard new investment. Higher tax rates should encourage further investment unless still further increases are expected. In any case some provision should be made for the inheritance problem, and consistent adjustment of the estate and inheritance tax structure would be an early priority.

All sorts of individuals and groups need information about potentials for wealth and progress in creating wealth. One possibility is to employ separate measures and even separate concepts tailored to the needs of each group. Most accountants however hope for a more general measure that may lose in specificity but gain in broader application. In the latter case the needs of all groups are given some consideration in the composite construction. Many feel the latter approach has been reasonably successful in spite of reservations about realization, conservatism, and special needs for an equitable taxing base.[10]

Recently politicians have been locked in a bitter debate over the desirability of eliminating the capital gains tax. Some argue that its removal would increase investment and make the American economy more competitive. Others insist that such preferred treatment is likely to have little effect since a large part of capital gains is connected with the sales of existing securities—simple transfers of wealth. It is clear that a reduction or complete removal of the tax would make capital more mobile and that preferential treatment for any group tends to encourage movement into the preferred group.

Some decades ago many of us were astounded when some very bright people "discovered" that a capital gains tax reduced the mobility of capital and tended to erect a locked-in-barrier. It should be obvious that *any* barrier to a transfer of interests is such a deterrent. (We neglect here considerations of equity and justice that may arise from changing price levels or from possible inequities due to past inabilities to adjust to different tax rates or to smooth value changes adequately from period to period.)

Irving Fisher's conception of taxable income as consumption expenditures may be ideal for those who wish to promote investment through the taxing process. Put simply his tax is a straight consumption tax not greatly unlike a graduated sales tax levied on consumption items. Clearly the incentive to invest is greatly increased and since there is a tax on consumption this element will be discouraged. In this sense investors become "locked-in," not to particular investments, but to investment in general.

Turn now to some further consequences of defining regular income (other than taxable income) in terms of consumption expenditures. There is little to commend such a proposal as a measure of well-offness, and Fisher did not support this definition beyond the field of taxation. The opportunity for manipulation of periodic earnings is one consequence. Moreover, the measure is precisely wrong for most uses of income reports. Those who are accumulating wealth and increasing their potential for more wealth show the lowest income (progress) and these who consume their resources and decrease their potential show higher income. In addition this measure is a poor index of management effectiveness.

One effect of consumption as a measure of general income is that the amount of income varies for each recipient according to his unique spending habits. Thus it becomes difficult to design a common measure that would apply to groups of interested parties. Fisher's plan can be expanded easily. A corporation's income can be measured by the amount of property (non-stock) dividends. In a similar way partnership and sole-proprietorship income can be measured in terms of owner withdrawals. Recipients themselves report income only when they spend their dividends (or withdrawals) on items defined as consumption goods. These definitions encourage operating entities to keep dividends and withdrawals at low levels in order to defer taxes. One effect is to increase retained earnings and capital accounts, and there may be a further tendency toward larger business organizations. Internal financing becomes cheaper.

NOTES

[1] Traditional accountants account for value and value changes in the past with actual exogenous conditions. Analysts assess the firm's ability to adapt to and extrapolate for expected future environmental conditions. Fisher's income tends to meld the two operations.

[2] However modifications on the downside sometimes are recognized when historical cost is modified for *lower* expectations through cost or market or write-

downs for damaged and obsolete goods. Surges of optimism reflected in higher managerial expectations are not considered to be sufficient reason for taking gain on unsold goods regardless of the external evidence for substantial values added.

[3] Irving Fisher's most rigorous exposition is found in *The Theory of Interest* (London: The Macmillan Company, 1930). Of even more interest to accountants is his *The Nature of Capital and Income* (1906).

[4] Yuji Ijiri, *Triple-Entry Bookkeeping and Income Momentum* (Sarasota: American Accounting Association, 1982), SAR 18.

[5] John B. Canning, *The Economics of Accountancy* (The Ronald Press Company, 1929). Other supporters of the discounting approach to income include: Carl Nelson, George Staubus, Harvey Hendrickson and Robert Sprouse, who at one time were members of the Berkeley-Minnesota axis.

[6] This has some similarity to Ijiri's concepts of momentum and force as I understand them. He employs averages for shorter and shorter intervals, but does not attempt to derive expectational functions that are discounted or differentiated. He applies his processes to individual transactions but apparently does not derive force by differentiating momentum. I have difficulty with his adding units of force to units of net asset potential. A strong case can be made for knowing the rates at which actual results are converging toward norms. See for enthusiastic support: Robert K. Elliott, "The Third Wave Breaks on the Shores of Accounting," *Accounting Horizons,* June 1992, pp. 61–85.

[7] Presumably the income would be comparable to Ijiri's investors' momentum. In his case the momentum accountant would not be interested in the valuation of the business as an asset—the value of the potential—and he would attribute the equivalent of income to investors' momentum. See Yuji Ijiri, *Momentum Accounting and Triple-Entry Bookkeeping: Exploring the Dynamic Structure of Accounting Measurements* (Sarasota: American Accounting Association, 1989), SAR 31.

[8] In his later years Irving Fisher defined taxable income in terms of consumption (withdrawals) and thus was an early advocate of capital growth. He was in favor of no tax whatever on reinvestment. Thus he did not need to worry about income realization in liquid funds.

[9] Sidney S. Alexander defines "pure economic income" as the difference between beginning and ending expectations discounted at year-end rates, which in his words is "the difference between equity at year-end and hindsight value of [year-end] equity at year-beginning." He then continues: "The difference between the hindsight value of year-beginning equity and year-beginning equity as valued at the beginning of the year may be termed 'unexpected gain.'" See "Income Measurement in a Dynamic Economy," Study Group on Business Income, *Five Monographs on Business Income* (New York: American Institute of Accoun-

tants, 1951), p. 61. Efficient marketeers might assess the unexpected gain as a risk allowance.

[10] My own feeling through the years has been that taxing authorities have so many special needs (e.g., ease of extraction, self-assessment, bounties and subsidies) that our profession should split off a special set of measures that are separate from the usual concept of business income. In short the many special needs of the taxing authorities merit a new concept that may be so different that it no longer should be termed income. Of course the desirable degree of polysemy for any term always is debatable.

Some Accounting Leaders and Paradigms

METHODOLOGY: SEARCHING FOR THE MASTER, PROFESSIONALISM

[T]he teleological basis of information policy utterly fails to solve the problem of authority, nor does it really remove the alienation of subject and observer-of-the-subject. All it does is to suggest a new question: What are the costs and benefits of trusting the master?[1]

For any service activity finding and designating a host group for whom the service is to be rendered is of prime importance. Some accountants have let serious discussions of the problem go by default by depending on some seemingly neutral methodology while others (like Churchman) have spent numerous hours and pages trying to establish a "guarantor" not only for simple cost-benefit studies but for all knowledge. In fact philosophers have devoted a major portion of their efforts to this problem, but unfortunately accountants only recently are concerned with this area. In accounting the dominance of physical foundations and even the comfort of "scientific observations" are now well eroded, but no important foundation has yet arisen to fill the void. Conceptualism in which the investigator himself plays an important role in concept formation has risen rapidly, but the extreme metaphysical doctrine that factors relevant to reality are completely determined by the individual has not yet been accepted. This essay is devoted to these problems with a down to earth identification of some accounting leaders with various research paradigms. In the process the approaches of Paton, Littleton, Chambers, Mattessich and the agency-contracting disciples are reviewed.

237

LOOKING FOR FUNDAMENTALS AND BASICS

The Institute[2] has (at least since 1932) been committed to finding the basic cornerstones of the profession and Paton had advanced an unsophisticated set of postulates for accounting as early as 1924. The approach is an old and well established one that dates even before Euclid, whose study of geometry has been the envy of the world. Frege, Peano, Russell and others have performed a similar service for mathematics. Geometry, in Euclid's day, and later practical mathematics are activities for measuring and calculating and in this aspect are similar to accounting. In pure mathematics (and in structural linguistics) the axioms and postulates may indeed be stipulations, but at any rate they are stipulations that help develop an understanding of the practical bodies of knowledge they embrace. This background is given to help understand the near pathetic endeavor by recent accounting leaders to observe some portion of an external world and select those features and only those features that are basic for the entire field of accounting. These basic observations, plus the limited deductive apparatus of a simplistic two-valued logic are thought to be sufficient to explain, if not justify, the field of accounting theory.

Progress has come mainly from Mattessich, Chambers and Moonitz. The technique is similar in each case and consists of looking at certain happenings in the environment. By some (by no means clear) ability they have been able to identify and isolate vital happenings and establish relationships that are relevant to their objectives. They then employ them as *basic* statements from which further theoretical structures are derived. The additional device for moving from these general (exogenous) basic propositions to their own specific accounting guidelines is said to be one of deduction or, in the Mattessich schema, interpretation.

Now deduction is a logical process that gets new propositions from established propositions by accepted laws of transformation. When propositions and rules are stipulated and the correct application of all rules is made (or further stipulated), the conclusions are *valid* in a logical sense. (They are not necessarily useful even when "*true*" practical interpretations are made.) The conclusions are entailed and there is no question of error or ambiguity. This ideal has been transferred to the practical service activity known as accounting. Somehow if the profession can find the propositions that are *really* basic and apply the accepted rules of logic any "deduced" professional guidelines are assumed to be desirable when applied to objectives in the practical domain.

It is clear that an idealized set of guidelines for a service profession may have some association that can be applied deductively to the objectives of the profession. Some deduced theorems and related lemmas should be useful for finding consequences for various alternate lines of conduct. In order to select and recommend practical guidelines, judgments about their relative abilities to satisfy the objectives for their masters *must* be made.

Mattessich approached the problem by separating positive elements from the elements calling for more obvious value assessments. Deductions about consequences were placed in an if . . . , then . . . logical format in which the objectives of the profession became "if's" and the "thens" became the guidelines deduced by logic from the consequences (and indirectly from his basic postulates). A pragmatist would not arrange his investigatory machinery in this fashion. But Mattessich was never a pragmatist. In his later years he pays more attention to values and to objectives, but his framework for investigation is essentially that of Carnap and the logical empiricists.

Return now to the process of observing the environment for propositions that are *basic* for the accounting profession, identifying them and demonstrating unequivocally that they are relevant and sufficient to support professional guidelines. Chambers found his fundamental propositions, and they led him to market economics and finally to current cash equivalents. In this respect he is a relative of Paton except he deduced exit values rather than current entrance costs. Both Chambers and Paton deduced strong support for their income concepts but for some of us it is difficult to decide whose "deductions" are the more convincing.

It is not clear to this observer precisely how Chambers uses logical deductive methods to develop his accounting superstructure from his own basic observations. But it is clear that he found his foundation blocks in market economics, and moreover he found them in aggregate market actions; not in the objectives of individual actors in such markets. He actually argues that the objectives of individuals are beyond inquiry, and through some poorly disclosed logical process concludes that aggregate market actions themselves are adequate surrogates for individual objectives. There is no doubt that Chambers is a strong supporter of traditional scientific methods, but building a meta-structure for a profession is a job primarily of construction and not of deduction. However his emphasis on deduction is uncompromising, even to restating the high points of each chapter in an Aristotelian logical structure.

Mattessich too turns his eyes on the world-environment in search of basic postulates that could provide a basis for his accounting structure. His first restriction of the observing arena was to the field of economics, and he decided that there was indeed a constellation of the two. The field of national income accounting and measurement along with Vatter-like fund accounting provided a fertile digging area. The input-output analysis of Leontief and the primitive distribution framework of Quesnay offered further grounds. No doubt his early training in engineering sharpened his interest in these mechanical models. Yet Mattessich was far more than an engineer and was eager to widen the scope of his operations. He also was better trained in philosophy and scientific methods than other accounting theorists of the time. In his early works his Viennese education seemed to steer him strongly to logical positivism and to the works of Carnap and others of the Vienna Circle. His later work at Berkeley with that university's aggressive computer center no doubt reenforced his interest in mathematical modeling and the need for tight structures that fit the new computer age. The broadening influence at Berkeley probably came from Churchman, whose most important contribution may have been to tilt the scales of management science away from formal models (narrow operations research) and toward the need to assess values in all decision models. In any case Mattessich's work at British Columbia indicates more interest in extending his early models into the area of values.[3] Yet he seems never to have lost his contention that basing a general accounting framework on observed postulates from the environment is a necessary requirement for theorizing in any discipline.

Mattessich leans heavily on logical and mathematical methods once he has identified the elusive fundamental entities and reduced his observations to postulates, definitions and primitive terms. It is clear that he must be classified (along with Feltham, Demski, Gonedes and others) as a synoptic (the term is Braybrooke's) model builder, but Mattessich is far more. He is not only a student of the philosophy of science but he makes wide use of scientific methods—the hypothetico-deductive framework. His philosophical base in logical positivism helps him avoid metaphysical missteps, and keeps his searching eye on environmental entities that satisfy scientific and measurement criteria. These entities—to no one's surprise—are found primarily in the economic sector. Unlike others who have tried their hand at finding postulates, Mattessich actually does "prove" various theorems that can be given interpretations in the field of traditional accounting.

Mattessich probably believes that his main contribution to accounting theory is in the postulational area. But most observers feel that his major contribution (an important one) has been his ability to synthesize prevailing thought in economics, philosophy and science; and bring the synthesis to bear on the mundane field of accounting. This writer in particular has found Mattessich's theoretical work both intriguing and exciting, and has found it useful for formulating his own views of the field.

The Moonitz experience at finding basic postulates is somewhat less happy. Moonitz is one of the most analytical and incisive minds in our profession. But he is not primarily a philosopher, and he was severely handicapped by the previous bumbling of various Institute committees. Moonitz seems to have been influenced by the inductivism of Littleton. He began his familiar search by assuming first that the *family* of accountants could be identified. Once this bit of underbrush was out of the way, he could observe what they actually were doing. This start limited the field of observation to the environment in which accountants carry on their practical work. The orientation therefore is turned toward practitioners and what they *do* rather than toward academicians and philosophers.

Limiting the entire field to those parts covered by the activities of accountants is a useful device, but several practical problems still remain. For example which activities of accountants constitute accounting and therefore are relevant to their professional work? This problem certainly is not insurmountable. But there is a more difficult task: What device can be employed to identify the few strategic activities that are *fundamental* and *basic* enough to serve as cornerstones for the accounting superstructure. Thus Moonitz was confronted with the persistent problem that faced Wyatt and Sorter: *Which* events *are critical* and *which* events are to support accounting transactions? Even worse: What facets (aspects) of the selected events are critical enough to be measured and reflected as accounting information?

Moonitz, like the others involved in the postulate game, had difficulty moving from the basic objectives identified in his host system to specific postulates that could be said to underlie the accounting system. The transition from the A-postulates from the environment to the B- and C-postulates is not clearly explained. Apparently he was attempting to apply a functional format along traditional pragmatic lines. But his observations of what accountants do, somehow overpowered the search for functions that society expects the profession to perform. In this area he betrays a positivist orientation that tries to separate facts from values instead of the pragmatist view that involves ends in view (objectives) in all steps of an investigation. Moonitz is confronted with the elusive task facing all positivists: The necessity for a service activity sooner or later to move from observations of what *is* to conclusions as to what accountants *should* do. Moonitz himself fails to meet this problem squarely, and even in the Sprouse-Moonitz extension, only limited attention is given to the functional nexus.[4]

Finally, Mattessich, Moonitz and Chambers came up with specific recommendations for the profession. Mattessich presented a double-entry structure that could be adapted to all sorts of social goals and objectives. Chambers went further and came up with a set of specific accounting rules associated with exit markets and (for him) an income definition superior to all others. Moonitz, with the assistance of Sprouse, came up with a more detailed set of measurements that depended primarily on current entrance costs. After allowance for covariance between current entrance costs and current exit costs, the recommendations of Chambers and those of Moonitz-Sprouse are remarkably similar.

Meanwhile Ijiri was observing the social environment for possible guidelines for accounting actions. His mathematics may have been more complicated, but his formalization encounters identical problems even though his level of rigor is slightly higher. In any case he reaches the conclusion that historical cost accounting generally is satisfactory if not superior to the more rapid incorporation of market changes through current market schemes.[5]

For a down to earth pragmatist with the usual human yearning for firm foundations, there is something saddening about observing these outstanding world scholars ponder so deeply over an impossible question. One of the beauties of philosophical inquiry is that the outcomes can always be faulted from various points of view. Sometimes there is a fine line between the joys of important discoveries and the Zen-like realization that argument among experts may indeed become sterile.

LITTLETON

The Moonitz approach followed closely the pattern set by Littleton, who also began his search by observing what practicing accountants were doing. Once practicing accountants are identified, their activities can be observed and some sort of need-response relationship between social needs and accounting practices can be inferred. Littleton's empirical grounding then can be applied to observing activities and tracing their possible consequences. With his response-need assumption he can infer the social needs practicing accountants are trying to fulfill—their functions. Strict empiricists may feel uncomfortable by the need to make these inferences, and their discomfort may be greatly increased when Littleton takes the next step and moves from the relatively clean factual observations of what is *being* done to what *ought* to be done.

An accumulation of specific instances requires a classification scheme, so that certain groupings (aggregations) can explain the rules that practitioners are in fact following. Perhaps instead, Littleton observed the uniformities in accounting processing rules and then looked to the range of specific situations that each rule *may* have been designed to cover. In any case he assumed antecedent-consequent relationships between environmental events and accounting responses. The nexus through consequences served to separate accounting transactions from other events and to delimit the scope of inquiry. This philosophical approach is essentially that of pragmatism and is based on the simple idea that generalized accounting rules give an orientation toward similar future events by grouping responses to analogous events in the past.

At this stage Littleton apparently has a list of rules used by practicing accountants and a tabulation of specific instances to which the rules have been applied. If he can tabulate all these rules and generalize their applicable ranges, he can outline the entire domain of accounting. Of course he can never be sure that he had tabulated all past specific instances, and worse cannot be sure that his past sample can safely be extrapolated to cover all future instances that might appear.

Littleton's most difficult task is yet to come for he needs some way to coordinate his observed practices with a theoretical structure. He may have anticipated the accounting positivists, and attempted to stop his theory construction by asserting that his objective is to show only how various alternative practices appear to be selected. However he came close to falling into the fatal positivist trap by pretending that he is dealing only with facts when he is constructing a type of decision-making model based on rationality, opportunity and self-interest. Such constructed individuals (e.g. economic men, scientific observers) can of course be given characteristics so that their programmed actions can be used to support and *explain* almost *any* set of inferences from *any* set of facts. Further, facts (themselves simplistic inferences) are needed to indicate that the models selected are relevant to the explanations sought.

While Littleton avoided the construction of an hypothetical rule selector in the individual sense, he did rely on social groups to follow Darwinistic survival patterns to make his selection. He, like some naturalists, could then make the weak but legitimate claim that practices that survive are *good* theory. (To Littleton theory is defined to be what most scientists would call principles.) Deinzer has pointed out that Littleton's faith is based on a hidden assumption that the development of practices is in "good hands" and that the survival practices will converge and automatically become good theory, i.e., a desirable set of principles.

Littleton goes beyond most technical positivists in that he is genuinely concerned with *good* theories, but he is in the camp of some positivists in that he infers good theory from what is observed. Some positivists have argued that ethics is evaluated in terms of its consistency with biological laws that govern human behavior and that this evaluation is a simple part of science. Any other shoulds or oughts are secondary or even irrelevant.

In summary it seems that Littleton holds several beliefs. First, surviving practices are better than non-surviving ones. Second, rules applied to practical instances are better than those applied to hypothetical ones. Third, (by inference) rules themselves should be selected by practitioners rather than by academics. Finally, the ultimate arbiter for good or bad theory is historical survival as expressed in practices carried on by people identified as accountants. Followers of Littleton, however, are not constrained to accept his criterion for good theory. Thus Dopuch, for example, can be a Littletonian, and at the same time be a rigid empiricist and *de facto* positivist.[6]

Philosophically Littleton was a disciple of Dewey and his main contribution (other than being an excellent educator) may be bringing Dewey-type pragmatism to accounting. Dewey has said that theory apart from practice is futile, if not trivial, and even wondered whether anyone can talk about empty words devoid of meaning. His entire conception of intellectual endeavor is tied up in problematic situations with individuals immersed in a mess of ends-in-view, past meanings, yens for resolutions, conjectures and hypotheses all combined with conditioning features from the environment. Moreover Littleton shared Dewey's irrepressible faith in *progress* as a guiding vector pointing toward better human relations. Thus Littleton came honestly to his belief that changes in accounting practices are indeed in good hands, and can successfully lead theorists in their quest for principles that lead to a better profession.

Meanwhile a similar pragmatic approach was being promoted by the outstanding Dutch accountant, Theo Limperg, who had taken a strong stand in favor of a functional approach to public accounting. In addition he was uncomfortable with limiting the functions of managerial accountants to simple errand boys for management. Limperg grounded his theory on the cannons of *good business administration*. His host group thus was firmly based on businessmen and whatever helped them accomplish their goals was sufficient warrant for professional acceptance. Clearly he did not appeal, like Spacek, to natural laws or, like most modern accountants, to governmental agencies or broad social customs.

Limperg understood that there were sharp limits to the power delegated to the public accounting profession. Once the audit responsibility was accepted, the auditor no longer had authority: to perform partial audits with stated (or unstated) exceptions, or to abandon the task of evaluating the shortcomings to readers who normally have access to much less information than the performing auditor. Apparently the mandate from "good business administration" also required auditors to exercise their very best judgment and perform their function to the best of their ability in order to support their claim on the social dividend. Furthermore Limperg was a good pragmatist on principles. Professional accountants can not be expected to be familiar with all specifics that may arise in their practices. Principles then are guidelines to assure conformance with good business administration when unfamiliar situations arise. Modern business is complicated and accountants need some sort of compass to navigate unfamiliar waters. However where principles have not been established to cover particular situations, accountants must depend on their general training, integrity and ability to follow the what's-good-for-business beacon. At this point individual ethics and professional discipline become dominant.

PATON AND HIS POSTULATES

Discretion triumphs over valor and this writer has delayed this critique of Paton's postulates and theories until Paton is no longer able to defend himself and overwhelm us again with the force of his personality and his unmatched rhetoric.

It is essential to understand that Paton's world view is not one of sociological conflict, but one of general cooperation and functional harmony. True enough his idealized market system is competitive, but the undesirable aspects of competition were softened if not avoided by restricting competition to the framework of free markets. (In this respect Paton, like Friedman, followed the competitive model started at Chicago by Henry Simons.) Once the dysfunctional characteristics were neutralized or removed by purifying markets, the desirable features shine through, and the greed of human beings can be safely harnessed to carry on the world's work. Unfettered greed was of course condemned, but Paton never was able to agree with idealistic socialists that individual self-interest and fierce competition for the world's goods can easily spread to other aspects of human relations and encourage a dominant group of human beings who are ugly and without compassion.

To Paton the scope of accounting was largely restricted to the business sector and primarily to big business where worthy outsiders do not have direct knowledge of corporate affairs. In this area he was a product of the industrial revolution, where managers and entrepreneurs are consciously separated from suppliers of capital. Responsibilities are delegated and a new information system becomes necessary to keep all parties informed of their duties and accomplishments. Collecting and reporting such information becomes the function of financial accounting, and the goal of accounting is to help society manage and control organizational affairs.

Paton believed that accounting must be concerned with accountabilities and responsibilities, and his interest focused on income as the coordinating structure and the very core of accounting. In this area the Patonian position has some strange and unexpected aspects. Auditing is concerned primarily with seeing that activities are unified according to organizational plans and oriented toward reducing uncertainties, yet Paton showed practically no interest in auditing as a proper subject for university study. Furthermore he displayed little interest in managerial accounting as a device for aiding lower-level managers, and requiring them to report their actions faithfully. Finally institutional and governmental activities, where duties and responsibilities require careful coordinating, also were of little interest. Presumably he felt this field is too political, and the clerical chores too routine for serious university study.

Although he identified the dominant duties of the profession and the groups to be served, he seldom discussed the characteristics of the *masters* for whom the profession toils. Presumably they are businessmen and financial administrators who prefer more wealth rather than less, are reasonably rational and therefore understand normal literary and mathematical discourse. Certainly they are capable of reacting to accounting reports so that Paton's theories always carry a behavioral or hermeneutical bent. It is the function of accounting to gather, process and report financial aspects of business activity to help these rational users. Moreover it becomes the task of a theorist to help the profession clean up centuries of accumulated rubbish, improve its logical structure and revise its terminology (semantics).

It probably is too simplistic to assert that Paton looked entirely to financial decision makers for guidance and neglected accounting practitioners. Certainly he considered the latter group, and evidently was not enthralled with what he saw. Unlike Littleton he saw few idealistic role models in the practicing profession. He seriously criticized their terminology, quarreled with their user models, challenged their measuring rods, lamented their failure to follow established economic doctrines and growled at their training methods and inconsistent rules. He regretted their departure from rational decision making processes, and their adherence to traditional usages that are no longer appropriate. To assume that good theory (principles) could be derived from *generalizing,* classifying and structuring such practices was unthinkable. A strong turnaround in the direction of neoclassical economic theory was necessary and revolutionary methods were appropriate. Yet there is irony here, for the main structure of the profession survived and the foundations remained substantially intact.

A brief summary of Paton's attitudes and guidelines may be in order.

1. He understood clearly the need for a service profession to perform the functions expected by society. He was a strong normative accountant.

2. He limited his worthy users primarily to members of the investment community.

3. He clearly saw the need for complicated industrial complexes to delegate authority and to develop reports that highlight delegated responsibilities and indicate accomplishment.

4. He was concerned with terminology and felt that the language of accounting reports should be consistent with good language elsewhere. For the better part of a century he fought to rid the profession of verbal garbage and out-dated stereotypes.

5. He was not directly interested in psychology and clearly was not a modern hermeneut, but he was a skilled rhetorician, was keenly interested in the techniques of persuasion and should be classed as one interested in pragmatics.

6. Paton had a positivist side in that a substantial part of his theorizing consisted of tracing the probable consequences of alternative accounting rules. Too often the consequences ended with showing the differences in numerical measures that would result (e.g., cost or market, anticipated discounts) and seldom were extended to probable behavioral reactions. Yet in order to make normative rec-

ommendations, he found it necessary to relate the differences in consequences to the attitudes of dominant users. The behavioral aspects were given less attention than the tracing of consequences.

7. He recognized the fact that environmental conditions and general attitudes change and that accordingly guidelines (standards) must change to meet the new conditions. Paton was an uncompromising current value advocate, but in ordinary times was comfortable with historical costs matched with revenues as an adequate surrogate for values expired and received. It is interesting to note that his early espousal of current costs came during and shortly after World War I, 1918–1930. His espousal of historical costs was strongest during the depression when price levels were reasonably constant, and his renewed emphasis of current values came after World War II.

8. In some instances Paton simply changed his mind. At least it is sometimes difficult to correlate his changes with clearcut changes in the business climate. His change in the recommended treatment of income taxes probably could be correlated with the increase in importance of this tax, and his decreased interest in discounting and the isolation of implicit interest in business transactions may be related to the decrease in interest rates and therefore the importance of interest between the wars. Even his apparent vacillation on mergers, consolidations, poolings, reacquired securities and the like may be related loosely with various hijinks in the financial world.

Recently attention has been devoted to Paton's accounting postulates as set forth in Accounting Theory, Chapter XX ("The Postulates of Accounting").[7] These postulates are in the form of an ex post summary of the assumptions he needed to develop his early theories, and there is little evidence that he used them as the basis for strict deduction. Apparently he felt that his conclusions cannot be proved in some mathematical manner. While they are simple assumptions, they are slightly more general than propositions within the traditional body of accounting theory.

Interestingly he does not consider his most useful statement to be a postulate at all. His following expression may be too broad to serve as a mathematical premise, but it is pure Dewey and serves as a guideline for the development of Patonian theory:

> Accounting is a highly purposive field and any assumption, principle, or procedure is accordingly justified if it adequately serves the end in view—assuming that end to be reasonable . . . (p. 472).

It is this statement that sets forth accounting as a service activity, stipulates the need for objectives, requires the tracing of consequences and thus shows the path for professional justification.

Herbert Taggart, a Paton student disciple and longterm colleague, summarized what he believed to be Paton's postulates:

1. ". . . the existence of a distinct business entity . . ."
2. ". . . the continuity of this entity . . ."
3. ". . . an equation . . . between the total of the properties and the total of the representations of ownership . . ."
4. ". . . that a statement of assets and liabilities . . . in dollars and cents is a complete representation of the financial condition of the enterprise . . ."
5. ". . . that the value or significance of the measuring unit remains unchanged . . ."
6. ". . . that cost gives actual value for purposes of initial statement."
7. ". . . that the value of any commodity, service, or condition, utilized in production, passes over into the object or product for which the original item was expended and attaches to the result, giving it its value."
8. ". . . that costs accrue . . ."
9. ". . . that a loss in asset value falls upon or extinguishes the most recently accumulated proprietorship."
10. ". . . that all disbursements to shareholders absorb earnings before tapping investment . . ."
11. ". . . that units of raw material or merchandise consumed or sold are always taken from the oldest in stock . . ."[8]

There is no question that Paton's selection of postulates was an amateurish effort, but it should be remembered that at this time deductive systems were rare. Only a few of the better universities had introduced mathematics as a deductive system that requires interpretations in areas such as geometry and mechanics. Joseph H. Woodger had not begun his work on postulational biology, and the social sciences were still further behind. Why Paton failed to develop this promising beginning still remains something of a mystery. Paton was clearly a deductive theorist as was his mentor in economics, Fred M. Taylor. Moreover he had two internationally recognized physicists in his immediate family, and the physics of the time was making fantastic advances in constructing deductive theoretical structures.

Paton never claimed that his postulates were "fundamental truths" that endure forever. In fact he was so leery of such absolutes that years later in his joint effort with Littleton he preferred "standards" over "principles" on the ground that the latter term implies more permanency than is warranted. It is clear that Paton himself changed his mind about some of his "postulates." Taggart points out the obvious weaknesses in postulates four, five and eleven, and many other critics (including this one) feel uncomfortable with at least some aspects of numbers six, seven, eight, nine and ten. Some critics freely accept only the "existence" of postulate one, and argue that the continuity assumption must be determined for each engagement and that the "fundamental equation" may just as well be expressed as assets equals sources of assets, or assets equals responsibilities or even inputs equals outputs.

In a similar way the assumption that initial cost equals value to the entity is demonstrably false, but it helps block the admittance of certain types of subjective values before Paton wishes to recognize them. The assumption that costs accrue is an attempt to employ statistical lags and leads to divorce cost from expenditures and permit cost to be matched with services rendered and recognized. Interestingly there is no similar postulate for revenue recognition on a value added basis although there is extensive discussion of this area.

His selection of seven, nine, ten and eleven are clearly unfortunate choices and shows his philosophical commitment to realism and his concern for the influence of physical things. At times in his *Theory* he shows the influence of Irving Fisher and emphasizes that accountants deal with values and that values are expectations, but he seems unable to escape the arguments of classical economists (and Marx) that value is somehow stored up and encapsulated in physical things. The idea that value passes from product to product or from one stage of production to another is at best an inappropriate analogy. In later years he had second thoughts about the assumptions that costs adhere "like barnacles" to physical constructs. This adherence theory is, of course, a convenient assumption and a useful tool for teaching cost accounting. Even Vatter made wide use of "embodiment" and the "release" of service potential from Promethean-like restrictions.

That losses fall on the "most recently accumulated proprietorship" is an outrageous postulate and there is no clearcut evidence either to accept or reject this last-in, first-out assumption of flows. This assumption does not even have a physical basis and certainly has no basis in value expectations. (He rejects this thesis for inventories.) The older capital-revenue doctrine is based on the idea that revenues are to be matched with ordinary expenses and unusual items are to fall on capital investors. Even in this old-fashioned approach the distinction is between unusual and usual losses and not on the recency of the loss.

The physical aspects of postulate eleven obscure the important feature that accountants deal with values, their changes and their future potential. The FIFO rule is no doubt selected because of a prior belief that identified unit cost is *the* proper method of handling costs and that the FIFO substitute will give its closest approximation. This position is early Paton for then he was interested in getting the balance sheet to approximate current values as well as measuring income by matching current costs with current revenues. In most cases he preferred the latter method, but was never interested in using base stock methods or LIFO to match the income items and applying reserve techniques to bring the balance-sheet figures up to current levels.[9]

PROFESSIONALISM AND AGENCY-CONTRACTS

This discussion is a summary of attitudes expressed elsewhere over the years.[10] So far information economics has not fulfilled its early promise. This research employs the latest technical tools, but has not yet led to extensive empirical studies or to extensions into the world of practical affairs. These sophisticated mathematical and statistical models are far from generalized metamodels for they are based on idealized maximization structures and on the behaviors of strongly oriented psychological creatures. Its current extension into the agency area may at least lead to expansion into further empirical areas. Perhaps the cost of information and other variates will be expanded further to approximate the costs of organizational dysfunction, decentralization and political pluralism.

The extension of fresh viewpoints from the area of contracts to the selection of alternative accounting rules has been interesting. The tone of the present discussion is slightly negative for I always have been skeptical of those who want to base professional behavior and professional ethics on individual self-interest whether expressed through selfish one-on-one bargaining or through organized markets. The conception that all conflicting and cooperating features of an organization may be represented by bargaining and contracting is a neat structure that permits wide use of traditional capitalistic economic analysis. This framework is especially useful when the accounting profession is indifferent to the alternative rules and surrenders decisions to contending parties that might be helped (or disadvantaged) by the selections. The chief criticism here is that the approach, as I understand it, *assumes* that the profession is indifferent (or powerless). It is my contention that the accounting *profession* should take an *active* part in rule selection by reacting to the pressures from the general social order. The existence of professional codes of ethics is evidence that professionals are *not* passive observers and are *not* willing to accept the unrestrained expressions of market self interest without weighing them in terms of professional responsibilities.

This section is concerned with the problem of selecting a host system for a service profession—deciding who counts, whose voices are to be heard, who holds legitimate rights to the output of the system. So far the agency-contractual approach has made no *explicit* provision for a strong professional organization, although clearly it could do so. Previous market literature is filled with models of behavior similar to those advanced by agency theorists. To repeat: Professional codes of ethics are usually created precisely to combat the what's-in-it-for-me motivations of self-seeking bureaucrats and businessmen, and it is not acceptable to omit them from any explanatory model.

It is clear that modern contract theory is consistent with and an expansion of the use of free markets and bargaining arrangements to determine who gets information, i.e., who are the *directors* of the accounting profession. Modern agency advocates are nominal positivists and should not be permitted to *advocate* particular solutions. Predicting the consequences of decisions should not be confused with advocating particular choices. Clearly the influence of the profession as a protector of the public interest can be incorporated into the agency paradigm but this decision requires an extension of strict positivism. There can be no question that the agency-contract structure has attracted able minds to the profession, and has provided a useful framework for classifying forces and demonstrating how these forces might work in choice situations. So far they have not incorporated professional resistance, and so far as I know there has been no attempt to show why such resistances arise and how they can operate to influence market-oriented conflict resolutions among contending forces with inconsistent values.

The modern agency-contract framework is no doubt near the strict positivist position, but it does examine some of the forces at work to determine the selection of alternative accounting rules. As usual no one can remain true to the positivist ideal, and agency researchers move quite a distance from description in the direction of explanation. Now explanation is an endless regress, and it is only fair to point out that these researchers have stopped at a low explanatory level that fails to account for social pressures through legal restraints and professional influences.

Agency research strategy begins with a positive note by taking situations that involve clearly-defined choices, but almost at once it departs and attempts to *explain* a possible process that might underlie (cause) the observed actions. The capitalist market mechanism is posited with all contractors following rigid behaviors that seem appropriate for an "ideal" contracting man. He is *assumed* to be rational (in the Western economic sense) with some understanding of the consequences that might result and with the ability to conduct rigorous cost-benefit studies. Clearly this agent-contractual man is a mental construction for there is no serious attempt to use *positive* means to support the construction. In fact it is next to impossible to decide whether human beings are always trying to maximize their well being and whether they are rational and understand all consequences of their actions. Studies in this direction may be made in various ways, but there is no evidence that these positivists have attempted to make them. A simple study might indicate what choices were available. Another might deal with choices actually made. A further study might indicate what rules already have been vetoed by legal sanctions or professional guidelines and therefore do not appear among the alternatives. Additional studies might examine the characteristics of those who are the actual agents and contractors. As usual the important decision-making dimension requires consideration of appropriate value systems.

The study of value systems is a vexing problem for positivists. They can use questionnaires and related methods, but their "factual" reports then are limited to these reports. This is about as far as a strict positivist is able to generalize with safety. To infer value systems that are consistent with actual choices says something about the need to make inferences. A positivist may reach conclusions about the consistency of actual actions with any posited set of values, but the value systems actually employed by actors in the contracting scene are difficult for *positivist* inquiry. In a similar manner postulating an agency-contracting man whose behaviors are programmed to be consistent with a set of observed actions is an interesting and useful activity. Positivists should be cautious about concluding that there is such a man. Positive research may question prime targets, and they may devise experimental situations in which the actors' values may have bearing. But a positivist should be cautious about inferring that any actor actually holds these values. Empiricists may bring statistics to bear and reach conclusions that are acceptable by their own standards. Others may make inferences and hold beliefs on less evidence, but a strict positivist should remain skeptical. Remember that facts themselves are subjective interpretations so that positivists, in the limit, cannot even establish the facts of a situation without accepting evidence and making inferences that they themselves condemn.

Some accountants always have been more or less neutral and depended on other institutions to provide the ethical basis for the profession. The modern version of this attitude castigates accountants for assuming a "privileged" position in society and from this advantaged position dictating guidelines that have the potential for creating a highly dysfunctional economic order. This modern critical viewpoint puts a new-left spin on the older traditional view of the responsibilities of the profession.

Earlier advocates of a weak accounting profession with little ethical responsibility usually shifted the ethical problem to law-makers and assumed that the accounting responsibility for ethics consists in seeing that the appropriate legal pronouncements are met. Perry Mason for example states: "Is there any *accounting* reason why adjustments of paid-in capital can not be made in any way desired by the stockholders as long as legal requirements are met and full disclosure is made of the facts? . . . . Why is this an *accounting* matter?"[11] In this formulation codes of ethics for the accounting profession are confined to seeing that accounting practices agree with legal mandates. The ethical task therefore is assigned to the legislative and judicial operators so that accounting ethics turns out to be a minor adjunct to these establishments with powers to force compliance. The auditing branch thus is limited to establishing conformance with legal requirements, and accounting theory is confined primarily to finding the consequences of various alternative rules and reporting them. It is clear that the accounting profession *can* be defined in this manner and that such a division of responsibilities *can* be made to work. It is not clear that aggressive accountants will be satisfied with such an allocation of duties and responsibilities.

Of course it is impossible to avoid making ethical judgments and Mason's judgment is that the sanctioned legal machinery is superior in this area than guidelines coming from the accounting profession. In the agency-contract literature it seems that the market place manned by programmed agency-contracting operators is to be accepted unconditionally. The very existence of these rigorous studies may suggest implicit approval, but the researchers themselves generally have avoided expressing preferences.

The DR Scott model is interesting in this connection. Scott was certainly not an avowed positivist. However his belief that properly collected and reported external *facts* lead to "automatic" decision making and to some sort of robotic management is at least congenial, and may go beyond positivism or empiricism. Some institutional economists (e.g., Wesley Mitchell) held a similar position and sometimes seemed to argue that the facts would somehow sort themselves out and disclose their inner harmonies when subjected to statistical and other methodological techniques.[12] Strangely, Scott had some beliefs in common with the Chicago empirical school in accounting. Davidson, an early guru of this movement, is repeated here:

> George [Schultz] used to talk about the little bits of evidence—accu-
> mulating them, letting them pile up until decisions were easy. . . .
> [O]ften the facts will seek you out. . . . If all the evidence is not yet in,
> we [Chicago Business School researchers] do not publish. . . . [I]f the
> supporting evidence is present, the conclusion becomes redundant.[13]

The above quotation by one of America's most respected writers leaves some important questions unanswered, but it does express in clear terms the underlying assumption of strict positivists and empiricists. Yet, the "bits of evidence" may render the conclusion more not less difficult, but there is an even more damaging flaw. Conclusions are *constructions* of the human mind. While the evidence (sooner or later) relates to sense impressions, there is no way that an accumulation of instances can make the mental act of concluding redundant. Davidson might as well argue that scientific laws and law-like statements are not needed. Finally his use of the logical term "all" is question begging. There is no way except by stipulation that a researcher can decide that *all* the evidence is available—a necessary condition for the Chicago group to publish. Not many modern scientists and other researchers now accept a strictly empiricist view, and the above quotation must be among the starkest and most ex-plicit statements of primitive empiricism within or without the field of accounting.

It is true that before agency-contract researchers became active, there was a surprising lack of attention to the field of accounting-rule se-lection. All thoughtful accountants whether in practice or in academe were well aware of the tremendous pressures brought about by interested groups who stand to gain or lose by rule selection. DR Scott in the twen-ties reiterated time and again the influence of accounting rules on groups and the corollary that being neutral to all interests is an impossible task.

In my own experience Man Maloo was the first to give detailed at-tention to the area.[14] He had been toying with the idea as a dissertation topic for several years, but so far as I know, was not familiar with the embryonic positivist work if indeed such work then existed. Maloo's own statement of his objectives:

> A positive theory of evolution of selected accounting ideas is posited . . . for emphasizing the social character of the accounting change process in which environments affect accounting and are affected by it. . . . [A] set of hypotheses is generated and tested through the Hegelian Dialectical process. . . .
>
> The central thesis is that many accounting changes have certain favorable consequences for some institutions and unfavorable ones for others. When an accounting problem emerges, various interest groups offer and analyze different accounting alternatives related to the problem. . . . [I]nstitutions take definite positions as initiators, proponents, opponents, and reactors (*ibid.,* pp. ii, iv).

Maloo's more general approach like the market approach is based essentially on a conflictual model using institutions instead of individuals. He assumes that these organizations have within them some degree of homogeneity as to objectives and indeed are formed to further these objectives. Examples were numerous: Insurance organizations trying to protect the insured; utility regulators protecting the public from rate gouging; trade associations trying to further client interests; managerial associations wanting good report cards; stock exchange committees and the SEC representing the investing public; governmental agencies hoping to promote fairness in taxes and in pricing for all the public; accounting institutes promoting defensible and profitable positions; college professors hoping for a consistent structure that does not violate intellectual integrity.

Maloo then identified many accounting problem areas (e.g., leases, current costs, tax allocation) and sought to trace their consequences on variables of concern such as income and capital requirements. He then sought to predict how each of these associations and groups would line up on such problems if they followed their professed objectives. He then compared their historical actions to the predictions to arrive at some belief about their consistency and possible extrapolation.

Maloo's methodology was not quantitatively sophisticated and some of his Hegelian adaptations may have been clumsy and ill-fitted to further his objectives, but he deserves to be remembered as an early inquirer into the process of accounting rule selection and therefore into the broader areas as to how society determines its commissions to service professions. More specifically he was interested in how such professions react to these organized pressures, and by their reactions tentatively to "decide who counts."

RELATED PROFESSIONS

The search by all service professions for legitimacy is a commonplace and is by no means confined to accounting. Legal systems look for guidance from the customs and folkways of their cultures. These cultural foundations are often expressed through past laws and edicts set forth by accepted governing groups and through the legal process itself, i.e., the common law routine. On occasion however these political groups (and the process) lose their legitimacy and the legal system frantically looks for more "fundamental" sources for its authority and this search usually extends to natural laws or to some higher authority. At such times the ideas of justice, fairness and the like become dominant and are advanced to support revolutionary topics such as the duty of citizens to revolt against onerous governing institutions and to sponsor just laws and just wars. Of course individual justice and fairness, like history, are influenced by the prevailing power elite.[15]

In the legal profession much of the current agency-contract struggle takes place behind the scenes at the legislative level. The self-interest bargaining by individuals and political groups for favorable legislation resembles the contract framework. The resulting legislation is the result of decisions delegated to legislative groups and is the result of reacting to various pressure groups with conflicting (and cooperating) interests. These pressure groups share some common characteristics and may indeed be represented by some assumed "political man" who is similar to the financial bureaucrats who contend for favorable accounting rules. In a real sense the resulting legislation serves as guidelines for sharing benefits and controlling behavior and like agency contracts they are based on prediction and retrospection.

Political scientists have done much preliminary work in this area and they are well beyond accountants on the duties and obligations of legislators themselves. For example legislators are supposed to represent the interests of their hometown constituents in bargaining wars for pork allotments, but they also are given further responsibilities for the welfare of wider groups, e.g., the national interest. So far political scientists have not done well in setting measures and norms for tradeoffs in these areas.

The allocation in politics apparently is left up to each politician's own conscious. In accounting however exogenous professional groups tip the balance from unregulated self interest to the interest of a wider public. This wider public may transcend national interest to the welfare of humanity itself.[16] To many accountants the profession should not be a passive reactor to the pressures of quarreling contracting agents and small self-interest groups. Accounting leaders become accounting statesmen dedicated to the wider interests of humanity.

Modern agency-contract theorists have a specific and detailed model to explain the actions of their agents and contractors in a bargaining situation, and there is no question that the use of contracts to structure the numerous relationships is a useful device. Yet the contracting facade is much like the abstraction of markets to guide the distribution and production of goods. Serious scholars will wish to go behind prices and markets and agency agreements to find the cultural forces at work behind the activities. Agency-contract theorists have done this kind of explanation, but when they do, they go beyond the boundaries of strict positivism.

SELECTING THE HOST: ONE MORE TIME

It may be of interest to review again the ways in which the accounting profession might select its masters from among parties contending for information. Until the recent avalanche of articles in the agency-contract area it usually was assumed that the profession itself had some ability to select its own rules and had some independent *responsibility* to do so. In my own view professional leaders should listen to all contending parties, weigh the merits of the claims in view of social standards and reach their own decisions. It is further assumed that this power and this responsibility are implicit in the commission given by society. Clearly this commission does not cover all situations and set forth complete operating details.[17]

Recently Arrington and Puxty have emphasized some differences in orientation.[18] My own view is slightly over-simplified as follows. "From Devine's perspective . . . the task of accounting is to embrace certain interests and go about the business of enhancing those interests. . . . The theorist then sets about the task of finding ways to improve the efficiency of that service" (*ibid*, p. 38). This characterization is true as far as it goes, but a coordinate task is in the direction of *selecting* the interests, and it is this part of the professional exercise that requires direct weighing and comparing along problematic value lines. There is no point to our profession unless some valued group or person is helped through our actions. From some perspective our existence must make a meaningful difference—be more than a sum-zero exercise.

Arrington and Puxty then present Neimark's view as an "alternative," whereas I had believed that our conclusions were similar although our orientation was different. For example, she appears as an excellent example of a researcher who takes a conflictual approach, and is at home with the sociology of conflict; while my own orientation is functional (cooperating) pragmatism. Certainly the following Neimark statement (except for the assumed necessity for new alliances) is consistent with my long-time commitment:

> a growing number of accounting researchers . . . are situating public interest accounting at the very center of an accounting problem that concerns itself with the basis for adjudicating exchanges between corporations and various social constituencies and factions. . . . In siting the accounting problematic in this fashion, [they] . . . are not redefining accountancy, for adjudication of exchanges has always been the social function of accounting. What they are doing . . . is to make explicit the allegiances that underlie contemporary and historical accounting practice and research in order to increase the social self-awareness of accountants and to encourage them to assume both a new set of alliances and greater responsibility for the profession's social role.[19]

Arrington's assessment of my own attitude is more clearcut and less ambiguous then it appears to me. My emphasis has been on the *necessity* to make choices and my consideration of "pathologies" has been almost entirely confined to the absurdities of professional orientation and argument. Indeed the hard decisions about who counts must be made, but the profession cannot revert to technical matters once the decisions have been rendered. My own interest has been more or less confined to intellectual pathologies, and I have seldom railed at the American form of government or at traditional socialist idealism or at people expressing their self-interest through capitalistic ventures or union activity. I am convinced that progress often comes from resistance to the prevailing ideology, whatever it is, and have championed the right to revolt against all intellectual and social precepts. Nevertheless I have struggled manfully to separate my views from specific (non-intellectual) value systems. Thus my attitudes on preferred income or valuation measures have generally been fluid. Moreover I have tried to be a practicing functional-ist without succumbing to the inanities of far out *total* system advocates even though the systems approach is essentially a functional paradigm.

In this spirit I object mildly to Arrington's advancement of Neimark's approach as an alternative. Listen:

> The second alternative [to my orientation] is what we will call an emancipatory attitude toward accounting's relation to interests. Here, the theorist is less concerned to "build" an accounting that serves a given interest and more concerned to critique how existing regimes of accounting create and sustain social pathologies that are injurious to other interests (*ibid.*, p. 38).

The above section emphasizes again that resolution of conflicting claims for information is necessary, and once the particulars of the resolution are known an important task of the accounting profession is to determine the consequences of various rules and relate them to accepted objectives.

Clearly all sorts of people (including embezzlers and ordinary thieves) are willing to pay for information, and just as clearly there may be worthy needs that are under funded. Many have concluded that a straight market process of selection is inadequate and must be supple-mented by additional screening devices. It is impossible to give every possible user the information that he might desire so that there is a scarcity of information relative to demand. Information therefore ac-quires value and in capitalistic systems the market process is the most common device for making such selections.

It must be emphasized that shortrun scarcity with respect to shortrun demand gives rise to only one type of value—economic value. It is by no means clear that accountants should restrict their efforts exclusively to this particular value. After all there are a myriad of alternative ways of sharing scarce goods and the use of market mechanisms is only one of these possible mechanisms. There also is the problem of sharing with fu-ture generations, so that environmental and longrun issues clamor for attention. So far the market process—although it works after a fashion—has left many theorists in abject despair. There are further complications arising from the use of scarcity values to the exclusion of all others. The value to human beings and other forms of life, of good air, safe water and the like may be infinite for all generations. Accountants can improve their services to humanity by furnishing information in these areas. The same may be said about esthetic values, moral values, humanistic values, ethical values and countless other assessments. Attention to these objectives and to the specifics of attaining them should provide intellectual material for accountants for the next millennium or so.

SUMMARY

This negative look at the market for settling distribution claims does not deny that the accounting profession in the past (and no doubt in the future) has been acutely tuned to the squeak of the money wheel. Those with the highest bids undoubtedly have exerted the most influence, and have gone home with most of the informational merchandise. Unorganized bidders without adequate means to compete have been largely ignored unless they enlist government agencies to coordinate and advance their claims and to furnish funds. It is unfortunate that embezzlers, money launderers, narcotic tradesmen and the Ivan Boeskys of high finance usually have more than adequate resources and often know which pressure centers are subject to influence. They create their own symphony of squeaks, but it is not obvious that a service profession should listen to them. Mastering the strategies of market finance may create canny and effective operators, but it is doubtful that such skills will contribute to an effective service profession.

The feeling that the accounting profession is more or less inert and not an important player in the selection of accounting principles is not a recent one. The frantic search for principles in the thirties with brilliant scholars scanning the world of ideas for *fundamental* concepts was itself recognition that the accounting profession was in need of stronger support for its claim to legitimacy and a stronger hand in the principles game.

With respect to auditing professional leaders were slow to react and in truth the most widely used auditing text of the World War II years was a poorly organized combination of a 1936 rulebook and some badly thought out concepts of traditional accounting theory.[20]

The accountants of the thirties were well aware that the profession had a number of functions that society expects it to perform and that different users often have different needs, and therefore that they should exert some influence on the rule- making process. For example there was considerable argument over the need for including certain income tax matters in the definition of *accounting* income. Taxing authorities have very special needs that include ease of extraction, ease of preparation, wealth redistribution and various bounties and penalties. It is highly doubtful that the taxing authorities are interested in the traditional uses of income that require keeping capital intact to provide a base for comparing firms in different activities and for evaluating management. Many accountants, including this one, insist that tax needs should be met with new names appropriate for the occasion so that traditional definitions (e.g., income) need not be bastardized. The optimal degree of polysemy is more than a semantic distinction, and the term income already has so many variations of meanings so obscure that it requires individual explication each time it is employed. Other accountants admit that the traditional measures of accounting income already include responses to all sorts of needs but that the additional needs of tax collectors can be accommodated within the definitional framework. When necessary, they argue, discrepancies between GAAP and any particular income measure can be explained in the reports.

NOTES

[1] C. West Churchman, *The Design of INQUIRING SYSTEMS: Basic Concepts of Systems and Organization* (New York: Basic Books, Inc., 1971), p. 164. See also his *The Systems Approach and its Enemies* (New York: Basic Books, Inc., 1979).

[2] American Institute of CPAs.

[3] That he never abandoned his emphasis on formal models based on postulates and the mechanics of logic and moved completely to an American pragmatic position is clearly reflected in his later works. In discussing his own earlier efforts he states, "Yet I did not make any attempt to present a *body of systematic interpretations* of my theoretical framework. The reason for this omission rested in my conviction that I lacked the methodological and empirical prerequisites to tackle such a complex task. . . . [And] I admitted my ignorance about the pertinent means-end relations." The quotations are from his "On the Evolution of Theory Construction in Accounting: A Personal Account," in *Modern Accounting Research: History, Survey and Guide,* Research Monograph 7 (Vancouver: The Canadian Certified General Accountants' Research Foundation, 1984), p. 34.

[4] As was pointed out earlier Mattessich was careful to separate his positive notions and his *interpretations*. Unfortunately Mattessich too made his search for *basic* observations *before* he set forth his guidelines for making the selections. Apparently both Mattessich and Moonitz were searching for something *more* basic and general than observations from the narrow area of accounting. Mattessich apparently hoped that his general structure would serve all sorts of interpretations for various kinds of accounting and other information systems. Moonitz

seems to have limited his interpretations (applications) to a more traditional definition of accounting.

⁵ See Yuji Ijiri, "Axioms and Structures of Conventional Accounting Measurement," *The Accounting Review,* January 1965, pp. 36–53 or *The Foundations of Accounting Measurement: A Mathematical, Economic, and Behavioral Inquiry* (Englewood Cliffs: Prentice Hall, Inc., 1967). It may be that Ijiri's conclusions were influenced by historical factors. Certainly he was influenced by Cooper, who in turn was a disciple of Kohler, who always was an adamant defender of historical costs. Incidentally this reviewer always has been reasonably sympathetic to the historical cost application as a useful surrogate for values except in times of rapid price changes. In short my own preferences tend to be more situational.

⁶ For a fantastic shift in the "winds of doctrine," see a more mellow Nicholas Dopuch: "The Impact of Regulations on Financial Accounting Research," *Contemporary Accounting Research,* Vol. 5, No. 2, pp. 494–500.

⁷ W. A. Paton, *Accounting Theory, With Special Reference to the Corporate Enterprise* (New York: The Ronald Press Company, 1922); republished by Accounting Studies Press, Ltd., Chicago, 1962; and reprinted by Scholars Book Co, Houston, 1973; pp. 471–499.

⁸ *Ibid.* In the 1962 republication, this was included after the "Publisher's Preface" in "Remarks on the Republication of Paton's *Accounting Theory,*" pp. 5-6; in the 1973 reprint, this was included in the "Foreword to the Reissue," p. ix.

⁹ Why Paton selected Postulate eleven remains a question, but it indicates a long-term ambivalence toward physical manifestations, fungible goods and the rest. Consider: "The accountant . . . is dealing *primarily* with economic data, with values, not with physical *certainties* . . ." (emphasis added), *ibid.,* p. 471. Perhaps he should have substituted "entirely" for "primarily." The fact that he even considered physical objects to be "certainties" betrays his naturalistic leanings. In retrospect it seems incredible that he let my own subjectivistic dissertation go through with only minor suggestions. He did however discourage my earlier attempt to develop a dissertation around postulating the profession. Perhaps he already was disillusioned about the benefits of strict deductive reasoning.

¹⁰ More directly this discussion is the result of scanning a volume put together by Richard Mattessich, *op. cit.* It includes the following excellent articles as summaries of current thought: Gerald A. Feltham, "Financial Accounting Research: Contributions of Information Economics and Agency Theory," pp. 179–207; and John E. Butterworth, Michael Gibbins and Raymond D. King, "The Structure of Accounting Theory: Some Basic Conceptual and Methodological Issues," pp. 209–250.

¹¹ Perry Mason, "The 1948 Statement of Concepts and Standards," *The Accounting Review,* April 1950, pp. 137–138 (emphasis in original).

[12] Allan Gruchy states: "by pouring the voluminous data of business cycle history through the narrow sieve of statistical analysis, Mitchell endeavors 'to create order amidst the confused facts of observation. . . .'" *Modern Economic Thought: The American Contribution* (New York: Prentice-Hall, Inc., 1947), p. 269.

[13] Sidney Davidson, "Where is the Evidence?" *Issues and Ideas,* Spring 1971, pp. 29–30.

[14] Man Chand Maloo, *Toward a Theory of Evolution of Selected Accounting Ideas* (Tallahassee: Florida State University Dissertation, 1977). Incidentally Charles A. Tritschler also was an early pioneer in this field: "A Sociological Perspective on Accounting Innovation," *International Journal of Accounting Education and Research,* Spring 1970, pp. 39–67.

[15] In the Bork and other supreme-court hearings strict constructionists were seldom successful in trying to deny the influence of cultural changes in favor of higher authorities. That the constitution is only a temporary bulwark is illustrated by the current efforts to expand the first amendment by those espousing the dominance of individual rights over the will of individuals acting in groups. The constitution, like the direct word of the deity, cannot possibly cover every contingency. Most arguments so far have stopped with the constitution. Yet the constitution itself is based on natural law concepts and on behavior recommended in Judeo-Christian literature. Various religious groups, like the constitution, act as stabilizers to dampen sudden shifts in popular opinion.

[16] The problem of ethical pressure on accountants has been troublesome for decades. In the fifties my colleague Robert Dinman pointed out that practicing auditors "address" the problem by being advocates for clients when the public is protected by legislative or administrative agencies, and by becoming activist protectors of the public interest and against clients when the public is not otherwise protected.

[17] While to a large extent the social objectives *must* come from without the profession, I have always contended that most management science advocates (e.g., Churchman and Mattessich) have made an overly sharp distinction between an organization and its environment and have considered the objectives of *accounting* to be determined by these *exogenous* forces. Following DR Scott, I have held that the accounting profession itself plays an important part in the process and makes *selections* from alternatives offered. It therefore has to shoulder some responsibility for the results of such selections. This view certainly is not supported by the new agency-contract researchers, but it is consistent with most contributors to *Accounting, Organizations and Society,* to *Critical Perspectives on Accounting* or to *Advances in Public Interest*

[18] C. Edward Arrington and Anthony G. Puxty, "Accounting, Interests, and Rationality: A Communicative Relation," *Critical Perspectives on Accounting* (1), 1991, pp. 31–58.

[19] Quoted from Arrington and Puxty, Ibid., p. 38. Original in M. Neimark, "Marginalizing the Public Interest in Accounting," *Advances in Public Interest Accounting,* Vol. 1, 1986, pp. xii-xiii. My quarrel with Neimark, Tinker and the host of new traditional *language critics has never been in the area of the problematic nature of any accounting discourse* or about the force of ideology, the need for reification or the desirability of accountants to consider the social consequences of their recommendations and actions. My own criticisms might be characterized as "non-specific" antagonism to ridiculous argumentation. Their criticism has been far more specific with moderate to intense opposition to institutions not supported by traditional Marxism and strictures of the new left.

[20] The University of Michigan in the middle thirties did not even offer a course in auditing even though it was already clear that a major function of the profession is to decrease uncertainty and add confidence to reports from insiders. Auditing—largely from the 1936 rulebook—was combined with income tax in one three-hour course designated as Public Accounting. For more detailed information in the broader area see Kenneth S. Most, *Accounting Theory* (Columbus: Grid Inc., 1977). For example:

> the Federal Reserve Board and the Federal Trade Commission in 1917 requested the AIA to put forward proposals for standardized financial statements. The resulting memorandum received the endorsement of the Federal Reserve Board and, after being submitted to the banking community [!] nationally for their reactions, it was published in the April 1917 issue of the *Federal Reserve Bulletin.* This memorandum became the publication *Uniform Accounting* and was republished in 1918 as *Approved Methods for the Preparation of Balance Sheet Statements.* The Federal Reserve Board published a revised edition, *Verification of Financial Statements* in 1929.... A 1936 revision of this publication was published by AIA; entitled *Examination of Financial Statements by Independent Public Accounts* ... (p. 65).

Some Accounting Personalities— Major and Minor

A half-century of knocking about in the accounting field has led to observing many personalities. Unfortunately a number of interesting accounting leaders escaped my direct observation. I was genuinely disappointed, upon arriving at the Wharton School, that Kenneth MacNeal was and had never been connected with the school. His *Truth in Accounting* expressed some ideas that badly needed to be expressed, although his arguments violated all my own views of semantics and persuasion. I only observed Roy B. Kester, and unfortunately an opportunity to revise his well-known texts came only after his demise. Henry Rand Hatfield was something of a hero in spite of occasional negative remarks by former colleagues and associates. His wit was intriguing and his sense of scholarship was an example to neophytes in the profession. William Morse Cole expressed enough wisdom to suggest an interesting and well-rounded background. There is no doubt that I would have found DR Scott a delightful colleague. His broad social interests and knowledge were an inspiration even though our paths never crossed. Stephen Gilman's broad knowledge of accounting and its modern history influenced my own approach to the field, although we never had an opportunity to discuss such matters. Rufus Rorem's informal readings in theory demonstrated a wide interest and refreshing orientation to the field. All later generation managerial accountants must share my regret at not being able to discuss the nature of cost with J. M. Clark.

The sketches below do not pretend to be adequate summaries of views and influences. The discussion of Paton—the accountant of the century—is a summary of some personal glimpses and is in no way intended to be an exposition or analysis of his contributions. The discussions of Woodbridge and Saliers are more complete, for these important educators have not received critical attention by the accounting profession. By most assessments both were below standard classroom expositors, but both were in large part responsible for setting the tone for accounting instruction at important universities. The sketch on the Wharton School is devoted to the general orientation of the department and less with personalities. This discussion deals with the intermediate period at Penn and leaves the accurate historical account of early instruction and personalities to the excellent work by Lockwood.[1]

FREDERICK WELLS WOODBRIDGE

Whereas MacFarland and many other professors were impressive classroom performers, Woodbridge was far from impressive, especially for lower division students. His delivery was halting, his voice tended to tail off, and he apparently had little sense of timing, i.e., covering required material within rigid time constraints. Suggestions near the end of a gruelling afternoon or evening session for class adjournment to a neighboring tavern were common. Such sessions were usually pleasant and instructive and carried on with the grace that might be expected from one who had spent most of his life in the old west well before and after Pancho Villa "invaded" the United States and Zapata travelled the easy road. Among the virtues of the old west, he certainly adopted a deep sense of honor and a fierce sense of loyalty. (A stint at a military school—that upper-middle-class institution for reshaping rebellious young males—may have reinforced these values.)

With the help of post-war (I) educational opportunities, he landed at the University of Washington and later became an assistant professor at the University of Texas. Leaving Mount Rainier and the Northwest brought sadness and even tears. But the opportunity to travel over Texas in the middle twenties and to instruct ranchers about costs, profits and record-keeping helped offset his attachment to the Northwest. The opportunity to visit remote ranches along with the usual university duties was especially welcome, for Woodbridge had the rare ability to relate to all sorts of individuals, including workers, intellectuals, socialists, Republicans, rebellious students and faculty elite.

After a short stint at Lehigh University, he drifted back to Southern California in 1928 and devoted a quarter century to the University of Southern California with loyalty and devotion. USC, in spite of a big time athletic program that covered many sports, lacked endowment and suffered extreme financial difficulties during the depression. President von Kleinschmidt earned the loyalty of many professors (including Woodbridge) by cutting salaries only 10 percent and retaining faculty until ordinary retirements and separations closed the gap.

Running a university in a talent-rich urban center had a major advantage, for a convenient pool of part time teachers was available for low salaries and university prestige. This fortunate situation permitted flexibility in staff reductions and helped the university to enjoy some academic standing often with only one full-time professor in many departments. Retired professors from other institutions were employed, e.g., Irving Fisher who then was building his advocacy for a consumption tax and was especially interested in accounting and its problems with income definition and measurement. Extensive use also was made of nearby Hollywood for artistic talent. (It is fashionable to belittle the artistic culture of Hollywood, and many fail to realize the amazing artistic and writing talent that was and is available there.)

Woodbridge taught theory courses to both undergraduates and masters candidates. There were no doctoral programs in business, but candidates in economics, public administration and law could write dissertations in the field of accounting. These theory courses were analytical but somewhat circumscribed and devoted to narrow accounting concepts. In spite of his contacts with Fisher, Garver and other economists, he never seemed able to integrate economics with accounting as effectively as Paton and some others.

Overall Woodbridge had the attitudes of an engineer rather than those of an economist or social scientist. He was analytical and even though he himself was not a competent mathematician, he encouraged students to develop mathematical (as well as linguistic) skills and to stand ready to apply them to accounting problems. He always insisted that cost accounting was a production job, not a clerical one, and devoted much classroom time to finding possible reasons for the variances disclosed by the accounting system.[2]

Woodbridge's indirect experience in cost accounting was outstanding. Apparently the first N.A.C.A. Chapter arrived in Los Angeles shortly before he arrived. He served for decades as the chairman of its educational committee. In the course of these decades he came to know practically every cost accountant and accounting installation in Southern California and encouraged all local controllers to write technical how-we-did-it articles for the *Bulletin*. His knowledge of variable costing and flexible budgeting was well above average for traditional cost accountants. He was sympathetic to longterm basic standards with all sorts of adjustments to current levels by ratios, but he did not display the extreme fascination shown by Camman or Lockwood.

One result of this widespread practical knowledge was Woodbridge's early use of startup variances and his appreciation of learning in repetitive activities. It is true that he was not interested in some idealized equation to express the learning phenomenon for different situations, but he had a firm understanding of its accounting aspects. So far as I can remember he never used a direct "learning variance," but he was aware that variances employed during learning periods were usually erratic. In a well-remembered problem-case, he made use of a change-over variance to hold excess costs during this interval. His solution accepted managerial estimates for the appropriate speeds at various stages of operations. For example, if during the training period, assembly lines need to run at 60 percent of capacity, the standard costs for completed product were set at full capacity operations with the costs of the early slowdown treated as an overhead cost of the model run. The efficiency of the learning process itself could be monitored by comparing the changeover variances at different scheduled speeds.

On the theoretical level Woodbridge was both traditional and *avant garde* with the latter appearing in the more technical aspects. His most modern touch was clearly in the area of information and the accountant's duties in this area. The first chapter of his elementary text and at least the first two meetings of elementary accounting classes were devoted to organizational structures, lines of authority, information needs and document flows.[3] This user approach was reenforced in the elective systems course, where he often expressed outrage with textbooks that began with technical matters and a mechanical approach to the chart of accounts instead of immediate stress on the organization of the firm and the needs that the accounts are designed to serve.

Woodbridge had worked with the National Association of Credit Men and tended to emphasize shortterm debt-paying ability and the needs of financial institutions just when the profession was moving toward income measurement and the need of absentee owners to appraise hired managers. As a result, the impression often was that his attitudes were staid and traditional. The emphasis on shortterm credit and shortrun debt-paying ability is evident in his handling of receivables that recommended a scheduling of maturities on the balance sheet itself.

He was impressed with narrow profit margins (a common position for standard-cost advocates), and insisted that current assets and liabilities be expressed at current costs. Clean inventories (with small net profit elements) at recent costs should approximate the cash flow over the normal inventory turn. While inventories at current cost may be slightly understated in terms of net cash flow, receivables tend to be slightly overstated due to expected future discounts, allowances and returns. In a similar manner payables are slightly overstated. The general price-level problem did not interest him beyond the feeling that it was management's duty to balance dollar assets and liabilities to hedge the purchasing-power elements.

Woodbridge was a diehard base-stock advocate, except that he wished to bring the inventory in excess of base stock to current values by means of an unrealized capital provision (reserve). The objective is to present a balance sheet value that has some relation to debt-paying ability and an income report based on current costs. Depletion of the base stock was charged to operations at current costs with appropriate adjustments to the reserves.

In true base-stock fashion the basic amount of inventories is not available for current-debt paying and is considered to be a fixed asset. He in fact carried the concept further and insisted that the basic amount of current receivables would never be collected by the going concern, and that the basic amount of liabilities was permanent capital that need not be repaid. Woodbridge bravely carried this theme to its conclusion and insisted that the basic amount of cash (change funds and precautionary balances) is not a current asset. In fact he argued that the necessary change funds are as fixed as the cash registers themselves. As a result he clearly had reservations about the usual current ratios, and concluded that his version of modified current items tends to express current values adequately and can easily be adopted to the matching process.

While Woodbridge could hardly be called an income extremist, he favored matching current costs with current revenues, and was not convinced by Irving Fisher's persuasive arguments for discounting streams of expectations. His mild distrust of the subjective and his search for objective evidences were characteristics of accountants of this period. (Observe however that he was a mild advocate of cost or market whichever is lower even though the evidence for lowering expectations is somewhat indirect.) He was disturbed by such distinctions as income determination versus income administration, for, he argued, it does not make sense to construct concepts that require modification before they can be applied to their primary tasks.

Woodbridge also was concerned with abnormal as opposed to normal earnings in terms of the expectations they create. He recognized the difficulties of agreeing on what is to be considered normal. In cost accounting for example, he was sympathetic to—if not an active advocate of—the position that standard costs are the real costs of product with cost variances being the cost of something other than product. A good part of the accountant's task is to reach useful conclusions about the nature of something. With respect to earnings he was more thorough than most accountants of the time. He not only wished to segregate non-recurring items on the operating report to avoid misunderstanding at the operating level, but he also separated the surplus accounts to help those who wished to estimate the sources of capital accumulation. Unusual earnings were to be closed to a windfall (non-recurring) surplus account. The sources of dividends also were segregated and those based on unusual earnings were labelled as extras to discourage continuing expectations, and were charged to the specially designated surplus account.

Woodbridge was also disturbed at the sloppy way of handling capital and drawings accounts and wished to make the treatment nearer to that used in corporation accounting. To further this aim he distinguished between "vested capital" and more temporary sources of capital. Corporate stock dividends move some capital to the vested section, and similarly a declaration of intent by proprietors serves as the basis for moving portions of the current accounts to designated capital accounts. Most accountants of the time used a similar but less formal approach. If the owners wish as a matter of policy to determine whether they are living within their business means period by period, the personal or drawing accounts were closed at the end of each period. If however owners take a longer view of living within their means, the accounts are allowed to remain open. Woodbridge's idea of a formal commitment replaces this behavioral rule, and proprietorship bookkeeping moves nearer to corporate accounting.

After retiring at Yale shortly before World War II, Irving Fisher moved to California and became visiting professor at USC. During this time he was developing a formula that redefined income as consumption. As near as I can recall Woodbridge was reasonably sympathetic with Fisher's emphasis on income as discounted expectations. It is true that his own accounting training had been primarily from a documentary auditing viewpoint, but his experience with cost accounting and budgeting had generated a respect for budgets, variances from plans and the need for accounting to shift its emphasis from history as history to the use of the past to furnish clues to future action.

Apparently Woodbridge was not enthusiastic about a definition of income in terms of consumption expenditures. Clearly he was committed to the notion of keeping capital intact and measuring income from a stable base, and on many occasions he complained of pressures from outside the profession to harness the concept of income to some special (single) objective and forget its importance for all sorts of possible users. He was favorably disposed to the treatment of dividends as expenses (although he did not advocate this position to undergraduates), but was unable to accept withdrawals and dividends as measures of income. To abandon the entire income construction to the whims of those who declare dividends and divorce the concept from changes in wealth and corporate control was clearly more than he was prepared to accept.

Many of the following beliefs were widely shared in the profession of that time and are only summarized here. In Woodbridge's case he held them tenaciously and defended them without reserve.

He was balance-sheet oriented and grounded his judgments on the economic concept of wealth. For example he was convinced that one of the justifications for the profession is to account for levels of wealth, set forth the sources of wealth, indicate restrictions on the use of wealth, report significant changes in wealth and contribute to the safeguarding of wealth. Assets are classified to indicate the type of services to which wealth has been devoted, and to a lesser extent to the probable uses to which wealth will be put. Liabilities are restriction on the free disposition of resources, indicate important sources of wealth and show preferences for the types of contracts that procure it.

Equities performed similar functions, but Woodbridge made a much wider gap between equities and liabilities than Paton and entity theorists. Keeping control of the wealth was an important objective and maturity agreements therefore took on great importance.

The operating report was to a large extent a control device, although the function of linking balance-sheet statements of wealth was not neglected. Revenues were no big deal other than showing inflows of wealth from various operations. In fact Woodbridge was probably more interested in segmented statements, for they indicated certain information about relative markets and could trigger detailed management studies about demand elasticities and responses to promotional alternatives. Expenses were conceived in the traditional manner of the time and coincided with the definition of costs in the Patonian structure. Expenses indicated how wealth has been distributed by expenditures to potential sources of services. In a broad sense expenses are expenditures (sacrifices) that have not been assigned to activities. To Woodbridge a cost has to be a *cost of something* that resulted from the wealth creating process. Thus cost of goods sold was an ideal title and indicated that some resources designated as expenses had been matched with services recognized for the period. To be consistent he argued that plant expenditures are potential costs and the current depreciation charge is a cost of capital deterioration. Losses are defined in the usual fashion as decreases in wealth (expenses) without return. Income is of course excess of new wealth recognized over wealth expired (correlated) over the agreed time interval.

Certainly Woodbridge could not be considered at the leading edge of organization theory, but he did relate accounting instruction to the life-cycle approach to corporate management. According to his view the early stages of corporate organization are related to producing goods. As a result he presumed that the people most likely to be in charge of businesses would be inventors, engineers and plain production men who could get on with the work. Management in such firms is usually top-down. Accounting appropriate for the needs of such people is traditional standard cost accounting. Cost accounting at that time is oriented more closely to production workers and the results are related to standards, load factors, capacity and efficiency variances, plant departmentalizations and layers of employees ranging from snappers to plant managers.

According to his historical theory, the second stage of the organizational life cycle is a selling and marketing period. Competitors sense profitable opportunities and start competing with existing firms. Patents and related monopolistic grants can hold off competition only to a limited extent and for a limited time. Competitors move as near the protected products as legally feasible and attempt to improve them to support their competing patents. At this stage the people who rise to the top of the organization are men who understand the selling and marketing of goods. In the Woodbridge accounting scheme, the appropriate accounting shifts accordingly. Accounting information now emphasizes sales by lines, territories, etc., to sales returns, allowances and rebates, and to the estimation of cost and benefits of alternative marketing strategies. For this reason Woodbridge may have been one of the early supporters of what later became known as distribution cost accounting. Furthermore he felt that greater opportunities for cost saving and profits come at this stage from developing and monitoring marketing activities. Certainly marketing costs are less closely paced by machines and less controlled by direct (non-accounting) methods of supervision.

The third stage of organizational development corresponds closely to the Marxist (and populist) concept of finance capitalism. At this stage lawyers and financial specialists rise to the top of corporate administration. Legal defenses and aggressions became important, and all sorts of mergers and consolidations along with patent litigation and labor conflicts become dominant. At this stage the complexion of accounting again changes to cover more complicated financial arrangements such as poolings, mergers and looser combinations and reorganizations. Also at this level the uses of standard cost accounting change. Capital is less scarce so that incentive schemes that share fixed cost savings with efficient workers are less directly applicable and less acceptable to strong laboristic groups. Attention moves to stock options, fringe benefits and ownership sharing plans with new problems of dilution and less specific allocations.

EARL A. SALIERS

Saliers was something of a professional anomaly. His dignified mein and well cared for Van Dyke helped him look and act the part of a scholar. Moreover he had the proper credentials: Ph.D. from Yale in economics (when doctorates were rare indeed) and a student of Irving Fisher. Fisher was then an intellectual leader in the prestigious field of social sciences rather than in the grubby soil of business. Saliers attention began and remained with the field of depreciation and his popular *Depreciation, Principles and Applications* ran through three editions from before World War I to 1939.[4]

An anomalous aspect arises because in spite of impeccable theoretical grounding, Saliers remained a practical accountant with an easygoing simplistic approach to the field. In fact he avoided theoretical disputation whenever possible.[5] There also was an other-worldliness about his behavior that belied his intense interest in the practical aspects of accounting.

Saliers had a simple, straightforward writing style with short sentences and little jargon or constructions designed to impress the reader with his brilliance. He was one of the authors of the Northwestern University loose-leaf accounting series and of a subsequent handbook on office management and procedures (A. W. Shaw, 1929). This handbook too was thorough and comprehensive with little theoretical content. His text for elementary and notes for intermediate were used at Louisiana State University in the late thirties and followed his usual pattern. His joint effort at the intermediate level was a survey of practical procedures and was generally undistinguished.[6]

In some important ways the first edition of the *Accountants' Hand-*

book[7] has been seriously underrated. Its strongest point no doubt was the distinguished list of contributors. These contributors included Irving Fisher, M. J. Shugrue and James P. Adams in economics; L. P. Alford in management; Thomas Conyngton and William Diebold in business law and organization; J. T. Madden, P. W. Pinkerton, among others in accounting; P. E. Bacas in auditing and G. L. Harris in cost accounting.[8]

My overall judgment is that the section devoted to depreciation, written by Saliers himself, is among the weakest. His technique is the usual one found in handbooks—numerous quotations from practical leaders in the field to impart a feel for authoritativeness and general acceptance. Saliers himself cites few conflicting sources, and often uses citations mainly to buttress traditional positions. He himself tends to avoid conflict by the simple technique of either giving opposing sides without comment or omitting opposing views completely. For example for the definition of depreciation, Saliers gives three quotations. One is on the decline-in-value approach, another is on "expired capital outlay" (cost) and the other is on "exhaustion of capacity for service" (physical). His conclusion is that "No satisfactory general definition can be given . . . ," and his reason for the conclusion is "since the term is usually employed in a limited sense" (*ibid.,* p. 471).

His lack of analysis may be illustrated by the following: "**Unit depreciation** refers to a unit of plant. **Composite depreciation** refers to plant as a whole; it is the sum of depreciation of the units" (*ibid.,* p. 471; bold face in original).

Perhaps more serious is the lack of understanding of the elementary aspects of decision theory. Consider the following observations on obsolescence. "Obsolescence becomes effective only when production can be carried on more cheaply by replacing a given unit the underdepreciated or unrecovered cost of which is considered as a part of replacement cost. It is measured by the amount by which cost less salvage exceeds amount of depreciation already written off" (*ibid.,* p. 472). This rationale probably influenced Saliers to adopt the income tax recommendation to add the "loss" on trade-in or replacement to the cost of the replacement asset. For tax purposes this procedure may reduce the nuisance of collection, but other defenses are hard to construct.[9] Saliers, so far as I know never did defend this position, but the usual defenses take one or both of the following turns. First it may be argued without genuine force—that future periods benefit from the removal of obsolete technology and therefore future periods should bear the burden of exchange. His "loss" on the old unit is spread over the remaining life of the old asset and *not* added to the new and depreciated over the life of the new. Second it may be maintained with even less force that a going concern cannot suffer a capital loss. This argument apparently stems from the older division between capital and revenue expenditures so that only regular replacements should be charged against revenues. However even if this position is accepted, it still does not follow that the amount should be continued as an asset rather than taken as a reduction in capital.

Saliers' discussion of various deprecation methods also is fuzzy. The sinking fund method is discussed as follows. "The rate of depreciation is made a **function of an interest rate** and is purely theoretical. A fixed sum of money is set aside each period to accumulate at compound interest" (*ibid.*, p. 500; bold face in original). Interestingly he was well ahead of Moonitz and some others in pointing out that the annuity method with a zero rate of interest was equivalent to straightline depreciation.[10] There is some evidence that Saliers was familiar with the smoothing aspects of overhead rates and with the possibility of leaving under- or over-absorbed overhead on the balance sheet to counter the feeling that each period is a closed system for plant capacity and production. His discussion of depreciation (*ibid.*, pp. 495-6) uses two supplementary rates to ensure that product costs in fact absorb *all* factory costs period by period. On at least one occasion in answer to a direct question he asserted that all fixed costs should be added to the cost of product regardless of the amount of production and did not retreat when asked if he would recommend the procedure when only one unit is manufactured. Apparently all costs are product costs, and little attention was given to the allocation problem between production and idleness or to the further possibility that idle-time costs might even be assets because they represent the cheapest method of keeping capacity available for future production.

In summary it is clear that Saliers' claim for historical remembrance derives from clear expositions of simple practical matters rather than from theoretical originality.

WHARTON-INTERMEDIATE PERIOD

There is evidence that the conception of accounting at the early Wharton School was at best undistinguished, and in the intermediate years its leadership was not adequate for so distinguished an institution. Perhaps the charge in the original deed of trust from Joseph Wharton in 1881 was responsible for the limited esteem granted bookkeeping and accounting:

> one Professor or Instructor of Accounting or Bookkeeping, to teach the simplest and most practical forms of bookkeeping for housekeepers,

for private individuals, for commercial and banking firms, for manufacturing establishments, and for banks; also, the modes of keeping accounts by executors, trustees, and assignees, by the officials of towns and cities, as well as by the several departments of a State or National Government; also the routine of business between a bank and a customer.[11]

Certainly this charge was in part responsible for the broad emphasis on accounting systems for diverse industries that has always been a trademark of accounting graduates from Wharton.

According to Dowlin, classes started in 1881 "with one full-time professor of political economy and a part-time instructor in accounting. . . . from a downtown business office, and it is a legend . . . that a faculty member always accompanied him to class, to maintain order."[12]

Edward P. Moxey, Jr. the first professor of accounting and first chairman of the department was a product of this down-to-earth approach to the field. More theoretical scholars might have wished for a more academic leader with a broader background and with less interest in the practical problems of running an accounting office.[13]

While accounting as a discipline may have seemed to be pretty primitive at that time, such is not exactly the case. Sprague, at New York University, was busy getting his thoughts together for his well-known *The Philosophy of Accounts* (1908). Hatfield was absorbing the German experience and working toward *Modern Accounting* (1909), a treatise that for the time was truly modern. Cole (1908) and Esquerré (1914) at Harvard, were developing some sophisticated discussions, and Kester, Montgomery, and May along with some British accountants were stirring the theoretical waters. In the meantime Scovill was advocating interest as a cost of production. At the December 1916 organizational meeting of what later became the American Accounting Association, it is noticeable that Moxey was not among its founders and that no one appears to have represented the Wharton faculty.[14]

One of the most obvious manifestations of Moxey's fantastic organizational ability and concern for details is found in the teaching at Wharton that survived two decades after he was no longer active. Classroom performance has always been top-notch and classroom ability has remained an important factor in hiring and promoting. Young instructors not only were encouraged to teach well—they were given all sorts of teaching aids to improve their performance.[15]

Like the early Johns Hopkins Medical School, the Wharton School placed a well-known professor as the head of each department and paid him well in order to keep him interested primarily in university teaching.[16] (The relative values even then may be indicated by a reported $7,500 for business area leaders at Wharton, with perhaps at most $5,000 for professor at other high-level institutions. John Hopkins apparently followed a similar policy by paying fabulous ($16,000) salaries to the four heads of medical instruction.) Apparently Moxey was something of an exception for he was primarily a professional accountant and apparently remained so. Clearly he fitted better into the business elite rather than into the broader intellectual community.

Many young Wharton instructors of the time unfortunately did an informal apprenticeship in Moxey's firm. According to reports Moxey and his partners would arrive at their accounting office precisely on time and were presented with the *Inquirer's* crossword puzzle for the day. After ten minutes or so the partners were ready to issue work orders for the day. Many boring audits were of municipalities and savings-and-loan organizations. In the process juniors were armed with pencils of at least three colors and with infinite patience. After an appropriate (seemingly endless) wait the senior in charge would grunt with appropriate pitch and intonation and the assistant would select a pencil of the proper color and make a tic on the designated form. The traditional "tic and holler" approach to auditing was turned around.

There is evidence that the Moxey influence was to retard the development of accounting at Wharton in important ways. According to reports he believed that there were only two "principles" of accounting—double entry and control. Double entry in its simpler phases was covered in the introductory course in principles, and less obvious applications were treated in a course devoted to specialized systems. Control was attended to in auditing and reinforced in the systems course. The Wharton tradition (unlike Harvard's concentration in two years) was for spaced learning with technical courses interwoven with liberal arts courses over four years. Introductory accounting for many decades was a compact five semester-hour course that was given to entering or second-semester freshmen. It was held that accounting is an indispensable analytical tool and should be available to students early in their business studies.

The second principle (control) was approached uniquely and effectively at Wharton. One appropriate course was constructed around systems, but not systems in the sense of designing and installing devices for planning and control. Instead the course was devoted to application and criticism of systems already designed for major industries and different areas of government. The course content differed slightly from time to time and even from semester to semester, but usually included accounting for governmental units, utilities, brokerage houses and related financial institutions and railroads. Attention was directed to controls, types of statements, organization charts, etc. Thus the course was devoted to cases where the application of double entry and control was not obvious. In any case the systems course at Wharton has traditionally been a strong part of the curriculum, and for decades a working knowledge of system applications was a mark of the Wharton accounting graduate.

Incidentally, the Wharton tradition for spacing accounting courses over the entire four-year program remained strong until near the end of World War II. Harvard, Stanford, Michigan and some other schools adopted an opposing tradition and accepted graduate students with all sorts of majors and concentrated the teaching of business and accounting over approximately two years of intensive professional training. Actually it was not until the early-middle 1940's that Wharton designed a graduate two-year accounting major for all sorts of diverse majors. Until this time most non-business undergraduates who registered as Wharton graduates were required to take the long undergraduate sequence in accounting before entering the more challenging graduate courses.

A further development at Wharton that was closely related to Moxey concerned the library kept by the Accounting Department in addition to the excellent Lippincott library of business and the general university libraries. One interesting aspect of this department library was bound typed volumes of all C.P.A. examinations ever given including those given by the individual states before uniform examinations were adopted. Nevertheless, this legacy was an outright anomaly at Penn by the end of World War II. The school was moving away from the narrow professional orientation that had once dominated advanced courses. In fact it become extremely difficult to get Wharton approval for such courses as CPA review even when such courses were enjoying widespread popularity at many universities. (The matter was handled by registering such general titles as "Advanced Accounting Theory" and "Advanced Accounting Problems." These titles committed the designers to no specific topics and made a stated commitment only to some degree of rigor and to required prerequisites.)

George A. MacFarland was one of the more interesting of the Wharton accounting teachers over the intermediate period. His timing and classroom performances were simply unbelievable. His sixteen to twenty first-year lectures were polished gems and models of persuasion and communication. For one thing he looked the combination professor and dynamic business leader with marine-cut grey hair, a deep tan, impeccable haberdashery and rock-solid poise. Moreover he knew how to motivate students while (in the process) extolling Wharton's good points so that students were glad to be a part of the tradition. References to well known business leaders, e.g., "the current president of Sun Oil who once sat in the second row of this night-school course" impressed eager freshmen. Finally, his lectures were well-organized, coherent, entertaining and relevant.

Unfortunately MacFarland knew very little technical accounting and taught only the elementary course. Certainly his publications reveal little interest in theoretical matters. His introductory text with Robert D. Ayars was consistent with his interests. A student who finished MacFarland's introductory accounting course certainly was no theorist or philosopher of accounting, but he did have a good knowledge of how a simple accounting system worked and how it could be applied to business decisions and to the administration of small businesses.

An example of the disinterest in theory may be found in the earlier edition by MacFarland and an associate (1914), which stated without explanation or discussion that reserves for depreciation were liabilities of the concern. This statement has interesting overtones, and I have harassed numerous students by asking them to defend this statement.

Only a few more alert students could put together the continuity assumption and the desirability of expanding the definition of liability from a narrow legal concept to a concept that included expected demands on funds.

The experience with MacFarland and the Wharton School helped shape my own attitudes toward university policy about professional ranks and salaries. Earlier I had encountered a serious attempt to avoid academic ranks at what is now the University of Missouri–Kansas City.[17] Generally I have held that rank and salary should be more or less separated with the former related to research and international recognition and the latter influenced by number of children, level of living and related variables. There is no reason why good classroom men, such as MacFarland, should not be recompensed adequately and asked to spend twenty hours or so in the classroom with no pressing demands for research. Moreover there is no reason to pay them inadequate salaries or ask them to devote time to activities that they perform badly.[18]

Jeremiah Lockwood may be remembered by some for his love of

basic standard costs that provided room for virtuosity at the concert level, but my own appraisal of his contribution to accounting is in his rational defense for fixed cost allocation.

Schools of business were slow to adopt the newer approach to costing that emphasized differential (incremental) costs and pricing schemes based on such costs. J. M. Clark published a coordinated volume devoted to these and related matters in 1923, and there is evidence that his fellow colleagues in accounting at Chicago (notably McKinsey) may have been explaining and advocating such methods at about the same time.[19] Certainly Wharton followed the path of slow incorporation. The usual arguments are familiar enough. "Don't give away our profits." "Cutthroat." "Unfair." Clark himself pointed out that the supply and demand forces that establish market prices also could drive prices down to variable costs when operations are at less than full capacity.

Lockwood's defense may not have been new or original for there were scattered behavioral discussions in earlier engineering literature, but his support is based firmly on psychological considerations that fitted well into his conception of standard costs and their uses. His fixed cost assignments helped to induce psychological barriers for those who were quick to lower prices when conditions are not good. This approach was influential in my own thinking about behavioral accounting and ultimately to accounting as a system of metaphorical constructions.[20]

Lockwood's interest in fixed-cost assignment seems to have sprung from his early experience in a local Peerless automobile dealership in Philadelphia. He was intrigued with its concern with the usage of "floor time." The opportunity to approach a potential customer was considered to be a valuable resource that should not be squandered. In this context a salesman who pointed out that he had made *some* contribution over out-of-pocket costs did not satisfy management. As a result, standards were set on sales expected per unit of floor time, and then were translated into fixed charges for scarce space resources. A profit calculation replaced a margin calculation. He observed similar attitudes in department stores with expected sales per linear-foot of shelving, per square-foot of floor space and per work station. I have no way of speculating how much he may have been influenced by the then current trade association attitudes toward fixed costs for space charges, for advertising lineage and the like. In any case it was not long until he was teaching the motivational effects of fixed-cost assignment.

Lockwood was familiar with the works of the leading cost accountants and efficiency experts of the time, and had considerable knowledge of the numerous wage incentive plans that were popular. During the early decades of this century, capital was still scarce and consequently a high value was placed on labor efficiencies that tended to utilize capital more intensely. As a result many of the wage-incentive plans of the day included provisions that "shared" the fixed cost of providing facilities with laborers who could utilize them efficiently.

In any case Lockwood associated the use of fixed-cost assignments directly with motivational schemes, and it was only a small step from motivating workers to influencing those who set prices. It probably did not occur to him that marginal costing would become so important in the economics of imperfect competition for he was committed to full costing of both activities and products. The great depression of the thirties called the attention of all cost accountants to idle capacity and the need for flexible budgeting. Lockwood too saw this need and in spite of his commitment to basic standards and full costing became adept at adjusting budgets "to level" by means of variable cost allocations.

Finally Lockwood must have been among the first Wharton accounting professors to come from outside the public accounting area. He helped to set the later Wharton tradition which encouraged young teachers to spend summer vacations working off campus in brokerage houses, railroads, utilities, municipals and manufacturing. This trend was consistent with the school's emphasis on a strong systems orientation where the application of double-entry methods for recording and controlling were not obvious, but even more importantly it brought into focus managerial problems peculiar to various businesses.

Ideal standard costs were associated with basic standards, and required substantial modification before they could be used for inventory costing or as a surrogate for actual cost. Some extremely awkward percentage adjustments were the result. The ideal cost used by those supporting basic standards interested me only to the extent that the ideal represented the normal expected costs *if* technology and worker adjustment to the technology were at best current levels. This concept permits one to break out a technology variance and to broadcast periodically the cost of having out-of-date facilities. In turn this variance can be analyzed further into all sorts of components including the costs from labor inertia and general lack of adaptability.

HARRY A. FINNEY—MASTER TEXT WRITER

My personal experiences with H. A. Finney were limited and usually accompanied with generous portions of Johnny Walker, and as a result these observations may be of minor interest. As a member of the Paton brotherhood, I was not overly sympathetic to Finney's practical how-to-do-it orientation. Finney had been an English major and written correspondence-school materials for Seymour Walton and the Walton home study series.[21] His style was clear and straightforward, (I always felt that at the intermediate level, Newlove and his associates were at least as concise.) Neither series was strong on the whys and wherefors stressed in more theoretical works such as Paton, Hatfield and Kester. Both series suggested at least one acceptable solution and provided interesting problem material. By adding appropriate requirements and extensions many of these simplistically stated situations could be extended into Paton-type semi-cases or even to full-blown materials for the case method.

It is far too easy to be patronizing toward the early writers of accounting texts, but the truth of the matter is that until at least the eighties few changes have been introduced except to add formal "authoritative" options for traditional usages and to add simplified managerial decision models to traditional cost accounting. In fact some retrogression may be found in partnerships, estates and trusts, consolidated statements, branches and agencies. It is true that consolidations have been enlarged to include pooling (a questionable alternative at best) and foreign exchange has taken on a more impressive title—international accounting. Certainly grammar and general language usage have improved very little, and advanced accounting texts remain an embarrassment to academicians. Some changes are due to the inclusion of computer methods and programming as an alternative for low-level bookkeeping. In general the fantastic predictions of the sixties that accounting in twenty years would no longer be recognizable have scarcely been borne out. Even discussions of the uses of accounting output have changed little beyond pointing out simplistic facts such as: "Any service function should be user oriented."

Finney generally was tolerant to other views and approaches, although he confined his own interest to writing texts that were usable and therefore salable.[22] There certainly is no doubt that Finney had an uncanny ability to appraise the market potential of accounting manuscripts. In summary his contribution to the body of substantive accounting was marginal and his creativity was confined chiefly to assessing the education aspects of the profession.

WILLIAM ANDREW PATON—
SCATTERED PERSONAL REMARKS

It is difficult to discuss Paton. He has already been discussed, rediscussed, memorialized, pored over, listened to, published, republished, argued with, argued over, imitated and practically worshiped. His teaching at the university level covered approximately a half century and his publications extend over an astounding eight decades.[23]

We begin with a somewhat negative aspect—an unheard of heresy. It seems obvious that he was too bright and too persuasive to profit greatly from intercourse with most of his colleagues. Certainly he dominated fellow members of the accounting department, and it appeared even in my own days that his intellectual give and take with fellow economists was not as productive as it might have been. With respect to economics (and even more so to sociology and political science) his ideas were so conservative and tied to the free market ideas of Fred M. Taylor and Henry Simons that his departmental discussions with other economists did not lead to exchanges of new ideas as one might expect. It was not that Paton's knowledge of economics was denigrated by his colleagues for until Joan Robinson, Edward Chamberlin and Keynes his knowledge of economics and his ability to express its concepts were outstanding. He was an implacable enemy of socialism in all forms and somehow failed to follow Taylor's leadership in showing that a socialist government can guide production by a relatively free price system.

While accounting colleagues were reluctant to get into serious intellectual discussions much less arguments with Paton, he still managed an easy personal relationship with them as well as with public accountants and practitioners generally. Apparently with very few exceptions (perhaps George O. May and a few other leaders from an earlier generation) Paton was able to say "no" without arousing animosity, to point out procedural failings and faulty theories without leading to rancor and to adopt a satirical approach toward practitioners without wearing out his welcome.[24] As late as 1983 he was able to say some outrageous things about the SEC that brought down the house even though a poll of the audience might have disclosed some severe disagreement.

Practitioners have felt that the Paton medicine for the profession is indeed good medicine, but unfortunately they also considered the disease to be far from acute. In any case the ratio of action to advice has been low and often delayed. His recommendations on terminology (retained earnings for surplus, equity for liability and capital, income for profit and loss, allowance for reserve for deprecation or bad debts and net revenue for gross profit) were more or less adopted, but for a half century a listener or reader could identify a Paton-trained accountant by his use of some of these terms. Substantive recommendations suffered a similar delayed fate with some outright rejections and some changes in the thinking of Paton himself. His recommendation for price-level adjustments dates from the twenties and was more or less adopted a half century later. His form of income statement had little influence and he himself changed his position to a modified one-step format. His emphasis on current values (after his own lapse with Littleton during the depression) has recently surfaced with slight modifications, and with intriguing extensions in the direction of exit values. His disinterest in the liquidity aspects of income realization bore extreme and (unpalatable) fruit in current real-estate accounting and in the requirement for marginally useful fund-flow statements. His emphasis on an entity framework instead of the corner-store proprietary orientation has certainly been reinforced by the accelerated trend toward large concentrations of economic power.

Paton's formal venture into economic reform (1953) seems to be one of his unsuccessful ventures. By this time the work ethic of protestant America was pretty well eroded, and the state became the accepted device for keeping one's brothers. Thus, Paton's call for a return to laissez *faire* went largely unheeded, and he was deeply hurt by the reception of his clearly written and closely reasoned tome. On occasion most human beings yearn for simpler times and simpler ways. In engineering terms, the initial conditions unfortunately are no longer relevant.

Lack of acceptance no doubt led to some disappointment, and increased his tendency toward dogmatism. This ambivalence between many-faceted argument and dogmatism followed him much of his life. In his prime of intellectual vigor (*circa* 1940) he expressed confusion over this point by complaining that some accountants called him dogmatic while others complained about his "wishy-washy" stands on some controversial topics. When Paton made up his mind about a position he was likely to hold it firmly (at least for a time) and to support his opinion by strong assertions that often appeared to be more assertive than argumentative. If, however, he happened to be undecided about a position he was more than eager to consider different arguments and listen to diverse arguments. In these cases he was indeed wishy-washy and could hem-and-haw with the very best.

Paton, like any good scientist, was not reluctant to change positions. He abandoned his unsuccessful effort to reformulate profit and loss and surplus statements to show distributional claims on revenue in favor of a modified single-step statement. He shifted his position on treasury stock acquisitions; he modified his recommendations for handling intercompany gains, and he may still be searching for a useful worksheet format to aid hapless bookkeepers.

In spite of many dogmatic overtones, Paton could be quite forgiving when counseling serious doctoral candidates who for some reason or other might be in trouble with universities and their bureaucracies. In my own case he not only smoothly covered a small lapse in my preliminary credentials, but signed off on a rapidly completed dissertation (after some grumbling about "roughness") because of my willingness to "pitch in and get something done." Apparently once he made up his mind that a candidate was worth "fooling with" he became an enthusiastic supporter who encouraged early completion. On the other hand he gave little special consideration to new candidates, who were thrown into the furnaces of fierce course competition and apparently forgotten until they proved themselves worthy of attention. His immense responsibility to his students was obvious in many ways. For example he would forgo what could have been a lucrative weekend of lecturing or consulting in order to return some candidate's miserable manuscript before the deadline.

Even more surprising in view of Paton's reputation for dogmatism was his willingness to let a well-argued contrary opinion go unchallenged in dissertations. In my own case, he condoned with only a moderate number of snorts and groans a spirited defense of cost or market, whichever is lower, and LIFO—both of which he detested.[25] Base stock was anathema although separate inventory reserves were not completely rejected.

Interestingly he was willing to reach into the future and create reserves for expected bad debts, discounts to be taken and even goods to be returned. At the same time he was unwilling to accept reserves for fire-loss anticipation (self-insurance). Apparently he considered the event (fire) more important than the expectation. (Assets in "statistical jeopardy.") Perhaps it was the ridiculous term "self-insurance" that colored his decision, for, as I remember, he accepted anticipation reserves for plugging oil wells, rehabilitating destructive strip mining, cleaning up toxic wastes and related "aftercosts."

In reviewing my own case his only questionable advice concerned by dissertation topic. I was greatly impressed by his *Theory* chapter devoted to the postulates of accounting and wanted to develop the logical foundations of the accounting structure as my own dissertation. As preparation I completed a course in Philosophy of Science, audited a course in symbolic logic with Andrew Paul Ushenko and another in the *Foundations of Mathematics* with Raymond Wilder, and subsequently worked up a tentative outline for such a dissertation. Paton apparently feared that committee members from the Philosophy Department might give trouble and that my limited background in Philosophy might be a serious obstacle to approval. (I could not conceive of more trouble than Paton himself was reported to give.) Moreover he believed that a young neophyte should get identified as a coming expert in a particular aspect of the profession lest he alienate himself and wander beyond acceptable professional boundaries.

Paton's position on most accounting issues is well known. Perhaps comments on some issues that later became popular may be of interest. Certainly he anticipated the Durand-Modgiliani-Miller controversy by at least two decades. Paton discussed possible profits from trading on the equity in calculating the value of goodwill from the viewpoint of the entire business and as an alternative from the viewpoint of common equity holders. He developed a case or two to cover this area and treated the matter as an arbitrage situation. He acknowledged the tendency of arbitrage to reduce the differences in calculated values of goodwill by suggesting different discount rates to reflect the differences in risks. Yet he did not argue that the situations were invariably arbitraged and that creditors always extracted the full value of their positions. Presumably the market prices of senior securities recognize such situations so that taking or not taking over senior securities at current market should not make much difference in goodwill calculations.

Some of his goodwill calculations anticipated the imperfect competition of Chamberlin and Robinson. (Perhaps they were more closely related to the arguments of J. M. Clark.) In any case Paton discussed layers of earnings with the "excess" or "super" layer related to the corresponding areas in imperfect competition. He even emphasized that this region of super earnings may be shortrun-stable or longrun-unstable. (A tentative forerunner of Feltham and Ohlson?) The erosion of this portion of excess earnings results from all sorts of forces: patent expirations, advertising gimmicks, higher cost pressures generated by reported higher profits (also stronger labor demands), less stringent cost control and general corporate slack.

Paton also was aware of pressures to adjust the value of the business at each statement date by summing the market value of the equities and setting up an adjustable goodwill account with offsetting credits and charges to something like market-value income or equity-value gain. He was discussing these points in seminars at least a decade before Lerner suggested the procedure (1940) and at least two decades before Bodenhorn gave it wider publicity. Paton's attitude was more or less typical. He could see no reason why the investor himself could not do this job without special help from the accountant.

Accolades to Paton sometimes have stressed minor points that he sometimes defended with the stubborn tenacity of a true Scotsman, but his outstanding problem-case accumulation has been largely neglected. The Michigan Business School began in the early-middle twenties as a graduate school patterned after Harvard with early case books (and many professors) imported from Cambridge. Paton was a non-Harvard carry-over from the department of economics—a home-grown young man whose early texts were supplemented by highly analytical, more or less traditional problems rather than Harvard cases. Michigan business professors soon developed their own cases patterned closely after the Harvard mold. By the early thirties, Paton had for his advanced courses some combination problem-cases that must have been among the most exasperating and diabolical devised for student use.

The technique (except for a very few drill exercises) was to take verbatim or slightly modified statements from the Board of Tax Appeals, the Committee on Stock List of the NYSE (prototype for the SEC), Interstate Commerce Commission, Public Utility Commissions, Stockholder reports, leading textbooks and financial journals; and in the best Harvard tradition present a few hazy, vague questions and directions. Among a half dozen or so such directions, there usually was an instruction to prepare accounting entries to reflect the petitioner's position and perhaps to repeat using the recommendations of the court. Students who survived were wary citizens indeed and, not surprisingly, the current saying was that "Michigan numbers its accounting majors in hundreds while many comparable universities number them in thousands."

Paton's selection as accountant of the century is well deserved and is to be applauded, although my own efforts to summarize the importance of his contributions may differ slightly from the general assessment.

His greatest contribution, in my estimation, results from his *rigorous* application of theoretical economics as the central accounting paradigm. This framework not only afforded a more consistent general structure, but it also shifted emphasis from accounting as a routine service function for small businesses and bankers to an independent social force in modern industrial society. Broad social and economic objectives became the objectives of accounting, and the functions of accounting shifted to meet these broader objectives. While it may be an exaggeration to hold that Paton directed accounting to the now-popular theme of "user needs," it is not too much to argue that he helped guide the perception of such needs to serious consideration of all *economic* interests in the social order.

The second important contribution stems from his driving personality that encouraged rational discourse, furthered cogent argumentation and set an example for all who wished to conduct serious inquiry. As a result Paton was an outstanding educator in academic circles, and as a bonus he was influential among hard-headed practitioners. Incidentally along the way he produced some of the best literary expositions in the accounting field. To paraphrase: His reasoning was the reasoning of a logician, but his expression was the expression of an artist.

NOTES

[1] Jeremiah Lockwood, "Early University Education in Accountancy," *The Accounting Review,* June 1938, pp. 131–144.

[2] In this connection he had more of a modern behavioral bent than Paton and other leaders. For example, he was not particularly interested in anticipating future sales returns and matching them with current revenues although he recommended this procedure. Typically he was more interested in the possible causes of returns reported by the accounting system, i.e., over-selling, impossible delivery promises, poor packing, careless shipping orders, poor order filling and defective merchandise.

[3] "[E]mphasis is placed upon the primary importance of understanding the flow of authority (responsibility), the work flow, and the resulting flow of data (original papers, etc.) from the point of activity to the points where the data are needed. . . ." F. W. Woodbridge, Book Review of R. I. Williams and L. Doris, eds., *Encyclopedia of Accounting Systems* (Englewood Cliffs: Prentice-Hall Inc., 1956), *The Accounting Review,* October 1957, p. 683.

[4] Saliers' publishers were The Ronald Press Company along with A. W. Shaw, Northwestern University and Richard D. Irwin. Incidentally in the early years of the profession Ronald published most of the theoretical (prestige?) works as well as all sorts of practical helps such as C.P.A. examinations and solutions, along with handbooks that covered many aspects of business and accounting. Consider for example: Paton's *Theory,* Esquerré's *Applied,* Sprague's *Philosophy,* Yang's *Goodwill,* Canning's *Economics* and Gilman's *Concepts.* Furthermore the influence of Northwestern's loose leaf materials and its College of Commerce was a major factor in business training during the twenties.

[5] As a staff colleague he simply did not engage in controversial discussions with the more argumentative members of his staff. He reviewed DR Scott's undistinguished *Theory of Accounts* rather than his *The Cultural Significance of Accounts.* In his "Depreciation" section of the first edition of the *Handbook* discussion of income tax aspects and lists of acceptable rates for various industrial assets took up more than one-and-one-half as much space (57 pages) as his dis-

cussion of other matters (37 pages). The discussion of depreciation included full-page charts of various calculating methods, illustrations of plant ledgers and other practical items.

⁶ See Earl A. Saliers, *Fundamentals of Accounting* (1935) and the revision with Arthur W. Holmes, *Basic Accounting Principles* (1937). Holmes, himself went on to combine some auditing procedural steps from the Federal Reserve Board's *Examination of Financial Statements* with some nonanalytical accounting theory into an auditing textbook that went through at least seven editions—a commentary on the quality of early text materials for auditing. His *Auditing Principles and Procedure* text was a modification of *Basic Auditing Principles* that also went into at least three editions.

⁷ Earl A. Saliers, ed. (New York: Ronald Press Company, 1923); reprinted (New York: Garland Publishing, Inc. 1986).

⁸ Some comparisons between the first and second editions may be of interest. Changes introduced by William A. Paton were thorough going and only the number of sections (31) remained without substantial shakeup. Paton clearly did much of his own writing and severely edited the works of others. Indications are that 19 sections were contributed by others and strictly edited by Paton. Paton also used a much wider group of "consulting" editors, whose work according to informal hearsay ranged from substantial to nothing of consequence. (In the first edition the publisher also gave credit to seven additional consultants including R. B. Kester.)

The carryovers of advisors and contributors to the second edition were few. None of the original contributors were identified as specific contributors to the second; and only James P. Adams, John T. Madden and Paul Pinkerton were carried forward as consulting editors. Many sections were changed, combined and rearranged; and the sections on business law and economics were noteworthy casualties.

⁹ Editor's Note: This section reflects arguments that continue to be advanced against the Saliers-income tax approach that was implemented as GAAP in 1973 by APB Opinion No. 29, *Accounting for Nonmonetary Transactions.*

¹⁰ *Ibid.,* p. 504. See Maurice Moonitz and E. Carey Brown, "The Annuity Method of Estimating Depreciation," *The Accounting Review,* December 1939, pp. 424-9. This article was my introduction to this interesting relationship.

¹¹ Quoted from *The University of Pennsylvania Today,* edited by Cornell M. Dowlin (Philadelphia: University of Pennsylvania Press, 1940), p. 53. Much of the early part of this essay is based on this volume. Those interested in the details of the university along with its troubles and considerable accomplishments may wish to refer to the more complete *History of the University of Pennsylvania, 1740–1940,* by the famous historian, Edward Potts Cheyney (University of Pennsylvania Press, 1940).

[12] *Ibid.*, pp. 37, 53. The part-time accountant remains unnamed, but the full-time professor was Robert Ellis Thompson, who was "the only professor on the Wharton School faculty from 1881 to 1883" (*ibid.*, p. 42). It is clear that the broad social science approach that helped integrate, political science, geography, sociology, economics and led to such interdisciplinary publications as the *Annals* came from Thompson.

[13] For an alternative approach consider the development of operations research and management science at Penn. Edgar A. Singer, Jr., joined the Philosophy Department in 1896 after being "an assistant in psychology [at Harvard] under William James . . ." (*ibid.*, p.11). Singer's broad scientific interests joined with others in philosophy and near-philosophy (especially Isaac Husic in jurisprudence) took root in Thomas Cowan and others, and influenced Churchman, Ackoff and other future management scientists. The closeness of the Moore School of Electrical Engineering with its development of ENIAC might have been important for operations research and computer integration, but seemed to have little influence on accounting at Wharton. The engineering influence may have been important. So far as I know neither Churchman nor Ackoff were actually trained in engineering, although Churchman and perhaps both taught statistics in the Wharton School—evidence again of the broad orientation of the school itself.

[14] See Stephen A. Zeff, *The American Accounting Association: Its First 50 Years, 1916–1966* (American Accounting Association 1966 and 1991), p. 7.

[15] The Lecture-Note Fund at Wharton was a first-rate production and reproduction service. This efficient operation encouraged good classroom presentations by providing up-to-date readings and supplementary material. The Lippincott Library also performs an outstanding service for faculty and students alike. It seems in retrospect that the fund and the library both helped attain a very high level of classroom performance, but for some reason did not do much for original research.

[16] The earlier leaders were E. S. Mead, father of Margaret and Richard (later professor of marketing at the University of Southern California) as professor of finance, Emory R. Johnson was the leader in transportation with S. S. Huebner in insurance, Moxey in accounting and Simon Nelson Patten in economics.

[17] Apparently the experiment was considered by the faculty and administration to be a failure, for the university began operations in 1933 and by 1941 the usual array of academic ranks had been instituted.

[18] The Johns Hopkins University tried various schemes along these lines. By 1942 the university based its general standard on one-half time for transmission of knowledge and one-half for developing new information. Various degrees of skewness were recognized in some research. Earlier the university had experi-

mented with two parallel lines with the adjective "collegiate" used to recognize teaching merit rankings. Thus Abraham Cohen was a collegiate professor of mathematics for his excellent texts in calculus and differential equations, even though he did substantial work in Lie Groups and (for the time) other mathematical exoteria. Apparently the designation of collegiate became another name for second-rate, but the scheme has merit and can be made to work in most combination graduate and undergraduate schools.

[19] See J. Maurice Clark, *Studies in the Economics of Overhead Costs* (Chicago: The University of Chicago Press, 1923). Some indication of James O. McKinsey's attitudes may be found in *Managerial Accounting* (Chicago: The University of Chicago Press, 1924). This volume seems to have been the direct ancestor of Vatter's later attitudes. It also is interesting to observe that Clark's later accounting colleagues at Columbia were less interested in variable costing. See for example James L. Dohr, Howell A. Ingraham and Andrew L. Love, *Cost Accounting, Principles and Practice,* 2d rev. ed. (New York: The Ronald Press Company, 1935).

[20] Another former colleague, Howard E. Cooper of Johns Hopkins, should be mentioned as a full coster, but his answer to the famous article by Jonathan N. Harris suggests that Cooper was interested more directly in the pricing aspects. Nevertheless see his earlier "Some Controversial Phases of Standard Costs," *N.A.C.A. Bulletin,* September 15, 1933. pp. 81–108. The Harris claim to historical immortality is "What Did We Earn Last Month?" *N.A.C.A. Bulletin,* January 15, 1936, pp. 501–27. My own interest in this aspect of cost accounting was enhanced by Clem N. Kohl in "What Is Wrong with Most Profit and Loss Statements?" *N.A.C.A.Bulletin,* July 1, 1937, pp. 1207–19.

[21] Incidently my own learning beyond *Twentieth-Century Bookkeeping* and before Paton was from the Walton texts. Ironically, after requiring Paton's Advanced Accounting (New York: The MacMillan Co., 1941), Michigan reverted to Walton's C.P.A. materials as the backbone of the introductory course in public accounting.

[22] In approximately 1957 Finney was induced to leave his horse farm (financed no doubt by some of his more than a million textbook royalties) to address the students and faculty at the University of Florida. He was (unexpectedly) interested in the staff which included doctorates from Kester, Newlove, Littleton, DR Scott, Paton and a former teaching assistant under Hatfield. All except one, as I remember, had previously taught at least one course using a Finney text or had taken at least one course using a Finney text. Few were aware of his *Consolidated Statements* (New York: Prentice-Hall, Inc., 1922; reprinted by Garland Publishing, Inc., 1982) where he championed the case for minority interests as outsiders and his later review of Moonitz' substantial effort to emphasize the entity orientation.

[23] Incidentally my own favorite is his first major publication with Russell Alger Stevenson, *Principles of Accounting* (New York: The Macmillan Company, 1918). A mimeo, lithoprinted version from Ann Arbor is dated 1917. (Editor's Note: The author's "Preface" of the version reprinted by Arno Press Inc. in 1976, is dated September 1, 1916 and states: "A revision . . . will be published early next year. Extensive appendices will be added. . . .")

[24] In a private conversation at the annual meeting of the American Accounting Association (1983) he indicated that he was well aware of this ability and emphasized that he had devoted attention as a young man to developing this facet of his personality. Hatfield (whom Paton considered of an older generation) also had this ability to a lesser degree. His satiric discussion of stupid remarks made by leading members of the profession in the field of depreciation is an excellent illustration, and his discourse on bookkeeping as a proper subject for university study seems to have intrigued university intellectuals. Yet Hatfield was willing to accept accounting practices to the extent that his joint effort (1938) with Sanders and Moore was appraised by Paton as "junk."

[25] Cost or market advocates were "throwing logic to the winds," but once when discussing my modest defense he reminisced that under questioning after a speech he once had a fleeting glimpse of market as a means of allocating cost. Perhaps later he could go further and view market as evidential support for expectation levels. This step was not likely however, for he remained convinced that writing down damaged goods to net selling price less disposal costs was sufficient and that an additional write down for any profit margin was an unnecessary "measure of conservatism." Incidentally he sharply rejected my identical arguments when presented as a contribution to his *Accountants' Handbook*.

Socially Necessary Costs— Congealed, Attached, and Embodied

This essay discusses the outmoded American doctrine of cost attachment (embodiment) and certain implications that might arise from such a position. Then it reviews the usual assumptions of standard cost accounting in terms of the decisions that must be made and the simplifications that make cost measures homogeneous. Finally it compares costing in the western world with the Marxist recommendation for calculating all costs in terms of socially necessary labor hours and the resulting values in use and values in exchange. The later discussions include some new left doctrines that are little more than speculative outlines and do not attempt to give a detailed historical account of parallel developments. Perhaps an occasional reader may wish to furnish scholarly details and expand the present simplistic framework. In any case the reader must remember that all accounting and indeed all thinking requires attributions and allocations.

The accountant's doctrine that costs attach and create stored-up value may flow from Adam Smith and a long list of followers headed by David Ricardo. Certainly these two eminent scholars were labor-value theorists in a broad sense and developed coherent structures based on value being either equal to or proportional to labor cost. It is more certain that accountants did not derive such metamorphic imagery from Marx. Most accountants are probably not acquainted with the Marx-Engels literature and even if they were, it is doubtful whether their identification with private enterprise would have permitted serious analysis of Marxist ideas.

It also is doubtful whether a substantial body of accountants ever actually held a strict labor theory of value. Certainly the evidence is mixed.

Enterprise accountants have always been vitally interested in identifying events that can be easily recognized and can be used as signals for recognizing value added, i.e., income added by the entrepreneurial function. In the recording tradition all costs—including labor costs—are allocated, accumulated and carried at their expenditure levels until the events support belief that value changes need to be recognized. In short early theorists looked at cost accounts primarily as temporary allocation centers to preserve expenditure costs until critical signals for value changes become clear.

While Adam Smith (and to some extent Marx) considered value to be *stored up* and more or less equal to labor cost, Ricardo argued that value is not precisely equal to labor expended but is roughly proportional to it. Presumably overhead and indirect costs change the amounts but not the proportions. Accountants never accepted the more rigid assumption of Smith. Their practices have been nearer to Ricardo, and application of overhead (supplementary burden) has often been related to direct labor hours or direct labor cost. Thus the accountant's cost of manufactured goods is often roughly proportional to direct labor cost and is occasionally used for pricing so that labor cost may actually become proportional to sales and to sales value. This association is carried through many standard cost systems where labor cost is normalized and overhead is trimmed to fit the labor mold through variances that are not permitted to affect the cost of product. Presumably product costs are price-determining and add value. Variances are not recoverable or are recoverable only indirectly through market imperfections.

In the Marxian framework the accountant's standard manufacturing cost may be roughly equivalent to the socially necessary cost of product. Remember however that selling and administrative costs for traditional Marxists are unnecessary labor and constitute an institutional distribution of surplus value to unproductive elements of society.

Accountants did not entirely escape the labor-value identification of the classical economists. In the Paton-Littleton monograph the concept of cost is emphasized, and in turn cost is defined in terms of "effort exerted." It is true that the required *effort* may include selling and administering costs and thus does not qualify for Marx socially necessary labor. For most modern accountants a definition of cost in terms of effort exerted is a poor substitute for cost as sacrifice—as alternatives necessarily foregone.

Furthermore accountants often identify cost at acquisition with value and, in the absence of entrepreneurial rationality, the two are said to be equal. Thus they completely neglect the fact that subjective value to the buyer must be at least as great as the expenditure (effort) and that the subjective value to the seller must be less than the exchange price. All are certainly aware that entrepreneurs can make bad buys, so that a loss may require recognition at acquisition. From these positions the reader may infer that Paton-Littleton considered the current market price to be a surrogate for (or limit to) *the* value of the effort expended. Marx too was not interested in excess subjective value and his "effort exerted" is firmly restricted to socially necessary labor effort.

Yet Littleton, at least, was never entirely comfortable with current market quotations even as upper limits and apparently also was not impressed with the fact that such market prices might represent social cost or that market prices might approximate at least one alternative for the enterprise, i.e., command over resources in liquidation. The result is that he advocated the concept of "bargained exchange" to represent value at acquisition. Thus market prices at acquisition are specialized bargained exchange prices that apply more generally to all exchanges resulting from two-person bargaining.

There is evidence that Littleton, Kohler and others were not happy with the term *value* and made a serious effort to avoid it. In fact Littleton and Vatter may have been among the first accountants to substitute the term *potential* as the primary defining property of an asset. The term potential is delightfully vague and need not be associated with values, costs or physical concepts.

The net result is that Littleton took the classical economist's view and turned to effort (not only labor effort) exerted as the active defining ingredient of cost. Classicists (and Marx) took an adequate amount of utility for granted as a necessity for value (or socially necessary cost). Capitalist accountants consider utility to be problematic and consequently subject to occasional review to determine whether expectations are adequate to support the *stored up* (attached, embodied) effort exerted. If utility fails to support carrying values measured by effort legitimately exerted, a loss (writedown) is recommended. When a product includes some socially unnecessary labor, Marx too would insist on a reduction of the *value* of the product and his accountants might be instructed to recognize a loss.

EMBODIED COSTS

Certainly it is not necessary to hold the simplistic—and juvenile—belief that costs (many of which are associated with intangible effort) go into and somehow physically attach themselves to products. Such imagery may attract attention, but these devices are near useless for explaining cost allocation and accumulation. Paton sometimes used the attaching metaphor, and made distinctions between fungible and non-fungible goods. Certainly he flirted with cost attachment as a legitimate postulate of accounting, but in general he avoided this crude illusion; he states:

> [T]he accountant makes the closely related assumption . . . that the value of any commodity, service, or condition, utilized in production, *passes over into* the object or product . . . and *attaches* to the result, giving it its value. . . . [H]ow valid is this assumption? . . . [I]t may be noted first that the physical essence of assets utilized in production does not always [sic] literally pass into the product. . . . [E]ven if the product were simply an amalgam, physically, of the commodities used in production, this would not mean that the original values had literally passed into the result.[1]

Balance sheet mechanics have encouraged the feeling that costs become values and by extension that costs *flow* through the accounts. Certainly costs in suspense are presented as assets, and assets in turn are usually associated with balance-sheet values. Paton is well aware of this tendency but finds it difficult to reject; he states:

> If he [the accountant] finds at the end of a particular period that a certain fraction of the total costs incurred are still within the business, or at least have had nothing to do with current sales, it is entirely natural, then, for him to conclude that these values attach to work in process and finished [goods]. . . . [L]ater they will be passed on as expense, conceived to be embodied in finished product sold.[2]

Marx may have been the original user of "embodiment" to express this concept of attachment. We only mention the matter here and defer a more detailed discussion by Marx:

> A use value . . . has value only because human labour in the abstract has been *embodied* or *materialised* in it. . . . Commodities . . . in which equal quantities of labour are embodied . . . have the same value. . . . As values, all commodities are only definite masses of congealed labour-time.[3]

Vatter, and later an able AAA Committee, advocated the concept of cost embodiment.[4] This concept is a variation of cost attachment and is equally unsatisfactory.[5] The term "embedded" has an even stronger sense of physical bonding, and in the Vatter case the physical image is reinforced by asserting that these costs are somehow *released* and presumably float away into a new world represented by non-personal dimensions. Since Vatter was not favorably disposed toward the income concept, it was not essential that *released* costs ever became associated with revenues. The objection to such terms may not be serious when viewed as a teaching or learning device, but the use of any imagery that later must be unlearned or relearned should be suspect.

It may be useful once again to emphasize that the important variable to be considered is value. In modern terminology it is values that are "privileged" and financial accounting is "grounded" in those particular values that are related to wealth. Physical properties are relevant only as conceptual devices for structuring value movements. As an example accountants may use inventory units as the primary device for transferring costs, but they invariably modify the physical framework for damaged and obsolete goods. These modifications acknowledge the primacy of values and treat physical flows as a convenient simplification.

SOCIAL COST

In neo-classical economics market values are approximations of economic (social?) significance. Current market values show relative economic valuations, and if the distribution of income and wealth is in line with social objectives and if there are not too many monopolistic elements, market quotations can be used as a surrogate for economic significance. These relative market values express the opinions of an important sample population about relative social worth. Thus the market establishes rough social equivalences for all agents of production subject to its operation.

For a capitalist accountant the calculation of cost of product in terms of the market value of inputs approximates the social cost of the product. This social cost in turn serves as a benchmark for determining whether individual entrepreneurs are using resources effectively. Economists and socially inclined accountants favor the computation of all enterprise costs in terms of current market values in order to establish the value of the resources taken from the common pool and devoted to specific entrepreneurial effort. Approximate social cost as expressed by current market values is thus recommended for both private and national income determination and also for the calculation of unit costs, variances, losses and the like.[6]

While there may be some difficulty in accepting current market values as surrogates for social values, there is undoubtedly some correlation, and the result is likely to be better than the historical cost alternative recommended by many accountants. The most telling disagreement is likely to come from those with Marxist training. For the orthodox Marxist the equivalence value for all inputs is not determined directly by market forces, but by the amount of "socially necessary" labor involved in each alternative.[7] While it is possible to use an endless array of methods for finding input equivalents, the Marxist labor approach is among the most seriously advanced and defended. There are of course all sorts of compromise methods that indirectly influence market operations and their equilibrating function. Modification of exchange rates is an obvious technique that is widely used in developing economies, and all countries use tariffs, bounties and indirect methods of influencing demand-supply relations. In fact the accounting process of recording and amortizing original cost uses these coerced market values to determine original cost and then adopts modified value-in-use as the model for subsequent writeoffs.

Digress now to consider the possible weaknesses of using congealed (accumulated) past labor as a surrogate for and measurement of future expectations that are vital for any decision-relevant definition of value.

The main objection to the stored-up-labor concept as a surrogate for value is similar to the objection to the accounting recommendation for using historical cost to represent value. Both concepts use something about the past to serve as proxies for expectations about the future. A Marxist divides past labor into a part that is socially necessary and a part that is wasted, and *defines* value in terms of the former. Western accountants often take past expenditure (market price at the time of acquisition) as the primary defining property of value and modify this amount to reflect new information that affects original expectations. It is often pointed out that both methods look the wrong way and that such looking is fatal to an effective value system. Some methodological sleight of hand is of course necessary—in the absence of pure clairvoyance—for no one can use the future for decision making or judgment formation or to believe (with varying probabilities) that the future itself will follow a semi-stable pattern.

In short no one can measure the future, but we can often *measure* the forces and expectations that influence decisions. Measurement techniques and various probability assessments may be applied, but such techniques are applied to *existing* beliefs. What the investigator is doing is assessing and putting numbers on beliefs based on analogies from the past. Such beliefs about the future are individualistic, so that relevant individuals or groups must be identified and specified as legitimate determinants of value. But more importantly even beliefs about the future already belong to the past. In short we are not measuring the future, nor are we in some mysterious manner (ala Chambers) evaluating the future. What we are doing is quantifying certain existing *beliefs* about continuity and assuming that the future will somehow follow a predictable path.

To summarize decision makers assess and measure expectations that are already held. They may use all sorts of methods, models and simplifications to express these beliefs; and in a broader view these may be better than such crude surrogates as congealed necessary labor, prudent historical invoice cost or current (recently past) market ratios. The necessary considerations for making decisions are not written in stone and their situational importance forms a proper subject for argument.

SOCIALLY NECESSARY COST

Consider briefly some characteristics of accounting cost that resemble the widely discussed socially necessary labor cost of Marx and Engels. As it turns out many requirements for the socialist concept are already in place in American business and cost accounting practices.

Accountants ordinarily use expenditure cost at acquisition to measure sacrifice unless actual expenditure cost exceeds the best market prices available. Without some limit, businessmen could keep adding unnecessary (even foolish) costs without end. This tendency has been evident in public utility operations, where a fair return on necessary investment is a goal and a return on unnecessary expenditures is dysfunctional. To combat this possibility American courts have established the doctrine of an allowable (prudent) cost ceiling. This guideline requires utility commissions or the courts to judge the *necessary* cost to provide the required services and disallow recovery and return on unnecessary costs. It is clear that businessmen should not be allowed to capitalize stupid acquisition or construction costs without limit, but how should limits be set?

In most cases the rough (general) guideline adopted by the courts is that the total costs to be capitalized should not exceed the *reasonable* reproduction or replacement cost of the service potential. Current market prices for the services installed are often adopted when such quotations are available. Bid quotations and various appraisals are sometimes substituted when market prices are not available.[8]

In a similar way the standard cost of manufactured items is considered by many accountants to be *the* cost, the *necessary* cost or the *actual* cost of product. Any excess costs are *defined* to be the cost of something other than product, e.g., inefficiency. In effect accountants and engineers set the standards and thus determine the "actual" cost of the *product* and refuse to consider other sacrifices as costs of production. Accountants for trading concerns put limits on such inefficiencies as cross shipments and excess acquisition costs, and refuse to add them to inventory cost. In simple cases current cash prices often are suggested as appropriate upper limits and discounts not taken are treated as outright losses rather than legitimate additions to asset cost. The practical effect is that asset acquisition cost itself becomes an exercise in definition and allocation.

Any standard cost system also must meet problems of quality, including the quality of inputs such as materials, machines and labor. In a capitalist economy standard cost sheets include these inputs at normal standards for both prices and quantities. A similar problem arises in Marxist economies from the need to determine the socially necessary labor content of each type of material, machine and other service. Clearly the system must set standards for labor input so that product cost includes only the "necessary" amounts of labor. There is nothing unusual about this process, and it is found daily in standard costing in the western world. Since Marxist inputs are in labor or in congealed labor of various types, the socialist loss from inefficient labor might include some portion of materials and overhead as well.

The determination of socially necessary labor costs for a planned economy requires little new thinking, because the foundation exists in ordinary capitalist standard cost accounting. In the latter case the standards usually are estimated by engineers and cost analysts, but competent planning boards should be able to perform a similar task in a broader social context. Furthermore changing from capitalistic standard allowances to estimates of socially necessary costs is not an impossible task. The introduction of physical measures adds few additional difficulties, for capitalist accountants often determine standard allowances in terms of physical units before translating them into a common monetary unit.

The socialist accountant may not make the translation into monetary units for he can express all accounting measures (e.g., earnings, assets and liabilities) in terms of standard labor units and thus make the labor unit perform the measuring function of money. Soviet accountants did express their output to the general public in ordinary monetary units.

This transformation of labor-unit equivalents to monetary units without market direction is a critical task, but the more difficult task is the determination of socially necessary equivalents among different types of labor—fresh inputs as well as congealed inputs for services such as shelter, insurance, supplies and management services. Again, this is not an impossible approximation, but it is more critical than comparable determinations by Western accountants who have ready access to market prices to help determine tradeoff equivalents.

MORE ON DETERMINATION
OF SOCIALLY NECESSARY LABOR

Over- and under-production of specific items exist side by side in any economic order. In Mandel's example the rise of the automobile led to over-production of carriages.[9] Each potential customer has spending power based on his own necessary labor already exerted, but unless demand for every product clears its market, the economy is not in equilibrium. "[I]n the carriage industry *more labor is expended than is socially necessary,* [so] that a part . . . is socially wasted labor. . . ."[10] Clearly the situation is different in the auto industry: "it is therefore a sector expending fewer hours of labor than are socially necessary and it receives a bonus from society in order to stimulate an increase in production. . . ."[11] The latter group is getting more return than the measured necessary hours.

This explanation fits well into the theoretical framework of a capitalist society. The standard cost to make and sell should be recoverable along with a return for the entrepreneurial function. Unfavorable variances are considered to be losses unless ill-informed or government buyers bail out inefficient producers or uncritically accept cost-plus contracts. Mandel's auto industry would show favorable variances until the standards are adjusted downward, and even then the firm would receive bonuses (profits?) until sales prices are adjusted.

In the Mandel case it is clear that the concept of socially necessary has shifted considerably, and the market through the bonus process indirectly influences what is and what is not socially necessary. (If the labor cost can be recovered through bureaucratic price setting, does it automatically become socially necessary?) As an added capitalist feature, bonuses from higher selling prices of the autos may be an incentive to reduce unnecessary labor in the carriage industries and to encourage workers to migrate to automotive work. Clearly Mandel is more market oriented than Marx and his traditional followers.

It seems obvious that what is socially necessary will be influenced, if not actually determined, by market actions in a Mandel economy. This modern use of markets as aids to socialist planners apparently started with Fred M. Taylor in 1928 and was expanded by Lange, Lippincott and Lerner in subsequent years.[12] These early theorists pointed out that socialist planners could watch inventory balances to find which posted prices would maintain inventory stocks. Planning boards can also adjust prices to provide for taxes and for modernization and thus establish new levels of socially desirable costs that may be necessary in the longrun to meet budgeted plans. Shifts in the application of labor from unnecessary to necessary could follow a marginal process until the *average* labor return is approximately equal in each necessary operation after recognition of changes in relative skills and relative intensity of congealed labor in capital goods.

This set of procedures is based directly on the capitalist price system and uses inventory balances to monitor operations. There also is a volume (output) control working here. Presumably Mandel's inventory of carriages would pile up and signal the need for lower output and fewer necessary labor hours. The inventory of autos would be quickly depleted at prices set at their current necessary labor hours. Capitalists would normally raise prices in the shortrun until plants could be expanded. It is difficult to speculate about the reactions of authoritarian planning boards. They might be reluctant to raise prices above the new level of socially required hours, and if so, their adjustment would probably come through greater output. In the shortrun waiting lists and black markets should be expected. Of course planning boards might raise market prices above exchange value until capacities can be adjusted. Such excesses might be distributed as bonuses or be used to finance government activities or to provide the funds necessary for the needed expansion.

In the Marxist structure capital goods for expansion is composed of congealed socially necessary labor, but there is question about the types of necessary labor to be used to calculate the congealed value. Clearly it is an *average,* but is it an average for the auto industry alone? An economy-wide average? Any old average? Firms below the average are wasting labor and therefore social resources. The average that determines the socially necessary amount must therefore include some socially *unnecessary* effort from less efficient firms. The Marxist solution might use the average for the pertinent industry, with appropriate adjustments to reflect the effects of new technologies. Otherwise socially necessary would be defined to be a weighted average for existing technology.

Many cost accountants have followed a similar path, and have often recommended that standards be set at average levels of performance. These averages contain (buried in the calculations) normal interruptions and some inefficiencies that are always present when human beings are involved, e.g., judgmental errors, physical lapses, malingering. Not many capitalist accountants employ ideal standards based on perfect human beings and the latest technologies. Instead they argue that a reasonable amount of inefficiency should be recoverable when competitors operate in a competitive business environment. In Marxist economics inefficiencies that are too gross may not be allowable while average failure may be included in commodity values.

MARX'S COST-PRICE (KOSTPRIJS)

Even in a Marxist economy marginal calculations should be highly desirable.[13] No one in any kind of economy wishes to match scarce resources with incompetent managers and combine their resources without regard to social significance. In capitalist production, substitutions consider not only hours but also prices as determined by markets. Communist planning boards presumably take planned labor hours of various kinds and determine in some manner the substitution ratios of each item of direct and congealed labor. These substitutions may be made *ex cathedra* by the planning board on any basis whatever, but such substitutions must be made. One method of establishing the exchange value of commodities uses average profits to determine the relative proportion of factors. It is true that in Marx's time little was known about marginal analysis. The planning board can be instructed to determine the average amounts for each kind of labor along with various combinations of labor, materials and equipment for all industries. The difficulties of such a planning process are too obvious for further comment.

Now Marx and some followers (e.g., Mandel) did set a process for directly finding the amount of socially necessary labor so that surplus value can be determined as a remainder by simple arithmetical methods. Clearly some scheme must be devised to keep from adding value by malingering and wasteful methods (a social cost ceiling), and just as clearly a method must be devised for finding equivalences for all sorts of different types of labor working in different circumstances. Mandel recommends something similar to American trade association estimates that are occasionally used by American accountants who substitute industry averages for engineered standards; he states:

[T]he exchange of commodities . . . rests on this fundamental basis of an accounting system in work-hours and consequently follows this general rule: *the exchange-value of a commodity is determined by the quantity of labor necessary to produce it.* . . . However, the general definition must be qualified in several respects. . . . If the exchange-value of commodities depended only on the quantity of labor . . . expended *by each individual* in the production of a commodity, we would arrive at this absurdity: the lazier or more incompetent the producer . . . the greater would be the value of the shoes!. . . . Whoever puts more time into producing a pair of shoes than the average necessary hours—an average determined by the average productivity of labor and recorded in the Guild Charters, for example!—. . . has wasted human labor, worked to no avail for a certain number of hours. He will receive nothing in exchange for these wasted hours.[14]

It should be observed first that Marx's "cost-price" is introduced only indirectly as a feature of socially necessary cost. It is similar to the Dutch *Kostprijs* or the cost accountant's current standard cost to make and deliver. In this connection a short review of Marxian terms may be in order. Constant capital (c) is that part of the cost of production devoted to capital consumption (depreciation) and cost of materials. Variable cost (v) is the socially necessary cost paid to labor, and (s) is the surplus value produced by the laborers and not returned to them by capitalists. Cost-price is denoted by (k) and the commodity value of production is designated by capital (C).

Thus as Marx-Engels state "the formula C = c + v + s turns into the formula C = k + s, that is, the commodity-value = cost-price + surplus-value."[15] No doubt our accounting concept of "keeping capital intact" owes much to Marx and perhaps to the early classical economists, but tracing the history of this concept is not a part of the present study. Clearly Marx himself felt that the concept of cost-price was more significant than a bookkeeping device for measuring profit; he states:

[T]he cost-price of a commodity is by no means simply a category which exists only in capitalist book-keeping. The individualisation of this portion of value is continually manifest in practice in the actual production of the commodity, because it has ever to be reconverted from its commodity-form by way of the process of circulation into the form of productive capital, so that the cost-price of the commodity always must repurchase the elements of production consumed in its manufacture. The category of cost-price, on the other hand, has nothing to do with the formation of commodity-value. . . .[16]

While Marx probably was not interested in capitalist bookkeeping techniques, Marxist countries that permit some degree of capitalist endeavor should be interested in incorporating some modified capitalist accounting principles. The following illustration makes use of Marx's own numbers (p. 26):

Capitalist Producer A
Suggested Statement of Operations (Period covered)

Revenues (Commodities transferred at Marx's Commodity value)		$ 600
Less Cost-Price of Commodities transferred:		
Depreciation and other measures of capital consumption..............	$ 20	
Cost of materials and supplies at current cost...............................	380	
Labor Cost (Amount paid to laborers) (v).....................................	100	
Cost-price of production...		500
Surplus-value (for which capitalist paid nothing)...........................		100
Distribution of Surplus-Value among capitalists:		
To: Landlords...	x	
Creditors (as Interest)	y	
Entrepreneurs (as profit)...	z	$ 100
		Zero

Observe that the entire amount of surplus value is distributed to various parasites, and that the rules for distributing the swag are treated as variables. In any event the rules for distribution make a large part of the problem known as the Marxian Transformation Problem.

Compare this analysis with the early Patonian income report that treats revenue as the entire take from the social product by the entity group, and treats the remainder of the income report as a distribution of this amount.[17] (National income accountants may be interested in comparing and contrasting their own recommendations.) Clearly the preferred rules for making the Paton and Marx distributions are widely different. Capitalist economists feel that they know the rules employed in their own economies, but those who discuss the transformation problem are not so sure that Marx had an acceptable formula for transforming surplus value into profit in a capitalist economy. It is generally agreed that a Marxist economist should not permit commodity prices as determined by the price system to determine the amount of surplus value in a Marxist society. There must be an independent method of finding surplus value.

In any case, economists should be interested in the methodology employed to find the value that is socially necessary for the production undertaken. It is clear that in the illustration the $100 paid to the workers is easy to verify for it is the sum of the payments made to those defined as laborers.

The excess or $100 that makes up the surplus value can easily be found when commodity value and other determinants are known. The amounts received from customers and other transferees (in this case $600) should be easy enough to determine in any economy, although the amount may include all sorts of taxes, subsidies and the like. In a capitalist society the case is usually clear enough, but even here transfer-pricing problems need to be considered. If the Marxist accountant knows the amount of the receipts, the amounts paid and allowed for materials and facilities (c), and the amounts paid to labor, the amount of surplus value is revealed as a simple remainder. Inasmuch as factors other than labor are assumed to contribute nothing, the $500 of cost-price is the amount necessary to replace the "consumed" means of production. Managers who cling to the older labor-intensive methods will find that competition has driven product prices down to the extent that they suffer losses and are unable to pay for the newly created unnecessary labor. The Marxist framework, according to Mandel, also has a tendency for all competing socialist units to adopt the newer methods and to converge on the concept of "*average*" profit that is so essential to Marxist thinking.

DEPRECIATION AND THE ORGANIC COMPOSITION OF CAPITAL

The accountants' concept of organic capital is concerned mostly with depreciation and various amortizations. The usual argument is that a portion of capital assets is circulated and recovered in the sales price of products so that a part of buildings and equipment become current assets through the realization convention. This imagery is fanciful at best and may seriously hamper the cause of understanding. In point of fact the sales amount usually is larger than the out-of-pocket costs so normally there is a positive cash flow—to use the latest financial buzz. Accountants usually earmark a part of the excess as a return *of* capital and treat the remainder as return *on* capital. Even if all the profit (return *on* capital) is disbursed there remains the current funds that represent capital deterioration. In practice these funds may be used (except perhaps for dividends) at the discretion of management. One possible use is to replace and modernize capital goods and consequently the composition of capital may be changed, modernized and even expanded without increasing the amount of the original capital fund (investment). This convention is more than a bookkeeping allocation. A successfully operating firm may make substantial alterations in the composition of its capital goods without going into the capital markets. In this manner substantial provisions for technological changes and obsolescence may be financed without recourse to budget extensions.

To the extent that a Marxist treats capital assets as congealed labor and values them in terms of necessary labor, he should be prepared to adjust for technological changes that affect the congealed labor in existing capital assets. Old inefficient technology wastes labor hours and through obsolescence loses some of its own (congealed) value. This view is consistent with the procedure used by capitalist accountants who modify their standards to accommodate such changes and argue that partial obsolescence is reflected in current market prices for used equipment. Presumably Marxist accountants can retain original cost or elect to adopt current costs without the help of markets.

Consider now some technical Marxist commentary from Mandel. The tendency to keep overall capital intact is clear enough, but some details are confusing to accountants even though they have been well indoctrinated in this direction.

> The value of every commodity consists of two parts: one part represents *crystallized or conserved value* and the other *newly created value*. Labor-power has a dual function, a dual use-value: that of preserving all existing values in the instruments of labor, machines, buildings, while incorporating a fraction of this value into current production; and that of creating a new value, which contains surplus-value, profit, as one of its components. . . .
>
> We call the equivalent of wages variable capital. . . . We call that part of capital which is transformed into machines, buildings, raw materials, etc., whose value is not increased by production but merely preserved by it, constant capital. . . . [T]he fundamental tendency of the capitalist system . . . is to increase the weight of . . . constant capital, with respect to variable capital. . . . [T]his organic composition has a rising tendency.[18]

Clearly the accountant's notion of recovered depreciation through the successful sale of product is related to organic composition in the Marxist sense. Consider:

> As soon as the stock of goods produced in a given period is sold, the capitalist is reimbursed with a sum of money which constitutes the counter-value of the constant capital expended in achieving this production, that is to say, the raw materials used together with the fraction of the value of machines and goods amortized by this production. . . . In addition he is in possession of the surplus-value produced by his workers. What happens to this surplus-value? . . . . A . . . part of the surplus-value is accumulated and is utilized by being transformed into capital [reinvested earnings].[19]

As one might expect the term profit is little used in socialist literature, and for Marx and his disciples surplus-value serves reasonably well. Mandel realizes that surplus value is essential for growth of capital assets: "*realizing surplus-value is the necessary condition for accumulation of capital,* and capital accumulation is simply the capitalization of surplus value" (p. 43). Mandel has already pointed out that not all surplus value is transformed into capital goods, for the capitalist must live and therefore uses some of such value for extending his useless existence. Presumably in a socialist state, the state appropriates enough surplus value to keep its administrators and related bureaucrats alive, to finance capital goods expansion and often to support huge military establishments. Capitalist countries extract a part of the value of commodity production through taxation and through inflation. In a socialist bureaucracy it should be convenient to use some sort of direct levy on the prices at which commodities are exchanged.

In a capitalist system, the capital-goods problem is handled automatically by market surrogates instead of by bureaucratic fiats. If a new product is introduced or new labor saving technology is available the competitive price system will encourage entrepreneurs to substitute new methods and reduce costs. In the absence of markets bureaucratic decisions are in order.

DIGRESSION: MARXISM AND THE NEW LEFT

It seems to be obvious that accountants are expected to account for and explain important activities. Moreover they are supposed to help control human beings and machines, so that some understanding of machines, human beings and the essentials of control are necessary. Similarly if accounting is supposed to help users, then accountants ought to be able to identify users and predict their informational needs. What then is the current interest in esoteric ontology all about? In the framework of Rorty and more traditional pragmatists, if all we can hope for is that some events work for us then there should be a discernable and specifiable *us*—an entity. In its broadest sense the entity includes everyone with an interest in the operations of the organization.

Chua feels that important consequences follow the adoption of a philosophical program. She argues (apparently following Miller and O'Leary) that standard cost accounting as presently applied "socializes workers into constantly being watched, monitored, and governed."[20] Apparently the ideal is complete decentralization so that each group and even each individual is given information primarily for his own guidance. Many others agree that hierarchical relations should be reduced and information directed to satisfy individual needs.

Chua believes "that the accounting discourse constitutes part of the 'ideological apparatus,'"[21] and she offers no hope for weaklings who need physical or objective crutches to support their tottering arguments:

> [T]here is no neutral, objective world of facts which acts as the final arbitrator, the adequacy of a theory (or explanation of intention) is assessed via the extent to which the actors agree with the explanation of their intentions.[22]

The recent revival of the pragmatic outlook has been impressive. New-age pragmatists often place emphasis on historical and emergent aspects, but these features too are part of the pragmatic tradition—especially that of James, and Dewey in his early Hegelian phase.[23] In any case accountants are cautioned to look no longer for physical facts to support belief. This is an old insight and even physicists of Mach's time treated the physical universe as structures constructed from sensations.

The New Left philosophers hold what Chua calls an "interpretative" view. (Can there be a non-interpretative view?) These theorists do not wish to admit the importance of a coherence theory of belief that makes the truth of a proposition depend on the accepted truth of related propositions. This attitude also is not new and stems essentially from the phenomenological tradition. Yet rejection of the coherence standard for warranted assertions requires partial abandonment of the holistic (systems) framework, which makes the "meaning" of a part dependent on its relationship to the system. In physics and perhaps many other disciplines the "truth" of many assertions and hypotheses can be inferred only from the success of the entire structural system and not by verification of individual statements.

Rejection of functionalism and acceptance of a conflict model does not necessarily call for the rejection of a coherence approach to belief. Conflict, with its Hegelian dialectic, has not resulted in the rejection of a systems orientation but the newer approach (based on dissension and divisive interests) is more individualistic and more situational.

For traditional Marxists the relevant group is the inner circle of intellectual conspirators who at some later time should expand to include the entire working class. In turn the working class itself should expand to include the rump proletariat and finally most remaining citizens. Yet it is difficult to see why a Marxist should be sympathetic to Chua's subjective "perspective" or to the positions of the New Left. The usual Marxist is committed to an outside reality, group cohesion and individuals restrained by objective institutions that are conditioned by the modes of production. These institutions become the superstructure for the legislative and legal machinery that supports the technological infrastructure.

For Marxists there is (in the old Platonian sense) an ideal set of institutions and structures, but the present plight is simply that there is a moving social reality that somehow remains objective even though it changes and must be observed from an historical perspective. This perspective itself is based on a definite pattern—the dialectic. (We neglect the early Marx of the *Notes* in which he is more subjective and more concerned with alienation and psychological factors.) Certainly Marx and his followers have expressed little doubt about the future course of the institutions—the course of the historical synthesis and little question about the ends that would lead to docility and reduction of conflict.

Marx was certainly one of the founding fathers of ideology and was in the forefront of those trying to establish the important force exerted by environment. Since he was something of a naturalistic philosopher, he certainly did not deny the reality of the substantive world with its substances and things. Yet for active advocacy he often emphasizes reification of theories and social structures with constructions such as class, labor, commodity. Examples of Marxist efforts to emphasize environment over heredity are numerous: the rejection of such doctrines as original sin; the later Lysenko fiasco in genetics: advocacy of an elite group of party members trained to break through capitalist indoctrination. (This anti-hereditary bias has partially permeated the American school system to the extent that some current teachers, who know better, simply refuse to admit that some students are more gifted than others.) This argument cannot be positively refuted for no set of environmental conditions are *exactly* identical and it is always possible to hold that no environments are literally the same. The irony of this position is shown daily by many schoolteachers who stoutly deny the importance of heredity while working daily with wide differences in mental sharpness, musical ability and athletic agility.

The traditional Marxist vigorously claims to be scientific, and to be scientific in Marx's time assumes an external world that can be described and predicted by finding uniformities and correlating them into laws. He observed conditions, found uniformities, constructed typologies, correlated outcomes in causative (antecedent-consequent) form and predicted future conditions. It is difficult to determine the extent to which Marx and his followers could separate belief in an objective scientific world from that of the propaganda world designed to confute idealistic socialists and the rise of subjectivism. It is entirely possible that they realized their world of reality was largely subjective and that they used the scientific argument as persuasive support. After all, claiming support from objective reality at that time was (and unfortunately still remains) an exceptionally persuasive argument.

In any case the New Left has adopted a different strategy. It is far less materialistic and certainly does not agree with the renaissance conception of God as a material entity. It may believe with Hawton, "that ideology is a mass-rationalization of motives," but it has not been scientific enough to "regard this proposition as an hypothesis [to be] verified by history. . . ." It is more in tune with those who regard "science itself as an ideology. . . . [I]f the concepts used by science are social products, they must be modified by their social environment." These newer dialecticians certainly do not support the use of science to test assertions about ideology.[24] We conclude this digression by returning to the central concepts of accounting. The accountant's careful constructions for assets, revenues, expenses and income are subjective enough but they have their counterparts in the social sciences. Economists use national income, gross national product, supply, demand, money and a host of other concepts that have no physical counterparts. Psychologists are fond of aspirations, needs, desires, traits, mental sets and similar usages. Sociologists do all sorts of amazing things with status, role, alienation, society, socialization, internalization and the like. Physicists manipulate atoms, sub-atomic particles, forces, strains, inertias, velocities, space-time cusps and related constructions. Accounting has no claim to originality here.

Each profession requires typologies and operations to recognize, classify and measure its constructions. In some cases the operations are so habitual that practitioners do not recognize the mental nature of the concepts. In many cases these mental ideas are thought to constitute the very nature of reality, while less familiar operations are unreal and fictitious.

The auditor, to repeat again and again, verifies the "existence" of revenues, income, etc., by checking whether the outcomes of applying the stipulated rules of measurement are consistent with reports. This type of verification is an important part of the entire auditing process, which is concerned with applying appropriate operations to such definitions. This kind of auditing is precisely what scientists do when checking the work of other scientists for accepted scientific practices. The physicist, to take an example, takes a series of experiences classified as substance, atom or time and applies operations to measure, mass and otherwise assess them according to accepted rules.

It is argued here that the audit procedure in accounting is similar to the intersubjective process of checking work in the hardest of sciences. It remains to remark on the similarities, if any, of applying accounting rules to actual business events and conjectures to the similar task of carrying on original scientific research. The accountant is a given set of practices that act as laws, and his task is to recognize events, to abstract their attributes until the remaining portions fit his typologies—his set of constructions used to define his trade. The hard-scientist applies his kit of scientific constructions to events, or tries to bring about events that would fit his typologies. Normally businessman try to produce events that lead to desirable changes in accounting constructions, so that it often takes both the accountant and the businessman to execute the tasks performed by the scientist.

NOTES

[1] William Andrew Paton, *Accounting Theory, With Special Reference to the Corporate Enterprise* (New York: The Ronald Press Company, 1922); republished (Chicago: Accounting Studies Press, Ltd., 1962); reprinted (Houston: Scholars Book Co., 1973), pp. 490-1. Paton also recognized that value added by entrepreneurship may be accruing, but generally rejected the view that specific

costs do *in fact* attach to identifiable products. Unfortunately Paton was never able to free his theories completely from physical analogs.

² *Ibid.,* pp. 492-3.

³ Karl Marx, ed. Frederick Engels, *Capital: A Critique of Political Economy,* Vol. I, "A Critical Analysis of Capitalist Production," Translated from the Third German Edition by Samuel Moore and Edward Aveling (New York: International Publishers Co., Inc., 1967), pp. 38–40, emphasis added.

⁴ Editor's Note: The "able AAA Committee" appears to be the Committee on Accounting Concepts and Standards that issued "Inventory Pricing and Changes in Price Levels," Supplementary Statement No. 6, December 31 1953. This Committee concluded that "the measurement of accounting profit involves the matching precisely of the identified costs of specific units of product with the sales revenue derived therefrom." It also "recommended that if and when techniques for reflecting in accounting reports the impact of changes in the general level of prices have become generally accepted, the *artificial LIFO* method be abandoned entirely for reporting purposes in favor of a realistic flow assumption." *Accounting and Reporting Standards for Corporate Financial Statements and Preceding Statements and Supplements* [Madison: American Accounting Association, 1957], pp. 36–37. This committee's "identified cost" concept appears to be a variation of "embedded cost" or "attached cost.")

⁵ See William J. Vatter, *The Fund Theory of Accounting and its Implications for Financial Reports* (Chicago: The University of Chicago Press, 1947). Observe however that "Assets . . . are embodiments of future want satisfaction . . ." (p. 17); and not embodiments of past labor or effort. Thus he separated himself from the Marxist position by changing the nature of the embodiment. Precisely how "future want satisfaction" becomes embodied remains ambiguous, but at least his argument is oriented to the future.

⁶ Many on the fringes of welfare accounting (and economics) have been accused of being soft-headed ethicists rather than practical business people. The telling objection to welfare economics is that it neglects all sorts of human values and includes only economic wealth defined in terms of scarcity relative to utility. Idealistic institutional economists are on a fruitful path when they insist on studying the value systems that lie behind the forces of supply and demand that establish market transfer prices. Certainly not all values that support the notion of the good life are captured in the positivistic market net. To paraphrase and extend Whitehead's oft-quoted statement: Colors too are relevant—relevant far beyond the tentacles of any marketplace.

⁷ The concept of socially necessary labor cost in the traditional Marxist sense has been discussed by Anthony M. Tinker, Barbara D. Merino and Marilyn Dale Neimark, "The Normative Origins of Positive Theories: Ideology and Ac-

counting Thought," *Accounting, Organizations and Society,* (2), 1982, pp. 167–200.

[8] According to Hatfield, French regulating agencies set the top limit at *budgeted* cost rather than expenditure cost shortly after the turn of the century. The behavioral consequences of such a policy may seem strange, but such a limit might retard some wild estimates that have appeared recently for world-fair facilities and athletic stadiums. See Henry Rand Hatfield, "Some Variations in Accounting Practice in England, France, Germany and the United States," *Journal of Accounting Research,* Autumn 1966, pp. 169–182. (From the University of California collection of Hatfield papers, Stephen A. Zeff, Editor.)

[9] Earnest Mandel, *An Introduction to Marxist Economic Theory* (New York: Pathfinder Press, Inc., 1970).

[10] *Ibid,* p. 21.

[11] *Ibid.,* p. 22.

[12] See Benjamin E. Lippincott, ed., *On the Economic Theory of Socialism: Oskar Lange, Fred M. Taylor* (Minneapolis: University of Minnesota Press, 1938). The Taylor contribution was his *Presidential Address,* Annual Meeting, American Economic Association, 1928.

[13] Mandel Illustrates this process (*op. cit.,* p. 22 *et passim*). Apparently Marx was not greatly concerned by marginals and was willing to live with convergences to averages. We are not concerned here with the widely discussed Marxist necessity for the falling rate of profit in capitalist countries and Lenin's miraculous discovery of imperialism as a natural development to combat this depressing effect. The Marx-Engels position can be found in Karl Marx, *op. cit.,* Vol. III, "The Process of Capitalist Production As a Whole," pp. 142–210.

[14] Karl Marx, Vol. III, *ibid.,* pp. 17–18.

[15] *Ibid.,* p. 26. He adds: "The capitalist cost of the commodity is measured by the expenditure of *capital,* while the actual cost of the commodity is measured by the expenditure of *labour.*" (*Ibid.*)

[16] *Ibid.,* pp. 26, 28.

[17] William Andrew Paton *Advanced Accounting* (New York: The Macmillan Company, 1941).

[18] Mandel, *op. cit.,* pp. 41-2. Compare this with the accountant's division of funds from operations into return *of* capital and return *on* capital.

[19] *Ibid.,* pp. 43-4.

[20] Wai Fong Chua, "Radical Developments in Accounting Thought," *The Accounting Review,* October 1986, p. 625.

[21] *Ibid.* Here she paraphrases C. Lehman and A. M. Tinker, "A Semiotic Analysis of: 'The Great Moving Right Show' Featuring the Accounting Profession," Paper presented at the Interdisciplinary Perspectives in Accounting Conference, University of Manchester, July 8–10, 1985, p. 9.

[22] *Ibid.,* p. 614. Of course accounting can be utilized by subversive groups and for conspiratorial propaganda. Most modern accounting is capitalistic and not laboristic, anarchist or Marxist.

[23] The revived *us* orientation with an elite group making up the *us* has a long history. For treatment in the modern dissident fashion, Chua points out that Feyerabend emphasizes linguistic uses and the ideology of the "tribe" and that Gadamer "rejects the feasibility of a 'disinterested observer' and implies that competing theories can only be judged by (unspecified) historically-bound criteria that are temporarily agreed upon by a community of scientists" (*op. cit.,* p. 614).

For a better understanding of these anti-Popperians, see Paul Feyerabend, *Against Method: Outline of an Anarchistic Theory of Knowledge* (New York: New Left Books, 1975). Also see H. G. Gadamer, *Truth and Method* (London: Sheed & Ward, 1975); H. G. Gadamer, *Philosophical Hermeneutics* (Berkeley: University of California Press, 1977); and H. G. Gadamer, *Reason in the Age of Science* (Cambridge: MIT Press, 1981). At last we are seeing an integration of some existential tenets into the Anglo-Saxon philosophical tradition, but these tenets sometimes become almost undistinguishable from related beliefs held by pragmatists.

[24] The quotations above are from Hector Hawton, *Philosophy for Pleasure* (London: Watts & Co., 1949), p. 131. That ideological dogma often gets in the way of inquiry in Marxist thinking is emphasized by Alexander Vucinich; he stated: "The [Soviet] economist could not apply the refined mathematical methods. . . . Even when he had quantitative data at his disposal, the economist of the Stalin era was discouraged from using the methods that transform 'economic qualities' into 'mathematical quantities.'" "Science," *Prospects for Soviet Society,* Allen Kassof, ed. (New York: Frederick A. Praeger, Publishers, 1968), p. 326.

Index

326

Index

Responsibility
professional, 245–46, 251–58,
264
social, 258–62, 264
Revenue(s), 140, 185, 273
Revolution(s), 196–206, 214
Revsine, Lawrence, 71
Rex, John, 213
Rhea, R., 65
Rhetoric, 9, 53, 110–14
Ricardo, David, 295–96
Richards, I. A., 7
Ricoeur, Paul, 39–41, 44, 47, 70
Risk, 223, 227, 232, 236, 288
Ritzer, George, 174, 179–82,
187–88, 192
Roberts, Oral, 14
Robinson, Joan, 24, 196, 285,
288
Rorem, Rufus, 267
Rorty, Richard, 311
Rose, Arnold M., 183
Rules and guidelines, 253–54,
256
Russell, Bertrand, 8, 11–13, 39,
45, 50–51, 76, 125, 127,
238

Sacrifice(s), 5, 296
Saint Anselm, 72, 180
Saliers, Earl, 132, 153, 268,
275–77, 290–91
Sanders, Thomas H., 294
Sartre, Jean-Paul, 70, 106, 213
Saussure, Ferdinand de, 71
Scarne, John, 26
Schär, Johann F., 123
Schlatter, Charles F., 131
Schmalenbach, Eugen, 107, 133
Schmidt, Fritz, 14, 61, 133, 154,
202
Schultz, George, 100, 136, 255

Schumpeter, Joseph A., 123
Schutz, Alfred, 180, 213
Schweiker, William, 70
Science, 11–14, 51
Scott, D. R., 24, 61, 63, 100, 133,
136, 144, 201, 214, 254–55,
264, 267, 290, 293
Scovill, Hiram T., 278
Segovia, Andrés, 68
Self-evident truth(s), 15, 105–107
Semantics, 1, 8, 12, 24, 39, 40,
112, 139–41, 144, 215, 246,
262
Shannon, Claude E., 37
Shugrue, M. J., 276
Silverman, David, 213, 215
Simon, Herbert A., 22, 65, 98
Simons, Henry C., 245, 285
Simpson, N. F., 70
Singer, Jr., Edgar A., 122, 127, 292
Situationalism, 3, 8, 9, 45–46, 62,
64
Skinner, B. F., 12, 180
Smith, Adam, 295–96
Smooth(ing), 4, 5, 277
Social cost, 299–303
Social Darwinism, 135, 141, 195
Sociology, 8, 35, 38, 60, 84, 174,
177, 196, 207, 313
Social science(s), 65, 85, 174
Solipsism, 3, 12, 107
Solomons, David, 62, 202
Sombart, Werner, 144
Sorter, George H., 241
Spencer, Herbert, 195, 210
Spencer, William H., 196
Spengler, Oswald, 196
Sprague, C. E., 132–33, 153, 278,
290
Springer, Durward, 153
Sprouse, Robert T., 72, 137, 152,
203, 235, 242